THE
ENTREPRENEURS

THE
ENTREPRENEURS

*Explorations Within
the American Business Tradition*

by ROBERT SOBEL

Weybright and Talley

NEW YORK

To Harold Yuker

Contents

Introduction

Like other aspects of American society, business has its galaxy of major figures, notables whose names and exploits are familiar to the general public as well as to specialists. John D. Rockefeller, Andrew Carnegie, J.P. Morgan, and Henry Ford are known to the same people who have knowledge of George Washington, Abraham Lincoln, and the Roosevelts.

The reasons are clear enough. These were exceptional individuals whose work had major impacts on their times. They were dramatic leaders, bold and original, interesting as human beings as well as powerful influences. Finally, they were and are useful symbols, the kind of people textbook writers like to utilize to illustrate points they wish to make about the nation and its people at particular times.

All have been subjects of major biographies, articles in popular magazines, and even motion pictures and television programs. They were giants who became semilegendary. They were unique.

And for these reasons, those who would understand the American political and business traditions may be misled if they do not also consider the efforts of less spectacular or overlooked figures. Both traditions encompass the efforts of lesser politicians and entrepreneurs, from county legislators to Cabinet members, from operators of candy stores to dealers in whale oil. These are subjects so vast as to be beyond the grasp of a single scholar, or even a team of scholars.

Such is not the purpose of this book. Rather, it has more modest goals, one of which is to present the lives and works of nine important businessmen who have not received their proper due from historians and continue to be either ignored or unappreciated.

In part this neglect was a result of their having been overshadowed by other figures in their industries, who lived and worked at approximately the same times as they did, and have been deemed more important by writers during the past few decades. Samuel Slater, not Francis Cabot Lowell, is considered the father of the American factory system, for example. There are several biographies of Slater, but none of Lowell. Yet in many respects Lowell was a more significant and influential figure and was certainly a greater innovator. Eli Whitney is viewed as the genius whose inventions transformed the American South and created the Cotton Kingdom, and his name is known to every high school student in the land. Not so Cyrus McCormick, the man credited with inventing the reaper, which did for wheat what the gin did for cotton. Emperor Wheat defeated King Cotton in the Civil War, but in terms of reputation, Whitney has bested McCormick.

Similarly, there are impressive histories of such major retailing firms as Sears Roebuck, Macy's, and J.C. Penney, which extol their founders. Meanwhile, John Wanamaker, the dean of them all, is the subject of second-rate works, some of which were commissioned by his store. E.H. Harriman was a major force in railroading, and is rightly considered as such by historians. So was James Hill, who in his own way was even more successful. The only good biography of Hill is half a century old, while there is no published history of his railroad, the Great Northern. There are several definitive biographies of Andrew Carnegie, ruler of steel, but none of James Buchanan Duke, who dominated tobacco to a greater degree. Duke merits such a book, and one could be written from existing sources. None is in the works.

There are several fine biographies, and even a motion picture, on the life of Alexander Graham Bell, the inventor of the telephone. There is only one biography of Theodore Vail—who more than anyone else was responsible for creating the telephone industry—and that by a close friend, a literary historian. In writing of his experiences at the one hundredth birthday party of Adolph Zukor, the motion picture giant, Peter Bogdanovich, the critic and director, noted that many artists attended. "Without their talents, and the talents of scores of others, what would have become of Mr. Zukor?" he asked.[1] The question can be turned around. Without the development of motion pictures as a business—accomplished by Zukor, Marcus Loew, and others—who would have provided jobs for the artists? What would have become of Rudolph Valentino and Clara Bow? Zukor has been the subject of several books, all of them lightweight, and in addition he has written a chatty but unrevealing autobiography. There is no biography of Marcus Loew, yet new works on those who profited from his genius appear regularly.

Scores of books and articles have been written on Henry Ford and the Model T, yet there is only one popular work on Donald Douglas, creator of the most successful line of passenger planes in history, who did for civil aviation what Ford did for autos.

Finally, the most famous conglomerateur—and indeed, the most noted businessman at present—is Harold Geneen of ITT. Certainly Geneen was and is a skillful manager and creative if contentious force. But the man who more than anyone else developed the conglomerate form, Royal Little, certainly deserves more than passing mention. This book attempts to take a small step in that direction.

There is another, even more important reason, for selecting these businessmen. The efforts of each illustrate specific aspects of the American business tradition. These

[1] Peter Bogdanovich, *Pieces of Time* (New York, 1973), p. 253.

were ambitious and talented individuals, from a variety of backgrounds, and each came to his main theater of operations almost by chance. This is not to say that luck and fortune dominated their lives and determined their destinies. Rather, the nation almost always presented many opportunities to aggressive and intelligent individuals such as these. How they reacted to them is a significant aspect of this work. Of course, the vast majority of Americans have been unable, often for reasons over which they had no control, to seize the chance when it presented itself. On the other hand, these men, while talented, were not necessarily exceptional.

The individuals selected became leaders of industries that tend to be ignored, overlooked, or slighted in most works on American economic history. Textiles, farm machinery, retailing, railroads as regional developers, tobacco, telephones, motion pictures, and aviation have received less attention than those industries dominated by huge figures, such as petroleum, steel, investment banking, and automobiles. Perhaps it is too early to expect definitive works on conglomerates, for although much has been written on the subject, most of the books and articles are highly specialized and technical, overly general, or frankly sensationalist. Similarly, some industries suffer from what to those who are interested in business must seem the wrong kind of attention. Motion pictures and aviation are obvious examples, where the tinsel often outweighs the substance, a point that is expanded upon in the chapters dealing with Loew and Douglas.

Of course, all the businessmen discussed are interesting people in their own rights, each with a clear philosophy of business that was developed in the crucible of experience, and each the developer of a structure to carry it forth. This too was taken into consideration in the selection of subjects.

Clearly the number of businessmen considered here could have been increased. The ones ultimately selected were culled from an original list of over one hundred. A good case could be made for others. It was difficult selecting Duke over Charles Schwab, Douglas rather than John H. Patterson of National Cash Register, Little over several other conglomerateurs, Loew over William Fox or Carl Laemmle, and so on. The selection of these nine rather than an alternate set is a matter upon which reasonable people may differ.

But there is another matter to consider. There are interesting interconnections between the men discussed in this work, some of which are direct, most of them not. Francis Cabot Lowell was of the Boston aristocracy, as were his associates. Their grandchildren financed railroads that competed with Hill's Great Northern, and their children were among the initial backers of the Bell telephone. A direct descendent of Lowell's became interested in the commercial aspects of flight and offered to support the work of the Wright Brothers, while others were involved in the workings of Textron, Royal Little's conglomerate. Textron absorbed Bell Aircraft, an aviation firm started by Lawrence Bell, who had been one of Douglas's associates at Glenn Martin Company. Douglas and other aviation pioneers were able to survive the depression years of the 1920s and 1930s in aviation by taking jobs (usually stunt flying) in motion pictures, among them the epics produced by Metro-Goldwyn-Mayer, owned by Loew. The motion picture industry was based, initially, on the inventions of Thomas A. Edison, who also developed telephone equipment superior to Bell's. Had he the interest and inclination, Edison might have become a leading tycoon in both industries. For his part, Bell turned to aviation in the last years of his life, conducting many experiments in flight in Nova Scotia. Buck Duke, the tobacco tycoon, spent his last years erecting Duke Power and Light, made possible, of course, by Edison's work in electricity. That same discovery enabled John Wanamaker to electrify the Grand Depot. Had this not been done, the enterprise might have failed, bringing an end to Wanamaker's mercantile career. Electricity was also needed for telephones and, later on, in the mass production of cigarettes, thus establishing a link between American Tobacco and AT&T. Another came in the person of Peter Widener, who attempted to raid both the Duke and Vail companies at various times in his business career. Each man dealt with the threat differently, and in ways totally in character with his other activities. Vail tried his hand at several occupations before entering the telephone industry. At one time he attempted to invent a reaper superior to the McCormick, and several years earlier, James Hill served as regional salesman for the devices. Finally, Textron emerged from the same Rhode Island community that nurtured Almy and Brown, the predecessor of Lowell's Boston Manufacturing Company.

These portraits of men at work are not substitutes for full-scale biographies. They are interpretive essays, efforts at understanding the ways in which the protagonists operated, how they got to where they were going, and why they decided to go there in the first place. Also considered are such matters as the development of personalities and strategy in the business crucible, and the impact of change upon individuals and institutions. The goal throughout has been analysis as well as exposition, for clearly the former cannot exist without the latter.

Students of American history will recognize that the concept is not novel. It was most successfully utilized by Richard Hofstadter in his classic *The American Political Tradition and the Men Who Made It*, published in 1948, which inspired not only this work, but many others. If I am indebted to Hofstadter in matters of form and intent, I owe still more to Alfred D. Chandler, Jr., in the area of analysis and approach. In *Strategy and Structure: Chapters in the History of the Industrial Enterprise*, published in 1962, Chandler investigated the behavior of corporation leaders in developing strategies, and then how they constructed tactics to carry them through. Hofstadter dealt with such political giants as Jefferson, Jackson, Lincoln, and Franklin Roosevelt. Chandler investigated major corporations, including General Motors, Standard Oil of New Jersey, DuPont, and Sears Roebuck. In this work, I have selected less prominent individuals in often neglected industries and areas of industry.

THE
ENTREPRENEURS

I

Francis Cabot Lowell: The Patrician as Factory Master

And this is good old Boston,
The home of the bean and the cod,
Where the Lowells talk to the Cabots,
And the Cabots talk only to God.

John Collins Bossidy wrote this toast and offered it first at a Holy Cross alumni dinner in 1910. By then, however, the power of the Lowells and Cabots and others of their kind had become diluted. Still, they stood for tradition and a sense of *noblesse oblige* old Bostonians prized. In addition, the Lowells, Cabots, and others of the early Boston aristocracy—such as the Jacksons, Appletons, Thorndikes, Lawrences, Saltonstalls, Quincys, Adamses, Forbeses, Searses, and Derbys—had money and, to a degree, political power. Both had been accumulated during the colonial period, the Revolutionary era, and the early national experience. After that, the families tended to live on reputation and past glories, but these were sufficient to keep them safely ensconced at the pinnacle of Boston's social aristocracy to the present day. Certainly it was the case when Bossidy delivered his toast.[1]

[1] Frederic Cople Jahar, "The Boston Brahmins in the Age of Industrial Capitalism," in Frederic Cople Jahar, ed., *The Age of Industrialism in America* (New York, 1968), pp. 188–91.

Francis Cabot Lowell was a fitting symbol of this early power, combining as he did the genealogies of two of the leading families. His name evokes much of early American history, especially that of Boston in its golden age, just before and after the Revolution. On hearing it, one assumes him to have been a person of importance, even before knowing of his accomplishments. So he was, more than any other Cabot or Lowell, even though his was a short life.

Francis Lowell is generally credited with establishing the factory system in America. Yet factories dotted the Pennsylvania, New York, and New England landscapes before he was born–if we define a factory as a place where workers are brought to fabricate goods. Lowell's name and references to his life appear in few American history textbooks, however. More specialized works in economic history often assign him a paragraph, noting his involvement with the textile industry. Some do not even mention this; one wrongly states he was the founder of the city that bears his name, when in fact Lowell, Massachusetts, was not incorporated until after his death in 1817.

Monographs offer more information, but not enough for us to obtain a multidimensional picture of the man and his works. A few articles have been written on his life, and eminent scholars have told of it in specialized studies dealing with the origins of the American textile industry. For the most part, however, these tend to repeat the same information known to writers a century or more ago.[2] Francis Lowell left no major collection of papers, although the records of his firm—those that remain—are on deposit at

[2]The most complete scholarly work on the subject is George Sweet Gibb, *The Saco-Lowell Shops: Textile Machinery Building in New England, 1813–1949* (Cambridge, 1950), but this book devotes a relatively small section to Francis Lowell. Hannah Josephson, *The Golden Threads: New England's Mill Girls and Magnates* (New York, 1949) is a popular account that covers some of the same ground. Caroline F. Ware, *The Early New England Cotton Manufacture: A Study in Industrial Beginnings* (Boston, 1931) is an excellent monograph on the industry.

the George F. Baker Library at the Harvard Business School. It is unlikely that new findings regarding Lowell will be unearthed.

In other words, we already know all we are likely to of one of the key figures in the American business tradition, and this is sparse indeed. There is no Lowell biography, and none in the works.[3] No portrait of the man exists; all we have is a silhouette, apparently cut while Francis Lowell was in his twenties, one that shows his regular features marred by a somewhat weak chin. At the time, the Lowells were considered important in Boston, though not yet at that pinnacle where they would talk only to the Cabots. It was Francis Lowell's father who gave the family eminence, but it was the son who provided the economic power.

Boston was a vital city in the late eighteenth century, during Lowell's youth. Then, as he reached maturity, it began to decline. New York and Philadelphia were growing more rapidly, and one of the two seemed destined to become the economic and even the intellectual center of the new nation. Boston appeared more staid, less receptive to change, than did its rivals. It did change, and the leadership for the transformation came from Lowell and his associates. They could not prevent the victory of New York, but they did enable Boston to continue to prosper and remain a key American city.

This was so because the Boston aristocrats were pliable, far more so than was realized only a half century ago, when they were the butt of many jokes. The aristocratic families provided religious leaders for Massachusetts Bay when the locus of power was in the church. Then, as land grew in importance, they dominated agriculture and land speculation. These were the families that sent sons into commerce at a time when Boston and Salem were developing the Oriental trade, and afterward some of them became leaders of the Revolutionary cause. They were proud of their line-

[3]There is a family history, however. See Ferris Greenslet, *The Lowells and Their Seven Worlds* (Boston, 1946).

age, carefully marrying their daughters to sons of families
with equal—or, hopefully, slightly higher—status. The
families often worked together in matters religious, political, and economic, and in the process provided Boston with
a continuity of leadership unmatched in the New World.[4]
The Winthrops and Mathers were in the foreground during the early years, and then gave way to the Saltonstalls,
Endicotts, and Otises, among others, who in turn bowed
gracefully to and intermarried with the commercially in-
clined Jacksons, Lees, Tracys, and Lowells. The Adamses
led the way in the Revolution, with most of the others in
the van. At each turn in the stream of history, another
family or group of families seemed to take command; but
at the same time, the others joined in, acting as though the
present leaders were really cousins, as indeed they often
were.

In the last years of the eighteenth century a member of
one of the families, John Adams, was President of the
United States. His administration was short-lived, as the
Federalist Party, to which most of the aristocrats belonged,
went into decline. Four years of John Adams were followed
by eight each of Thomas Jefferson, James Madison, and
James Monroe—twenty four years of Virginians. Not until
1825 would another family member, John Quincy Adams,
become President, and he would be the last of the Boston
aristocrats to occupy the White House.[5] But while the Virginians held political power, another of the Boston fami-

[4] Mary Caroline Crawford, *Famous Families of Massachusetts*, 2 vols. (Boston, 1930),
is a somewhat inadequate survey of the families over three centuries. But it is
difficult to imagine a similar work for New York or Pennsylvania, one in which
the author could trace such a continuous lineage of power and prestige.
[5] John F. Kennedy would be the next Massachusetts President, but of course the
Kennedys and Fitzgeralds were not accepted as aristocrats by the old families
until quite late, even though in manners and styles they were not very different.
Senator Leverett Saltonstall of Massachusetts would view Senator Kennedy as a
quasi-kinsman, but others of the Boston aristocrats still viewed him as the grand-
son of "Honey Fitz," one of those out to smash what remained of their power.
Joseph Kennedy was acutely aware of this and took special delight in besting the
brahmins at their own game. See Richard Whalen, *The Founding Father: The Story
of Joseph P. Kennedy* (New York, 1964), for a view of the Boston elite as seen from
the other side of the fence.

lies, the Lowells, together with allies in the Jackson, Appleton, Thorndike, and Tracy clans, made a bid for economic
power that in its own way was as important for the nation's
future as any event that occurred in Washington. During
the Age of the Virginians, the Boston aristocrats turned
their attention, slowly and at times painfully, from commerce to manufacturing. This change took place not from
desire and a search for profits but because of a necessity
forced upon them as a result of the foreign policies of the
southern Presidents. At the time the families resented the
change, one that transformed would-be merchant-adven-
turers into factory masters. Later on they would realize
that control of factories was not without its compensations.

But the beginnings were in commerce, international
trade that returned large profits that would later be used to
create the factories. Federalist Boston was a major commercial center. It may have lost the battle for Atlantic su-
premacy to New York, but Boston was besting Salem and
the Rhode Island ports in the contest for the Pacific. Oriental goods flowed into Boston, and from there were trans-
shipped to other parts of the United States and Europe.
"Upward of seventy sail of vessels sailed from this port on
Monday last, for various parts of the world," wrote the
Columbian Centinal on October 26, 1791. "The harbour of
Boston is at this date crowded with vessels," noted one of
the aristocrats three years later. "Eighty-four sail have been
counted lying at two of the wharves only. It is reckoned
that not less than four hundred and fifty sail of ships, brigs,
schooners, sloops, and small craft are now in this port." As
Boston's commerce grew, so did its population, which rose
from 18,320 in 1790 to 33,787 in 1810.[6] Vessels laden with fish
and lumber bound for the West Indies would dock side by
side with those newly arrived from Europe, prepared to
transship brandy, bar iron, and cloth to the Carolinas. A
cargo of rum and molasses would be sent to Montreal, and

[6]Samuel Eliot Morison, *The Maritime History of Massachusetts, 1783–1860* (Boston, 1921), p. 124.

there the ship would take on wheat for Cadiz, the money
for which would be used to purchase salt for Africa. A
Boston-based ship might carry rum and provisions to the
Cape of Good Hope and exchange it for tea from China,
which would be taken to Guiana and sold with whatever
remained of the rum for ivory and gold dust. Then on to
the West Indies for sugar and cotton, and back to New
England. Or the ship might go directly to India, selling
stores for tea and ivory, and afterward crisscross the western Pacific, trading from port to port for several years
before making the return voyage to Boston.

The men who controlled this vast and, for the time,
complicated trade were carefully trained for their tasks.
Before the Revolution many went to college, and then to
the countinghouse of a merchant, usually one belonging to
a friend of the family or a relative. Perhaps they would
make a few voyages, not as ordinary seamen, to be sure, but
as supercargos, intent on using the experience as a prac-
ticum for their work in the office later on. Assuming all
went well, the young men would be set up on their own,
backed by family capital. Others, from families with less
wealth, would go to sea as cabin boys, work their way up
to seaman and finally captain. Armed with savings and
experience, they would become shipowners and merchants
too.

This changed somewhat after the Revolution, as Boston,
no longer under the protection and control of the Crown,
went off on its own. Young men from the families no
longer felt the need to obtain a college education, one
whose classical emphasis might serve them well in London
and polite society at home but had little significance in the
countinghouses and on the foredecks.

Patrick Tracy Jackson, the son of one of the most prominent of the Boston families, which at the time was in somewhat sad straits financially, nonetheless went to Drummer
Academy, but then rejected the university. "His own instincts prompted him to take up a merchant's life, and at

that period the best opening for such an occupation was rather through the countingroom or the deck of a merchantman than through the halls of Harvard."[7] In any case, Jackson's two older brothers were in the university, and the family could scarcely have afforded the expense at the time; in 1788 Patrick's father, Jonathan, wrote to John Lowell that he was finding it "difficult enough for us to get along from day to day without any extra calls."[8] Young Jackson was apprenticed to a merchant, William Bartlett of Newburyport, where he learned his trade in the countinghouse and served as supercargo on a voyage to St. Thomas. Afterward he left Bartlett and worked under his brother, Henry Jackson, embarking on voyages to Madras and Calcutta, India. With his savings from these expeditions he established himself as a merchant in Boston in 1807, specializing in the East Indies trade. Patrick Jackson's path to a business career was not unusual; it was taken by many of his contemporaries, with the goal being a merchant's office near the docks in Boston.[9]

Francis Lowell's story followed a similar line. The Lowells could trace their lineage back to the sixteenth century, and in 1639 one of the members, Percivall, a Bristol merchant, immigrated to America. His great-great-grandson, John, graduated from Harvard in 1721, and went on to a distinguished career in the ministry. His son, also named John, graduated from Harvard in 1760, and married three times—first to a Higginson, then, after her death, to a Cabot, and finally to the widowed daughter of Judge James Russell. John Lowell represented Newburyport in the Massachusetts Assembly before and during the Revolution and served in the Continental Congress. After the Revolution John Lowell became United States Judge for the District of Massachusetts and from there went on to be ap-

[7]James J. Putnam, *A Memoir of Dr. James Jackson* (Boston, 1905), p. 128, as quoted in Kenneth Wiggins Porter, *The Jacksons and the Lees: Two Generations of Massachusetts Merchants, 1765–1844* (Cambridge, 1937), I, 8.
[8]Henry Lee Shattuck Collection, quoted in *Ibid., loc. cit.*
[9]*Ibid.*, pp. 9–11.

pointed Chief Justice of the Circuit Court.

John Lowell had three sons, one by each of his three wives. The eldest, also named John Lowell, was a political writer of local repute, while the youngest, Charles Lowell, entered the ministry and had a long career. Francis Cabot Lowell, the middle son, who was born in 1775, became a businessman.

Little is known of Francis Lowell's youth, but since he was the son of a successful and moderately wealthy father, we may assume it was a period of relative calm and leisure, tempered by admonitions to lead a useful and productive life. He grew up at a time when Boston's docks were undergoing extensive rebuilding, and he must have been aware of the vitality of the Indies trade and the opportunities that lay in commerce. His friends, especially those of the Jackson clan, were interested in becoming merchants, and he considered such a career at an early age. But unlike Patrick Tracy Jackson, Francis Lowell did go to Harvard, a member of the class of 1793, although he was suspended in his senior year for lighting a bonfire in the Yard contrary to regulations.

Lowell showed little inclination toward religion and philosophy but excelled in the sciences. "He has a happy genius for mathematics," wrote the Reverend Zedekiah Sawyer of Bridgewater to Judge Lowell. "I presume few if any of his class equal him in mathematics and astronomical attainments. He is very accurate in calculating and projecting eclipses."[10] This talent, along with his natural inclinations, led Francis Lowell to business.

Upon graduation Lowell shipped out as supercargo on several voyages, most of which took him to Europe. Then, having undergone this conventional training for commerce, he established an office on the Long Wharf in Boston and proclaimed himself a merchant. Lowell had every reason to expect success. Trade was booming, and at the

[10]Greenslet, *The Lowells*, p. 93.

time it appeared that America was destined for agriculture and commerce, with Boston the key to the European and Oriental trade. He had the right name, sufficient capital, intelligence, and the proper training and connections. As though to solidify the last, in 1798 he married Hannah Jackson, Patrick Tracy Jackson's sister, after which Lowell's ties with the Jacksons became much closer. Jackson had concentrated on the China and India trade, while Lowell knew Europe. Together they would make an excellent team. Jackson would travel through the Orient, dealing for Lowell and helping make both their fortunes and reputations in that part of the world, while Lowell worked through others in Europe. Each man used several contacts in his work, as was the practice for sedentary merchants of the period. But their ties were close, and their fortunes interrelated.[11]

Lowell proved an excellent businessman. In 1802 he owned more than twenty separate parcels of land along the Boston docks as well as land in Maine, held for speculation. His dealings were worldwide, conducted in large part on ships owned by his father—*Perseverance, Regular, Thomas Russell, Horace, John, Ocean,* and *Hannah*—and which Francis managed. Shortly after the Judge died, also in 1802, Francis's brother John wrote that this commerce had "accomplished the restoration of my father's dilapidated fortunes."[12]

Boston's commercial life depended upon the seas, and the merchants hoped for peace so the lanes would be free. In time of war, blockades by one or another nation would disrupt trade. Lacking peace, the Boston merchants tended to side with Great Britain, for the Royal Navy controlled the high seas. With the coming of the French Revolution

[11]See letters from Patrick Tracy Jackson to Francis Lowell in Porter, *Jacksons and Lees*, pp. 594–95, 607–10, 613–14.
[12]Greenslet, *The Lowells*, p. 83.

and, in early 1793, the declaration of war by France against
Britain, some of the Boston merchants, including a few
who had been rebels in 1775, proclaimed their pro-British
sympathies. "Broadly speaking, one may say that in 1793
maritime Massachusetts was making up her mind on the
American policy toward the European war. By 1795 she
found her opinion to be flatly pro-British; in 1796 she imposed it on the rest of the state, and in 1797 on the rest of
the nation."[13] With John Adams in the Presidency and
Thomas Pickering of Salem, Massachusetts, as secretary of
state, the Boston families felt their interests would be protected. So they were. Peace and neutrality were maintained.

Conditions changed somewhat in 1801 when Jefferson entered the White House, supposedly with a pro-French inclination. But in the following year Britain came to a temporary peace with Napoleon, and despite some misgivings
Massachusetts voted for Jefferson in 1804. Soon after Jefferson's second inaugural, Britain and France were at war
again, with each country proclaiming a blockade of the
other. Jefferson's response was the proclamation of an embargo, to go into effect on December 22, 1807, which prohibited all vessels except foreign ships in ballast from depart-
ing from the United States for foreign ports. The embargo,
which would be in effect until March 15, 1809, was designed
to keep America neutral and free from contamination by
the European war. Most of the price, however, was to be
paid by the Boston merchants, who were supposed to cease
operations for the duration. Massachusetts had more than
a third of the registered tonnage in foreign trade at the
time, and her fishing fleet consisted of nine of every ten
American ships in that business. The merchants and fisher-
men rebelled against the embargo. Some engaged in smug-
gling, as their fathers had done when the British attempted
to control their trade, while others worked for the defeat
of the Jeffersonians or, failing that, a change in policy in

[13]Morison, *Maritime History*, p. 173.

Washington. This came on Jefferson's last day in office, when he agreed to repeal the embargo. Still, Jefferson was to be succeeded by Madison, another Virginian and Republican, and a man not considered friendly to the Boston aristocrats. Frustrated in politics and fearful for their businesses, some Boston merchants searched for new outlets for their energies and investments.

Textiles were obvious candidates. The American South was the world's leading grower of cotton, most of which was exported to England for the manufacture of yarn and cloth. Of course, some was spun and woven in America by crude methods, in most cases by the ultimate wearer of clothing cut from the cloth. But prior to the invention of the cotton gin in 1794, cotton cloth was a luxury item, so Americans wore linen and woolen garments, as well as clothing made from leather and animal skins. Even then, most northerners and city dwellers in general purchased imported cloth. "The inhabitants of the trading towns, men, women, children, have their whole supply of clothing from Great Britain," reported Sir Francis Bernard, the Massachusetts colonial governor, in 1768. "Most of the women in all other towns have the principal part of their clothing of British manufacture; the men have more or less."[14]

Such was the situation before and during the Revolution. It was one that some Federalist leaders, Secretary of the Treasury Alexander Hamilton in particular, hoped to rectify. In his Report on Manufactures, delivered in 1791, Hamilton urged the nation to become self-sufficient in all its needs. "The expediency of encouraging manufactures in the United States, which was not long since deemed very questionable, appears at this time to be pretty generally admitted," he wrote.[15] Hamilton envisaged a nation where

[14]Victor S. Clark, *History of Manufactures in the United States, 1607–1860* (Washington, 1916), p. 207–8.
[15]Alexander Hamilton, "Report on Manufactures," December 5, 1791, in United States, *American State Papers, Finance* (Washington, 1832–1859), I, 123.

the farmers would grow crops to be sent to the cities for processing, while manufactured goods, made in new urban centers, would be taken by farmers in return. Such a situation would enable the new nation to stand alone and not become a captive of the manufacturers of Europe. It would also provide Hamilton with a business class he felt certain would support his programs.

Hamilton was incorrect in stating that the need for manufacturing was "generally admitted." Those who had seen the newly constructed factories of England feared such a system would degrade American workers and help create a new feudalism, while free farmers, land speculators, and the commercial interests saw manufacturing as a competitor for capital and labor, one that would destroy the dream of "an American Garden."[16] In 1885, nine years prior to the invention of the cotton gin, Thomas Jefferson spoke eloquently of his feelings on the subject. "Cultivators of the earth are the most valuable citizens. As long therefore as they can find employment in this line, I would not convert them into mariners, artisans, or anything else. . . . I consider the class of artificers as the panders of vice and the instruments by which the liberties of a country are generally overturned."[17]

Even the development of the cotton gin did not change the situation. Instead of resulting in the development of domestic American cotton textile industries, it only served to increase the amount of the fiber exported to England. In 1810 most American cotton textiles were produced by household manufacturers. Of the 14.8 million yards produced that year, over 9 million were turned out in South Carolina, Georgia, and Virginia. That year Rhode Island produced 461,000 yards, and Massachusetts, so little that it wasn't even reported.[18]

---

[16]The emotional opposition to industrialization is well covered in Leo Marx, *The Machine in the Garden: Technology and the Pastoral Ideal in America* (New York, 1964), and Marvin Fisher, *Workshops in the Wilderness* (New York, 1967).
[17]Paul L. Ford, ed., *The Writings of Thomas Jefferson* (New York, 1892–99), IV, 88.
[18]Rolla M. Tryon, *Household Manufactures in the United States, 1640–1860* (New York, 1917), p. 166.

By that time—largely as a result of the problems attendant upon the European wars combined with the continued work of the Hamiltonians—the desire to create a vigorous manufacturing sector had grown. Soon after, even Jefferson was obliged to concede that "To be independent for the comforts of life we must fabricate them [textiles] ourselves. . . . He, therefore, who is now against domestic manufactures must be for reducing us, either to a dependence on that nation [England], or to be clothed in skins, and live like wild beasts in dens and caverns:—I am proud to say I am not one of these. Experience has taught me that manufactures are now as necessary to our independence as to our comfort."[19]

Attempts to develop a domestic textile industry antedated the wars. Societies for the encouragement of industry were formed in New York, Philadelphia, Boston, and other cities prior to the ratification of the Constitution, while the legislatures of several states went so far as to exempt manufacturing establishments from taxes.[20] But these and other inducements proved insufficient to attract capital. Even had Americans been willing to enter textiles, the technological barrier might have stopped them. Great Britain, leader in the field, took extraordinary steps to prevent others from learning her secrets, using methods similar to those that would be employed two centuries later in America to safeguard atomic secrets. In 1718 Parliament passed an act forbidding woolen workers from emigrating on danger of losing all properties owned in England, while foreigners who attempted to lure them abroad would be subject to a £100 fine and three months imprisonment. These penalties and fines were increased later on, and cotton, mohair, and linen workers were also included among those covered by the provisions of the act. Parliament also attempted to prevent the export of textile machinery. Despite this, several American companies, most notably those

[19]Ware, *The Early New England Cotton Manufacture*, p. 10.
[20]Samuel Batchelder, *Introduction and Early Progress of the Cotton Manufacture in the United States* (Boston, 1863), pp. 51–55.

in the Philadelphia area, conspired to import both men and machines, but with little success. In particular these Americans wanted to learn the secrets of Richard Arkwright's mechanized water frame, which made continuous spinning possible and lowered the costs considerably. Here too, the efforts failed. The secrets were too valuable to remain secrets for long, however. They would come to America, to emerge not in Philadelphia but in Rhode Island.[21]

Moses Brown of Providence was interested in cotton textiles. Like the Boston aristocrats, the Browns had arrived in America in the second quarter of the seventeenth century, but unlike them, they were Quakers, and appeared more interested in commerce than in government or religion, or at least saw business as a proper place from which to serve God and man, as well as their own interests.

In 1787 Moses Brown, then forty-nine years old and a recognized leader in the Oriental and Baltic trade, turned his attention to cotton manufacturing. He visited small shops in Connecticut and Massachusetts in order to learn all he could of the processes. Two years later he formed a partnership with his son-in-law, William Almy, who shared this interest, and the firm of Brown and Almy purchased a broken-down spinning jenny and a carding machine and set up shop in Providence. Brown poured a considerable amount of money into the enterprise, with poor results. The machines didn't work as expected, and most importantly, the water frame proved a failure. Brown and Almy had the money and zeal for the enterprise, but lacked knowledge and technology, both of which remained in England.

[21]David J. Jeremy, "British Textile Technology Transmission to the United States: The Philadelphia Region Experience, 1770–1820," *Business History Review*, (Vol. xlvii, No. 1 Spring, 1973), pp. 25–27. Jeremy notes that from 1773 to 1776, some 6,000 emigrants left Britain for North America, and of these, 315 were engaged in the textile trade, with 58 settling in Philadelphia. *Ibid*, p. 35.

Not for long. Samuel Slater, a young Englishman who had been an apprentice of Jedediah Strutt, one of Arkwright's closest associates, decided to immigrate to America in 1789. Slater, only twenty-one at the time, knew that British regulations forbade the emigration of skilled mechanics such as he and so, disguised as a farm laborer, he slipped out of the country from London. Slater worked for a brief period in New York, attempting to apply his knowledge of textiles there, with little success. He was about to take off for Philadelphia when he learned of Moses Brown's experiences in Rhode Island. Slater wrote to Brown in early December. "A few days ago I was informed that you wanted a manager of *cotton spinning,* &c. in which business I flatter myself that I can give the greatest satisfaction, in making machinery, making good yarn, either for *stockings* or *twist,* as any that is made in England," he wrote. Slater noted his connections with Strutt, his familiarity with the Arkwright water frame, and his interests in innovation. Brown answered the letter immediately. He had retired from the firm, he said, but was close to its successor, Almy and Brown. "An experiment has been made, which has failed, no person being acquainted with the business, and the frames imperfect." Brown urged Slater to come to Providence. "We should be glad to engage thy care as long as they [*sic*] can be made profitable to both, and we can agree."[22]

With this letter in hand, Slater set out for Rhode Island. Less than three months later he was taken in as a partner. Slater contributed his knowledge to the firm, while Almy and Brown provided capital. The company was housed in a shed. Raw cotton was purchased and taken there to machines set up and tended by local children and supervised by Slater. There they turned out cotton yarn, which was

[22]E.H. Cameron, *Samuel Slater: Father of American Manufactures* (Toronto, 1960), pp. 37–39. For a full account of the Brown involvement, see James B. Hedges, *The Browns of Providence Plantations: The Nineteenth Century* (Providence, 1968), pp. 159–85.

sold to local weavers, who produced cloth by hand.

Later on the Almy and Brown facility would be considered the first true textile factory in America. This was the case, but one should not infer that the partners were true industrialists, or even factory masters. Almy and Brown were merchants, and Slater an engineer; they did not develop much beyond this. The major difference between the Almy and Brown factory and earlier attempts to produce yarn by bringing workers together in one place to undertake the task was the machine, and machines alone do not make factories. Rather, Almy and Brown merely mechanized what formerly was a hand operation, and did so better than anyone else at the time in America. But there is little evidence they appreciated the implications of mechanization, understood the development of a labor supply, the intricacies of distribution, or even the role new, related inventions might play in their business. It was as though, at the time of the development of the automobile, the village blacksmith began to repair cars, forging his own parts, ignoring the possibilities of gasoline sales and related services, and considering the new invention as a variety of horse and buggy. Almy, Brown, and Slater were men in textiles, but they were not textile men.

The venture was a success. Almy and Brown made profits, and the firm's example prompted others to enter the field. The beginnings were slow, however; in no year until 1810 did more than four new facilities open in New England.[23] Part of the reason for this lay in the fact that not many investors were willing to risk their funds in manufacturing, and part lay in the fear of British competition. "The quantities of Brittish Goods . . . on hand Exceeding the Markett Obstruct the sale of Our Own Manufacturys. . . ." wrote Brown in 1791, and he urged a protective tariff to safeguard the young yarn industry. Even here, Brown was unable to carry his plan to a conclusion, for he failed

[23]Ware, *Early New England Cotton Manufacture*, p. 37.

to attempt to influence politicians in passing the legislation.[24]

Nor did Almy and Brown innovate in any major fashion. They concentrated on the production of yarn, ignoring possibilities in cloth. In 1794 John Bell of Glasgow invented a power loom, one he claimed would weave yarn into cloth. The device failed to perform as advertised, but the experiments continued. Yet Brown showed little interest in the device. Not until 1808 did the firm make a move in the direction of cloth, and then it did so by bringing handweavers into the shop, where they plied their trade side by side with the spinning machines. And this was done only when the practice of putting out yarn to home workers broke down due to increased demand. "We have several hundred pieces now out weaving," noted the company in 1809, "but a hundred looms in families will not weave so much cloth as ten at least constantly employed under the immediate inspection of a workman."[25] As demand increased, Almy and Brown added more weavers, which created problems of quality control and management the company could not overcome. Still, Almy and Brown made excellent profits during the embargo, and the managers seemed content with that.

This, then, was the situation in 1812, on the eve of the second war between America and Britain. A textile industry had begun in the northern states—perhaps it would be more accurate to call it a yarn industry. English machines and techniques were known, and there was a small labor force —some English, like Slater, others trained in the yarn factories—at hand. The demand for cotton cloth was high, and the prices attractive. Profits awaited those who could wrest additional secrets from England and bring them to America. The political climate had never been better, with even

[24]Hedges, *Browns of Providence Plantations,* p. 167.
[25]Ware, *Early New England Cotton Manufacture,* p. 51.

the Jeffersonians admitting the need to encourage domestic manufactures, especially cotton cloth. Into this situation came some of the Boston aristocrats, their outlets in commerce crippled, their energies hindered, but their ambitions unslaked. Building on the foundations set down by Almy and Brown, using their capital and training wisely, along with connections in Washington, they would develop not only a textile complex, but a new industrial form.

A handful of the Boston aristocrats had tried their hand at manufacturing in the late eighteenth century. George Cabot, Israel Thorndike, Henry Higginson, and several others—including two of Francis Lowell's uncles—had invested in and helped manage the Beverly Cotton Manufactory, which was incorporated in 1789. Within two years the firm employed forty workers who operated nine spinning jennies and sixteen looms, turning out yarn for sale in much the same way as Almy and Brown did in Rhode Island. The venture was not profitable; the partners lacked experience and interest, the machines continually broke down, and the firm was inadequately capitalized. It closed down in 1807—on the eve of the great boom in cotton cloth —having lost some $14,000 for its investors.

Francis Lowell was not personally involved in the Beverly experiment, though he doubtless knew of it. His land speculations in Maine, the ownership and management of a distillery, and real estate in Boston kept him quite busy. In 1808 he became a major factor in the construction of the India Wharf, designed to provide services for the Orient trade. Soon after, he entered into a partnership with the Jacksons, one designed to develop further the Oriental markets and also export flour and provisions to Spain. Then came the embargo, and Lowell's businesses were crippled. Some of his colleagues turned in anger to politics, intent on smashing Jefferson's power and, later on, Madison's as well. Others became smugglers, while a few turned to real estate. There is no evidence that Lowell considered any of these alternatives. Instead, in the autumn of 1810, Lowell, his wife and three children, together with young Augustus Thorndike, set off for a vacation in England.

Overworked and never robust, Lowell let it be known that he was going to England for reasons of health and for a vacation. To be sure, these were factors, but an Atlantic crossing in late autumn at that time was dangerous, certainly rough. Furthermore, relations between the United States and Britain were strained, with talk of war in the air. Lowell's commercial interests did not extend to England, so he was not going in search of new markets. It would appear, then, that he took the trip for some other reason, probably a desire to learn more of England's textile industry and perhaps pirate some of her secrets.

The Lowells rented a furnished house in Edinburgh and from there toured England in the fashion of so many other well-to-do American visitors. They spent considerable time in London, seeing the sights and attending several plays. Lowell also looked up some relatives who, after taking the Tory side in the Revolution, had been obliged to leave America. On his travels, Lowell met several British politicians, and he listened to their talk of the war and the possibility that the United States might enter as a belligerent. As a merchant, he was interested in British commerce, and Lowell spent several weeks in Bristol, talking to his English counterparts. He also visited iron foundries in Lancashire and Edinburgh and was impressed by their size, noting the rather sad state of labor in the new industrial towns.

We know Lowell visited cotton mills in Scotland. While in Edinburgh he met with fellow Bostonian Nathan Appleton. "We had frequent conversations on the subject of Cotton Manufacture," wrote Appleton almost a half century later, "and he informed me that he had determined, before his return to America, to visit Manchester, for the purpose of obtaining all possible information on the subject, with a view to the introduction of the improved manufacture in the United States. I urged him to do so."[26]

Lowell wrote home almost every day. In letters to members of his family and friends, he described the sights and gave his impressions of them. Many of the letters went to Jackson, his brother-in-law and business partner. In these he wrote of commercial matters and commissions he had obtained. Toward the end of 1811, however, mention of cotton manufacture appeared, and in a few of these letters Lowell conveyed his enthusiasm for what he had seen in British factories. Perhaps these were carried to America by friends, for Lowell would scarcely trust the ordinary mails, which might be opened by inspectors who would then learn of his interest in the carefully guarded secrets. In no letter, however, did he mention the specific mills visited.[27] It is fairly certain that in some of them he saw power looms, such as those constructed by Edmund Cartwright as early as 1787, and which he perfected during the years that followed. The looms were famous; weavers had burned several to the ground, claiming they were taking their jobs from them—and so they did.

Lowell probably visited New Lanark, which was only thirty miles from his Edinburgh house. There Robert Owen had constructed a factory where workers were well paid and housed. Owen attempted to demonstrate that profits and philanthropy could go hand in hand. Later on, some historians would conclude that it was Owen's business acumen, not his hopes for utopian factories, that was responsible for his success. At the time, however, it appeared that a factory master need not squeeze the last particle of labor from workers in order to achieve financial success. This, too, Lowell remembered.[28]

[26]Nathan Appleton, *Introduction of the Power Loom and Origins of Lowell* (Lowell, Mass., 1858), p. 7.
[27]Good studies of British factory management are Stanley D. Chapman, *The Early Factory Masters: The Transition to the Factory System in the Midlands Textile Industry* (London, 1967) and R.S. Fitton and A.P. Wadsworth, *The Strutts and the Arkwrights, 1758–1830: A Study of the Early Factory System* (Manchester, 1958).
[28]Josephson, *The Golden Threads*, p. 20.

The Lowells went to Paris in November 1811 and spent the winter there. On returning to London in the spring of 1812, they learned of the imminence of war between the United States and Britain. Shortly thereafter they prepared to return home. The British searched the Lowells' baggage twice and found nothing of contraband.

The war came in June, while the Lowells were on the high seas. Halfway across the Atlantic their ship was captured by a British frigate and taken to Nova Scotia. After some difficulty, the Lowells hired a small boat to take them to Boston. "I decided on entering Boston Harbor it was more beautiful than anything I had seen in my absence," wrote Hannah Lowell.[29]

Francis Lowell arrived to find his commercial enterprises badly crippled. He and other merchants might have been able to survive a short war, but there was no evidence in late 1812 that the conflict would be such. The commercial correspondence of the time indicates that the Boston merchants felt ruin was on the way, and some of them at least toyed with the idea of separation from the Union. "Should the war have been continued God only Knows what may be the consequences," wrote Henry Lee, then in Calcutta, to Patrick Tracy Jackson on January 30, 1813. "You and all other commercial men largely in trade I suppose will be ruin'd, the only good effect which can result will be the separation of the States, and that is quite uncertain."[30]

Jackson was in bad shape financially. He and Lowell had prospered during the previous two years, in part through commissions Lowell arranged while in England, and the rest a result of success in land dealings and the Orient trade. Profits were placed in reserve, and not plowed back into the business. Perhaps this was done in anticipation of hard times when and if war came. More likely, however, was the partners' desire to accumulate funds for a textile venture.

Others had the same idea. With the coming of war the

[29]Greenslet, *The Lowells*, p. 130.
[30]Porter, *Jacksons and Lees*, II, 1076.

already flourishing yarn mills worked overtime. Thomas Jefferson had spindles installed at Monticello, and other installations, most run by slaves, appeared in the cotton South. The knowledge and capital were in the North, however, and it was there the greatest advances were being made. Nine cotton mills were erected in Massachusetts alone in 1812, more than had been opened throughout New England in any previous year. Forty-five more would be opened in New England in 1813 and 1814, and of these, twenty-five would be in Massachusetts, nine in Connecticut, and six in Rhode Island.[31]

Massachusetts led the way because the state had adequate water power, a good labor force, but most important, sufficient capital (much of which had been derived from commerce and was now shifting to manufacturing) and an entreprencurial class. Of course, most of the Boston merchants preferred to remain in commerce, while others concentrated on politics in an attempt to end the war and revive their fortunes through a reopening of trade. Others, led by Francis Lowell, took the plunge into cotton textiles.

We cannot be certain when Lowell gathered his group or, for that matter, whom he contacted regarding his project. Certainly Jackson was there at the start, as was Nathan Appleton, and it is fairly certain Lowell received advice from his uncles, who had been badly burned in the Beverly enterprise but nonetheless could offer information on problems awaiting new manufacturers. Sometime in mid–1813, the group decided to form the Boston Manufacturing Company, to be located in Waltham, Massachusetts. Appleton, the only one of the founders to write a memoir, said that Lowell and Jackson "came to me one day on the Boston exchange, and stated that they had determined to establish a Cotton manufactory, that they had purchased a water power in Waltham, (Bemis paper mill,) and that they had obtained an act of incorporation, and Mr. Jackson had

[31]Ware, *Early New England Cotton Manufacture*, p. 37.

agreed to give up all other business and take the management of the concern."[32]

Understanding that one of the reasons for previous failures was insufficient capital, Lowell set out to raise what
was for the times a prodigious sum: $400,000, to be taken
in shares, and of which $100,000 would be called at first.[33]
Two thirds of the capital would be invested in machinery
and real estate, while the remainder would be used to initiate operations.

Boston Manufacturing issued one hundred shares of
capital stock, which were taken up by twelve shareholders,
all of whom were Boston aristocrats, close friends and relatives. Jackson, who had prospered through his association
with Lowell, took twenty shares, which meant he contributed $20,000 in cash to his brother-in-law's creation,
with a potential call for an additional $60,000. His two
brothers, James and Charles, accounted for an additional
fifteen shares between them, while Lowell purchased another fifteen for his own account. So half the shares were
owned by the closely knit Lowells and Jacksons. Israel
Thorndike, Sr., a prominent merchant from an old Boston
family, who had been associated with the Beverly enterprise and had close relations with the prestigious Cabots,
purchased ten shares, and his son, Israel Thorndike, Jr.,
took another ten. The Cabots, already smarting under mercantile restrictions and remembering the Beverly failure,
refused to enter the company. Appleton was asked to purchase ten shares, a modest investment for a man rumored
to be worth in the neighborhood of $400,000. But Appleton
was wary, even though he had been a major mover in the
organization of the company. "I told them that theoreti-
cally I thought the business ought to succeed, but all which
I had seen of its practical operation was unfavorable; I,

[32]Appleton, *Introduction of the Power Loom*, p. 7.
[33]This arrangement was common practice at the time. An investor would undertake to purchase shares with a par value with the understanding that only part
of the par value would be called initially, with the rest callable at some future
date, if and when necessary.

however, was willing to take five thousand dollars of the stock, in order to see the experiment fairly tried, as I knew it would be under the management of Mr. Jackson; and I should make no complaint under these circumstances, if it proved a total loss."[34] Then two of Jackson's brothers-in-law, John Gore and James Lloyd, purchased ten and five shares. Uriah Cutting took five; he had profited from a business arrangement with Lowell and hoped for more of the same. Benjamin Gorham and Warren Dutton, two more of Lowell's relatives, came in for a total of five shares between them.[35]

Boston Manufacturing was not only a creation of the Boston aristocrats but of a small group of relatives and business associates. In this, at least, it was not a modern enterprise but rather a family undertaking. Francis Lowell had studied the English mills carefully, and he understood the problems other mill owners had faced in America. He was conversant with yarn operations and recognized the need to attract skilled labor to his factory. Lowell had done well for friends and relatives who had backed his judgment in commerce. Ever since his college days he had been considered somewhat of a mechanical and mathematical prodigy. To fail to offer support for the new textile venture would not only indicate a lack of confidence in his abilities but would risk insulting a relative and friend. This personal consideration, added to a natural desire for profits, must have entered the equation when the company was organized. Those who rejected Lowell's advances must have done so out of a sincere distrust of the venture. Perhaps they would have given freely of their funds had Lowell planned another yarn mill; after all, they knew something of that, and could look to the Almy and Brown experience for assurance.

[34]Appleton, *Introduction of the Power Loom*, p. 8.
[35]Gibb, *Saco-Lowell Shops*, p. 9. Henry Lee, who also refused to come into the company, wrote that many potential investors tried to discourage Lowell. They "used all their influence to dissuade him from the pursuit of what they deemed a dangerous and visionary scheme." Josephson, *The Golden Threads*, p. 26.

But Lowell had other ideas, and these appeared strange, somewhat utopian, and certainly beyond their experience.

We have no way of knowing what Lowell told his backers and potential investors in 1813, but from what he did in setting up his firm, and the assurance with which he moved, it appears evident that, from the first, he operated under some kind of master plan. Lowell wanted to purchase ginned cotton and transport it to his factory. There it would be processed, spun into yarn, and then woven into cloth. All operations would be mechanized; unlike Almy and Brown, Lowell would not have handweavers, or, for that matter, hand operators, in his establishment. Nor would he rely upon occasional labor, or the children of local farmers. Instead, like Owen, he would recruit young girls from nearby farms, who would work in the factory for a few years to help their families or earn money for their dowries, and then move on. The plant would be supervised by a factory master, a man who understood machinery and would develop new machines when they were needed. The plant itself would be self-sufficient except for power, which would come from flowing water.

The British factories would provide Lowell with a guide, but no more than that. To him they seemed a crude attempt to mechanize what had formerly been done by hand, without changing the form of the organization to meet the needs of the new technology. A hundred years earlier, farm wives in their huts had produced yarn from flax, wool, or cotton, which was then taken to other farmers' wives and woven into cloth. All the British had done was to bring workers to a single place where they produced yarn, and then take that yarn to other places where it would be made into cloth. Slater, who had been trained under Strutt in Britain and brought that method to America, perfected it and helped mold an industry on its basis. Lowell would carry the process a giant step forward: he would change the structure of the factory to meet the needs of existing technology and create new technology when called for. In the process, he would also improve upon the foreign models, adapting the factory system to the American social and economic climate. As one student of the subject wrote, Lowell would "create the prototype of the big modern corporation, organized for mass production and integrating all processes from the raw material through the finished product under one management and, as far as possible, in one plant."[36]

Boston Manufacturing was officially incorporated on February 23, 1813, and the subscriptions completed by early September. But the organization of the company did not await completion of the financing. Late that summer Lowell began the search for a plant site—one near a river for water power—and he settled on the old Waltham paper mill. Then he sketched plans for his buildings, which would include a mill, a machine shop, and houses in which his workers would live.

Of these, the machine shop was central. Lowell would have to construct his own spindles and power looms, drawing in part from the American experience, recalling what he had witnessed in Britain, and adding new ideas as he went along. For this task he would need the help of a master mechanic, whose task it would be to actually put the machines together and superintend their operations. Lowell's choice was Jacob Perkins, a well-to-do merchant who had organized a successful nail factory and had a reputation as one of Massachusetts' leading inventors.[37] Perkins rejected Lowell's offer gracefully; he had plans of his own in

[36]Ware, *Early New England Cotton Manufacture*, p. 60. Another scholar wrote: "Previous to the starting of the Waltham mill the processes of spinning and weaving were carried on in separate establishments in both England and America, those who wove buying their twist of those who spun. It was the original purpose of Lowell and his associates to construct a weaving mill to do solely by power what had previously been done by hand, but it was learned that it would be cheaper to spin the twist rather than buy it, and accordingly the mill was built with about seventeen hundred spindles." Thus economy too played a role in Lowell's actions, one of the results of higher labor costs in America. Perry Walton, *The Story of Textiles* (New York, 1925), p. 192.
[37]Greville and Dorothy Bathe, *Jacob Perkins: His Inventions, His Times, and His Contemporaries* (Philadelphia, 1945), pp. 13–15 ff.

the textile industry. But he did recommend Paul Moody, a thirty-four-year-old mechanic who had helped construct some of the nail machines in Perkins's shop, and before that had been a handweaver. Moody was not an aristocrat but rather a self-taught mechanic of great skills. Lowell asked him to take on the task of superintendent at Waltham, and Moody accepted in October 1813.

Soon after, Lowell and Moody began work on a model for their power loom. They were eclectic in their approach, utilizing whatever idea or innovation seemed to fit in best. Lowell would provide the plans and drawings, while Moody would carry them out, although many of Moody's ideas went into the plans while Lowell helped in their execution. As the power loom emerged, it appeared quite similar to the Cartwright models then in use in Britain, but in several respects was superior. Lowell would travel around the area seeking new ideas by observing American looms. At one point he and Moody tried to purchase a patent for a winding machine from a Mr. Shepherd of Taunton. At first Shepherd tried to drive a hard bargain. "You must have them, you cannot do without them, as you know, Mr. Moody." Paul Moody then turned to Lowell and suggested an improvement, one that would make the purchase of the patents unnecessary. "I am just thinking that I can spin the cops direct upon the bobbin." Quickly realizing the Moody proposal would work, Shepherd agreed to accept Lowell's offer. "No," said Lowell, "it is too late."[38]

Lowell and Moody did purchase some machines from other textile shops. In March 1814, they bought a loom from E. Stowell for $100, and there were other, smaller purchases, all of which presumably offered additions to the Lowell-Moody loom. In the autumn of that year the power loom was ready to be seen by the investors. Writing in 1858, Appleton recalled the moment. With "admiration and satisfaction" they sat for several hours, "watching the

[38]Appleton, *Introduction of the Power Loom*, p. 10.

beautiful movement of this new and wonderful machine, destined as it evidently was, to change the character of all textile industry."[39]

Still, Lowell was not satisfied with his product. That winter he took a trip through the South and central states, seeking new ideas from other inventions. In February 1815, Jackson wrote to Lowell. "See if Stimpson has got a patent for his loom. As you return, go to Paterson, New Jersey. If Stowell is there, he can show you all worth seeing. See the looms in Baltimore if you can." Lowell did purchase a loom from Stimpson for $200, and perhaps some of its innovations later appeared on his own machine.[40]

Meanwhile, Jackson concentrated on construction of the buildings, especially the mill. He spent over $3,000 on machinery and tools during the year ending in November 1814, and half of this went into the loom. With the help of Jacob Perkins, a water wheel was installed at Waltham, along with dams, flumes, and a raceway. All of these, together with the building costs, came to more than $37,000. In December, the Boston Manufacturing Company placed its first order for cotton, and at the same time the machinery was installed in the mill. Not for another nine months, however, would the first cloth be ready for market.[41]

With the work of the machine shop almost completed, Lowell turned to the problems posed by the mill, the most important of which was the recruitment of a work force. According to plan, he spoke with local farmers regarding the possibility of their daughters coming to the mill. This operation required tact. The farmers tended to resent the new facility, which they regarded as an intrusion on the landscape. Furthermore, they were wary of permitting their young daughters to work and live in Waltham unless proper moral safeguards were assured. Some came to visit the site. There they saw a row of boardinghouses, clean and

[39] *Ibid.*, p. 9.
[40] Josephson, *The Golden Threads*, p. 21; Gibb, *Saco-Lowell Shops*, p. 14.
[41] Gibb, *Saco-Lowell Shops*, pp. 25–26.

neat, with each under the supervision of an older woman who would serve as a housemother or matron, and whose task it would be to assure the health and moral well-being of the workers. As Appleton wrote:

> There was little demand for female labor, as household manufacture was superceded by the improvements in machinery. Here was in New England a fund of labor, well educated and virtuous. It was not perceived how a profitable employment has any tendency to deteriorate the character. The most efficient guards were adopted in establishing boarding houses, at the cost of the Company, under the charge of respectable women with every provision for religious worship. Under these circumstances, the daughters of respectable farmers were readily induced to come into these mills for a temporary period.[42]

As previously mentioned, Lowell did not envisage a permanent mill force but rather expected the female operators to work for a few years and then leave for marriage. At that time they would have a small amount of savings and their future husbands would be assured of their purity, since Lowell meant his boardinghouses to be free of any hint of scandal. Lowell's plans for mill operators drew great attention at the time and later on and was considered a combination of old-fashioned Puritanism, with its stress on virtue and work, and the utopianism copied from Robert Owen. It may have been more than that. The mill work was hard and the hours long, even in comparison with work on the farms, where during the long winters there was some time for rest. The workers might be worn out after a few years at Waltham, after which they could be replaced by a fresh group of workers. Also, the work was not of the skilled variety, and so experience was not necessarily desirable.

[42]Appleton, *Introduction of the Power Loom*, pp. 15–16.

The female operators did not grow more valuable over time, but merely older. By May 1817, there were 125 employees at Waltham. Of these, 36 were weavers, earning $0.62 a day, 17 were carders at $0.44 a day, and 12 spinners, at $0.51 a day, with all of these jobs performed by the farmgirls. These wages were approximately the same as those in similar enterprises.[43] Boston Manufacturing had its utopian streak, but it was, after all, a business enterprise, out for a profit.

The situation was different at the machine shop, which was the key to the operation. Not only did the shop provide looms and other machines for the Waltham installation but it sold them to other textile factories that appeared during and after the war. Boston Manufacturing did well in textiles but even better in machines, and in time the company seemed to be a machine shop with a textile mill as a subsidiary, rather than a textile operation with a machine shop to provide needed devices. The machine shop workers, almost all of whom were mechanics, were the vital element at Boston Manufacturing, even though they received less publicity than did the farmgirls. Unlike the mill operators, they became more valuable with time, accumulating skills at innovation and production. Lowell recruited them carefully, and Moody took pains to keep them content. Some came from other shops, others were trained at Waltham, while Lowell attempted successfully to lure a few from England. In 1817, Boston Manufacturing had twenty-six machinists, each with an average daily wage of $1.43, well more than double that paid weavers. The roper received $2.31 a day, the two mule spinners, $3.14. Even the common laborers were paid $1.02.[44] As a leading authority on the subject put it, "The success of the Boston Manufacturing Company was the success of the machine shop. . . ."[45]

But the primary reasons for the enterprise, at least at the beginning, were the production of cotton cloth and its successful and profitable marketing. Unlike earlier mills,

---

[43]Gibb, *Saco-Lowell Shops*, p. 54.
[44]*Ibid.*, *loc. cit.*
[45]*Ibid.*, p. 60.

Boston Manufacturing hoped to develop a few large wholesale outlets rather than sell small quantities of cloth to
many small jobbers and commission brokers. This decision
was made more through need than design. In 1815, the only
large seller of domestic cloth in the Boston area was Mrs.
Isaac Bowers, who couldn't take much of the Waltham
product, due in part to the continued popularity of home
weaving and the desire of the upper class for imports. For
a while Lowell sold his cloth through an auctioneer. Then,
as the demand for domestic cloth rose, Appleton decided to
take charge of distribution. He controlled a commission
house, B.C. Ward and Company, which was near failure as
a result of a loss of foreign trade. Ward and Company
agreed to take all of Boston Manufacturing's cloth, which
it would sell for a commission of 1 percent. This was less
than was usually paid for the service, but Ward and Company expected to do well since the demand was so high. So
it did.

The combination of an increased demand for domestic
cloth and the lower costs per unit made possible by mechanical innovations at Waltham resulted in large profits for
the firm. In 1815, Boston Manufacturing showed sales of less
than $3,000. By 1817, the figure was well over $34,000, and
the company paid a dividend of 17 percent.[46] Certainly the
investors could congratulate themselves on their success,
which had come faster than any had expected in 1813. Even
Lowell was surprised at the results; he told Appleton
"that the only circumstance which made him distrust his
own calculations was, that he could bring them to no
other result but one which was too favorable to be credit-
able."[47]

The success of the Waltham mill, combined with the continued demand for cloth, resulted in the establishment of
other mills in the Northeast, and this meant increased sales

[46] *Ibid.*, pp. 27, 738.
[47] Josephson, *The Golden Threads*, p. 28.

for Lowell's machine shop. Many merchants maintained their political activities, and toward the war some of them went so far as to advocate outright secession. Others, equally angered by the loss of commerce, grudgingly abandoned the docks and went into manufacturing. They would remain factory masters after the war had ended. These were the men who molded the Massachusetts textile industry, making it the leader in the nation.

Most went into yarn; not until after 1816 did cloth manufacture increase significantly. But as late as 1820, Rhode Island outproduced all other states in yarn, with almost 2 million pounds spun and over 63,000 spindles in operation. New York had more spindles than Massachusetts, which was in third place nationally. By then, however, Massachusetts had grabbed a strong lead in cloth, with most of its looms in the Boston area, while its yarn facilities were developing at a faster rate than those of any other state. In 1826, Massachusetts had 135 factories, 25 more than Rhode Island. The lead increased during the next half century. Massachusetts reported 194 mills with 71,000 looms and 3,700,000 spindles in 1874. Rhode Island was a distant second, with 155 mills, 25,000 looms, and 1,300,000 spindles.[48] Lowell, the innovator, had created an industry that easily bested that of the less imaginative men of Providence.

Nor was manufacturing the only area in which Lowell developed techniques that the Browns and Slater only talked about. After the war ended in 1814, British textiles began to arrive in America once more. At the same time, the British dumped India yarn, spun by low-cost labor, on the American market in the hope of smashing the domestic yarn industry. Half the mills in Providence and Fall River were idle in 1816, while the number of Massachusetts companies seeking charters fell from thirty-four in 1814 to

[48]Frederick M. Peek and Henry H. Earl, *Fall River and Its Industries* (Fall River, 1877), pp. 82–85.

twenty-three in 1815 to eight in 1817. Established mills in the Boston area laid off workers, and several closed down after vain efforts to meet British prices.[49]

The Lowell mill, really the only one in the nation to produce large amounts of cloth, was an exception. It was better capitalized than the yarn facilities and more ably run. In fact, Lowell was able to meet the British competition, and actually sell cloth below the English price and still show a profit.

Jackson had developed into a skilled manager by then, while Moody had emerged as one of the nation's leading inventors and innovators. Today we would describe the three as a "management team." Jackson and Moody helped develop new production-line techniques far in advance of any in the industry. As for Lowell, he continued to oversee all operations, in spite of his failing health, and with Moody developed new machines for use in the industry.

Lowell assumed a new role after the war, that of spokesman for the manufacturing interests of the nation in general and the textile industry in particular. This brought him into conflict with his old colleagues who had remained in commerce, as manufacturers and merchants lobbied for beneficial legislation in Washington. Lowell sincerely believed that without a strong manufacturing sector the nation would suffer. At the same time, he recognized strength in that part of the economy would benefit the Boston Manufacturing Company.

Early in 1816, Lowell and Appleton journeyed to Rhode Island. In all probability it was a business trip, for Lowell was ill at the time, while Appleton rarely did anything not connected in one way or another with work. It may well have been that the two men wanted to explore the possibility of selling looms to the yarn spinners around Providence. Boston Manufacturing was the only significant cloth plant in America at the time, owned patents on key

[49]Ware, *Early New England Cotton Manufacture*, pp. 69, 299.

machines, and now wanted to benefit from its position by leading the yarn mills into cloth.[50] But there was no market for machines in Rhode Island. Instead, only a few of the mills were in operation, the rest having closed as a result of inability to meet British competition. Clearly help would be needed, for without it the yarn spinners would be doomed.

The textile interests looked to Washington for aid, and it was there that Lowell went after his visit to Rhode Island. Secretary of the Treasury Alexander Dallas had introduced a new tariff bill in February. Dallas recognized the need and demand for protection of domestic industry. He divided all manufacturing into three classes: the first consisted of those firmly established, which required absolute protection; the second those more recently established, which would also be protected but to a lesser extent; while the third was made up of products where imports would be needed, and so would not be protected. Dallas believed yarn and cloth belonged in the second category; Lowell and his colleagues insisted their products be placed in the first; most of the New England merchants thought yarn and cloth were natural foreign monopolies, and so should be placed in the third.

The original Treasury schedule called for a duty of 33.3 percent on all cotton products, but mercantile representatives on the Committee on Commerce and Manufactures in the House of Representatives managed to reduce the duty to 25 percent. Adjustments were made in other parts of the schedule in a clear struggle between the manufacturing

[50]Prior to this time, Lowell and others would purchase machines solely in order to acquire knowledge of their operations. In June 1816, Lowell attempted to conclude a swap of machines with David Greenough, a part owner of two mills. "It is perfectly indifferent to us whether you relinquish this bargain or not[;] if you think our prices too high[,] build for yourself[,] or if you think the price of your frame too low[,] keep it," he wrote. Not until February 1817, did Boston Manufacturing make its first outright sale of a loom and other machinery for use, the purchaser being Poignand Plant & Co. The price was $2,078 for machines that cost $1,670. The profit margin of some 20 percent was attractive, and encouraged Boston Manufacturing to seek additional sales. Gibb, *Saco-Lowell Shops*, pp. 40–41.

interests on the one hand and the commercial and agricultural representatives on the other. It was every man and industry for himself. William Irving of New York demanded protection for the clock manufacturers of his state but opposed an upward revision of the coal tariff supported by James Pleasants of Virginia, for example. Daniel Webster, already becoming known as a weather vane for New England, represented Portsmouth, New Hampshire, at the time, a mercantile town dependent upon the seas for its life. As such, Webster opposed protection that might cut into trade. On March 25, he recommended that the tariff on cotton goods be set at 30 percent for two years, 25 percent for the next two years, and 20 percent thereafter. John C. Calhoun, then a nationalist and as such a supporter of domestic manufactures, was willing to accept this compromise, but representatives from the textile and yarn areas of Rhode Island and Massachusetts were not. Then followed a debate, in the course of which Robert Wright of Maryland demanded that all who owned shares in textile or yarn companies be forbidden from voting on the schedule. Wright withdrew his motion later on, at which time the wheeling-and-dealing for compromises began.

Lowell was in Washington to petition Congress in behalf of the cloth interests. While there, he formed an alliance with the southern cotton growers, on the basis that American cloth produced from American fibers needed protection against foreign cloth from foreign fibers. This alliance could be seen in his memorial to Congress:

The articles whose prohibition we pray for, are made of very inferior materials, and are manufactured in a manner calculated to deceive rather than serve the consumer. No part of the produce of the United States enters into their composition. They are the work of foreign hands on a foreign material. Yet they are thrown into this country in such abundance as to threaten the exclusion of its more useful and substantial manufacture.[51]

Lowell was a skilled negotiator. The final committee bill contained a special proviso—one might call it the Lowell Proviso—which contained an olive branch for the Massachusetts commercial interests:

> Provided, That all cotton cloth, or cloths of which cotton is the material of chief value (excepting nankeens imported direct from China), the original cost of which at the place whence imported shall be less than twenty-five cents per square yard, shall be taken and deemed to have cost twenty-five cents per square yard, and shall be charged with duty accordingly.[52]

If passed, the Lowell Proviso would have guaranteed profits in textiles. At the same time, a declining tariff on other cotton goods, yarn in particular, would have placed that industry under increasing pressures, obliging the yarn spinners to seek other outlets for their energies—perhaps in cloth. If this took place, they would require machines. Since the only significant producer of textile machinery in the United States was the Boston Manufacturing Company, Lowell and his associates would have done well indeed.

Of course, Lowell's congressional allies paid a small price for the proviso. The section dealing with China cloth was put in to satisfy the merchants in the Orient trade in Boston and elsewhere. Webster, who spoke for them, called it "an act of strict justice." Later on he met Lowell, writing, "I found him full of exact, practical knowledge, on many subjects." For the moment, Webster stood for the New England shipping interests. But the moment changed, and as manufacturing grew, so did Webster's enthusiasm for

[51]Josephson, *The Golden Threads*, p. 30.
[52]Edward Stanwood, *American Tariff Controversies in the Nineteenth Century* (Boston, 1903), pp. 139–140.

factories. Soon after, he went on the payroll at the Boston Manufacturing Company.[53]

Thomas Telfair of Georgia saw through the deal and objected vigorously. Was Congress to take a direct hand in the economic destiny of the nation? Were the legislators to favor one group of businessmen over another, or for that matter consider the question directly? This, he said, would be "taxing the community one day to foster the interest of the manufacturers, and on the next to secure to the mercantile class a high profit. . . ."[54] He, for one, was opposed.

The debate raged, with neither side willing to settle for what it had received. Thomas Pickering of Massachusetts, who spoke for the Salem commercial interests, was strong for the merchants; he wanted to remove the Lowell Proviso. On the other hand, Solomon Strong of the same state, a representative of the factory owners, attempted to increase the textile tariff even more than already existed in the draft.

Votes on several motions indicate that the commercial interests were far stronger than the manufacturers in 1816. But the textile men, combined with the cotton growers and some of the China merchants, got pretty much what they wanted in the final version of the bill. The cloth duty would be 25 percent for three years and 20 percent thereafter. The Lowell Proviso would be retained but would not go into effect for three years. The tariff was high enough to ensure profits at Waltham, yet low enough to encourage the yarn spinners to seek purchases of weaving machines, presumably from the Boston Manufacturing Company. Lowell was delighted. So was Calhoun, whose cotton supporters shared the victory. Lowell saw the American future in terms of factories; Calhoun thought the factories would serve the farmers, still by far the largest group in the nation. "When our manufactures are grown to a certain perfection, as they soon will be under the fos-

[53]Josephson, *The Golden Threads*, p. 31; Gibb, *Saco-Lowell Shops*, p. 61.
[54]Charles M. Wiltse, *John C. Calhoun, Nationalist, 1782–1828* (New York, 1944) p. 65.

tering care of government, we will no longer experience these evils," said Calhoun of the protective tariff. "The farmer will find a ready market for his surplus produce, and, what is of almost equal consequence, a certain and cheap supply of all his wants. His prosperity will diffuse itself in every class in the community."[55]

So it appeared in 1816. The pathway to a balanced economy seemed fixed, and Calhoun believed it would result in harmony between the nation's sections and economic pursuits. It was not to be; the alliance of cotton and machines would barely outlast the generation. Within four decades the descendants of the Lowells and the Calhouns would be at one another's throats.

We don't know Lowell's views on the subject. It is certain he worked effectively for his firm, the textile industry, and manufacturing in general. That, for him, appeared to have sufficed. Boston Manufacturing's machinery sales increased, rising to $8,700 in 1818 and $28,800 in 1819, at which time machinery profits were $14,000. The company also began licensing its patents, and by 1821 this provided substantial profits too. In 1817 the company's net sales were $34,000; five years later they were $345,000.[56]

Lowell lived long enough to see Boston Manufacturing a thriving concern, but not much beyond that. In 1815 he began to talk of recurrent pains, and when his wife died that year he fell into moods of depression. Never a robust man, he now seemed to fall apart physically. Lowell tried several spas, with no change in health. The trips to Rhode Island and Washington exhausted him. Lowell died in August 1817, at the age of forty-two.

Like most significant figures, it might be said of Francis Lowell that had he not existed, he might have been invented. Certainly the Boston aristocracy had others who

[55]Stanwood, *American Tariff Controversies*, p. 151.
[56]Gibb, *Saco-Lowell Shops*, pp. 27, 47.

might have recognized the need for a shift in economic direction in order to maintain the group's power. Francis Lowell, who led a segment of the aristocracy from commerce to manufacturing, happened to be the one who accomplished the task. Given the impetus and inspiration of the Boston Manufacturing Company, the "Boston Associates," as its leaders were known, continued to expand, individually and collectively. Within thirty years of Lowell's death, the Associates controlled 20 percent of all the cotton spindles in New England, 30 percent of Massachusetts' railroads, 40 percent of the state's insurance, and 40 percent of Boston's banking. Boston itself remained a major city, in large part through the efforts started by Lowell and his associates; the aristocrats would live off the capital given them by that generation for the rest of the century. Until late in the nineteenth century the Boston Stock Exchange, not its New York counterpart, was the major market for industrial securities in the United States.

Could this have been started by anyone else but Lowell? British industrial secrets had been pirated into America long before the Lowells made their European trip. Had Lowell not brought back the secrets of the power loom, someone else might have done so. Within the Boston Associates there were others—Jackson and even Appleton, for example—who might have accomplished the task. Appleton denied this, however. "For, although Messrs. Jackson and Moody were men of unsurpassed talent and energy in their way, it was Mr. Lowell who was the informing soul, which gave direction and form to the whole proceeding."[57] Yet Moody's industrial genius was evident, as were Jackson's abilities at management and Appleton's at finance and investment. The Boston Associates did not falter with Lowell's passing; as we have seen, it grew rapidly.[58] Nor was Lowell the only significant manufacturing representa-

[57] Appleton, *Introduction of the Power Loom*, p. 15.
[58] For a summary of the other companies formed by members of the Boston group, see Ware, *Early New England Cotton Manufacture*, pp. 299–300, 320–21.

tive in Washington during the tariff debates of 1816. His skills at manipulating, lobbying, and the organizing of forces were undeniable; the results speak for themselves. But others had them too. Nail, iron, coal, clock, and other producers and manufacturers received their due from Congress that year. Lowell was a leader, a man who spoke for an industry that was turning out some $40 million worth of product a year, but he was not the only one available.

In essence, Lowell was an unusually talented man, one with more foresight than most, and a greater vision than many of his contemporaries. He was bold, imaginative, and flexible—the qualities one expects to find in a business leader. Lowell did not have a monopoly of these virtues, although he possessed them in the right mixture and was present in the right context at the right time. The American business tradition was not carried out by solitary geniuses—or at least, very seldom did such a person appear and gain power—but rather armies of them. Seen in this light, Francis Lowell was not an indispensable man. He was, instead, a necessary one.

II

Cyrus Hall McCormick: From Farm Boy to Tycoon

The United States was an agrarian nation at the time of the founding of the Boston Manufacturing Company, and it would remain essentially agrarian to the end of the century.[1] Lowell's factory at Waltham, the Almy and Brown operation in Providence, and the dozens of others that dotted the landscape in the 1820s and 1830s were viewed in somewhat the same way as space launchers are today—as intrusions on the countryside, on a land clearly meant for farmers. America had excellent soils, inadequate capital resources, and was chronically short of labor. Such transportation as had been developed was geared to the agrarian sector, used by farmers to bring goods to market, and by merchants to carry supplies to the farms. Nature and economics appeared to have destined the land for grains and cotton, not for factories. So Jefferson appeared correct in appealing for a nation of farmers—or at least he would appear to have been accurate in his projections during his lifetime. Even Hamilton, with his bias toward manufactur-

---

[1] By 1870, the United States was responsible for almost a quarter of the world's manufacturing output. Still, such production was a small part of the world's economy, and smaller yet for America. More than nine out of ten Americans still found employment on the soil at that time. Douglass C. North, *The Economic Growth of the United States, 1790–1860* (New York, 1966) pp. v ff.

ing, asked little more than self-sufficiency for the nation in
all goods. Neither man spoke of an industrial America.
How could they, given the technology of the period in
which they lived, the mood of the populace, and the heri-
tage of European civilization they shared?

Of the merchant class and himself one of the precursors
of an age of industry, Francis Lowell might be viewed as
little more than an appendage of the cotton culture, existing to process ginned cotton into cloth and so serve the
plantations of the South. This, it would appear, was the
view of men like Calhoun, who visited Waltham and sur-
rounding towns in the 1820s and 1830s to see what the Yan-
kees were doing with their cotton. Just as a previous generation of the Boston aristocrats had carried and sold the
products of agrarian America overseas, and then imported
goods for sale to farmers, so the men of the 1820s and 1830s
—their sons and grandsons—would process the raw
materials of the farms into finished goods, and most of these
would be consumed by farmers. Industry depended upon
and existed to serve agriculture; the American business
tradition had its roots in the soil.

Two northerners, Eli Whitney and Francis Cabot Lowell, had pioneered in developments that helped make cotton
king in the South. A Virginian, Cyrus McCormick, developed the technology that created emperor wheat, which a
generation later would triumph in the battle between the
two crops. In the process McCormick accomplished much
more. If Lowell was the father of the American factory
system, McCormick was the precursor of and model for the
big businessmen who followed him, men whose ties to the
soil were indirect and in some cases nonexistent. Yet
McCormick, like Lowell, had his origins in products of the
soil.

McCormick is generally credited with being the inventor
of the reaper, a device that cut wheat in such a way that the
grain would not fall from the stalks, leaving it in the field
for a binder, who would then gather it and arrange the

stalks in orderly sheaves. Later on, McCormick helped develop a machine that would bind the stalks as well, and his name is associated with a variety of other devices used in the wheat fields. But even McCormick's most ardent champions concede that had he never lived, effective reapers would have been invented, while lingering doubt as to his inventive genius remains to this day.

In Chicago he is still considered one of the founders of the modern city that emerged from the great fire that leveled the wooden town in 1871. McCormick's role in rebuilding Chicago was significant, but not central, and in any case Chicago did more for him than he for it, while the fire proved a blessing in disguise in that it enabled McCormick to create a modern factory instead of modifying an already obsolete facility.

Some historians view the Civil War as an economic contest between cotton and wheat, and so credit McCormick with a central role in the North's victory. The war was far more than that, however, and McCormick's loyalty to the Union cause was suspect at the time.

The popular literature of a half century ago pictures McCormick as the man who unveiled American inventiveness to the Europeans, with the reapers of his design changing the face of agricultural Europe, causing social changes of a major magnitude, and creating relative prosperity for the masses of the old continent. But the Europeans had developed reapers and other farm equipment too, some of which were superior to the McCormick machines and in most ways competitive in price, while McCormick's American competitors did better in the European markets than he for a while. The reaper would have been invented, the North would have won the Civil War, European as well as American wheat fields would have been mechanized, and Chicago rebuilt, all without the aid of Cyrus Hall McCormick.

Having said all this is not to deny that McCormick remains a major figure in the American business tradition. It is not McCormick the inventor, however, who made the major contribution. Instead, McCormick's most significant work came in the area of sales and distribution, servicing and credit, popularization and education. Without these accomplishments and armed only with a superior machine, McCormick might yet have failed. But with his innovations in distribution and popularization, together with a set of machines that in some ways were inferior to those of his competitors, McCormick triumphed.

McCormick's grandfather arrived in America in 1735 and settled in Pennsylvania. His fifth son, Robert, was born three years later, and grew up to become a farmer and part-time weaver. Robert McCormick moved south with his family during the Revolution, arriving in Virginia in 1779. Soon after, his first wife died, and Robert married Mary Ann Hall, the daughter of a local farmer. Their son, Cyrus Hall McCormick, was born in 1809.

In most respects Cyrus McCormick's childhood was like that of the majority of farm boys of that time and place. He managed to survive diseases, received some schooling, attended the local Presbyterian church, and courted the local girls. At an early age he went into the fields to work alongside his father, and learned to tell whether the soils were good or worn out, whether the crops that year would be successful or fail, and how to use horse and slave power effectively. By all accounts Robert McCormick was a good farmer, a man who learned his skills not only from practice but by reading agricultural journals and swapping information with his fellows. In one respect, however, he was different from most. A half century later, Cyrus McCormick wrote:

My father was both mechanical and inventive, and could and did at that time, use the tools of his shops in making any piece of machinery he wanted. He in-

vented, made and patented several more or less valuable agricultural implements, but, with perhaps less
inventive speculation than some others, most of his
inventions dropped into disuse after the lapse of some
years. Among these were a threshing machine, a hydraulic machine, a hemp-breaking machine, with a
peculiar horsepower adapted to it, and others.[2]

All of the machines Robert McCormick worked on were
related to wheat farming in one way or another, with the
sole exception of a method or device to aid in the teaching
of "performing on the violin." Later on, McCormick's son
recalled that he was always more interested in working
with his father in the shops than in the fields. By the time
Cyrus McCormick was in his early teens he and Robert had
become co-inventors in the shop, trading information and
seeking improvements as they went. None of Robert
McCormick's devices ever succeeded financially. He would
use them on his own farm and on occasion sell one or
another to a neighbor, all of whom appeared interested in
what he was doing. In the process, however, he was training his son and educating him in the arts of farming and
machines. This too was not unusual in the Virginia of the
early nineteenth century. By working with and observing
his father, Cyrus McCormick learned of machines, wheat,
patents, and the frustrations that accompanied farming,
inventing, manufacturing, and selling.

Robert McCormick was particularly interested in his
thresher, and so were his neighbors. He claimed it was
superior in design and construction to others, built a few
in his shop, and sold them to other Virginia farmers for $70
apiece. Actually, this thresher was not unusual in any way,
and probably no better in performance than others turned
out by rival farmer-inventors. Nor was the idea of such
implements novel. Throughout history wheat farming had

[2]"Sketch of My Life," by C.H. McCormick, August 4, 1876, as quoted in William
T. Hutchinson, *Cyrus Hall McCormick: Seed-Time, 1809–1856* (New York, 1930), p. 34.

been seasonal. A busy planting period was followed by the long, tedious, and steady work of caring for the crop. Then came the harvest, a few days during which the wheat was cut, gathered, and threshed. Afterward the farmers would settle down for several months, preparing for the next planting season.

The lone farmer had little difficulty caring for growing wheat or preparing for planting. He might need help at these times, and this usually came from members of his family. The harvest was the critical time. The wheat had to be cut and gathered at the right time, for otherwise it would break down and decay. It could not be left in its cut state in the field, but had quickly to be taken to the barn for threshing. On small farms the entire family would work around the clock during the four-to-ten day harvest season, hoping to gather and thresh as much of the crop as possible. Sometimes this labor was insufficient, and then the hogs and cattle would be turned loose to feed on the already rotting grain. This constituted waste, the fattening of livestock on expensive fodder. The short harvest season could bring disaster to larger farmers whose holdings could not be serviced by their immediate families. At such times as harvest they would seek occasional labor, paying whatever wages were then current. These farmers could not rely upon friends and neighbors for assistance, since all were busy with their own harvests and storage of crops. Thus, from the first, the wheat farmers recognized the need for farm machinery. These machines would be most useful at the time of planting. They would be vital at harvests.

The lack of help during harvests was one of the major factors holding down the size of farms in wheat areas. Slaves were not the answer: it would hardly pay to own a slave for those few days and not be able to use him effectively the rest of the year. Nor would occasional labor do except in areas with large numbers of unemployed men and women, and such was not the case in America. Clearly American farmers needed a well-designed reaper, one that would cut the wheat cleanly and not break down at critical moments. Many farmers were at work on just such a device. Robert McCormick joined them, and worked on a reaper as well as a thresher.

Medieval farmers must have dreamed of such machines. They would thresh wheat by stamping on it and then blowing the chaff away, or they would wait for the wind to do the job for them. These same farmers used scythes and sickles to cut the grain stalks. They would stumble through the wheat fields with large, ungainly scythes in hand and flail at the wheat. Or they would go more slowly, cutting clumps of stalks with the smaller but more effective sickles, taking more time in the process. Both hand tools were ineffective, and they knew it. At first they tried to design better sickles and scythes. Then they turned to the development of other hand tools. Later on they would try to invent reaping machines.

Actually, the Romans made stabs at developing reapers —they are mentioned in Pliny and Palladius. Crude "harvesting carts" were used by some English farmers in the late sixteenth century. With the coming of the agricultural revolution in England in the late eighteenth century, several models appeared, none of them very effective. By the early nineteenth century, dozens of inventors in England were experimenting with reaping devices.[3] Some produced working models, but few of them were able to sell many to skeptical farmers. It was one thing to advertise the miracle machines but quite another to convince customers they could do the job as claimed. Farmers were asked to purchase the machines at prices they really couldn't afford, with no guarantee as to performance and no recourse if they failed. Some of the inventors would take their devices into wheat fields, invite local farmers to watch, and then give demonstrations. Most of these ended in disaster, with the grain uncut or butchered; and more often than not, the

[3]G.E. Fussell, *The Farmer's Tools, 1500–1900: The History of British Farm Implements, Tools and Machinery Before the Tractor Came* (London, 1952), pp. 115–18.

machine broke down. One inventor tried a novel approach in 1814, when he advertised:

> J. Dobbs most respectfully informs his Friends and the Public, that having invented a Machine to expedite the Reaping of Corn, etc. but having been unable to obtain the Patent till too late to give it a general inspection in the field with safety, he is induced to take advantage of his Theatrical Profession and make it known to his Friends, who have been anxious to see it, through that medium. . . . To conclude [the performance] will be presented the celebrated farce of Fortune's Frolic. The part of Robin Roughhead will be taken by Mr. Dobbs, in which he will work the Machine in character, in an Artificial Field of Wheat, planted as near as possible in the manner it grows.[4]

As far as we can tell, the demonstration was unimpressive. In any case, that was the last the world heard of the Dobbs machine. English farmers continued to use sickles and scythes, the larger farmers employing jobless men and women, usually Irish.

A similar situation existed in America, compounded by the labor shortage and the resultant higher wages paid to occasional workers. Working with a scythe, an experienced farmer—followed by men or boys who would bind the wheat—might cut two acres in a good day. At prevailing wages, the farmer who hired workers could expect to spend three dollars an acre for his labor, which would be about 10 percent of the money he would receive for his wheat. Little wonder, then, that American wheat farmers sought methods to lower the cost. Increased labor was not the answer, so it would have to come from new tools, animal power, or machines. In 1823, Jonathan Roberts of the Pennsylvania Agricultural Society put it this way:

[4]Bennet Woodcroft, comp., *Specifications of English Patents for Reaping Machines* (London, 1853), pp. 16–17.

In practical husbandry the expense of labor is a cardinal consideration. Since the year 1818, farmers have very sensibly felt that labour has been much dearer than produce. We can not speedily look for their equalization; a mitigation of this effect may be sought in some degree by improved implements. . . . Nothing is more wanted than the application of animal labour in the cutting of grain. It is the business on the farm which requires the most expedition, and it is always the most expensive labour. Such an invention can be no easy task, or the ingenuity of our fellow citizens would, ere this, have effected it. But we have no right to despair where there is not a physical impossibility. A liberal premium might well be employed to obtain such an object.[5]

The farmers and inventors of America were well aware of this. Some knew of Jeremiah Bailey's reaper, developed the previous year, and Peter Gaillard's earlier model. But these and others proved unworkable or unreliable, and in any case the inventors were unable to market them in numbers. Alexis de Tocqueville, the perceptive French visitor to America who traveled through the land in the early 1830s and wrote of his observations in 1835, did not seem to believe one would be forthcoming, at least not until Americans had become an urbanized people. "To cultivate the ground promises an almost certain reward for his efforts, but a slow one," he wrote in *Democracy in America*. "In that way you only grow rich little by little and with toil. Agriculture only suits the wealthy, who already have a great superfluity, or the poor, who only want to live." As for the rest, "his choice is made; he sells his field, moves from his house, and takes up some risky but lucrative profession."[6] In other words, only those who could afford to hire gangs of workers in harvesting crops, and the subsistence farmer, working with his family at harvest, would survive.

[5]Hutchinson, *McCormick: Seed-Time*, p. 69.
[6]Alexis de Tocqueville, *Democracy in America* (New York, 1969 ed.), p. 552.

In the summer of 1831, Cyrus McCormick, then twenty-two years old, was working on an improved scythe, while his father attempted to develop a mechanical reaper. Robert McCormick had produced a reaper in 1816 but abandoned it for other projects. The new device appeared more promising, though like its predecessors it had flaws and probably was unmarketable. Robert McCormick was one of many farmers and inventors at work on reapers that summer. William Manning of New Jersey had his own machine, developed independently of the McCormick reaper, and Obed Hussey, a retired sailor, was developing the machine he would demonstrate two years later. Enoch Ambler and Alexander Wilson of New York and Samuel Lane of Hallowell, Maine, were preparing their reapers, as were others who are forgotten today.

Robert McCormick's reaper was not completed in time for the 1831 harvest, but another model, this one fashioned with the help of Cyrus, was given field trials the following year. About a hundred people attended the first demonstration, which started out poorly. Then a neighbor, William Taylor, offered to permit Cyrus to harvest one of his fields. The McCormicks accepted, and cut six acres of wheat that day. One observer, a teacher at a local school, proclaimed the machine was worth at least $100,000. Another, a farmer, noted that the machine handled the stalks roughly, shaking the grain off and onto the field. He wanted his wheat reaped, not threshed, he said, and would have nothing to do with the reaper.[7] On the other hand, a second farmer, James McDowell, Sr., ordered one to be built for him to be used in the harvest of the following year.[8]

In September 1833, McCormick advertised his reapers for sale at $50 each, but none were taken. By then the basic machine devised by Robert McCormick had been changed in so many ways that it could be called a Cyrus McCormick machine. Later accounts indicate it was as good as any then

[7]Herbert N. Casson, *Cyrus Hall McCormick: His Life and Work* (Chicago, 1909), pp. 37–41.
[8]Hutchinson, *McCormick: Seed-Time*, p. 89.

being produced, but no better. And like his fellows, Cyrus McCormick hadn't the ability to sell his devices yet. The construction of the reaper was an impressive but not difficult feat; farmer-inventors elsewhere had already shown it could be done. Selling farmers on the idea of using the devices was another matter, while making it possible for them to obtain them at reasonable rates taxed the imagination of all producers.

At one time it was common to talk of the conservatism of farmers generally, including the Americans in this catchall. Today we know such generalizations are meaningless or deceiving. The introduction of farm machinery in England in the eighteenth century provided the impetus for what later came to be called the industrial revolution, and this would not have been possible unless the English farmers were willing to accept modifications of their old methods. The libraries of men like George Washington and Thomas Jefferson reveal that large farmers of the late eighteenth and early nineteenth centuries were interested in new methods of planting, cultivating, and harvesting their crops, and several of the founding fathers invented new plows and scythes or experimented with fertilizers and labor usage. In most cases these inventions and experiments involved the perfection of old techniques rather than the introduction of new ones, and this was to be expected; the same developments were taking place in textile production, commercial dealings, and other areas of business.

The acceptance of complex farm machinery such as the reaper, thresher, binder, and seeder was something else. It involved the introduction of a new technology to farming, not the further development of the old. Convincing wheat farmers to accept this new technology—to reorient their thinking, as it were—would be difficult. But it had been done in cotton with the gin (a lesser change, to be sure, but a change that affected an entire society, and more so than would any of the wheat-related inventions) and it could be done with other crops. The fact that most of the inventors of reapers and other wheat machines were farmers themselves, like McCormick, indicates that many farmers were prepared to accept the changes, and even welcome them. Some argued that the machines frightened their horses, others that they broke down and couldn't be repaired easily, and most were troubled by the costs. Perhaps they would have accepted reapers more easily if they could be rented. Or they might have been willing to hire "reaping teams," which would sell a service rather than a device. Just as wheat farmers would not keep slaves for effective use during only two or three weeks of the year, they balked at the purchase of a reaper, which would be stored in the barn for fifty or so weeks, and then used intensively the other two. If the machine broke down during the harvest and couldn't be repaired in time to continue the harvest, then it might be said it caused more harm than good, offering farmers a promise of help when little was really forthcoming.

There is no indication that McCormick or any other farm machine manufacturer considered the sale of the service rather than the machine at this time. Even had they done so, they lacked the capital for such an approach. On the other hand, individual farmers in the 1850s did sell their land, purchase machines and hire labor, and then go from farm to farm selling their services. Other wheat farmers, in the Midwest in particular, would join together to purchase two, three, and more machines, and then work together to bring in the crops of the township. Some would run the machines, others would become experts at repair, and the rest would organize teams for binding and threshing. These organizational innovations came from the farmers, not the manufacturers. McCormick and other businessmen, who were really farmers-inventors-manufacturers-distributors combined, understood what was happening and adjusted their policies accordingly. Throughout the early history of the reaper industry, the feedback from salesmen to the factories was more important than the orders that came from the factory and went into the field. McCormick and others like him would organize the industry, but they would do so in response to the market. Those who learned to do this—McCormick being one of them—would succeed. The others would fail.

The wheat farmers of the late 1830s were skeptical of the machines but did not reject them out of hand. As de Tocqueville indicated, farming was becoming less attractive to young men of that period. "Every farmer's son and daughter are in pursuit of some genteel mode of living," wrote a contributor to the *New England Farmer* in 1838. "After consuming the farm in the expenses of a fashionable, flashy, fanciful education, they leave the honorable profession of their fathers to become doctors, lawyers, merchants, or ministers or something of the kind. . . ." Others went to the mills, such as those begun by Lowell and his followers, to earn more in a week than they could obtain on the farm in a month. A New Yorker, writing in the same period, complained:

> Thousands of young men do annually forsake the plough, and the honest profession of their fathers, if not to win the fair, at least from an opinion, too often confirmed by mistaken parents, that agriculture is not the road to wealth, to honor, nor to happiness. And such will continue to be the case, until our agriculturalists become qualified to assume that rank in society to which the importance of their calling, and their numbers, entitle them, and which intelligence and self-respect can alone give them.[9]

There was some hope that the native-born farmers who were fleeing to the cities or assuming new occupations in rural areas would be replaced by immigrants from Ireland,

[9]Percy W. Bidwell and John I. Falconer, *History of Agriculture in the Northern United States, 1620–1860* (New York, 1941), pp. 204–6.

England, and the continent. Many of these did go to the farm areas seeking land, and more for employment, but their talents did not impress local farmers, who complained of their lack of skills. As a result of this labor shortage, the costs of farm labor rose. In Massachusetts, for example, the average wage of a farm worker, without board, went from $0.78 a day in 1811–20 to $0.88 a day in 1831–40. The prices for wheat declined irregularly from 1815 to 1836, to the point where some wheat farmers wondered whether it paid to have their crops harvested. In such a circumstance, machinery—even if the machines had to be purchased—would not only be beneficial but, in some cases, obligatory. In writing of the introduction of new reapers, ploughs, drills, threshers, etc., Jesse Buell, one of the more astute observers of the agricultural scene, said: "A farm may now be worked with half the expense of labor that was wont to be worked forty years ago, and may be better worked withal."[10]

Tragedy struck the wheat fields in the second half of the 1830s. First there was the failure of the crops in 1836 due to bad weather. Late in the year wheat sold for $2.00 a bushel and flour for $12.00, twice the price of the year before. Some farmers did well, but most suffered and many went bankrupt. It was the culmination of a series of below-average harvests.[11] Successful and unsuccessful farmers alike strove to increase their productivity, to take advantage of higher prices and at the same time earn sufficient money to repay their debts. To some this meant the purchase of machinery. The editor of the *Farmers' Cabinet*, writing in December 1836, said:

> We have long been firm in the faith that the time would come when most of the operations carried on in the growth of corn and grain, would be done by machinery. . . . We have no doubt that ploughing will

[10] *Ibid.*, p. 281.
[11] *Ibid.*, p. 498.

be done successfully by steam, and that mowing and
reaping will be done by the same Herculean power.
For a long time our farmers were opposed to the
threshing machines,—this opposition arose from imperfect machinery, but still this very opposition re-
tarded the perfection of the very machines it opposed.
So in reaping and mowing, some imperfect attempts
have been made which were not perfectly successful;
and hence the whole scheme has been condemned.[12]

The crop failures coincided with, and in part caused, the
financial panic of 1837, which was followed by a depression
that deeply wounded the young industrial sector of
the nation's economy.[13] The increasing demand for farm
machines pulled McCormick and others into the business.

But not immediately. After obtaining patents on his machine, McCormick's interests were diverted by a venture
into iron manufacturing. For a while it seemed the business
would prosper, and had this happened, McCormick might
have remained in that field. Then the depression struck the
iron business with a hammer blow. The iron facility lost
money, and eventually went out of business. McCormick
turned his attention to reapers once more, determined to
recoup his losses through sales to farmers.

While McCormick attempted to make a go of it in iron,
Obed Hussey concentrated on the reaper. He traveled to
New York in 1834, where he found a manufacturer for his
device, appointed agents, and met with editors of agricultural newspapers to tell them of his work. For a while
Hussey's business languished. He sold several machines
from his Maryland factory, conducted field demonstrations
for skeptical farmers, and placed advertisements in farm-

[12]Hutchinson, *McCormick: Seed-Time*, p. 153.
[13]Samuel Rezneck, *Business Depressions and Financial Panics* (Westport, 1968), pp.
73–100, is the best description of the social and economic problems of the depression.

ers' newspapers. "My next year's machine will be much superior to any which I have before made," claimed Hussey in 1839, "and to which I apprehend but little improvement can be subsequently made." Hussey later claimed that his machine could cut twenty acres a day, rather high a figure and one he rarely could attain. Often Hussey oversold what amounted to experimental models, and so would lose credibility among some of his customers. His approach was that of a manufacturer. Hussey would produce machines and then try to sell them, using the money obtained from the sales to turn out slightly better models. He was the first man to enter the business as a would-be mass-producer, and for years claimed to have been the inventor of the reaper, challenging McCormick and others on this ground. There is reason to believe that his early machines were the best in America, superior to McCormick's in most ways. McCormick's early success came not from a better design or construction but from his approach to the market.

McCormick did not sell a machine outside his immediate neighborhood until 1840. Up to then he spent so much time on the iron business that he had little to spare for the reaper. He would construct a model, give the machine a field trial, make improvements, and all the while consult with his neighbors, speaking as one farmer to another. Even then McCormick seemed to feel he would have to sell the service rather than the hardware, and take account of farmer psychology. When one of his neighbors decided to take a machine, McCormick would build it, make the delivery himself, and then teach the farmer and his hired hands how to operate the machine, make simple repairs, and service it. By 1843, McCormick was able to advertise, "They all give satisfaction, allowance being made for defects which I had afterwards to correct," and later on—only after the machine had been thoroughly tested—would he warrant it to cut from fifteen to twenty acres a day.[14] His me-

[14]Hutchinson, *McCormick: Seed-Time*, pp. 175–79; Leo Rogin, *The Introduction of Farm Machinery in its Relation to the Productivity of Labor in the Agriculture of the*

thodology and business strategy were those of a farmer-inventor rather than that of a sailor turned businessman. In order to function successfully in the industry, McCormick had to teach himself about business. Hussey, who already knew something of business, had to learn more about farming and farmers. Both men applied themselves to these tasks in the 1840s, and each in his own way succeeded. Still, their basic approaches differed, with McCormick's being derived from the field to the factory, and Hussey's the opposite. It may be an oversimplification to say that McCormick tried to help the farmers and then allow them to transform the face of American agriculture, while Hussey was developing a vision of a new kind of agriculture that he tried to "sell" to the farmers. Often they came to the same conclusion in practice, and neither man articulated his beliefs in that way during his business career. But the difference in approach remained nonetheless, and McCormick's was more palatable to the wheat farmers than Hussey's, even when his machines proved inferior to those of his rival.

In 1842, after selling some machines outside of his neighborhood, McCormick decided to expand operations. He advertised that:

> for some time to come, he [McCormick] intends to devote his attention exclusively to introducing his machines in different parts of the country, by establishing agencies, selling rights (which he now offers for the first time), or otherwise; and will continue to have them *manufactured in the best manner,* on the same terms as heretofore . . . guaranteeing their performance in every respect; and if they perform as *warranted* to do, it will be seen, as stated also by others, that they will pay for themselves in one year's use . . . and if so, what *tolerable* farmer can hesitate to purchase?

United States During the Nineteenth Century (Berkeley, 1931), p. 133.

Hussey saw this and other McCormick advertisements and correctly viewed them as challenges. In a letter to the *Richmond Southern Planter* he noted "an account of another reaper in your State, which is attracting some attention."

> It shall be my endeavor to meet the machine in the field in the next harvest. I think it but justice to give this public notice that the parties concerned may not be taken unawares, but have the opportunity to prepare themselves for such a contest, that no advantage may be taken. Those gentlemen who have become prudently cautious, by being often deceived by humbugs, will then have an opportunity to judge for themselves.[15]

McCormick accepted the challenge, and a contest was arranged for July in Virginia. Hussey had difficulties in transporting his machines to the site, and in the end had to use the smaller and inferior of his two models. As a result, McCormick won the first round. The judges reported "great reluctance in deciding between them, but on the whole prefer McCormick's." On the other hand, they found the large Hussey machine "heavier, stronger, and more efficient."[16]

Other trials followed, with machines constructed by several manufacturers competing. No conclusive verdict was arrived at, but the trials of the early 1840s served to publicize and popularize the machines. Within a few years the question no longer was whether to purchase a reaper, but when, under what terms, and which model.

McCormick did well in the competition for sales, so much so that he had to license others, including A.C. Brown of Cincinnati and other small firms in New York and Missouri, to produce his machines for local distribution. Furthermore, he began to job out parts production to

[15] *Ibid.*, pp. 172–73, 187.
[16] *Ibid.*, p. 192.

others, since his small installation in Virginia could not handle the demand for machines. Too, he no longer was able to fabricate machines on demand but rather went into full production after the autumn harvests, worked through the year, and then turned his attention to sales in the spring. With this development, technology became less important than distribution. Shortly thereafter McCormick found it necessary to devote much of his time to the market for his products.

And he had a definite talent for the market. In 1843 McCormick sold twenty-nine reapers to Hussey's two, and although his rival's record improved the following year he continued to trail McCormick by a wide margin. By 1849 McCormick was selling some 1,500 machines in all parts of the country, while Hussey could sell but a hundred or so, most of which were taken by eastern farmers. It was then that McCormick's competitors began to charge that he was "flooding the country with his machines." Law suits followed, but none of them were decisive. Before the end of the 1840s, McCormick had emerged as the reaper king.[17]

Throughout this period McCormick, Hussey, and the other manufacturers attempted to improve their machines, preserve patent rights, and expand markets. Patent struggles occupied much of McCormick's time, both those instituted against him and those he initiated. The fact that McCormick resorted to suits in attempts to crush rivals indicated that he still did not have the confidence that he could vanquish them in the wheat fields. In addition, the suits illustrated the crude nature of the machines of that period. Nor was this his only concern. As his business improved, McCormick found he no longer could control it as he did in the early 1840s. When he produced only a handful of machines, all the parts were made in his shop. Now he employed several parts manufacturers, many of whom were unreliable. Furthermore, the early sales agents

[17] *Ibid.*, pp. 194, 265–66.

were irregular in their operations and reporting, and now McCormick had to spend time training and often disciplining his salesmen.

McCormick was distressed with the quality of machines produced by his licensees. The Brown machines in particular were not well received. Nor were those produced by Henry Baer in Missouri and Grey and Warner in Illinois. Given the distances and transportation difficulties, it would have been uneconomical to ship reapers from his Virginia installation. If the situation were permitted to continue, the McCormick machines might earn a bad reputation in the Midwest, one that would be difficult, perhaps impossible, to overcome. In the late 1840s, McCormick began to plan for a move westward.[18]

Plant-location theory did not exist in the 1840s; most manufacturers then and earlier had little to guide them except common sense and a feel for the market. Earlier, factory masters had selected sites on the basis of their homes, the availability of power, raw materials, and the labor supply. McCormick was one of the first American industrialists to face the necessity of making a major move in order to be closer to his markets.

And the customers for reapers were moving westward. Apparently McCormick, alone among the major reaper manufacturers, thought the move would be swift. Blight and harsh summers in the late 1840s conspired to push farmers westward, while the lure of new, cheap land pulled them there as well. The geography of the Mississippi basin and lower land prices there made large farms more easily obtainable than they were in the settled East, and the larger the farm, the greater the need for machines. In the late 1840s, upper New York was the nation's wheat center, and there were relatively few large farms there. Still, a more

[18]Casson, *McCormick*, pp. 66–67.

prudent man might have decided to move his plant there not only to serve an already existing market but to ship machines westward via the Erie Canal and Great Lakes. In 1848, western Pennsylvania and Ohio were among the four leading wheat areas, and a McCormick move to either of these two places would have been understandable. But to go further would have taken great foresight and a willingness to stake all on the belief that America would continue to expand rapidly. Apparently McCormick did have this vision and was determined to make such a move.

America had recovered from the depression by then, and the move westward not only continued, but accelerated. A new depression in the early 1850s, after McCormick had moved to his new plant, might have destroyed his company and made Hussey or someone else the reaper king of America, in which case McCormick would appear today as a footnote in some history books. There was no depression, but prosperity instead. By 1859 the leading wheat states in America were Illinois, Indiana, Ohio, and Wisconsin, in that order. During the decade Illinois' wheat production more than doubled, while that of Indiana almost tripled.

McCormick had visited the Midwest on sales and promotion campaigns, and as a farmer recognized the worth of the soils of the region. Clearly the producer of a bulky object such as a reaper, one that would require servicing and close relations with purchasers, would have to be closer to the market than Virginia or even western New York or Pennsylvania. Already McCormick had a small army of agents in the Midwest. Now he would move his factory closer to these agents.

Where should the factory be located? Cincinnati, the Queen of the Ohio, seemed a logical choice. It was a factory as well as commercial center, one with an ample supply of labor and, for the time, centrally located so as to serve both the old and new wheat areas. St. Louis, which dominated the Missouri-Mississippi, and in 1848 was the prime candidate for the title of "the New York of the Interior," was

another. St. Louis had a growing capital market, experienced commercial and financial leaders, and close ties
with New Orleans, then bidding to become the nation's
leading export port, hoping soon to surpass New York. If
McCormick had ambitions to sell his reapers abroad—and
he did—St. Louis would prove an admirable site. So would
Cleveland, closer to the upper Midwest, with a fine harbor.
There were a dozen other cities McCormick might have
considered and selected, with good reason. In the end he
chose Chicago.

Chicago was a small town in 1848, with a population of
around 18,000. It was in the midst of smallpox and cholera
epidemics, and although vigorous, seemed scarcely a rival
for the other cities of the Midwest. Chicago was a lumber
and grain town, and little more. Wheat farmers and lum-
bermen of the upper Midwest looked upon it as a natural
market for their goods, which would be processed in Chicago's mills, breweries, and lumberyards. Then the wheat,
flour, and lumber were exported, by lake, canal, and river,
to New York. Chicago shipped more wheat in 1848 than any
other midwestern city, and it may have been this that attracted McCormick. It also had a fine harbor, while the
Chicago River, though hardly comparable to the Hudson,
not to say the Missouri, Ohio, or Mississippi, provided it
with access to the interior. Chicago's leaders were dredging
the river at that time, and in 1848 the Illinois and Michigan
Canal was opened, connecting the city with the Illinois
River, and thus with the Mississippi. To Chicagoans it
seemed the nation had a watery spine, with their city at one
end and New Orleans at the other. They hoped to master
the river, and so the entire Midwest.

This vision might have captivated McCormick. He
visited Chicago as early as 1844, and had even formed a
partnership with C.M. Gray of the city to produce and sell
reapers for the 1848 harvest. Several of McCormick's key
agents operated out of Chicago, and his contacts there were
better than in any other city in the Midwest. Then, too, he

struck an acquaintance with William B. Ogden, the city's leading booster and wealthiest businessman, and Stephen Douglas, who was elected to the Senate in 1847, and spoke glowingly of new railroads as well as a financial center. These friendships may have been a decisive element in the move, for Ogden became McCormick's partner and Douglas his attorney. These two also helped bring federal funds to Chicago and were instrumental in the formation of the Board of Trade in 1848, another sign of commercial and financial growth.

Finally, McCormick was a devout Presbyterian, and Chicago had a strong and active Presbyterian community. He must have found this attractive.

Like the other midwestern cities McCormick might have selected, Chicago had its share of assets and liabilities. Most of the liabilities were real enough in 1848, while some of the assets were based on hope and dreams. The Chicago move seems logical and sensible today; at the time it was a bold stroke.

In 1847 McCormick prepared for the move, cleaned up his accounts by ending the partnership with Gray, and spent much time on his endless court cases regarding the reaper. Work was also begun on the new factory. In October 1848, McCormick, Ogden, and William E. Jones, another Chicago tycoon, announced the formation of McCormick, Ogden and Company. Ogden had already loaned McCormick money for the new factory, the final inducement in making the move. Now he would provide the capital for the installation's operations. McCormick planned to produce 1,500 reapers at the Chicago plant for the 1849 harvest. Each machine cost him less than $65, including agent's fee and allowance for bad debts. The reaper would be sold for $115, or if purchased on credit, $120. The sales campaign was a success. McCormick was a wealthy man.[19]

[19]Hutchinson, *McCormick: Seed-Time*, p. 317.

Late in 1849 McCormick bought out his partners and took complete control of his business. Never again would he have to worry about money. While Hussey and other rivals spent much of their time in obtaining backing, meeting bills, and trying to finance receivables, McCormick was free to operate his business. His brothers William and Leander were taken into the firm, and they handled office duties and production. Each year the reaper was changed, improved, and developed, and Cyrus McCormick was involved in what today would be called research and development. Some of his time was spent in litigation, but by now he had a small army of lawyers to do most of this work. Increasingly, McCormick concentrated on sales and promotion, and these became the key to his operations. It is by no means certain that the McCormick reaper was the best to be had. John H. Manny's machine was considered superior by many farmers, and Manny sold almost a thousand of them in 1854 and over two thousand the following year. Seymour and Morgan had a machine that was simple, inexpensive, and most attractive. Atkins-Wright, Wood and Company, Palmer and Williams, and several other reaper manufacturers offered features not to be found on the McCormick machines. Later on Wood and Company would develop an efficient wire binder and so initiate a major breakthrough in the industry, one McCormick was forced to concede and imitate. But none of these companies could match McCormick in sales and promotion.

McCormick's advertisements continued, more in number and larger than any that had previously been seen in the nation. These contained testimonials from satisfied customers, assurances of the machine's worth, and often detailed cost analysis as well. On occasion the advertisements would take note of events that might make reaper ownership worthwhile. For example, the gold rush began shortly after McCormick made his move to Chicago. Farm labor was attracted to California, and at the same time the influx of gold into the monetary stream helped bring prosperity.

Farmers needed mechanical help at harvest time, and now they could afford it. McCormick took note of both, offering what amounted to short lessons in economics in some of the advertisements. Such notices helped make the 1849 sales effort successful.

McCormick continued to give assurances as to the worth of his machines. The written guarantee and what for the time was a good service organization helped here. The farmer paid $30 down on his machine, with the rest of the price due within six months on condition that the reaper cut one and a half acres an hour. If the machine failed to live up to expectations, the $30 would be refunded. Too, McCormick operated on a fixed price. Other manufacturers would offer discounts, haggle with farmers, and in the end come down to a lower price in order to clinch the sale. McCormick's prices varied from year to year, usually reflecting increases in costs and improvements but always based on what he thought the market would bear. And seldom would a McCormick agent deviate from this price; if he did, it would come out of his commission.

McCormick recruited an able agent corps, provided them with literature, brought them to the factory to see how the machines were produced, and even instituted an *ad hoc* trainee program. He paid these men smaller commissions than did his rivals, but the McCormick agents more than made up the difference by volume sales. Also, he made his agents' tasks easier by his deep concern for goodwill. McCormick rarely sued a farmer for nonpayment, preferring instead to carry him until the next harvest. Agents' calls for spare parts were answered promptly, and McCormick would schedule more field trials—really company-paid picnics—than would his rivals. Bonuses, sales incentives, and higher commissions as rewards for success became common parts of the McCormick sales efforts. Some of the agents, A.D. Hager and D.R. Burt among them, developed into prototypes for the future. They knew their machines, cultivated the customers, and offered a good line of patter. In 1854, for example, Burt wrote of his experience in Iowa:

> I found in the neighborhood supplied from Cassville quite early in the season one of Manny's agents with a fancyfully painted machine cutting the old prairie grass to the no small delight of the witnesses, making sweeping and bold declarations about what his machine could do and how it could beat yours, etc., etc. Well, he had the start of me, I must head him some how. I began by breaking down on his fancy machine pointed out every objection that I could see and all that I had learned last year . . . gave the statements of those that had seen the one work in the grass . . . all of which I could prove. And then stated to all my opinion of what the result would be should they purchase from Manny. You pay one half money and give your note for the balance, are prosecuted for the last note and the cheapest way to get out of the scrape is to pay the note, keep the poor machine and in short time purchase one from McCormick. . . . Now gentlemen I am an old settler, have shared all the hardships of this new country with you, have taken it Rough and Smooth . . . have often been imposed upon in the way I almost know you would be by purchasing the machine offered you today. I would say to all, try your machine before you [pay] one half or any except the freight. I can offer you one on such terms, warrant it against this machine or any other you can produce, and if after a fair trial . . . any other proves superior and you prefer it to mine, keep [it]. I will take mine back, say not a word, refund the freight, all is right again. No, Gentlemen this man dare not do this. The Result you have seen. He sold not one. I sold 20. About the same circumstances occurred in Lafayette Cy.[20]

[20] *Ibid.*, pp. 361–62.

After such a sales pitch, the agent often would point out that McCormick would not press for payment if the crops were poor that year. "It is better that I should wait for the money, than that you should wait for the machine that you need." Of course, such an approach—low down payment, deferred payments in bad years—meant McCormick would have to carry a large number of accounts receivable. In some cases he lost large sums of money, such as when farmers were driven from the land due to continued drought. For the most part, however, the tactics paid off.[21] The 1850s proved a banner decade for McCormick, his first great period of prosperity.

In this period McCormick traveled to England to show his machines at the Crystal Palace Exposition of 1851, and then went on to travel the Continent, attempting to sell them on a worldwide basis. These early efforts were not very successful, and even later on, European models and those exported by some of McCormick's American rivals did better overseas than did the McCormick reapers. In America, however, McCormick easily led the field. His major problem in this regard was Manny, with whom he engaged in a running series of court battles involving patents. Manny was represented by a battery of lawyers, in-

Statistics for C.H. McCormick & Co., 1849–1858

Year	Machines Made	Costs	Number on hand	Number in Agents' Hands	Notes held by Company	Gross Sales
1849	1,490	$72,149	0	0	$2,590	$172,505
1850	1,603	?	5	0	2,976	89,017
1851	1,004	36,290	5	0	5,114	105,000
1852	1,011	38,702	17	0	3,753	112,531
1853	1,108	62,573	22	0	5,841	124,974
1854	1,558	86,737	9	0	12,855	209,374
1855	2,534	138,344	10	0	34,558	363,484
1856	4,095	194,398	56	100	125,415	574,011
1857	4,091	199,892	154	39	315,690	541,346

SOURCE: Hutchinson, *McCormick: Seed-Time*, p. 369.

[21]Casson, *McCormick*, pp. 79–87.

cluding Abraham Lincoln and Edwin Stanton, while Stephen Douglas spoke for McCormick. Manny won the case, in part the result of a brilliant defense and attack mounted by Stanton. McCormick was so impressed he engaged Stanton in future legal frays, while Lincoln received his first major fee from the case, money he would later use to help finance his senatorial struggle against Douglas. As for McCormick, he recovered from the suit and fought off attempts on the part of his rivals to strip him of all his patents by 1861.

The McCormick interests prospered in the field. During good times his agents outsold their competitors. During bad—such as the panic year of 1857 and the immediate aftermath—McCormick's willingness to extend credit won him additional sales, even when some of his competitors were forced to the wall. By 1860, McCormick was planning new machines and working to extend his markets in America and abroad.

McCormick was also interested in politics. A lifelong Democrat and a Virginian, he supported James Buchanan in the 1856 presidential election, and during the next four years spoke out in favor of reconciliation of sectional differences. Later on, his critics argued he had done so in the belief that a civil war would destroy his company. There is some justification for this claim. When the war broke out in 1861, McCormick ordered his treasurer to convert all the company's liquid assets into gold. He wrote of fears that the British would come to the aide of the Confederates, that Lee's army would invade the Midwest and in the process destroy machines not yet paid for as well as his prime market. Too, in 1861 there were reports of hardships on the wheat farms, and this did cripple sales for a few months. McCormick might well have anticipated this in the late 1850s when he worked for peace.

On the other hand, most of his machines were sold in the

North, not the South, and so secession did not mean the loss of a major market. McCormick's experiences during the gold rush taught him that any major loss of labor from the wheat fields would be translated into reaper sales, and this did occur when Lincoln began to form the Union armies. A case can be made for either interpretation of his motives, but the most likely explanation is that by ancestry and upbringing (his brothers' wives had relatives in the Confederate armies) he was a natural ally of the peace forces. There is an internal consistency in his politics throughout the 1850s and 1860s.

As it happened, McCormick and other farm implement manufacturers profited greatly during the war. The demand for harvesting equipment was such that the Chicago factory oversold its production by 500 units in 1862, causing grave distress in the Midwest that year. During the five years prior to the war, annual reaper sales (for all manufacturers) were approximately 16,000. In 1862, 33,000 reapers and mowers were sold in the United States. The following year's figure was 40,000, while 80,000 were sold in 1864 and a like number in 1865. At the start of the war, there were some 125,000 harvesting machines in operation in the United States; this number doubled by 1864, when three quarters of all farms of over 100 acres had a machine.[22] Although hundreds of thousands of men had been drawn away from the fields for the war, wheat production soared. Slightly over 4 million bushels were exported in 1860; in 1862, the figure was well over 37 million bushels, much of which went to England, the Confederacy's putative ally. Later on it would be said that in the Civil War the reaper defeated the cotton gin—that, among other things, England's need for grain was greater than her need for cotton, and so she remained neutral. This is an exaggeration, but it is true that without the reaper, the North could not have produced as much wheat as it did while

[22]Paul W. Gates, *Agriculture and the Civil War* (New York, 1965), pp. 227, 233.

at the same time taking men from the soil.

McCormick spent much of the war in England, attempting to convince the Europeans of the worth of his new machines. He competed not only with the European products but those produced by Manny, Wright, and Seymour and Morgan, among others. McCormick selected several foreign firms as licensees, but few of these arrangements worked out well. Walter Wood, an American, had better fortune with his combination reaper-mower, which easily outsold the McCormick models, and not even the improved self-rake reaper, which McCormick introduced in 1862, could defeat it. Not until the late 1860s did McCormick's work bear fruit, and then not for long. Trouble with licensees, difficulties in adapting his machines to European fields, and a general inability to adjust to the continental market caused the world vision to fade for the time being. It would appear that McCormick, so well attuned to the needs and desires of American farmers, could not comprehend their European counterparts. The age of international manufacturing had begun, but McCormick was not a major participant in it at that time.

McCormick's business activities brought him new fortunes in the postwar years. Now he expanded into real estate and railroads, natural activities for a man who wanted to enlarge the market for agricultural machinery. He continued to dabble in Democratic politics and took stands on public issues, especially those concerning farmers. In fact, he became an unofficial spokesman for agrarian interests within the party's inner circles where, as one of the few Democratic millionaires and contributors, he was given a voice. Fortunately, he did not live to see the development of agrarian radicalism, which McCormick might not have been able to square with his innate conservative nature. Too, he became engrossed with the Presbyterian Church's development in the upper Midwest, and as he grew older this took up more of his time.

Now honors came from American organizations and foreign nations. McCormick was hailed as an inventive genius. But the praise was for what he had done prior to the 1860s, and not for what he was doing in these last years of his life. After 1860, McCormick did little to develop the industry, except of course for contributing greatly to reaper production during the war. Indeed, one might argue that by continuing his litigations he may have done more to hinder than help technological innovation. In this period McCormick was more a follower than a leader. Others developed the binders and combines, and eventually the harvester; McCormick was in the rear. Yet all the successful companies that emerged or grew in the postwar period imitated McCormick's sales techniques and distribution and finance methods.

Cyrus McCormick's place in the American business tradition is secure. But what is it? A recent text called him "the first really big businessman in American manufacturing" and "an ideal example of an innovator."[23] This is true, and more. Despite his difficulties in the foreign market, McCormick was one of the first American manufacturers to make this country's goods respectable in Europe. The McCormick factory practiced the division of labor on a scale unknown before its coming. McCormick was instrumental in the growth of Chicago; even though he was never the city's leader, he was long considered its "first citizen." When he died in 1884, at the age of seventy-five, all the city's churches held memorial services, and the Board of Trade closed down in tribute. McCormick had led the way in reconstructing the city after the great fire of 1871, and had lent important aid to distressed businessmen during the panic of 1873. He could do this not only because he was wealthy but because his company was one of the best managed in the nation, a model to others, not only in farm machinery, but almost all industries.

Still, McCormick's major contribution was not in manu-

[23]Herman E. Krooss and Charles Gilbert, *American Business History* (Englewood Cliffs, 1972), p. 100.

facturing, invention, or finance. As has been indicated, others could and did develop farm machines at least as good as his, and in some cases, better. Manny and Hussey are all but forgotten today, probably because they did not create enterprises that survived. But John Deere, Jerome I. Case, John Oliver, and others who founded firms that remain in business to this day, are not considered McCormick's equal. Although these men all were innovators in invention, they were obliged to imitate McCormick in sales and distribution. As one scholar put it, he was a "merchandiser par excellence."

> He formed his own sales organization, guaranteed the reaper, and offered to sell it on installments. Exclusive agents were selected at key points throughout the marketing area—this was, in effect, the dealer system later employed by the automobile industry—and control of agents was just as tight under McCormick as it was to be under General Motors. He challenged builders of other reapers to field tests. It was like the automobile speed races of later years. . . .[24]

McCormick convinced farmers that he was one of them. Speaking in a language they understood, he showed farmers that the reaper was a sound investment and made them believe they would benefit by purchasing it. He knew his market and how to exploit it. As a salesman-distributor, he had no peer.

[24]Ben B. Seligman, *The Potentates: Business and Businessmen in American History* (New York, 1971), p. 101.

III

John Wanamaker:
The Triumph
of Content Over Form

John Wanamaker is by no means a forgotten man. Stores
bearing his name are still in operation, and if not in the
forefront of retailing, retain old customers and win new
ones. Several charities continue to benefit from his dona-
tions, as do churches and the YMCA. But the man himself
no longer is considered a keystone figure in American business history, as he was at the turn of the century. At that
time Andrew Carnegie symbolized steel and John D. Rockefeller, petroleum. E.H. Harriman was deemed the king of
the transcontinentals, while J.P. Morgan ruled on Wall
Street. Americans who knew little of the machinations of
these four could recite the maxims of John Wanamaker and
shopped in his stores. His name was synonymous with
retailing.

Wanamaker garnered as many honors and awards as any
of the great tycoons. He was a confidant of major politicians, a power in the Republican Party, and greeted overseas as the embodiment of the American Dream. Indeed, he
was the only one of the business greats to achieve national
political office, the only one to be completely untouched by
scandal, and when he died in 1922, at the age of eighty-four,

tributes from all parts of the world testified to his honesty and good works.

Many referred to his contributions to American business and noted that he was active to the end. This was true, but Wanamaker's great contributions to American retailing were made four decades and longer before his death. By the time Wanamaker became known as a business genius, he had run out of original ideas, and even before then, he was more adept at developing the innovations of others than presenting those of his own. Rival merchants, more aggressive and imaginative than he, pioneered in such areas as store location, manufacturing, advertising, and distribution. He took their ideas and concepts and made them work, popularized them, and obliged others to follow his example. This was no minor task, but hardly the accomplishment of a business genius.

Wanamaker succeeded, in part at least, because, more than any of the others, he captured the mood of his period in his life and work. He became famous in the High Victorian Age, and Wanamaker was a Victorian to the core. Although no great reader—his favorite novel was *Pollyanna* —he was an instinctive Social Darwinist, a believer in Protestant Christianity, the importance of the family, the value of hard work and the rewards that came with its practice. His writings and activities were of the kind that would warm the hearts of readers of Horatio Alger's novels, of middle-class housewives engaged in needlepoint and their sober, industrious, hard-working, and ambitious husbands. Wanamaker knew the tastes of the American Victorians, and he catered to them. He did so without guile or artificiality, or concern with "image." By being himself, Wanamaker endeared himself to the middle class of his time and was considered one of their own—a man to be trusted, and one who operated establishments worthy of trust.

Times and people changed, but not Wanamaker. So it was that his last years saw the leveling off and, in some cases, the actual decline, of his stores. The man who was so much in harmony with the spirit of one age seemed out of touch with the one that followed. Pollyanna had little in common with Jay Gatsby.

At one time Wanamaker was considered the first man to develop the department store. In fact, he took pains to deny this and even refused to call his establishments by that name. Instead, they were "new kinds of stores," a term he first used in 1877. But in terms of structure, they were not even that. Enclosed bazaars of the ancient Middle East had some of the qualities of department stores, as did medieval trade fairs. Retail establishments such as Wanamaker's existed in New York, Paris, and London prior to the Civil War, a fact that his most ardent biographers concede. It is also true that the new kind of store developed out of necessity rather than by design. It might not have appeared at all had Wanamaker been able to convince other Philadelphia merchants to go along with him and support a different kind of retailing. Having failed in this, the merchant had to go it alone or face possible ruin. He chose the former course, and in the process created his new store.

It was a great success. The Grand Depot, as it was commonly called, became the basis of his reputation. In time it did become a department store, though Wanamaker never admitted it. In other words, he became a department store pioneer in spite of himself, in what was a triumph of content over form. Likewise, Wanamaker opposed the establishment of chain stores but later entered the field; he disliked wholesaling but became a major factor in that business; he fought mail-order sales but later came to accept them; in fact, he entered most of the major retail areas of his time, usually against his wishes and too late to dominate them. At one time he had a chance to create a firm similar to Sears Roebuck, at another he could have made Wanamaker's into a company resembling J.C. Penney, and he rejected the opportunities, never regretting the choices made. During the last four decades of his business career Wanamaker was a moderate, if not conservative, retailer, and other men, more daring and imaginative than he, beat him at his own game, often by using techniques he had developed years before. If what Wanamaker achieved was impressive, what he might have accomplished is monumental.

He knew what he was doing—and not doing. This rejection of opportunity resulted not from a lack of imagination but rather from a conscious set of decisions regarding his fundamental beliefs, not only in retailing but in the broader aspects of life. To put it another way, Wanamaker considered his business career as part of his private life; all was of a piece, and he would not tolerate a double standard. Morality, not merchandising, was his true interest, and he viewed success in the latter as the fruits of his dedication to the former. Rockefeller and Morgan were active churchgoers, but they often practiced a different kind of morality during business hours. Even Carnegie violated his own published moral standards on occasion, and then wrote elaborate rationalizations after the fact. Compromises on such issues were alien to Wanamaker. "We cannot—indeed, should not—survive without the public's trust." Others said much the same thing, but Wanamaker came to exemplify the thought, and his policies reflected his beliefs. Truth in advertising and merchandising claims hardly existed when he entered retailing. Wanamaker changed this. He earned public trust early in his career and never lost it, and did so by advertising his creed widely, to a larger audience than that reached by any American businessman before him, and then delivering on his promises. Like Cyrus McCormick, he might be considered the father of a modern version of an old industry. Also like McCormick, Wanamaker's talents lay in the areas of distribution, organization, and advertisement rather than invention. As one scholar put it, "His genius lay in dramatizing the commonplace."[1]

[1]Ralph M. Hower, *History of Macy's of New York, 1858–1919: Chapters in the Evolution of the Department Store* (Cambridge, 1946). Hower exaggerates when he adds, "I have yet to find a single instance in which a Wanamaker 'first' can be substantiated for the period before 1900." p. 289.

Wanamaker was born in 1838 in Delaware County, on the outskirts of Philadelphia. His father, Nelson, was a brickmaker and worked in the family brickyard. Later on, adulatory books would be written claiming that John was from "poor but honest stock."[2] Actually, Nelson was a better-than-average businessman and in what for the time would be called the upper middle class. John was born during a business depression, for example, and the family suffered little in this period. Rather, it was well-known and respected in the community, the brickyard flourished, and John Wanamaker, Sr., the boy's grandfather, was the first president of the school board.

Nelson was a devout Methodist, and like his father an abolitionist who believed the churches should be the focus of social reform. John attended Methodist services but went to a Lutheran Sunday School, while his mother was a member of the Reformed Church and took him to services there on occasion. The Wanamakers moved to Indiana in 1850, where Nelson purchased a farm of 260 acres. John attended services at several evangelical churches in the area and participated in revivals. He also made his first purchase —a Bible that cost him $2.75—and the family became convinced he had a religious vocation.

The Indiana stay was short; Elizabeth, John's mother, was homesick, and the following year they returned to Pennsylvania. John began to explore the churches of Philadelphia and on one occasion attended Presbyterian services conducted by John Chambers, a fiery preacher. "I had gotten my message, and as the people went out from the meeting I stayed," said Wanamaker in 1918. "I went up to the minister and I told him that I had settled the matter that night, and had given my heart to God."[3]

Only thirteen years old, he became a temperance worker,

[2]For example, "No lack of family background, but circumstances over which his parents had little, if any, control, made his childhood one of comparative poverty." Herbert Adams Gibbons, *John Wanamaker* (New York, 1926), I, 6.
[3]Joseph H. Appel, *The Business Biography of John Wanamaker, Founder and Builder* (New York, 1830), p. 23.

studied the Bible after school hours, and began to teach Sunday school. The following year he got his first job, as errand boy for a Philadelphia publisher at $1.25 a week. The money was given to his mother, who returned a small sum for his own use, admonishing him, however, "You must save, you must learn to save." A half century later Wanamaker recalled that "I began by saving seven cents."[4]

Wanamaker impressed his employer and received several pay increases. He also earned the dislike of his fellow-workers, who considered the small, sometimes sickly boy who prided himself on walking several miles a day to work and never being late, and who always talked of religion and the demon rum, as something of a bore. The man whom business colleagues would call "Honest John" and "Pious John" had already taken shape, and then as later, those who remarked on his behavior did not always do so in a complimentary fashion. Young Wanamaker was humorless, ambitious, hard-working, and probably stuffy. But he also was an exemplar of the young Victorian man, the kind so prized and applauded by serious businessmen of the day. After he had become famous, one of his early employers recalled:

> We had two messenger boys in the office. If we sent one of them on an errand, we were certain that he would go straight to the place and return as quickly as possible. Organ grinders with monkeys, beautiful store windows and all that sort of thing, could not make the boy swerve from a straight path. With the other lad it was different. As soon as the clang of a fire bell sounded, out he would rush to the engine house or the burning building.
>
> Years passed. I left the city for a time during the Civil War. After my return in 1866, I was passing along the street, when suddenly, at the corner of Sixth and Market, I saw a sign that almost took my breath away.

[4] *Ibid.*, p. 27.

Above the door of a big clothing establishment in large letters I read the name, John Wanamaker. You can imagine my surprise at seeing our old errand boy transformed so quickly into a successful merchant.

A few days later I was walking down Delaware Avenue. Over on a pier beside a molasses hogshead I saw a man lying in a drunken stupor. I went and rolled him over. Can you guess who I found? Our other errand boy.[5]

Such stories are too good to be true, and this one doubtless was embellished substantially. But it does serve to make a point regarding those qualities admired by middle-class Americans of that day, the kinds of rewards awaiting those who conformed to the norm, and the fate of those who did not.

Clearly Wanamaker was a conformer with a vengeance. He would awaken early and work late, taking pride in the fact that he was the first to arrive and the last to leave. He would be efficient, honest, earnest, sincere, and conservative—these are the words that come to mind when thinking of him, and they are not to be despised. On the other hand, they do not describe a man from whom one can expect originality, innovation, boldness, and imagination—and he possessed few of these qualities.

Wanamaker's zeal, combined with a weak constitution, resulted in broken health and tuberculosis at the age of nineteen. He traveled to the West in a successful effort at a cure, and on his return to Philadelphia in 1857 obtained a job as secretary of the Young Men's Christian Association. Wanamaker found a vocation there. The Association grew, and he received much of the credit. Friends and members of his family urged him to enter the ministry, or remain at the "Y" to become its next president, a position that he certainly would have been offered had he remained.

[5]Gibbons, *Wanamaker*, I, 24.

Later, Wanamaker wrote that the idea appealed to him, but another calling offered a greater challenge. "I would have become a minister, but the idea clung to my mind that I could accomplish more in the same domain if I became a merchant and acquired means and influence with my fellow merchants."[6] Looking back, he saw himself as a missionary to the business community.

Wanamaker's salary at the YMCA was $1,000 a year, and he worked there for three years. In this period he saved $1,900—almost two-thirds of his salary. In 1860 he married Mary Brown, the daughter of a respected middle-class Philadelphian. His new brother-in-law, Nathan Brown, wanted to enter business, and had savings of around $1,600. The two men decided to form a partnership, retailing men's clothing. They rented two floors in an old building on Sixth and Market streets in Philadelphia known as Oak Hall, invested a third of their capital in fixtures and cloth, and opened for business in April 1861.

Later on he wrote of the reasons for the choice of merchandising as a career—in essence, he believed it a way to serve his fellow man or, as he put it, to apply Christian principles to business and provide well-being for his customers. But he never discussed the reasons for selecting men's clothing. Wanamaker knew something of the book and stationery fields, and through his father and grandfather of bricks and building supplies. He might have become a dry goods (as opposed to wet goods, or hard liquor) merchant, carrying a variety of products and changing them to meet the needs and desires of his customers. Instead, the partners invested all their savings in a field neither knew much about in 1861—when civil war appeared certain and the conventional wisdom was that the conflict would destroy business.

The selection of clothing indicates either that Wanamaker was more of a plunger than he seemed to be, or that

[6]Appel, *Wanamaker*, p. 39.

he had a greater knowledge of American manufacturing than many of his contemporaries. Wanamaker and Brown started in business during a period when the economy was in an upswing after the depression of the late 1850s. Perhaps the partners felt clothing sales would rise in such an environment.

Or it may have been that Wanamaker understood that a true men's clothing industry was in the process of development due to changes that would make mass production and distribution possible. Not only was the population rising rapidly but the development of the sewing machine and the science of human measurements—anthropometry—were being applied to the nascent industry.

The sewing machine had been worked on for decades prior to the 1850s. Walter Hunt, G.A. Arrowsmith, and J.J. Greenough had patents on models in the 1830s, but these continually broke down and were difficult to operate. Then, in 1849, Isaac Singer developed a machine that worked efficiently and was relatively trouble-free. The following year Allen Wilson introduced a model that in some ways was superior to the Singer machine. But Singer and, more to the point, his partner, Edward Clark, were able to sell their machines more effectively, while Clark emerged as a bold innovator in merchandising. In 1852 he rented a storefront in New York to exhibit the machine in operation, offering what amounted to free lessons to any who wanted them. Four years later Clark announced that owners of "inferior" sewing machines could trade them in against a new Singer and receive $50 toward the purchase price, which was then $100. Clark also developed the concept of time purchases. The buyer could trade in the old machine, and then pay $5 a month for ten months until the $50 was paid. "This business we do is peculiar," he said, "and we have adopted our own method of transacting it." By the late 1850s, sewing machines were quite common, not only in homes but in shoe and clothing factories. In their own way, Singer and Clark had revolutionized the clothing industry. Indeed, there really was none until the sewing machine made it possible.

Equally important was the development of anthropometry. During the first half of the century most Americans wore either homemade or tailor-fitted clothing, with the latter reserved for the wealthy. Ready-made clothing existed too; men's suits could be purchased in dry goods stores, and some "slop-shops" in large cities specialized in the ill-fitting and crudely made garments, which were sold to sailors, manual workers, and itinerants. The buyer would shop for his suit in much the same way as one purchased eyeglasses in those days—by trying on several until he found one that seemed to fit. Of course, prior to the development of the sewing machine, ready-made clothing, like the rest, was cut and sewn by hand.

The combination of a rapidly growing population, prosperity, and the sewing machine made possible the mass production of men's clothing. Most of the 130,000 sewing machines sold in the 1850s were used commercially, worked by young women in small wholesale establishments or by tailors in several of the retail shops. This created a new dimension for the industry. Earlier, clothing had been produced on demand—that is, the customer would walk into the shop, indicate his intention to buy a suit, be measured, and, later on, would pick up the completed garment. Afterward the clothing would be manufactured, with no idea who the customer would be, or his measurements. It had to be done this way; to operate under the old system would mean to use the expensive sewing machines sporadically. But it also meant the retail outlets would have to adopt new methods of sales presentation and, in time, enter the advertising field.

Furthermore, the shopkeeper, now in the ready-to-wear business, had to be concerned with sizing. This was a new problem in the 1850s, one that hadn't been considered prior to that time. The shrewd shopkeeper would carry a variety of "sizes," hoping that the "mix" reflected his clientele. Then, when one of the suits seemed to fit, he would send it back to his tailor for alterations, which were always needed. Suits made and sold in this fashion were far cheaper than the fitted variety, and so the shopkeeper who was aware of his clientele could sell a large number of suits, far more than he could under similar circumstances in the 1840s.[7]

Wanamaker was one of probably dozens of men's clothing dealers who realized that the new methods of production would call forth changes in distribution. Mass-produced clothing required mass distribution, and from the first the Oak Hall store was designed with that in mind. This meant a fairly extensive alteration operation and even manufacturing after a while, which further implied large-scale purchases of cloth. These, and the large stock of clothing to be carried, required good lines of credit, and to service them, Wanamaker would have to turn over his stock rapidly—to develop a positive cash flow as soon as possible. Advertising and public goodwill would be vital in achieving this. All of these elements of modern retailing were at work at Oak Hall.

Even before the store opened, Wanamaker and Brown hired a cutter, and then a tailor. Wanamaker traveled to New York to obtain lines of credit, and did so only after the usual amount of difficulty one might expect given the newness of his business and the uncertainties that came with the threat of civil war. As the price of wool increased, he contracted with shippers for his supplies instead of purchasing the cloth from local distributors; a campaign was mounted against Oak Hall by the distributors, indicating

[7]The problems and opportunities presented by clothing sizing and the development of anthropometry is discussed in Daniel Boorstin, *The Decline of Radicalism: Reflections on America Today* (New York, 1969), pp. 9–11.

that Wanamaker was one of the first to do this. Additional tailors were hired as the business grew, and this backroom operation was handled efficiently and intelligently. Wanamaker, who increasingly took management and decision-making powers for his own, had an instinct for this kind of business and learned rapidly. But it was in the area of advertising and goodwill that he clearly was a master.

It was the practice at the time for a dry goods operation to begin small, plowing profits back into stock, and waiting for word-of-mouth advertising to bring in the customers. Wanamaker reversed the operation. From the first he would advertise heavily, more so than the size of his operation or cash flow would indicate was wise. Then, as customers came to Oak Hall, he would sell goods at a low markup and use most of his profits for additional advertising. Wanamaker recalled selling suits, and then delivering them and receiving payment. Before returning to the shop he would stop by the newspaper office to place additional advertisements, paying for them with the money received from the clothing transaction. The first advertisements were simple and conventional:

OAK HALL CLOTHING BAZAAR
Southeast Corner Sixth & Market Streets

Wanamaker & Brown desire to say to their many friends and the public generally, that they open to-day with an entire new and complete stock of ready made clothing; and having purchased their goods under the pressure of the times at very low rates, will sell them accordingly.

WHOLE SUITS FOR THREE DOLLARS[8]

Other, larger advertisements followed, and at first they appeared little different from those of other clothing establishments. Then, as business grew and Wanamaker studied

[8]Appel, *Wanamaker*, p. 42.

the matter, he introduced some innovations. He would erect billboards on vacant lots, with the letters "W & B" painted on in bold script, hoping that curious onlookers would want to find out what they stood for. Boys were hired to distribute leaflets announcing that balloons would be released from the Oak Hall roof, and that anyone who brought one back would receive a free suit. Such advertising seemed lavish to his competitors, and somewhat dangerous, since the costs were so high, but Wanamaker persisted. Instead of placing a single advertisement in the Philadelphia City Directory in 1864, he took space at the top of every page, on condition that the cover carry a picture of Oak Hall—with the Wanamaker & Brown sign clearly delineated. Free calendars were lavishly distributed, and not just to prized customers, as was then the rule.

Innovations in advertising made Oak Hill the best-known clothing store in Philadelphia. Customers would come to look, but might not buy unless the merchandising policies were superior in one way or another to those of its rivals. Just as Wanamaker helped develop the old art of advertising to create a new form, so he used ideas of others to create a different merchandising climate.

In September 1873, Wanamaker attempted to set forth his business creed in a new advertisement.

People often wonder how it is that Wanamaker & Brown do so much business when other houses are so dull. There is nothing strange about it. The facts of the matter are simply as follows:

1. We advertise what we have for sale.
2. We have for sale what we advertise.
3. The people come and see that it is so.
4. The people buy our clothing because they are pleased with the garments we make.
5. The people are satisfied that they get full value

for the money they leave with us and they come again and send their friends.[9]

In effect, Wanamaker claimed, in four of the points, that his was an honest establishment and that he had gone to pains to let the public know of it. Point number 3 requires some explanation. Wanamaker practiced a "free entrance" policy at Oak Hall. In most other establishments the customer would be greeted at the door by a salesman, who would then stay with him until the sale was made, or the customer left without having purchased goods. At Oak Hall customers were encouraged to come and browse, or even look upon the store as a variety of tourist attraction. Then, when they were ready to purchase goods, or wanted to see a particular item, they would call a salesman, who would attend to their needs. This practice encouraged the timid—people who had never been in a large store before—to become accustomed to such shopping. But it was not an innovation. A.T. Stewart and other merchants in New York and other cities pioneered in free entrance in the 1840s. As with so many other policies, Wanamaker popularized what others had originated.

A year later Wanamaker published a large advertisement, the first to be copyrighted in America. In it he announced "these as the FOUR CARDINAL POINTS By which we hereafter steer our craft"

| FULL GUARANTEE | CASH PAYMENT |
| ONE PRICE | CASH RETURNED |

It was, he said, "A GREAT STRIDE UP AND OVER BUSINESS CUSTOMS."[10]

Actually, all four points were introduced by others. The guarantee, which gave the customer the right to return unsatisfactory merchandise, had been introduced by Stew-

[9] *Ibid.*, p. 61.
[10] *Ibid.*, p. 69.

art and others at least a decade earlier. Lord & Taylor in New York advertised a one-price policy in 1838, and Wanamaker, like other merchants, deviated from it to offer discounts to some classes of people, clergymen in particular. Cash payments in order to keep prices down had been in practice for a generation, and was common in Paris stores in the 1860s. The cash refund policy, of which Wanamaker was particularly proud, was employed at the Bon Marché in 1854.[11]

Wanamaker was different in two ways. First of all, he practiced what he advertised, unlike other merchants of the time who used advertisements to draw customers into the shop, and then presented them with different rules. *Caveat emptor* still ruled in the vast majority of dry goods stores in 1874, advertisements to the contrary. Although Wanamaker did not coin the phrase, he did believe "the customer is always right," and lectured his staff, especially new clerks, on acting in such a fashion. Others may have innovated; Wanamaker made the innovations credible, and in the process forced others to follow his example. Further, he advertised the principles effectively, most of the time writing his own copy, and in a way that was pleasing to his customers. For example, in his advertisement, he said:

> Fourth Point—"CASH RETURNED"—This is simply a concession on our part to our customers, to secure them full confidence in dealing for goods they know little about, and we thus prevent any occasion for dissatisfaction from any and every cause whatsoever. If the garment is not exactly what you thought, if your taste changes, if the "home folks" prefer another color or another shape, if you find you can buy the same material and style elsewhere for less money, if you conclude you don't need it after you get home, if the season changes suddenly and you wish you had

[11]Harry E. Resseguie, "Alexander Turner Stewart and the Development of the Department Store, 1823–1876," *Business History Review*, Vol. 39, No. 3, Autumn, 1965, pp. 301–22.

not bought it, bring it back unworn and uninjured, and the amount of money you paid will be returned on the spot. What more can we do for our customers than this, when we make our clothing so that they can draw the money value with it equally as well as with a check on the banks?[12]

Wanamaker would later extend his money-back guarantee to cover clothing that had been altered by his tailors, and so presumably could not be resold. He was the first merchant to do this, taking the risk that few such garments would be returned, while the expense of the goodwill engendered by the gesture could be written off to advertising.

Such advertisements and the deserved reputation for honesty made Oak Hall the city's leading men's clothing store. Wanamaker became expert in all areas of the industry and was known as one of the shrewdest buyers in Philadelphia, taking up goods when prices fell, and remaining away from the market when they were high. He would conduct clearance sales regularly, making certain his goods moved, and so the merchandise was fresh. In its first year, Oak Hall had sales of $24,000, made possible by Wanamaker, Brown, and a handful of tailors. In 1870, nine years later, sales were $2.1 million, and Oak Hall was manned by forty-three salesmen, seventy cutters, and twenty clerks.[13] Wanamaker's personal wealth was estimated at a million dollars or more.[14]

All of this had been done without recourse to bankers, and here too Wanamaker proved adept at developing old methods to his needs. Cloth would be purchased from suppliers with notes, and the material would be cut, sewn, and sold before the notes were due. In effect, he had the cash from the sale before having to pay for his raw materials. The system relied upon a quick turnover of goods, and it

[12] *Ibid.*, p. 70.
[13] *Ibid.*, p. 59.
[14] Credit Report, 1870, in Dun & Bradstreet papers, Baker Library, Harvard Graduate School of Business.

was here that the gamble becomes more impressive. Unscrupulous merchants would do the same as he, and then if they guessed wrong, would go out of business and leave town before the creditors could catch them. Wanamaker, who throughout this period continued his volunteer work at the YMCA, would have acted differently, paying creditors even had it meant his ruin. He was proud of his self-financing, saying at one point that "my customers, not the bankers, made me." Oak Hall and his subsequent stores were all privately owned. He would borrow money for supplies, but never sell equity in his companies. In this respect, as in most others, Wanamaker was a model of a "conservative businessman."

In terms of making a reputation for honesty, such actions made sense. But they also meant many attractive opportunities for growth were missed. By 1869 Oak Hall was the largest men's clothing store in the nation. Brown had died the previous year, and Wanamaker directed the enterprise by himself, attending to all details of purchasing, cutting, distribution, and advertisement, and doing so in such a way as to maintain his reputation and turn a profit. In other words, he was the paragon of a storekeeper. But was he more than that? In order to expand, Wanamaker would have had to delegate authority, and throughout his life he was unable or at least reluctant to do so. Because of this, he allowed several chances for mercantile greatness slip through his fingers. For example, he neglected an opportunity to enter, and indeed found, a mail order business. As his clothing became better known, Wanamaker began selling suits through agents, most of whom were postmasters. Later on, as business in the region developed, he would appoint a local tailor as agent. Such individuals would measure customers, send particulars to Philadelphia, and receive semi-fitted clothing in the next mail. The agents would undertake final fittings, and then deliver the suit to the customer. Wanamaker would go no further than this, although the next step—self-measurement and orders of clothing on approval—must have been obvious. He never gave reasons for holding back, but it seems he was unwilling to relinquish too much of his business to agents, knowing perhaps of the experiences men such as McCormick had with such individuals. Besides, he enjoyed meeting customers at the door of his establishment, and then seeing them leave satisfied with their purchases. He couldn't give up that pleasure easily.

In 1871, when Oak Hall found itself with a surplus of stock, Wanamaker learned that Pittsburgh was booming and New York was in good shape. So he opened a store in Pittsburgh and another on Fifth Avenue in New York, supplying them from the Philadelphia establishment. Other stores followed, in Washington, Richmond, and several midwestern cities. By 1873 it appeared Wanamaker had initiated a chain of men's clothing stores, the first in the country. Had he continued to expand in this direction, and then carried additional items in his stores, he might have come closer to controlling the dry goods trade in America than any merchant before or since.

Such an operation would have required Wanamaker to delegate responsibility to branch managers and, as was the case with agents, he refused to do this. An alternative might have been for him to be constantly on the road, traveling from store to store, making certain all was well. This too was out of the question, since it would mean the abandonment of work at the YMCA and his Sunday school classes. So he closed down the branches and instead concentrated on Philadelphia. Nor would he consider remaining in nearby cities, like New York, which could have been reached in a matter of hours by railroad. Had he opened a larger branch in New York, for example, he might have dominated that city's men's wear business in a matter of years. As it was, Wanamaker would not move to New York permanently until 1896, by which time he was unable to make a sizable impact on the city.[15]

Wanamaker did expand in Philadelphia, however. In 1869 he opened what he hoped would become a fashionable

[15]Gibbons, *Wanamaker*, I, 124–30.

clothing store on Chestnut Street, next to the Continental Hotel, then the most exclusive place in town. A magnificent edifice was constructed on the site, complete with thick carpeting, gilt-framed mirrors, and a doorman. He would not go to the country, but perhaps the country would come to him. A few months after the Chestnut Street store opened, Wanamaker said:

> We expected to have a local trade; but we have been led, we might better say compelled, to do what we might also call a national business. In nearly every state we already have customers, with unlimited prospect of further expansion.
>
> All of this has greatly encouraged and nerved us to the determination to push our original design of establishing in Philadelphia a clothing house which shall be unrivalled in the country—a place where can be found a class of ready-made clothing such as can be had nowhere else, and where custom work of the highest order shall be done on a scale at once extensive and elevated.[16]

The Chestnut Street store was a success, and was soon known as Philadelphia's leading men's clothing establishment. Within a decade it employed two hundred salespeople and six hundred tailors, cutters, and related workers. The store catered to the upper middle class—Wanamaker's natural milieu—which by then had become accustomed to ready-to-wear clothing. Oak Hall continued to prosper, dealing primarily with the lower middle class and bargain hunters.

Together these two establishments might have formed the foundation for manufacturing as well as retailing operations. Wanamaker had a national reputation by then,

[16] *Ibid.*, I, 112–13.

spread by those who had purchased his men's clothing. He might have set up separate facilities for clothing manufacture and sold his suits in other stores throughout the nation. After all, he did speak of "unlimited prospect of further expansion." But this opportunity was not seized; once again the man prevailed over the businessman. Wanamaker enjoyed overseeing all aspects of the business. He still couldn't bear to see his suits sold by others, at a time when New York and Boston merchants were experimenting with production and new means of distribution.

Wanamaker was a merchant, a churchman, and a patriot, and in 1874 all three interests converged. For some time he had been considering a third Philadelphia store, one larger than Chestnut Street, that would carry women's as well as men's clothing. In addition, he was involved with the planning for a religious revival in the city, to be headed by evangelists Ira Sankey and Dwight Moody. Finally, Philadelphia would be the host city for the Centennial observations of 1876. This was to be a major event, with American and foreign visitors crowding into the city. As one of Philadelphia's leading citizens, Wanamaker was selected to serve as chairman of the press and finance committees, and was on several other important planning bodies, all of which he took very seriously. This work, added to his constant movement between his two stores and service at the YMCA and Sunday school, taxed his energies.

But all of his interests meshed. Wanamaker took an option on the Pennsylvania Railroad freight depot at Broad and Market streets, at the time an out-of-the-way part of town, inaccessible except by horsecar. The site could be used for the revival, which would be held from November 1875 to January 1876. Afterward it might be utilized as part of the centennial. Then it could become the site of a new store.

In 1875, while in the midst of his work, Wanamaker decided to take an extended European vacation with his family. He had been to Europe once before, in 1871, on a buying expedition. Now he would take the Grand Tour, remaining away from work for several months, traveling to all parts of the continent. It was not a true vacation, however. Wanamaker visited large stores wherever he went—Whitely's in London, the Bon Marché and the Louvre in Paris, and their counterparts elsewhere. Most were department stores, one of several new retailing forms then developing. He was unimpressed with the concept, believing as he did in specialized retailing. Still, he must have gotten some ideas from the tour. On his return to America Wanamaker exercised his option, paying $500,000 for the depot. He also began to plan for his new store, one that would resemble the department store in some respects, but be different in others.

The fact that Wanamaker planned such an establishment in 1875 indicates that he recognized that retailing was changing, and that he would have to move with the times. By then Oak Hall, and even Chestnut Street, were old-fashioned establishments, prosperous though they were. American and foreign retailers were aware that social forces were at work that would transform their ways of doing business in the future.

The western world was becoming increasingly urbanized, and nowhere was the trend more obvious than in the United States, where the urban population almost tripled from 1850 to 1870, while the rural population rose by less than 50 percent. Industrialization provided the population with a greater variety of goods than ever before, usually at lower prices than their handmade equivalents, while advances in transportation made it possible for consumers to chose between goods produced in many parts of the world. America underwent a financial panic in 1873, followed by a long depression, then another panic in 1884 and a third in 1893. Still, in the large cities there were people with money to spend, and they had their choices of many different retail stores, all of which competed heatedly to obtain a share of the market.

These forces resulted in two major changes in dry goods retailing. In the first place, there was greater specialization than ever before, a situation that was noted as early as the mid-1850s. "The tendency, in all great commercial marts, is to simplification," wrote the *Philadelphia Merchant* that year, "and in many cases only a single class of articles is kept by the merchant—as in cotton goods, woolen goods, silk goods."[17] This was so because few of the old-line dry goods dealers could afford to keep a stock of a variety of goods. So they became, in effect, proprietors of specialty shops.

The second tendency was toward the department store, an institution that defied exact definition then and now.[18] Most scholars agree that all such establishments had central locations, many departments under a single roof, and transacted large volumes of business. One-price policy, low markups, and cash selling was the rule, as was aggressive, specialized advertising and promotion.[19] Such stores were owned at first by major dry goods dealers. There is much debate as to when and where the first American department store appeared, due in large part to these difficulties in definition. Many consider Alexander T. Stewart's Marble Dry Goods Palace, erected in New York in 1846, a step in the direction of the department store, if not the first of them. Stewart's Cast Iron Palace, a magnificent building opened in 1862, was a department store as people of the time understood it. So was Rowland Macy's establishment, and Jordan Marsh in Boston, and several other retail operations in other large cities. All carried wide varieties of goods sold

[17] *Philadelphia Merchant* in *Merchants Magazine*, June 1855, pp. 766–77, as quoted in Hower, *Macy's,* p. 84.
[18] For two histories of department stores, see Hrant Pasdermadjian, *The Department Store: Its Origins, Evolution, and Economics* (London, 1954), and John W. Ferry, *A History of the Department Store* (New York, 1960).
[19] Resseguie, *A.T. Stewart,* p. 303.

in different parts of the store, featured cash and one-price policies, and most offered money-back guarantees.

Oak Hill was not a department store, but a men's clothing establishment, while Chestnut Street was a larger and more elaborate version of the dry goods store. Both were under Wanamaker's direct control, and although doing well, each had reached its limit of growth in its present form. Understanding the changes that were taking place in retailing, Wanamaker was faced with the need to change or stagnate. He could turn his old stores into specialty shops and capitalize on his reputation for quality and fair prices. If this were done, he would lose business to other establishments but might become a leader in a narrow field. Or he might turn his enterprises into department stores, in which case he would enlarge his business. But this would mean giving department managers a fairly wide degree of latitude not only in management but perhaps in purchasing and related decisions as well. It would appear that Wanamaker was psychologically unwilling or unable to do this in 1875. Instead, he sought a way by which he could enjoy the benefits of both options and avoid the liabilities.

The railroad depot offered a way out. It was an old but serviceable structure, one that could be turned into a huge store in time for the centennial, and become not only a major tourist attraction, but a profitable venture as well. Wanamaker was thinking beyond the celebration, however. For a while he thought of closing down the old Oak Hall and Chestnut Street buildings and moving their operations to the depot. But he gave up on this, fearing that old customers might not want to shop in the new location. Then, in February of 1876, he approached other Philadelphia merchants, offering to rent them space in what he now called "The Grand Depot."

In effect, Wanamaker projected a huge indoor fair that would take up the several acres of ground at the depot, a collection of specialty shops under one roof. The idea was rejected, as the Philadelphia merchants would not take the risk, and in any case feared that he would dominate the Grand Depot, leaving little business for them. Yet Wanamaker did not give up on the plan, and spoke of it often during the next few years. He felt such an enterprise would combine the attractions of the specialty shop with the benefits then offered by department stores without sacrificing the special qualities of either. In effect, Wanamaker had rejected the notion of the department store in favor of what eventually would become the suburban shopping center of the post-World War II period. This was not because he was a far-sighted individual, however, but rather due to his unwillingness to accept the marketing realities of his own time.

Late in the year he abandoned his attempt to win converts, and changed the name of the Grand Depot to "Wanamaker's New Establishment," signaling a determination to go it alone. It would be a giant dry goods store, not a department store. Wanamaker would sell women's as well as men's clothing, household linens, and upholstery as well as fabrics. An elaborate "Store Book" was readied, telling visitors how to get to the site, and noting that they were welcome to come if only to look at "the largest dry goods establishment in the world." These were distributed to Philadelphians and visitors to the city at the beginning of the centennial celebration, along with free postcards featuring pictures of the depot and souvenirs. Through his position on the many committees planning events, Wanamaker was able to have many scheduled at Fairmont Park, not far from the store, and he made certain visitors knew that they could see the establishment after the day's activities and so witness two extravaganzas instead of one.

The centennial celebration lasted half a year, and drew close to a million visitors to Philadelphia, many of whom crowded into Wanamaker's New Establishment. The store was a success, at least as long as the celebration was on. What would happen when it ended? When Philadelphians alone would shop there, perhaps many who under ordinary circumstances would go to Oak Hall or Chestnut Street? The new store was in direct competition with the old, and could easily put them out of business. Too, it was possible that the Philadelphians would return to the old stores after the novelty of the new had worn off, and leave Wanamaker with a white elephant on his hands.

Wanamaker revived his idea of an indoor bazaar. Noting the great success of the New Establishment, he once again asked other merchants to sublet space from him at the depot. Now he called it "a new kind of store," one in which some parts of the business, such as advertising and purchasing, might be centralized, while actual management would be left to the individual merchants. As before, his overtures were rejected. Faced with the alternatives of closing down the establishment—and in the process suffering a large loss as well as admitting defeat—or creating the new kind of store on his own, Wanamaker decided upon the latter course.

During the winter of 1876–1877 he spent most of his time at the Grand Depot, planning and developing what he called, for a while, "The Wanamaker Composite Store." The basic edifice, which covered two acres of land, would be converted to the display and sale of all forms of clothing and cloth, and little else. The floor plan indicated what for the time was a lavish waste of space, with entrances on all four sides and eight vertical aisles leading to the center, where was located a circular counter, ninety feet in circumference, where silks were sold. Wanamaker came to look upon the project as one of the greatest undertakings in the world, and to view his mission as almost religious in nature. For a man who had devoted all his life to the church and merchandising, this was not unusual. Gathering his staff around to show it the design, he said, "It is a wheel, and each of you is a spoke. I am the motive power, and I shall see that the wheel keeps moving." It is not difficult to imagine him speaking as a prophet, for later on, when he recalled the task, he did so in semi-religious phrases.

"But you must each be in your place at all times, and do your duty, or I can accomplish nothing. But if we all do our part, this wheel will keep on revolving, and it will become the largest and best of its kind in the world."[20]

One may dismiss this as Victorian hyperbole, but the fact remains that Wanamaker risked all of his considerable fortune in the venture. Had it failed, he would have been close to bankruptcy. The building and renovations took most of his capital, and the huge stock was purchased with payments due within a matter of months.

Success would make Wanamaker the nation's leading merchant, or so he believed. And it also might put many of Philadelphia's other dry goods stores out of business. Wanamaker advertised the new store lavishly, and he drew customers. On the first day, March 12, 1877, some 70,000 people crowded into the Grand Depot, where they were waited upon and given guided tours by a staff of over a thousand clerks.

At first most of the visitors were just that—sightseers but not customers. Wanamaker had to put off his creditors, while his rival merchants predicted his collapse. "There's trouble in the big Market Street Wigwam," wrote one critical newspaper. "Protests, extensions, unpaid employees, etc." Wanamaker's trouble lay in overambition, it said. "He's in danger. He is walking on the thin crust of a volcano which threatens to blow him and his wigwam sky high, scattering hats and haberdashery, shoes and chemisettes, collars and cuffs, trunks and teapots, lawns and lines, boots and broadcloth, furs and flannels to the four winds."[21]

Wanamaker responded with more advertising and pep talks to his employees. In the end the Grand Depot was a success, the greatest of his career. His victory was not altogether the result of his dogged determination, or his insistence on his original principles. Rather, it came about

[20] Gibbons, *Wanamaker*, p. 170.
[21] *Ibid.*, p. 177.

because of changes in the economy, technological developments, and Wanamaker's ability to change his mind, albeit slowly and without acknowledgment, and transform the Grand Depot into a department store.

Wanamaker had opened the store during an economic depression. The store was far from any railroad passenger station and could be reached only by foot, horsecar, or carriage. The huge building had a basement and galleries, which together measured some three acres and could not be used due to the lack of safe lighting. These problems, the solutions of which were not at hand in 1877, were no longer present by 1880.

The depression had ended by then, the result of poor harvests in Europe, a strong upward movement in grain prices, prosperity on the farms, and ultimately, an economic revival in the cities as well. The Grand Depot never lacked sightseers, but at first not enough of them could afford to make purchases. Now this was changed. Sales rose, and with them, profits.

There had been electrical demonstrations at the Centennial, and Wanamaker was quick to recognize their significance for retailing. The following year he utilized battery-fed lights for "great illuminations" in the windows of his store. Edison's incandescent lamp was patented in 1880, and the Grand Depot was the first store to use the new lights. Now the basement and galleries could be opened, and in time ventilation and the use of pneumatic tubes for the transmission of sales were made possible. In 1882 Wanamaker installed elevators at the Grand Depot, making it even more accessible to customers. Meanwhile, he encouraged the city to extend transportation to his store, and with the coming of electricity, Wanamaker insisted that Philadelphia adopt the electric trolley.

At the same time, Wanamaker began to extend the line of goods offered the public. The change from clothing to a diversified stock came in stages. In 1878 chinaware was added. Sporting goods and refrigerators came in the spring of 1880, and carpets and jewelry in the fall of the year. Bedsteads, antique furniture, optical goods, gas stoves, and even an art gallery appeared in 1881, and the following year saw the introduction of a book section and a soda fountain. The expansion continued, with new items added every few months. By the mid-1880s Wanamaker's was a department store in every sense of the word, and the largest in the nation.

In addition to expanding his stock—horizontal expansion as it were—Wanamaker re-entered production. At first it was candy. He complained that suppliers could not sell him enough high quality merchandise, and so he opened his own plant. Then it was mattresses, with the same reason given. Other products followed, with all being sold at the Grand Depot. In all cases, Wanamaker advertised that as a result of savings in manufacture, the price of his own goods would be lowered. So the customer had the choice of purchasing a Wanamaker-made mattress or one turned out by a supplier, which sold at a higher price. The Wanamakers outsold the others, and so production was raised, and prices lowered again. He was not the originator of house brands, and other merchants used them more skillfully. But it was another example of his willingness to change if forced to do so.

The enlarged business meant that Wanamaker would have to delegate responsibility. Fortunately, he had by then found a man whom he could trust. Robert Curtis Ogden, two years older than Wanamaker, was in the clothing business in New York, where he operated a store not unlike Oak Hall. He too was a devout Presbyterian—the men met at a YMCA conference in 1861—and a Sunday school teacher. Ogden had the same moral and business background as Wanamaker, so it was not surprising that he was asked to join in the Grand Depot. At first Ogden refused, and later on he attempted to interest Wanamaker in setting up a New York operation, which he would head. This failed, but in late 1878, Ogden agreed to come to Philadelphia.

For the next four years Ogden managed Oak Hall, where he functioned as an extension of, not an aide to, Wanamaker. Then, in 1885, Ogden came to the Grand Depot.

The move signaled the beginning of a new period in Wanamaker's life. Ogden and Wanamaker's oldest son, Thomas, were given management roles at the Grand Depot. Brother William became president at Oak Hall, while another brother, Francis Marion, went to Chestnut Street, along with Isaac Shearer, a trusted friend. Two years later Wanamaker purchased the wholesale operations of Thomas J. Mustin and Company and followed this with the acquisition of Hood, Bonbright and Company, said to be the third largest wholesale house in the nation. Now he integrated operations at his three stores, using the new wholesale installations as supply bases. Not only that, his wholesalers aggressively sought business in other parts of the country. Wanamaker was not prepared to "invade" other cities with stores bearing his name, but his influence was felt beyond Philadelphia nonetheless. In addition, he entered the publishing, banking, and other service and manufacturing areas in the late 1880s. Marshall Field was erecting a larger mercantile establishment in Chicago, but the Grand Depot remained the most famous store in the nation.

Wanamaker was only forty-seven years old at the time he revamped his operations, and a man whose great gambles had turned out well. He had transformed himself from the owner-manager of a clothing store to the head of a fairly complex retail and wholesale operation, having delegated powers to others in ways he said he would never do. Up to this point, all of his ventures had succeeded, despite times when his capital was short. Now he had sufficient capital and, in Ogden, an able lieutenant. Given his resources, reputation, intelligence, and vigor, Wanamaker might have gone on to become the master of American retailing. This did not happen. His reputation grew in the years that followed, but many of his business decisions after the 1880s turned out badly.

Wanamaker's instincts regarding himself and the business, as expressed in the 1870s, were well-founded. He liked to have control over all aspects of operations. So long as he did, the establishments flourished. There can be little doubt that he would have preferred to remain in that kind of business. During one of his European trips in the 1880s he visited the diamond center in the Netherlands. Writing to one of his sisters of the experience, he said:

> Is the diamond-cutter to be envied? I've been watching one. He cuts and polishes. Then he puts aside the stone on which his skill has been expended and which he will never see again. He takes another stone—and goes through the same process. I am glad I will never be through cutting and polishing my store stone. I must keep at it like my religion—or I won't have a precious stone. God is good who doesn't ask me to put it aside, finished.[22]

Yet even then, Wanamaker was involved more deeply in church matters than before, and preparing for a political career. He had been an excellent manager at Oak Hall and had proved his skill at dry goods and purchasing at Chestnut Street. The Grand Depot experience was a daring move that succeeded—perhaps no other retailer at the time could have taken such a move and done so well. But he was a mediocre chief operating officer at best. The times required such individuals, and Wanamaker hadn't been able to move with the times.

In 1888 Wanamaker worked for the candidacy of George Childs, the Republican editor of the Philadelphia *Public Ledger*, who had minor Presidential ambitions. Later on he supported Benjamin Harrison, who defeated incumbent Grover Cleveland in a close race. For many years Wanamaker had been a contributor to Republican causes and had

[22] *Ibid.*, II, 33.

earned the friendship of Pennsylvania state boss Matt Quay. Now Quay tried to repay his obligations by suggesting that Wanamaker might be interested in a diplomatic appointment. Harrison, who shared Wanamaker's religious and social ideas, was prepared to make an offer, but the merchant wasn't interested in living overseas. Instead, the President-elect gave him the office of postmaster-general, and Wanamaker accepted.

The merchant proved a capable executive but a poor politician during his four years at the job. Mail delivery improved, and Wanamaker worked hard for rural free delivery. But he also advocated postal savings banks, then considered almost socialistic, and followed this with a plan for the nationalization of the telephone and telegraph companies, placing them under the Post Office Department. These suggestions had no chance of approval, especially in the administration of Benjamin Harrison. Had Wanamaker been a serious politician, he might have been attacked. Some suggested that the reason he was so intent on improving mail service was to enable the Wanamaker parcel post business to prosper. But in fact, his stores were still a minor factor in that field. As it was, most in Washington looked upon him as a dilettante, who was being rewarded for party favors and whose presence in the Cabinet would be approved by the public. So he was tolerated, but never had real power.

Harrison lost the 1892 election to Grover Cleveland, and Wanamaker returned to Philadelphia, where his family and Ogden had been running operations. The company had prospered in his absence, a fact he might have resented. The stores no longer were *his* but rather the *company's*. Perhaps he wanted a new challenge, one he could direct. Or it may have been that Wanamaker finally came to understand that expansion was necessary. In either case, he began to look beyond Philadelphia once more.

New York was the most obvious place for a new store. Chicago, the other great and growing center, was domi-

nated by Marshall Field, while Boston was too far a trip for
Wanamaker, who intended to supervise any operation he
might open. Furthermore, New York clearly was the most
powerful city in the nation, and the home of the old A.T.
Stewart operation, then being managed by Hilton, Hughes
and Company. Stewart had died in 1876, after becoming one
of the heroes of merchandising. But the operation he had
founded on Astor Place was on the verge of failure. The
shopping district had moved uptown, and the store itself
was old-fashioned. If Wanamaker could take over and then
revive the store, it would ensure his place as a master retailer, a status then being sought by Field and others, and
which he dearly wanted.

Wanamaker purchased the old Stewart business in 1896,
after a long and carefully developed plan of operation had
been worked out. He would take over the entire business,
including the Stewart name, and then revive it. To indicate
the continuity—the passing of power from one merchant
prince to another—he placed a tablet at one of the corners
of the store which read: "JOHN WANAMAKER FOR-
MERLY A.T. STEWART AND CO."

The renovation was a sentimental gesture, but bad business. If Wanamaker wanted to go to New York, he should
have gone fresh, and not have attempted to revive an old
store in what had become an out-of-the-way location. In
1877, he had been able to lure Philadelphians to the Grand
Depot, but at the time it was the only large store in the city,
and a tourist attraction as well. It was different in New
York at the turn of the century, where Macy's, Hearn's,
Altman's, Lord & Taylor, and many other stores, most of
them more modern and attractive than Wanamaker's, were
further uptown, with Gimbel's to appear soon after to has-
ten the move northward. Many of these stores, Macy's in
particular, had good reputations in the city, as least as high
as Wanamaker's in Philadelphia. So it was not altogether
surprising that the new store did not perform as expected.

It took Wanamaker almost a decade to concede this point.

Then, in 1907, he constructed another building across the street from the old one, and connected the two with a double-deck "Bridge of Progress." The new store was lavishly furnished, a rival for any in the city, while the bridge drew the curious to the location. Still, the march uptown continued, leaving the stores by themselves.

Wanamaker had been unable to dominate retail trade in New York. He might have done so had he made the move in the 1880s, or even in the early 1890s. By 1907 it was too late to seize the lead position.

He refused to admit defeat. Instead, he began to consider stores in other cities as well, reviving the idea he had abandoned a quarter of a century earlier. In May 1899, he visited Chicago, where he met with Marshall Field. Almost casually, he mentioned that Chicago appeared to be in need of additional retail stores. To this, Field replied, "Probably. But I've been thinking of expanding too. You come here and I think we'll open in Philadelphia." For the moment, the matter was closed. But Wanamaker returned to Chicago the following year, and was said to be interested in the acquisition of a site. Later in 1899 he appeared in Boston, and that city's newspapers announced that Wanamaker had purchased a block of property in a prime location and would soon begin construction on a new store. Then, in 1901, he returned to Chicago and met again with Marshall Field. This time a new rumor appeared, one to the effect that Wanamaker, Field, and Jordan Marsh and Company of Boston would soon announce a merger, "the greatest colossal mercantile combination which the world has ever seen." A week later there came an announcement that Wanamaker had taken options on a large block of land in Cleveland, and in 1902 he traveled to Chicago to confer with Daniel Burnham, the city's leading architect, known for his store designs.

Almost all the rumors of new stores in American cities and combinations with other merchants lacked foundation. This was an age of combination in business, and whenever two large factors in the same industry met, such rumors were started. On the face of it, a merger between Field and Wanamaker made little sense; each man insisted on control, and neither was likely to share it with the other.

But Wanamaker was serious about expansion, though in Europe, and not America. In 1899 he formulated a plan for an English affiliate, and he considered sites in Oxford Circus, at Trafalgar Square, and High Holborn for a new store. For many years he planned a store in Paris, and he also did some preliminary work on one in Berlin. Whether or not he would have proceeded with any of them had not the war interfered is debatable. He wrote first of European expansion in 1899, and did nothing about it for the next fifteen years of peace. Perhaps Wanamaker looked upon foreign stores as a way to spread the American ideal abroad; he certainly had more than his share of missionary zeal. In any case, nothing came of the plans. Others developed their stores; Wanamaker now seemed content to embellish the old, and he stopped innovating and expanding.

Wanamaker was no longer the leading merchant in America, but rather the first among equals, and even here his position was slipping, as Marshall Field and Isadore Straus began innovations in deliveries, sales promotion, store location, and retail methods. Increasingly, Wanamaker left the actual running of the business to others, concentrating on advertising, an area which he always enjoyed since it enabled him to spread his message of morality as well as sell goods. He wrote thousands of "business editorials," and delighted in presenting maxims to the public, all of which reflected his philosophy of life and values. In them can be found the YMCA enthusiast, the Sunday school teacher, and the Victorian, to an ever greater degree than the merchant:

"Happy is the man who chooses his life's work carefully and stands by it faithfully to the end."

"We cannot all be generals, doctors or preachers, but we can be plain, honest, unselfish men and women, helping each other to live a true life."

"No day seems long enough to those who love their work."

"To believe you cannot do a thing is the way to make it impossible."

"The first duty of a boy is to his conscience. The second duty is to his home, because there is a mother there. His third duty is to his country."

"The North Star is more valuable than any others because the little fellow is always in his place."

"What is success but to make sacrifices?"

"Almost every human being wants to do right."

"Our conduct is only a sample of our thoughts."

"It is the children and their mothers who keep the world sweet."

"It is always a mistake to be hasty in spending money."

"Some people never see the sun in a dew-drop."[23]

From time to time Wanamaker managed merchandising *coups*. He became a strong advocate of the Ford automobile and helped the manufacturer in his fight with the owners of the Selden patent. Wanamaker was convinced the automobile would change retailing, though he wasn't certain how this would be done, or when, and he wanted to play a role in its introduction. He sold Fords in his store, and offered to defend any customer who might get into trouble with the Selden people. Later on, Wanamaker attempted to sell airplanes in the same fashion. Toward the end of World War I, he became convinced that there would be a depression after the armistice, and ordered sales in all his stores to insure liquidity. The decline came, forcing many merchants out of business, while Wanamaker was secure.

[23] Appel, *Wanamaker*, pp. 225–32.

Wanamaker's later stores were as up-to-date as any in the land. In 1908 he had put up a new store at Chestnut Street, which was completed two years later and was considered one of the finest in America. The New York store was altered on several occasions, and was more elegant than Macy's or other rivals. But increasingly the stores' atmospheres were coming to appear dated. Wanamaker, who was in tune with middle-class Americans in the last half of the nineteenth century, operated in such a way as to reflect his beliefs, and those who shopped at his establishments appreciated this. His customers remained loyal to his values, and to his stores; Wanamaker's remained a potent force in Philadelphia and New York retailing prior to World War I, and even afterward. But the children of his original customers were not as loyal.

In part this was the result of his success. Other retailers imitated Wanamaker, so much so that there seemed little difference between his stores and methods of operations and those of many others. This was true not only in New York but in Philadelphia, where Strawbridge & Clothier, Lit Brothers, Gimbel's, and Snellenburg now provided strong competition. It was also due, however, to a certain rigidity to be found at the stores. Wanamaker would not countenance rivalries, such as those Macy's had with several of its 14th Street neighbors, and later with Gimbel's. He refused to engage in price-cutting competitions, although he did permit more sales when urged to do so by his managers. In other words, Wanamaker's featured a "fair price," while its rivals boasted of "lowest price in town." Similarly, Wanamaker insisted on a more personal style of advertising than what appealed to young people in the first quarter of the new century. Nor was he able to adjust to the arrival of lower-class shoppers in downtown areas, a movement which accelerated with the new century. Such individuals responded to a more garish form of advertising than Wanamaker wrote and approved, and would accept inferior merchandise if the price were low enough, while he always refused to deal in such items. Macy's, Gimbel's, and other of the department stores were able to sell merchandise to the masses without losing their essential middle-class tone, while newer stores, such as Orbach's and Klein's, were unabashedly lower class. Wanamaker would not make the change; nor would he open a lower-class outlet. He had built his reputation and fortune on a set of principles, and demonstrated them in all aspects of his life. He would not change them; and even had he desired, he could not have altered his manner of doing business. Toward the end of his life, he was hailed as America's leading retail genius. This was somewhat overstated, but certainly Wanamaker, as much as any merchant, could have claimed that honor. But as is so often the case, the praise came for accomplishments that were decades old, and not for the Wanamaker of the 1920s. Like so many nineteenth-century Victorians who survived, he was something of an anachronism toward the end.

IV

James J. Hill:
The Business of Empire

"The Railroads is the only sure topic for conversation in these days," wrote Ralph Waldo Emerson in 1848. "That is the only one which interests farmers, merchants, boys, women, saints, philosophers, and fools."[1] Emerson exaggerated, and yet there was good reason to talk of railroads that year. The United States had just defeated Mexico in battle, and one result of the victory was the extension of the nation's boundaries to the Pacific. Gold was discovered in California, and became the magnet that drew Americans across the Mississippi in large numbers. Zachary Taylor, one of the heroes of the Mexican War and to many a symbol of overarching power, won the Presidency on the Whig ticket in 1848, and although the party did not write a platform that year—Taylor alone sufficed to lure voters—the election clearly endorsed expansionism and all it entailed. The pace on the road to empire quickened.

Some political leaders opposed continentalism and the form it had taken. Daniel Webster, for example, was unsure of the vision prior to the war, and certainly saw little to be gained from acquisition of the West. "What do we want with this vast, worthless area, this region of savages and

[1] Edward Waldo Emerson and Waldo Emerson Forbes, eds., *Journals of Ralph Waldo Emerson* (Boston, 1909–14), VII, 504.

wild beasts, of shifting sands and whirlpools of dust?" he asked. California gold and the gradual fading of the myth of "the Great American Desert" west of the Mississippi silenced Webster. Empire was the new dream, and the railroad one of its prime symbols.

The railroad shattered the rural landscape when it first appeared, and as much as any other invention and development quickened the movement toward industrialization and urbanization. The railroad expanded markets, transported raw materials and finished products, and utilized huge amounts of both on its own behalf. In 1830 the nation had only twenty-three miles of track. In every year for the next century American railroad mileage increased, despite wars and depressions. Historians and economists still debate the economic impact and worth of the lines. There is evidence that in many parts of the country canals might have been better investments than railroads, and provided cheaper transportation.[2] Without powerful lobbyists who obtained land grants and other favors for the lines, they might not have been built when and where they were.[3] In 1843, Senator James Buchanan of Pennsylvania denounced these pressures:

> If you defeat them at this session, they will be here in greater force than ever at the commencement of the next. Their importunity will never cease whilst the least hope of success shall remain, and we have learned from our experience that they have both the ability and the will to select shrewd and skilful agents to accomplish their purposes before Congress.[4]

[2]Recently the railroad has been compared with canals in several works. The most significant work in the field is Robert W. Fogel, *Railroads and American Economic Growth: Essays in Econometric History* (Baltimore, 1964).

[3]The pressure for railroads, especially transcontinentals, was similar in some respects to those for space programs, in particular the moon shot. See Bruce Mazlish, ed., *The Railroad and the Space Program: An Exploration in Historical Analogy* (Cambridge, 1965).

[4]Robert Sobel, *Panic on Wall Street: A History of America's Financial Disasters* (New York, 1968), p. 77.

Whether or not the railroads were good investments for the nation, they did create large fortunes for individuals as well as great reputations for builders and operators. This was particularly true in the case of the transcontinentals— a misnomer, since these lines went from mid-America to the West Coast, and not from ocean to ocean. Even as Emerson wrote, plans for such a line were being formulated. On Independence Day, 1851, Mayor L.M. Kennett of St. Louis broke ground for the Pacific Railroad of Missouri, the first part of which would run from his city to Kansas City, and would then drive on to California. The Pacific of Missouri was poorly financed, badly planned, and led by men of little experience. It failed. But in 1869 the Central Pacific and the Union Pacific were joined at Promontory Point, Utah, making the transcontinental a reality.

Work on the transcontinental began during the Civil War, and continued while the fighting raged, an indication of Lincoln's view of its importance. Builders and operators became major public figures in the years that followed, while engineers were admired as romantic personalities, with songs written in their honor. The person who memorized the words of "Casey Jones" would have a son who sang "Lucky Lindy," and he in turn would be father to a child who wanted to be an astronaut. In trying to "draw the generations together," in his acceptance speech at the Republican convention in 1968, Richard Nixon alluded to this. "I see another child tonight," he said. "He hears a train go by. At night he dreams of faraway places where he'd like to go. It seems an impossible dream."

The real power, however, belonged to the tycoons, the men who financed and constructed the lines, operated and reorganized them, and took possession of vast tracts of land and viewed them as feudal fiefs. They did not war on governments; they simply bought them out. But they did fight one another, viewing intrusions by other tycoons as though invasions from a foreign power. America's true history, wrote Philip Guedella in 1936, "was always the history of transportation, in which the names of railroad presidents are more significant than those of Presidents of the United States. These names emerge—Gould, Vanderbilt, Hill, Huntington, and Harriman."[5]

Vanderbilt, the ruler of the New York Central, the despoiler of the Erie, the man who dominated Wall Street and sent his private army to conquer Nicaragua, was the first of these. After working with Vanderbilt on Wall Street and the Erie, Jay Gould went west, declared war on the Union Pacific interests and won, and then took possession of that line, along with the Kansas Pacific and others. Gould purchased newspapers and used them to destroy congressmen, and then bought the congressmen who replaced them. On a European trip he tried to see one of the Rothschilds, but was rejected. "Europe is not for sale" was the reply to his note. Huntington dominated the Far West, and financed the Central Pacific as leader of the "Big Four," which included Charles Crocker, Mark Hopkins, and Leland Stanford. California was their domain; no other tycoons dared intrude there without permission. E.H. Harriman began his railroad career by taking over the Illinois Central, and then he gained control of both the Union Pacific and Southern Pacific. He dreamed of constructing a line across Siberia, of dominating European lines, establishing a two-ocean fleet, and expanding his American influence to the East Coast—in the end, he hoped a globe-circling enterprise would emerge. Harriman did not realize this ambition, but he did become the most powerful of the rail tycoons, and he wore this power easily. Once, while in Vienna, he was scheduled for an audience with Emperor Franz Joseph. The Emperor was unavoidably detained. When apologies were offered, Harriman brushed them aside. "I, of all people, know the problems of empire," he said.

[5] Albro Martin, *Enterprise Denied: Origins of the Decline of American Railroads, 1897–1917* (New York, 1971), p. 22.

Like the others, James J. Hill had imperial ambitions, and he was more successful than most in realizing them. Hill could be as rough with his enemies as Vanderbilt, as devious as Gould when the occasion called for that quality, as arrogant and ruthless as Harriman, and as protective of his holdings as Huntington. He knew more about railroad construction than the others, who tended to concentrate on finance and management. His Great Northern Railroad was better designed, constructed, and financed than any other transcontinental. In fact, it was the only major line of its type that never went bankrupt.

In time Hill acquired other roads, among them the Northern Pacific, and he ruled his region with the authority of an absolute monarch. From the Great Lakes westward to the Pacific and from the Missouri River to central Canada, Hill was the master. He would share power on occasion, but never relinquish it. Hill had shipping lines in the north Pacific and more than any other American businessman of the time, dominated the Orient trade. He influenced state legislatures and outmaneuvered the federal government, but never received a major federal land grant. Like his fellow tycoons, Hill accumulated money and power, more than Huntington, somewhat less than Harriman.

Hill's career went through three stages. He began as a general tradesman, went on to become a railroader, and completed his work as one interested in regional development. He succeeded in all areas and constantly sought new ones. There was a depth to Hill not found in the others. He was the only one of the major railroaders who wrote seriously about major problems in such a way as to influence academic work on the subjects. Hill was a scholar, a self-educated one, who felt at ease among intellectuals, even though he rarely met them, disliking their natural habitat in the East and remaining in the Northwest as much as possible. He was the first American millionaire to collect French Impressionist art, and even wrote feelingly about it, but such things were of far less interest than the land itself. Hill understood the principles of ecology and warned against ravaging the land, even when he was guilty of doing so himself. "Population without the Prairie is a mob," he wrote, "and the Prairie without Population is a desert."[6] He hoped to bring the two together, to tame the mob and cultivate the prairie, with each contributing to the Great Northern's growth.

Settlers on his lands would receive benefits from the Hill empire. He would do all he could to help them prosper, understanding that such prosperity would help the Great Northern. Hill understood that greater wealth could be derived from economic development than from shady financings and the bleeding of already sick lines, practices common among many other railroaders. By 1905, Hill's lines served a population of over 1.5 million, a majority of whom had come to the area as a result of prodding and pulling by the Great Northern and the Northern Pacific. The rapid development of the trans-Mississippi West might have taken place without Harriman and Gould— indeed, development might have been faster and less inefficient had these men been involved in other activities. It was different with Hill. At the turn of the century he was known as "The Empire Builder," which also was the name of the Great Northern's Number One train.

Whether any one man—or, for that matter, group of men —should have as much power as Hill wielded at his prime is doubtful, but the question was academic in the age of the transcontinentals, when railroading and industry offered so much in the way of opportunity to the ambitious, the bold, and the cunning, with no major political or social force to stand in their way. The fact of the matter was that the power and wealth were there for the taking, and they were seized by a number of major businessmen. Hill used his power with skill, moderation, and a sense of proportion.

[6]Stewart H. Holbrook, *The Story of American Railroads* (New York, 1947), p. 186.

The same could not be said for most of the others. Perhaps this was so because most of them entered railroading as a result of the luck of the draw. Huntington was a wealthy hardware dealer when the chance to get in on the transcontinental bonanza presented itself; Harriman and Gould were Wall Streeters who, had they remained in New York, would have manipulated stocks and bonds rather than actual properties. Almost all the other transcontinental giants came to railroading and transportation itself through happenstance, and to regional development not at all. It was different with Hill, a man of the Northwest from the start, and one who always identified himself with the region.

Hill was born in a log cabin near Rockwood, Ontario, Canada, in 1838. As was the case with John Wanamaker, much was made of the circumstances of his birth later on, and it was claimed that Hill, like Lincoln and others, had risen from poverty to greatness through hard work and intestinal fortitude. But like Wanamaker's parents, Hill's were fairly well-to-do. They insisted on the best education possible for their son, who went to a local school and then on to Rockwood Academy, a private institution run by Quakers. By his own account, Hill was happy at Rockwood, enjoyed reading and especially ancient languages, and had some ambitions for a scholarly career. Then, in 1852, his father died, and Hill left school to obtain a job. For four years he clerked at a local village store during the days and, as he later recalled, read Plutarch and Byron at night. This reading and talk in the store of distant places made Hill restive. He wanted to travel overseas, to the Orient in particular, and planned to do so by signing on as a sailor at a United States port along the Atlantic.

Hill left Ontario as the age of eighteen, bound for New York. He arrived a few months later, but was unable to find a ship willing to offer him a job. From there he went to

Philadelphia, again being rejected. Hill saw enough of the Northeast to realize he didn't like the area; it was too settled for his taste, too unlike Ontario. Rather than remain there awaiting a ship, Hill decided to walk and ride across the United States, and leave from San Francisco or some other Pacific port. He set out in early 1856, hoping to catch a wagon train in the Minnesota territory before the last ones left in July.

He arrived in St. Paul (then called Pig's Eye) in mid-July, a few days after the last wagon train of the year set out for California. Out of money, he had to remain in the town for the winter, get a job, and save enough for the crossing in early Spring.

St. Paul was a small Mississippi River town in 1856, with a population of some 4,000–5,000, dominated by St. Louis businessmen who hoped to develop it into a key fur-gathering point for Minnesota and mid-Canada. Lumbering projects were also in the works, and already St. Paul had visions of dominating the upper Midwest north of Missouri. The territory had a population of below 150,000, but was growing rapidly; two years after Hill arrived it would be admitted into the Union as a state. The St. Louis merchants recognized this potential, and at the time of Hill's arrival had announced that regular steamboat runs to St. Louis would begin the following year. In other words, St. Paul was in the midst of a boom, and optimism ran high. Hill knew he would have little trouble finding employment in such a place. And in fact, he liked the town, which was not much different from similar settlements in Ontario except in that it offered greater promise. Too, it was a welcome relief from what he considered the stuffy atmosphere of the Atlantic port cities.[7]

The greatest opportunities in St. Paul lay in lumber and river transport. Perhaps because he still had hopes of crossing the Pacific and had never been on a ship with the

[7]Theodore C. Blegen, *Minnesota: A History of the State* (Minneapolis, 1963), pp. 156–57.

exception of ferries, Hill decided to seek a job at a shipping firm, and found one as clerk at the Dubuque and St. Paul Packet Company. The work there must have been interesting and the prospects good, for by the time the wagon trains were ready to leave in the spring, Hill had decided to remain in the city.

River traffic at St. Paul was busy in 1856, and busier yet the following year, when 1,090 steamboats arrived at the port, ten times as many as had come in 1850. But 1857 was the high point for St. Paul port; by 1860, traffic was down to 776 arrivals. Clearly hopes for the port had been overoptimistic. The river was closed by ice for almost half the year, and during part of the rest was barely navigable.[8] St. Paul was well located as a transportation terminal, but perhaps not for Mississippi traffic.

The Civil War destroyed what remained of the city's Mississippi dream. The commercial class that dominated St. Paul, connected as it was with St. Louis, was sympathetic to the Confederate cause, while the lumbering interests were pro-Union and by that time more closely connected with Chicago's growing mercantile class than with any other. The war also ended St. Louis' dreams of becoming the terminus for a transcontinental railroad; now Chicago went to the fore.[9] The victory was not only one of North over South, but the northern transcontinental over the southern, the railroad over the river, Chicago over St. Louis and New Orleans.

When the war erupted, Hill was working as an agent for the Davidson steamboat interests. He tried to enlist in the Union Army, but was rejected because he had lost an eye as a boy. So he stayed with Davidson until 1865, when he

[8]Wyatt W. Belcher, *The Economic Rivalry Between St. Louis and Chicago, 1850–1880* (New York, 1947), pp. 43–44.
[9]H. Craig Miner, *The St. Louis-San Francisco Railroad: The Thirty-Fifth Parallel Project* (Lawrence, 1972), pp. 29–42.

obtained an appointment as agent for the Northwestern Packet Company, another steamboat operation, which also had an interest in the Chicago, Milwaukee, and St. Paul Railroad. This was only one of his interests; by the end of the war Hill was involved with warehousing, the fur trade, fuel supply operations, factoring, and commission work, all highly competitive businesses with few rules of fair conduct to guide novice businessmen. Hill's successes in all these areas indicate that by 1866 he had become a hard-fighting and clever entrepreneur.

In that year Hill became a major supplier of stores and other goods for the St. Paul and Pacific Railroad, a small line with transcontinental ambitions that connected eastward with the Chicago, Milwaukee and St. Paul and the Illinois Central. "I acted as agent for the St. Paul & Pacific Railroad Company in St. Paul," wrote Hill many years later, recalling his life as a sedentary merchant.

> This began in the spring of 1866. I handled the freight by the ton and by the carload under a contract. I built a warehouse, or it might be said I extended their station—built an addition to it two hundred feet long and about sixty wide—in which I received freight from steamboats on the Mississippi River destined to other points, and local freight to St. Paul, and did any business that I might have to do in connection with these boats, giving the preference as to room to the business of the railway company. The floor upon which the boats delivered their freight was a story below the station, on a level with the car tracks. That arrangement was to save drayage. A large portion of the business was to St. Anthony and Minneapolis; and, prior to the construction of that warehouse, steamboats unloaded on the public levee, and freight was drayed to the railway at the expense of sixty cents to a dollar a ton. Adding to the cost of draying it from the station at St. Anthony to the merchants' stores, it would have

been about as cheap to haul the freight direct by team
from one point to the other. The railroad was anxious
to have this arrangement made for landing freight
directly from steamboats into the warehouse. There
was no charge made as agent of forwarder on any
freight handled by me going over the railway.[10]

Within a year, Hill was the leading handler of freight in
St. Paul, in part because of the continuation of practices
begun earlier with the railroads. He added no charges for
certain transfers, willingly erected warehouses at his own
expense, and offered competitive rates.

Now Hill extended his reach. He formed one partnership with a storage and commission firm in Dubuque, and
then another with Chauncey W. Griggs in 1869, for freight-
ing, merchandising, fuel, and warehousing enterprises. According to Griggs, the new firm of Hill, Griggs and Company was capitalized at $25,000.[11] Griggs operated this
business, as Hill expanded on his own into an agency for
the sale of farm machines, flour mills, and flour shipments.
He was on the road much of the time but also served as
president of the St. Paul Democratic Convention and, in
1871, ran for alderman even though he would not become an
American citizen until 1880.

Increasingly, Hill's interests were drawn to the north
and west, to the Red River valley. Winnipeg, near the
northern end of the river, was growing as rapidly as St.
Paul, and Hill thought it would become the metropolis of
the Canadian West. Accordingly, he formed another company for "carrying on a merchandising and transportation
business on the Red River of the North," and moved to
crack the Hudson's Bay Company control of steamboat
traffic on the river by building and operating his own line.
"My business, commencing in 1870, included the transportation of a large amount of freight by teams to the Red

[10]Joseph G. Pyle, *The Life of James J. Hill* (New York, 1917), I, 58–59.
[11]*Ibid.*, I, 112.

River and the building of flat boats by which the freight was transported down the river."[12]

Hill acted against the Hudson's Bay Company, invoking a neglected law that prohibited foreigners from carrying freight on United States waters. Not realizing that Hill was a Canadian himself, the company retaliated by setting up a dummy company under Norman W. Kittson, its agent in St. Paul. A rate war ensued, and both lines lost money. At this point Hill and Kittson met, and the result was the formation of the Red River Transportation Line which, with Hudson's Bay approval, monopolized river traffic. Now rates rose and remained high, with all but those who had to ship goods benefiting. Hill and Kittson celebrated by buying out Griggs and other partners and throwing their interests into a new firm, the Red River Transportation Company. This new entity contained an odd assortment of transportation, trading, milling, and related operations, ventures, and schemes; in some respects it resembled a modern conglomerate, although the financing mechanisms used by these later corporations did not yet exist, and in addition Hill's companies and interests were not as widespread as those of businessmen a century later. But the various parts of the enterprise meshed, and through the Transportation Company, Hill and Kittson prospered. In its first full year of operation, it returned a net profit of 80 percent.

Kittson remained in St. Paul directing operations, while Hill roamed the north country seeking new business. He was in the field in 1870, investigating a rebellion led by Louis Riel, who had organized trappers against the Hudson's Bay Company and the new Dominion. While there Hill met Donald A. Smith, one of the Company's governors and now special commissioner for the Dominion. Hill already knew Smith by reputation, while Smith had followed the Red River episode carefully, and respected his

[12] *Ibid.*, I, 98.

"adversary." The two men were impressed with one another at this face-to-face meeting, although they did little
more than share a meal at the time. Smith proceeded to
crush the rebels, while Hill went on to explore commercial
possibilities in Canada. But they corresponded afterward,
and one result of this was a closer relationship between
Hill and the Company along the Red River, and the promise of further cooperation should the opportunity arise.[13]

For a while it appeared another interloper might destroy
the harmony Hill and Smith were creating in Minnesota.
Jay Cooke, who had made a reputation and fortune as the
"financier of the Civil War," was now banker for the
Northern Pacific Railroad, the projected new transcontinental, which was supposed to extend from Lake Superior
to the Pacific Northwest. The line had been chartered by
Congress in 1864, but actual construction did not begin
until 1870. Cooke knew little of railroading but he did prove
adept at selling the line's securities, mostly to foreigners,
who knew less of the problems and of the nature of the
terrain. The success of the Union Pacific, together with
promises of large land grants, subsidies, and profitable construction contracts, lured them on, even though the economic need for a northern line was by no means clear at
the time.[14] Given its leadership, the Northern Pacific did
not seem a serious rival. In time new men might appear,
however, and then they could drain business not only from
Hill, but the Hudson's Bay Company as well. The potential
was there.

In 1872 Cooke challenged Hill in St. Paul itself. By that
time the St. Paul and Pacific was near failure, and believing
its extension from the town to the Mississippi worth having, Cooke took it over. He announced his intention to
bring the line to the Canadian border, and then make it

[13]Pierre Berton, *The Impossible Railway: The Building of the Canadian Pacific* (New
York, 1972), pp. 134–35.
[14]Eugene V. Smalley, *History of the Northern Pacific Railroad* (New York, 1883);
Henrietta M. Larson, *Jay Cooke, Private Banker* (Cambridge, 1936).

part of the Northern Pacific. Armed with this plan, his European salesmen were able to sell $15 million worth of bonds to Dutch investors to finance the acquisition. Cooke then spent more than $1 million on additions and improvements, a sign that he hoped to capture the Red River traffic from the steamboats.[15]

Hill was also interested in the St. Paul and Pacific, having worked with it since 1866 and recognized its potential not only as a rail line but as a complement to his other activities. He lacked the funds to purchase it, however, and was forced to watch as the Northern Pacific interests began developing it in such a way as to insure trouble for all of his other enterprises as well.

The nation was struck by a financial panic in 1873, caused in part by the failure of Jay Cooke and Company. The overblown and oversold Northern Pacific, along with other Cooke interests, was crippled, not to truly function again until two years later, when it was taken over by Henry Villard. As for the St. Paul and Pacific, it was bankrupt, with the Dutch creditors not certain they could salvage anything from the crash.

Hill had not suffered as a result of the crash; his varied interests were intact, although the firms' volume of business was somewhat lower than they had been prior to the panic and depression. Hill wanted to approach the Dutch bondholders and make them an offer for their holdings, but he knew he lacked sufficient funds for the undertaking. Still, he continued to study the line, and met with John Carp, a bondholders' representative, who visited St. Paul to determine the line's value. Hill took Carp on a tour of the line, making certain the visitor saw only the most rundown portions and would write a pessimistic report to his clients. He also discovered that John S. Kennedy, a New York banker, was the Dutch Committee's agent in America, and would be receptive to an offer—and deal.

[15]Julius Grodinsky, *Transcontinental Railway Strategy, 1869–1893: A Study of Businessmen* (Philadelphia, 1962), p. 33.

Hill spoke with Kittson about the possibilities. His partner opposed a takeover; they were doing well enough on the river, he said, and in any case they couldn't hope to raise money for the project. Hill persisted, and in the end Kittson was won over. But the money problem remained.

Donald Smith had come to the same conclusions as Hill regarding the St. Paul and Pacific, but for a different set of reasons. Smith realized that in time the territory would be opened by a railroad, and he meant for the Company to control it, either directly or indirectly, through an American partner or agent. Several attempts had been made to form a Canadian railroad, one that would construct a line that ran from coast to coast, but in 1873, hopes for such a road were dim.[16] The St. Paul and Pacific, while not a transcontinental, might serve as well for the time being. With the Company as a partner, it could be extended northward throughout British Columbia, while the eastern sections could be brought into Chicago in time. Later, Canadian mileage would be added; the Canadian transcontinental could be disguised as an American line in this fashion.

Smith went to see Kittson in the autumn of 1873 to explore the matter further, and to find out whether Hill, with whom he had worked so well on the Red River, might be willing to serve the Hudson's Bay Company's interests. Smith asked Kittson to find out all he could about the St. Paul and Pacific and, in particular, the attitude of the Dutch bondholders toward a sale. Smith, who also was an officer at the Bank of Montreal, indicated that he would be able to raise sufficient funds for an outright purchase if the price was right.

At the time of this meeting Hill had given up hope of acquiring the line; there seemed no way by which he could obtain the necessary funds. Now Kittson told him of Smith's interest, and Hill's spirits rose. When Smith passed

[16]L. Lorne McDougall, *Canadian Pacific: A Brief History* (Montreal, 1968), pp. 19–30.

through St. Paul in early 1874, he spoke with Kittson again, who took him to see Hill. The three talked for several days. Hill told Smith all he knew of the line, its problems and potentials, and the management. At the time the St. Paul and Pacific was in receivership, with one Jesse P. Farley the court-appointed operator. John S. Kennedy was still banker for the railroad and agent for the Dutch bondholders. Both men were on close terms with Hill; each benefited from his dealings with the line. Hill probably told Smith of these connections too. Finally, there were some $18 million worth of St. Paul and Pacific bonds outstanding, in the hands of the Dutch group. The foreigners would listen to terms; they would watch results on the bankrupt line; they would receive information from Kennedy. All that was needed was time—sufficient time for the partners to raise money, for the Dutch to become disheartened, and for a low price to be set and paid for the bonds. In addition, the partners hoped to lobby for a land grant from Minnesota, a bonus for their work.

The partners waited two years, during which time Smith worked for the Hudson's Bay Company, Kittson for his many projects, and Hill devoted most of his time to the railroad, which increasingly was becoming a passion with him. With Kittson's reluctant agreement he organized a "paper railroad," which would be charged with making new river connections for the St. Paul and Pacific if and when it was acquired. He saw John Carp the next time the Dutch representative came to St. Paul, and made certain Carp received all the bad news regarding the line from Farley. "I was induced to believe that it would last many years before all these troubles should come to an end," he later testified. Hill also operated through friends in the state legislature to get a land grant for the line, if and when it was reorganized.

Hill felt prepared to make his first offer to the creditors in early 1877. The Northern Pacific had been sold at foreclosure and the Dutch bondholders were now free to act on their own. Accordingly, Hill offered them $3.5 million in cash and the land grant for their bonds, with the understanding that the money would not be paid until the line was freed from debt. Since this would require a large amount of money, Hill knew the offer would not be accepted, but it would give him a chance to communicate with the Dutch and point out just how decayed the railroad was, how it had little chance of success. The figures would seem to indicate this was so, but Hill later admitted that he knew the figures were deceiving, that in fact the line was worth in excess of $20 million as it stood.

The next step was to bring in the Bank of Montreal, whose resources would be needed once a firm offer was accepted. George Stephen, president of the Bank, agreed to come into the partnership, and used his influence not only to raise money but to convince the Canadian government not to make grants to the newly reorganized Northern Pacific, which wanted to enter the territory. In the end, the Dutch accepted an offer of some $5.5 million plus preferred stock for their holdings. In March 1878, the four partners took control of the line.

In early 1879, Hill, Smith, Kittson, and Stephen organized the St. Paul, Minneapolis and Manitoba Railroad, with Stephen as president. The new line was chartered, and financed through the sale of stock and bonds. This paper railroad then purchased the assets of the St. Paul and Pacific, and after a series of complicated deals each of the partners emerged a multimillionaire, and still in control of the new line.[17]

Hill had spent almost eight years in conceiving, planning, and then executing the St. Paul and Pacific takeover and

---

[17]Pyle, *Hill*, I, 168–251 is a pro-Hill account of the negotiations and takeover. Using other information, Berton (*Impossible Railway*, pp. 179–204) indicated that Hill and his partners used means conventional at the time but which today would be considered shady to obtain the road, and then reorganize it.

subsequent reorganization. At the beginning of this period he was a man with many interests, all of which were connected in one way or another with the development of the region north and west of St. Paul. From his actions and statements in the early 1870s, it would appear that he viewed the railroad as another means to be used toward this end. As he studied railroading, traveled along the line, spoke with railroad men, and watched activities on other lines, his interests grew and developed into what might properly be called a mania. Now his other businesses—factoring, fur trading, steamboats—mattered little, and these were sold off or left to others to manage. Hill considered himself a railroad man, and although Stephen was the nominal head of the St. Paul, Minneapolis and Manitoba, Hill was its real leader.

Hill and his partners had concluded their deal at a fortunate time. By 1879 the depression that had begun in 1873 was ending, with grain production in the Midwest at record highs. Minneapolis was developing into a major flour-milling center, and the St. Paul, Minneapolis and Manitoba brought grain to its mills. The line had some 650 miles of track in 1879, most of it in bad shape, and indifferent rolling stock. Hill made improvements at once, supervising operations in the field. He was prepared for the bumper crops of 1879 and 1880; in the former year the line earned over a million dollars, and it did even better in 1880. Hill plowed most of the money back into the line, and all the while prepared to push his road westward, to the Pacific. He believed the land between St. Paul and Oregon was rich, excellent for winter wheat and also heavily forested. His line would open the area and then fill it with settlers who would ship their goods to market later on.

The area's potential, so obvious to Hill, also attracted the new owners and managers of the Northern Pacific, which would contest the St. Paul, Minneapolis and Manitoba for domination. In addition, there was a northern threat. The Canadian Pacific was chartered in 1881, and led by Stephen and others who viewed the line as a force that would bind the nation together. This was too great an enterprise for Hill to oppose. Even had he wanted to challenge the CP, he could hardly have done so, since Stephen was president of the St. Paul, Minneapolis and Manitoba, and other Canadians held significant equity in the line. For the time being, Hill had to cooperate with the CP—so long as that line remained out of territories he had marked for his own.

Along with other Americans, Hill became an investor in the Canadian Pacific. Indeed, he was a major stockholder and, for a few years, a director of the line. Stephen asked Hill to help plan the line's route from Winnipeg to Vancouver, and Hill obliged him, in the process earning another fortune and a Canadian agreement not to construct a road that competed with his interests south of the border for twenty years.[18] The presence of Hill, Stephen, and others on the boards of the two railroads lulled Villard and his colleagues at the Northern Pacific into a false sense of security; as far as they could see, the St. Paul was destined to be a local road, connecting with the Canadian Pacific and funneling American goods into Canada and vice versa. Villard knew Hill had always wanted to develop the Red River valley; at first he showed little desire to do anything else with the line. At one point Villard offered to buy the St. Paul, not suspecting that Hill meant to crush the Northern Pacific eventually. Hill did little to cause suspicions at Northern Pacific headquarters. In 1883 Villard and Hill agreed not to build in territory controlled by one another. Most of the St. Paul's construction was northward, not westward, and Hill concentrated on the Red River area. But Hill resigned from the CP board that same year, and in 1884 he made a trip into the West, which in retrospect clearly was a scouting expedition.

Hill was still interested in regional development in the mid-1880s, but by then his vision took in the entire West, on

[18]Glenn C. Quiett, *They Built the West: An Epic of Rails and Cities* (New York, 1934), p. 458.

both sides of the border. Once again, Hill took advantage of opportunities in his path. So long as he was wedded to the steamboat, only the Red River Valley could be developed. Now, with the railroad, he could drive westward, in a way completing the journey he had begun when he set out from New York in 1856.

Hill hoped to attract European settlers to the West. He would help them find farms after bringing them to his territory at a low charge. Then he would do all in his power to assure their prosperity, realizing that well-to-do farmers would need a railroad to ship their goods and bring in supplies. Hill would encourage other businessmen to enter territory served by his line, selling them land at low prices as a lure. These men too would need his line, and insure its prosperity.

He also had trans-Pacific ambitions. Hill believed that American development of the Pacific West would make trade with the Orient all the more important. Later on he would write that American manufactures would be hard-pressed to compete with European, due to high American labor costs, to which were added transportation charges. But the United States was closer to Japan and China than were the Europeans, and could develop these markets and turn them into major trading partners. "The first steps had to be taken and the whole burden assumed by the railroads," he wrote in 1910. "The birth and growth of our commerce with the Orient would depend absolutely upon a favorable transportation rate. Having to meet the competition of the world, we must sell more cheaply and deliver more satisfactorily than the rest of the world."[19]

The West had an abundance of raw materials; all that was needed to turn the area into a major industrial region was people, and the railroad would bring them there. In time, the West would surpass the East in terms of productivity and power. As the West grew, so would Hill; and to

[19]James J. Hill, *Highways of Progress* (New York, 1910), p. 162.

make both possible, a northern railroad was needed, with connections in Washington and Oregon, which were closer than the California ports to the Orient. Later Hill would enter the steamship business too, and establish depots in Asia.

In effect, Hill planned to bring people from Europe to work in the American Northwest, producing goods that would be sold in Asia. He had imperial ambitions, as did Harriman and other western rail tycoons. All of them, in varying degrees, encouraged settlement on their lands and were active in "colonization efforts." Hill's work in this field was not only more successful than most of the others but different in design. His eye was always on the region; the other rail magnates tended to concentrate on the railroad. They would build rapidly, taking their lines through land that was sparsely settled and had little need for a railroad in order to collect land grants and construction bonuses. Most western lines were poorly built, badly financed, and mismanaged; for the most part, the managers viewed them as vehicles to be exploited for their personal profit, not part of an economic infrastructure. As a result, all of the non-Hill transcontinentals went bankrupt at least once, and some several times, while construction and operating scandals were fairly commonplace.

Hill adopted a different strategy. He would construct carefully, planning routes in a far more scientific fashion than his rivals, and until 1887, build slowly. When one section was settled, he would go on to the next, The railroad accompanied colonization or, at most, kept only a few steps ahead of it. Hill was never faced with the problem of a large line that ran through a barren land empty of people, one that could never hope to meet current charges. In this, too, he was unique among the transcontinental leaders.

In contrast, Henry Villard of the Northern Pacific was a man of vision without the experience or knowledge to fulfill it. Where Hill would settle and then build, Villard tried to build and then settle. The Northern Pacific reached the Pacific Coast in 1883, but construction costs had been $14 million over estimates and the line had a debt of $19 million. Villard hoped to populate the land owned by the railroad by bringing in settlers, and the line had some hundred and twenty-five agents in Europe, seeking potential immigrants and handing out literature, while other agents in East Coast port cities met incoming ships and urged new Americans to settle in Northern Pacific lands. In 1881 an Oregon newspaper quoted an immigrant's conversation with a Californian who asked why he was going to the North. "Your people have few or no agents east to offer inducements to immigrants," was the reply. "You keep your state entirely in the dark."[20]

Villard's settlement program was insufficient to keep the line afloat. Burdened with debt, the Northern Pacific almost collapsed in 1884. As it was, Villard was forced to leave the line, and he returned to the East. C.B. Wright of Philadelphia, a land speculator who knew little of railroading, now became the leading power at the Northern Pacific, with Robert Harris, a former Erie Railroad vice-president, as his tool and new president. The line grew, but it also declined in power, while its direction was second-rate at best.

Meanwhile, Hill continued to extend the St. Paul, Minneapolis and Manitoba northward to Canadian Pacific connections and eastward to Duluth, in apparent accord with the agreement with Villard. All the while Hill was buying up land in North Dakota and Montana, for his own account, and in particular land in the copper area around Butte.

In January 1886, the Montana Central Railroad Company was organized by Hill's nominees, although at the time Hill himself tried successfully to mask his interest in the

[20]James Blaine Hedges, *Henry Villard and the Railways of the Northwest* (New Haven, 1930), pp. 128–29.

line. The railroad, which was to connect Great Falls, Helena, and Butte, was an advance agent for the St. Paul, Minneapolis, and Manitoba, which Hill planned to bring west as soon as he could get government permission to cut through Indian and military reservations. That year, Democrat Grover Cleveland, whom Hill had supported with a large donation, vetoed a measure that would have granted the line permission to go through the lands. Cleveland also rejected feelers for a federal construction grant and federal lands, indicating that if and when Hill received his right-of-way, it would be just that—permission to construct a line, with perhaps a few feet on either side of the track. Cleveland approved such a measure in early 1887, and this gave Hill access to North Dakota and Montana.

Hill had planned for this moment. He quickly sold his private land holdings in the states to the St. Paul, Minneapolis and Manitoba, and then merged the Montana Central into the larger line. Construction began at once in North Dakota, with a connection from Grand Forks on the state's eastern border to Minot in the center of the state the first leg. Hill reached Minot in late March, and immediately began work in the direction of Helena, Montana, which was reached on November 18. Construction costs were high, primarily because Hill built well. On the other hand, Hill did not participate in the leaching of assets from his line through construction firms, a common practice in the post-Civil War period, and so his line remained solvent. He also began attracting settlers to the territories he opened up, offering to carry immigrants to their new homes for ten dollars. Finally, Hill cut freight and passenger rates whenever he entered a territory, and always below those charged by his competitors. Unlike most railroaders, Hill refused to enter pools, regional compacts, and associations formed for the purpose of maintaining charges. "Mr. Hill is a law unto himself," wrote Northern Pacific President Robert Harris, doubtless with a degree of sadness. "He attends no meetings, keeps aloof from such and is therefore dangerous."[21]

During 1887, Hill supervised the construction and operation of 1,175 miles of track, more than any other railroader that year by far.[22] The line remained solvent, in part because the Minnesota wheat crop was excellent and the railroad showed high earnings in carrying it to market. In addition, he had been able to extract land at little or no cost from "cooperative" townships which gave him aid in other ways as well. Hill made certain they understood what might happen if they opposed him. When Fort Benton refused to grant Hill land in town for a station and right-of-way, he diverted his railroad away from the community in a huge arc, leaving Fort Benton more than a mile from the track and further from the station. After that, Great Falls gave him all he wanted.[23]

Hill moved to extend his line to the Pacific. Just as he had earlier formed the Montana Central as a mask for his interests, so now he organized the Seattle and Montana, which would build a line between these two places, and then be merged into the main holding. By this time Hill had earned one of the best reputations for carrying out promises in the industry. He had little difficulty in floating a $10-million bond issue in London, while Seattle interests paid dearly for the privilege of having the line extend to their city.[24]

In 1889, Hill decided the St. Paul, Minneapolis and Manitoba had "outgrown its clothes." He recapitalized the line, merged it with his other interests, and renamed it the Great Northern Railway Company, which became an official entity on February 1, 1890. In the Great Northern's first annual report, issued on June 30, Hill said:

When the Pacific extension has been completed, your company will have a continuous rail line from Lake

[21]Grodinsky, *Transcontinental Railroad Strategy*, p. 293.
[22]Pyle, *Hill*, I, 397.
[23]Holbrook, *American Railroads*, p. 178.
[24]Grodinsky, *Transcontinental Railway Strategy*, pp. 394–97.

Superior, St. Paul, and Minneapolis to the Pacific
Coast, shorter than any existing trans-continental railway and with lower grades and less curvatures. Its
cost and capitalization will also be much less than
those of any other line to the Coast. It is expected that,
with the foregoing favourable conditions, the heavier
products of the Pacific Coast region, which up to this
time could seek markets only by ocean routes, can be
moved eastward to the older sections of the country.[25]

For the next two and a half years Hill divided his time
between constructing the railroad to the coast and making
certain it had something to carry there. Though difficult,
the construction was the lesser of his problems. One hundred miles of track were put down in 1890, 162 miles the
following year, and the final 554 in 1892. The railhead at
Everett was reached in January 1893; the transcontinental
was completed, and the first trains arrived in Seattle in
July.

Even before starting on his final leg, Hill began work on
regional development in Washington state and Montana.
In 1889 he had organized two subsidiaries and taken over a
third, all of which were to drive north to the Canadian
Pacific. By the time the Great Northern had reached the
ocean, it was able to claim connections throughout Canada.
The idea was for the Great Northern to bring American
goods into Canada, while the Canadian Pacific's customers
would be able to reach American customers more easily.
Each line would divert business to the other if and when
its lines were crowded. But the region was still relatively
undeveloped, with insufficient work for one line. Relations
between the Canadian Pacific and the Great Northern
were strained, but the feeders did benefit the Hill line more
than they did the CP, and this too proved helpful.

Hill had promised his Seattle allies that he would bring

[25]Pyle, *Hill*, I, 462.

men representing "a thousand million dollars" to the city, all eager for investment opportunities. Still, as the Great Northern approached Seattle, the major question was, what would the line carry? The wheat trade of Minnesota and Montana went eastward, to be milled and then sold in the East or in Europe. The population of Washington, Oregon, and California was small compared with that of the East, and had little use for additional grain in any case. Even had this market existed, the land was not ready for planting, since much of the Far West was covered with forests.

Hill's idea was to help develop the lumber resources of the region first, by necessity sending most of the logs east where they could find markets. Meanwhile, he would try to develop commercial contacts with the Orient, and in time ship American logs as well as flour and other products there.

Since the Great Northern received no federal land grant, it had little of its own property to develop. Hill took care of this situation in a roundabout fashion. In 1891 he claimed some 75,000 acres of land in the Red River area, stating that Congress had passed a law in 1857 granting the land to the railroad that crossed the valley. He had a good case, though not an airtight one; the original line was defunct, and had been absorbed into the St. Paul road. Farmers had settled the land, and now Hill appeared about to evict them. The farmers appealed to Congress for relief, and after the region's politicians negotiated with Hill, they offered him land elsewhere to compensate for the Red River properties. Hill agreed, and selected valuable timberlands in Idaho, Montana, and Washington. Some of the land was leased to lumber companies, Weyerhaeuser Timber of St. Paul in particular, as Hill and Frederic Weyerhaeuser became allies. Several years later, Hill sold 900,000 acres of land to the company for six dollars an acre, not so much to make a profit on land sales as to develop the area, and in this way help his railroad. In many cases, Hill retained mineral rights, while in others he withheld land, for later sale to small farmers.

Hill brought thousands of farmers into the Great Northern territory in the 1890s. He sponsored cattle breeding projects, and even gave steers free to settlers to encourage them to enter the business. The railroad offered prizes for the best grain grown within twenty-five miles of the line, and Hill sponsored agricultural research, especially in the area of dry farming. Regularly he would cut carrying charges, observing that increased business more than compensated for the decreases. Of course, these and related actions hurt his major competitor, the Northern Pacific, which by 1893 was once again in shaky condition.

In May 1893, Hill said, "We are going to have a panic next September. It will take five years to get over it." The panic came in July, but Hill was ready for it by then, having husbanded his resources well. He would use them to take control of the Northern Pacific, in this way dominating all major rail traffic in the Northwest.

The Northern Pacific did collapse, one of many roads to do so in what was the most serious financial panic of the nineteenth century.[26] In reporting on the reasons for the failure, the Northern Pacific's leaders said:

> Regarding the rate war with the Great Northern, the character of the manager and principal party in interest of this road, Mr. James J. Hill, has to be reckoned with. People who know him thoroughly assert that it needs only an energetic decision to defeat him with his own weapons. The most important territory of the Great Northern is the wheat district of the Red River Valley, in which Hill is the successful competitor of the Northern Pacific. If the rate war could be carried

[26]Sobel, *Panic on Wall Street*, pp. 230–72.

to such a point that by a special reduction of freight rates in the Red River Valley the best business of the Great Northern would be threatened, peace could be quickly gained under a general restoration of freight rates. The very fact that the Great Northern traverses an immense territory—some 1,500 miles—which has so far hardly been taken hold of by settlers, makes this system especially vulnerable at those points from which it gains it actual vitality.[27]

The report did not note that Hill's operating costs per miles were lower than those of the NP, its books cleaner of debt, and its rolling stock and lines in better shape than any other comparable road. There simply was no way by which the NP could defeat the Great Northern.

Within a year 192 American railroads were in the hands of receivers, and these operated almost 41,000 miles of the nation's total of 178,000—almost a quarter of the rail miles. Now Hill moved to take control of the NP, hoping to merge it with the Great Northern, turn it around, and make another fortune while at the same time "harmonizing" the transportation system of the Northwest.

With the backing of his Canadian friends, Hill offered to buy out the defunct line. He was blocked by public pressures, but more important, a suit brought by a Great Northern stockholder based on a Minnesota law prohibiting unification of parallel railroad lines. If he couldn't purchase the NP for the Great Northern, Hill would buy it for himself. With the aid of associates, he obtained a major block of Northern Pacific stock for $4 million. Now that line—the Great Northern's main competitor—was part of his empire. And with this, reformist and public sentiment against railroad giants like Hill moved up another notch.

Having solidified control of the territory, Hill turned to the quest for foreign markets. Captain James Griffiths, a

[27]Pyle, *Hill*, I, 445.

resident of Washington state, had read that the Nippon
Yusen Kaisha line was interested in establishing a steamship service to the West Coast, and was considering San
Diego as its major port of call. He notified Hill of this,
discussions ensued, and in the end Griffiths was sent to
Japan to negotiate an arrangement for Seattle. The meetings in Tokyo were successful; the San Diego plan was
scrapped, and the line's first Seattle-bound ship, the *Miike
Maru,* unloaded its cargo in August 1896.

Now Hill turned to Seattle itself, making it a key port
and in the process dominating the city's political structure.
He also interested Weyerhaeuser in the city, and he too
began using it as a major terminal.[28] Hill, more than any
other individual, helped establish American trade with the
Orient in the late nineteenth and early twentieth centuries.
In 1896, the United States exported $7.7 million worth of
goods to Japan; nine years later the figure was $51.7 million,
while imports rose from $25.5 million to $51.8 million in the
same period. Total Asian exports went from $25.6 million
to $128.5 million, and imports from $89.6 million to $161.9
million. Hill later wrote:

> The business increased. The market was opened, the
> opportunity accepted, our trade with the Orient, no
> longer a dream, became a splended fact, as the statis-
> tics show. In the ten years between 1893, when the
> Great Northern reached the coast, and in 1903, the
> exports of the Puget Sound customs district increased
> from $5,085,958 to $32,410,367, or nearly 540 per cent. In
> those years our exports to Europe increased 50 per
> cent., to North America 80 per cent., to South Amer-
> ica a little over 30 per cent. . . . At this rate it seemed
> that the bulk of the trade of the Orient was ours for
> the taking.[29]

[28]Quiett, *They Built the West,* pp. 463–64.
[29]Hill, *Highways of Progress,* pp. 166, 169.

Hill worked with the Japanese steamship interests at first, primarily because he wanted them to make a major commitment to the American trade, but also because much of his time was spent in developing the land and resources along his route. In 1900, however, he set about to dominate the trade of the North Pacific area. Hill organized the Great Northern Steamship Company, which was capitalized at $6 million. Most of this money would be used to construct the *Minnesota* and the *Dakota*, planned to be among the largest vessels in the world at that time. These freight carriers were to dominate the run between Seattle and Yokohama and Hong Kong, bringing Oriental goods to America, and shipping American manufactures overseas. Then, to make certain his railroad would have sufficient goods to take to the Orient, he formed alliances with eastern manufacturers, hoping to interest them in sending goods westward. "Now a new market including from five hundred millions of people upward was worth considering," he later wrote.

> We could not export a large range of commodities to the Orient. A people whose labour is so cheap cannot afford many luxuries. Labour is so expensive in the United States that the Germans and the Belgians undersell our manufactured goods. But because this country can produce cotton, grain, iron ore and coal cheaper than the others, there are some things that, with low freight rates, we could lay down in Japan and China for less money than any other country can. If the Chinese should spend one cent per day per capita, it would amount to $4,000,000 a day, or nearly $1,500,000,000 a year. We could not spare food enough to sell them that much.[30]

---

[30] *Ibid.*, p. 167. This paragraph, read in 1974, seems quite contemporary given the developing relations between the United States and China.

Of course, the Chinese and other peoples in the Orient consumed large amounts of rice as well as wheat. Rice would not grow well in Great Northern territory, where the major crop was wheat. Hill's response was that he would teach the Orientals to appreciate bread. "But the Japanese and Chinese could be made customers for our flour in increasing quantity. A people once accustomed to the wheat loaf are slow to give it up."[31]

The Great Northern's major economic function in this period was to carry wheat, and in order to increase his revenues, Hill intensified the colonization effort. He regularly lowered the price of one-way tickets for immigrants, knowing that if they succeeded on the soil, they would pay him back through freight charges. "You are now our children," said imperial Hill in 1906, "but we are in the same boat with you, and we have got to prosper with you or we have got to be poor with you." In that year Hill sent out demonstration trains with lecturers to show farmers how to plant and cultivate the Montana and North Dakota soil. A department for agricultural research was organized in 1912, and two years later extension departments went into the farm districts. Intensive farming became the rule, and in the short run it brought benefits to both farmers and railroad. In the end, however, such planting destroyed millions of acres of good farmland. In 1909, Montana soils yielded more than twenty-five bushels of wheat per acre; ten years later, after the soil was ravaged, the figure was 2.4 bushels. Hill had created an empire; he had brought flour to the Orient and was a major factor in the Chicago grain pits. But in this case—in the aggregate—he had done more harm than good.[32]

Having provided his road with products for export, Hill turned to iron ore and steel. Realizing the potential of the

[31] *Ibid.*, p. 160.
[32] Blegen, *Minnesota*, pp. 370–72; Elwyn B. Robinson, *History of North Dakota* (Lincoln, Nebraska, 1966), pp. 241, 252; Joseph K. Howard, *Montana, High, Wide, and Handsome* (New Haven, 1943), pp. 167–77.

Mesabi Range, Hill began land purchases in the area in the mid-1890s. He acquired the Duluth and Winnipeg Railroad in 1897, and two years later, the Duluth, Mississippi and Northern, which also owned valuable ore lands and serviced the Mesabi area. Hill combined these properties to form the Great Northern Iron Ore Properties Company, which was run by his sons. He might have entered the iron and steel business at this point, but his interests lay elsewhere. In 1901, when J.P. Morgan put together United States Steel, Hill could have obtained a large price for his holdings, but he held back. Instead, Hill leased land to the company, selling it some 7 million tons of ore in 1901, Big Steel's first year of operation. Six years later Hill estimated that the Great Northern Iron Ore properties were worth in the neighborhood of $600 million.

In 1901 too, Hill became involved in a financial panic, in part of his own making, and one that indicated to many reformers that the power of the railroad barons had become too great. He wanted to take control of the Chicago, Burlington and Quincy, a major line that extended from Chicago to the Rockies, and southward into the Mississippi Valley. Once acquired, the CB & Q could easily be joined with the Great Northern and afford Hill entry into Chicago, the greatest terminal in mid-America. Afterward he might attempt a takeover of an eastern line, thus realizing his dream of owning a railroad that ran from ocean to ocean. But the desire for the CB & Q was not based on sentiment. The line would give him contacts with the cotton-hauling roads of St. Louis and Kansas City, the packing houses of Omaha and Chicago, and the ore lands of the Black Hills.

Harriman, head of the Union Pacific, had a similar vision, and he too attempted to win control of the CB & Q. This precipitated a struggle between the railroad barons, with J.P. Morgan working for Hill on Wall Street, while Harriman was represented by Kuhn, Loeb. Hill managed to obtain a majority of the shares, and when Harriman asked to participate in the holding, Hill rejected him. In retaliation, Harriman began to make purchases of Northern Pacific stock, hoping to undercut Hill in this fashion. On learning of this, Hill began his own purchases through Morgan. The struggle of these two titans shook Wall Street, precipitating a panic. The result was a standoff, with Hill able to claim more of a victory than Harriman. The two met once more, and agreed that Harriman would be given representation on the Northern Pacific board. But the line itself would remain in Hill's control.

The great age of western railroad building had ended by the time of the Hill-Harriman confrontation. Additional lines and feeders would be constructed, but these were set down more to fill in the outline of the transcontinentals than to open virgin territories. More than any other railroader, Hill recognized this. Rationalization and efficiency were needed in 1901, not the struggles and wasteful duplications and rate wars that had accompanied pioneering in the last quarter of the nineteenth century. In the aftermath of the Northern Pacific panic, Hill attempted to rationalize the western rails and at the same time create a huge enterprise none would dare challenge. Through Morgan, he and Harriman agreed to form the Northern Securities Company. Both men would deposit their shares in the Northern Pacific, and Hill would relinquish his in the Great Northern and CB & Q and receive trust certificates in return. Morgan would be in charge of the company; both Hill and Harriman knew no Wall Streeter or raider would dare cross his path. The Northern Securities Company would be capitalized at $400 million, and be so large that even if a financier wanted to attempt a takeover, he couldn't afford one. The board of directors would consist of fifteen members—six from the Northern Pacific, four from the Great Northern, three from the Union Pacific, and two "independents." Harriman was one of the directors, and in addition received seats on the board of the CB & Q in return for his cooperation. And cooperate he did, joining with the other directors to elect Hill president of the company and pledging his support to Morgan as its banker.[33]

The formation of this holding company—justified though it might have been in terms of efficiency and benefits—was viewed as yet another sign of the power held by men like Harriman and Hill. The country had suffered in 1901 because of their struggles, so the argument went. Now that they had united, perhaps freedom itself would be lost. Theodore Roosevelt, who had succeeded to the Presidency shortly before the holding company was formed, seemed to hold this opinion. "We do not wish to destroy corporations," he later said, "but we wish to make them subserve the public good." Roosevelt was no crusading reformer, but he saw a chance to win a reputation as one and so gain a constituency of his own, in preparation for his try at Presidential politics in 1904.

He might not have acted had not reformist elements in Minnesota obliged him to do so. On January 7, 1902, the state initiated an action against the Northern Securities Company, claiming it was a combination in restraint of trade under the terms of the Sherman Anti-Trust Act. Roosevelt did nothing for two months, waiting to see which way the winds blew. Then, on March 10, the federal government instituted its own suit. Morgan was angered, and went to Washington to see Roosevelt in an attempt to make him reconsider. The attempt failed. Two years later the Supreme Court, in a five to four decision, ordered dissolution. This too was a surprise. The Northern Securities lawyers had claimed that the company had resulted from a stock transaction, and did not affect commerce, and therefore did not fall under the purview of the Sherman Act. Only nine years earlier, in 1895, the Court had stated in *United States* v. *E.C. Knight* that such was the case. The

[33]Jonathan Hughes, *The Vital Few: American Economic Progress and Its Protagonists* (Boston, 1966), p. 384.

reversal indicated that the reformists had gained power. It was a signal for further actions against the great industrialists, a sign that, through government, the reformists meant to take away some of their power.[34]

Hill spent little time following the case. Instead, he moved to further develop the Oriental trade. Hill carried cotton to Japan at low rates in order to stimulate demand, integrated operations at the Great Northern and Northern Pacific and reduced charges, and even clashed with Harriman—his purported partner—as both men attempted to dominate the area between Seattle and San Francisco. It was increasingly evident, even before the Supreme Court handed down its decision, that Hill's period of greatest accomplishment had passed. He was still vigorous, but the challenges of the early twentieth century seemed somewhat less important and staggering than those of a quarter of a century earlier. Like other great railroaders, he had completed the major tasks of construction. The rest could be left to lesser men.

Hill stepped down as president of the Great Northern in early 1907, at the age of sixty-nine. This was to be another panic year, and as had been the case in 1893, Hill foresaw the crash that came in October. After carefully refinancing much of the Great Northern's debt, and putting its house in order, he warned of a "commercial paralysis" and subsequent depression.

Now his son, Louis, succeeded to the presidency, but he was not free to pursue his own plans. The father continually dropped in at the main offices, and on occasion made "surprise" tours of the line to check it out. His temper, always hot, grew worse in these last years. In a fit of anger he tore a telephone from a wall and threw it out a closed window. When Hill felt slighted by some political leaders

[34]Balthasar H. Meyer, *A History of the Northern Securities Case* (Madison, 1906) is the classic study of the episode.

in a town along his route, he ordered his son to remove the depot and place it elsewhere. Once he asked a clerk his name. The reply was "Spittles." Hill didn't like the name. He fired the man on the spot.

Hill also found time for his excellent art collection, delivering speeches, writing articles and books, receiving honorary degrees, cultivating a model farm, and breeding livestock. Always a restless man, at one point he considered moving to New York, and even purchased a fine house there. But Hill felt uncomfortable in the East, and he returned to St. Paul in relief. He died there in 1916, at the age of seventy-eight.

Railroads were still the nation's major carriers of people and freight at the time of Hill's death, but they were clearly in decline. In part this was due to the public's reaction to high-handed methods employed by railroad rulers in the post-Civil War period, a reaction which took the form of legislation mandating the establishment of regulatory commissions. Hill conceded that abuses had taken place, and although he might have noted that others had been far guiltier of them than he, he refrained from making the point. He did feel that the efforts of the reformers were misdirected, especially when they insisted on competition as such a shibboleth. Competition was fine when there was a territory to compete for, he said, but the situation was different in the early twentieth century. By then the lines were overbuilt, and combinations were necessary if the remaining roads were to run efficiently, lower charges, and still make profits. Unless they were permitted to do so, he charged, the railroads would lack sufficient funds for needed improvements. And without these, the lines would decay. Railroads were a major industry. If they suffered, so would every part of the economy. In late 1910 he told a reporter that railroad investment, already dangerously low, would continue to decline. "It isn't because they haven't the money," he said, "but because there are no inducements . . . for them to invest it."[35] Soon after, they would lack the money too. It was on such a basis that he defended the Northern Securities Company. Its goal, said Hill, was not power, but rationalization of transportation. It was still not possible to travel from coast-to-coast on a single line—the dream of Hill, Harriman, and other railroad tycoons—and indeed it would never be so. Hill's last crusade, one that made as much sense as his earlier ones, failed.

Perhaps Hill was an anachronism in 1916. He and men like him—not only in railroading but other industries as well—had ruled the nation in the half century following Appomattox. Presidents in this period tended to be part-time executives, and several were little more than ciphers, while the congresses often were under business domination. The railroad tycoons were able to form and then rule empires by filling vacuums no other force would or perhaps could enter. The taming of the trans-Mississippi West was accompanied by waste, corruption, and the accumulation of much power in few hands, perhaps more than was wise in a nation that professed to be a democratic republic. Whether the task could have been accomplished in any other way is difficult to say. But that it was done, and so rapidly, is an accomplishment of no small magnitude.

Hill was the best of the breed, and in most respects the fairest. He certainly wasn't a believer in majority rule—or any rule that went contrary to his visions, desires, and whims—and what today would be considered fair play. Hill was, after all, an empire builder, and proud of the title. Democracies have never been good at constructing empires, and worse at administering them. In the opinion of many at the time, America in the early twentieth century was faced with the choice. The nature of the decision is still debated today.[36] But it would appear that the business

[35]Martin, *Enterprise Denied*, p. 169.
[36]For discussions and analyses of this problem, see Gabriel Kolko, *The Triumph of Conservatism: A Reinterpretation of American History, 1900–1916* (New York, 1963);

giants were thwarted in many of their more brazen actions. Their successors would not have their authority. James Hill was a power in his own right, a major force. Louis Hill was a good administrator.

Hill's mark is still to be found in the Northwest, even though he left no true successor, no empire administrator, as it were. The fact that a man like him could rise as he did, and accomplish so much, may be considered a sign of national vitality. When the empire builders completed their construction efforts they received honorary degrees, medals, and tributes. Their successors, however, were obliged to accept the regulations and dictates of revitalized governments reflective of a public desire to regain control of the land. This, too, may be considered a sign of vitality.

Robert H. Weibe, *Businessmen and Reform: A Study of the Progressive Movement* (Cambridge, 1962); and James Weinstein, *The Corporate Ideal in the Liberal State, 1900–1918* (Boston, 1968).

V

James Buchanan Duke: Opportunism Is the Spur

German sociologist and historian Max Weber explored the nature of industrial society, and in several essays attempted to understand the American experience. He concluded that the powerful capitalists who dominated the business arena in the second half of the nineteenth century were exceptional men, but that their types had existed at other times and in other places. "Only the technological *means* which they used for the acquisition of wealth have changed," he wrote. Major businessmen came to the fore by seizing opportunities that lay about like uncut diamonds, and the United States of that period was rich in opportunity. Weber indicated that had not one set of ventures existed, such men might very well have found their fortunes in others. The powerful entrepreneurs dominated their times, but the times provided a stage on which they would perform.[1]

The tycoons justified their actions by whatever morality happened to be popular; Weber thought Protestantism the most common, although many used Social Darwinist arguments to provide a scientific tinge for their Calvinism. Of course, most businessmen didn't bother to explain their

[1]Max Weber, "The Protestant Sects and the Spirit of Capitalism," in H.H. Garth and C. Wright Mills, trans. and ed., *From Max Weber: Essays in Sociology* (New York, 1958), p. 309.

actions, either by faith or science. The work was the only justification they needed; it was an end in itself.[2]

Some of the tycoons of this period had international reputations, and became legends, to be praised or reviled in the magazines of their own times and history books today. The railroad barons—Hill, Harriman, and the rest—have already been discussed. Rockefeller emerged as the ruler of petroleum, and Andrew Carnegie dominated steel. The Guggenheims aspired to the same position in copper, while Philip Armour led a small group of meat packers hoping to form a trust in that product. United Shoe Machinery, National Biscuit, National Salt, American Sugar Refining, United Ship Building, National Cordage—each firm tried, usually succesfully, either to control its industry or at least write its rules for competition. Such was the case at International Harvester, the farm machinery giant erected around the Cyrus McCormick holdings, which produced over 90 percent of all binders, more than 80 percent of the mowers, and 70 percent of power rakes at the turn of the century. The trust did not attempt to destroy all its competitors but made certain they paid homage to the leader. Similar statistics could be cited for other trusts, and the attitudes of their leaders were much the same.

Naturally, no two trusts were alike, and each tycoon had his own story to tell, though few did at the time. All the trust managers claimed to have brought stability and order to chaotic industries. In some cases they were correct when observing that large-scale enterprise meant economies of scale, and this in turn was translated into lower prices for consumers. They claimed trusts were natural developments, organizations vital for the new industrial America. They would extol competition in public speeches, but practiced cooperation, especially with those businessmen they couldn't crush. The tycoons formed communities of interest, informal at times, but real nonetheless. These com-

[2]*Ibid.*, p. 308.

munities were the true power nexus of America at that time.

Bringing order from chaos was a worthwhile endeavor, though the side effects may have been worse than the disease. Even then, many of the giants didn't perform as claimed. Promised economies, standardization of products, and lower costs often were not realized. In some cases this was due to the nature of the industry, but if this were so, what of the rationales for bigness trumpeted at the time? Undaunted, leaders of these trusts pressed on, for to them, power was an end, not a means.

This is not to say they were evil men, or even short-sighted. Rather, they acted to engulf other firms in part through instinct, the rest being explained as self-preservation. In other words, get the other fellow before he gets you. Such men often were tactical geniuses, but they tended to ignore strategy. Because of this, some of their successes turned out to be failures in disguise, while their shortcomings were fortuitous in that they prevented the tycoons from embarking on foolish expeditions.

James Buchanan Duke was one such individual. In time he came to dominate tobacco, and if he was not the most powerful businessman of his time, he certainly was a prominent figure. Duke operated in a less vital field than did Carnegie or Morgan, but he controlled it more completely than either man did his. He did not dominate the upper South as James Hill did the Northwest, but his ambitions for a global role were better realized than were Hill's. Duke was a pliable man, one able to adjust to the world of finance capitalism, something Hill and even Carnegie either wouldn't or couldn't do. But the greater men had strategies, something Duke possessed only in vague outline at the height of his career. Duke was a builder; Hill, Carnegie, and Morgan were creators.

Duke is often cited as the man who switched the nation's tobacco habit from chew (plug) to cigarettes. Yet at the height of his power, around 1904, far more people used plug than any other form of tobacco, while pipe tobacco sales were climbing rapidly and cigars, the "status" product, eluded Duke's grasp. At the time cigarettes ranked a poor fourth.

Although famous as a great innovator and organizer, Duke did not rationalize his many operations or do as much as he might have to integrate its various components. In part this was due to the rapidity of his acquisitions program —in two decades he took over some 260 companies. Nor did Duke control tobacco as Rockefeller was coming to do in petroleum. He expanded into retailing in a weak and indecisive fashion, and never developed a strong program to control his raw materials. True, he was a master acquisitor, but to what end? Power and size alone seemed more important than anything else to Duke. To obtain them he sacrificed efficiency and had to forego the kind of order and internal stability he might have preferred.

Stories of Duke's managerial abilities abound. One concerns his calling an American Tobacco vice president to his office and asking what would happen to his operation if the man left the next day and never returned. Could any of his aides take his place? The executive gulped and answered that there were several who could take over if necessary. He interpreted the question as a prelude to dismissal. Instead, Duke raised his salary. A good manager, he said, always makes certain he is not indispensable.

If the story is indeed true, Duke did not practice what he preached. Although many of his aides were capable and intelligent, Duke did not delegate responsibility effectively. He alone understood all the cross-currents at the company and how the internal mechanism operated. If Duke had vanished, there would have been a time of chaos at American Tobacco headquarters. Indeed, when the trust was ordered dissolved, the government had to ask Duke to preside over the divestitures, since he was the only person who understood the American Tobacco structure.

Duke overshadowed Percival Hill, his second in command and, later on, his successor. He had almost no control over Richard J. Reynolds, whose firm was under the American Tobacco flag, but who had undisguised contempt for Duke as a man and manager. After the divestiture Reynolds took over at his own company once more, and soon after Hill became president of American Tobacco, still the largest firm in the industry. During the next ten years Reynolds made his company a major factor in the field, while Hill, heading the old Duke "team," consistently lost ground. Whatever virtues Duke had as a manager, creating an efficient and effective staff was not one of them.

Duke was considered a promotional genius by many. But he built on practices initiated by others, and later on was credited with advertising campaigns his staff had developed in his name. For example, he was supposed to have purchased 380,000 chairs, painted the name of one of his brands, Cameo, on their backs, and offered them free to cigar stores on condition they stock Cameos and show the chair in the store. In fact, this innovation was the idea of Edward Small, a Duke salesman. Duke approved the program and later received the credit. Small, an almost forgotten man today, later broke with Duke, as would Reynolds, and went off on his own. In a similar fashion, Duke was credited with introducing the stiff cardboard box that replaced the old paper packages that tended to crumble smokes in pockets. This too came from his staff, though once again, Duke gave the order to move ahead on the change. Nor was Duke the father of the "advertising blitz," in which massive amounts of money were spent to saturate an area with slogans and premiums in order to destroy the opposition. This came out of the Bull Durham organization. What Duke did was to perfect what he found upon entering the field.

Duke was not interested in self-advertisement. In part this was because he was guarded in matters relating to his private life, somewhat risqué by Victorian standards. There were some exceptions. After he retired, Duke purchased an estate in Somerville, New Jersey. All was fine, except that his grounds lacked a mountain. Duke wanted one, and soon after, bulldozers appeared to create a miniature Alps. The newspapers ran the story in much the same way they covered Rockefeller's dime gifts to children— proof that tycoons were really quaint, almost lovable, eccentrics. This was a rare exception to the Duke rule of privacy.

The rule was derived in part from Duke's awareness of his plebian roots. The Dukes came from poor farmer-yeoman stock; they were not plantation aristocrats. But while not of the southern aristocracy, he accepted its creed, and patrician southerners disdained self-congratulation. Also, Duke was a more retiring man than most of the great capitalists of his day. Even though he was considered a shrewd salesman, he did not encourage extensive personal contacts once he reached the top. Duke was indifferent toward what constituted society and did not mingle well with his fellow tycoons.

Much of this may have been caused by the times in which he lived. Duke was born in 1856, and named after the President elected that year. His father fought in the Confederate cause, and young Duke grew up during Reconstruction, a period when his part of the country was under the sway of what amounted to an army of occupation. Later on he would travel north to New York, to deal with Union Army veterans and their sons, many of whom viewed the young North Carolinian in much the same way as an Israeli might look upon a German today. Duke had to tread lightly all his life, and perhaps this explains why he seldom ventured beyond the social confines of the tobacco world. The United States had many major tycoons in the late nineteenth century. James Duke was the only one of these to emerge from the defeated South.

No major biography of Duke appeared during his lifetime, and the national magazines published few adulatory articles on him—the kind that Harriman, Hill, Carnegie, Edison, and even Rockefeller and Morgan were honored with. Shortly after Wanamaker and Hill died, biographers went to work on them, often with the encouragement of their heirs and families. Both men were the subjects of two-volume biographies that described them in glowing terms. A superior two-volume work on McCormick appeared a generation after his death. Not so with Duke. A one-volume book, a minor effort, appeared two years after he died, and then another, far more critical, a decade and a half later. Afterward, scholars wrote extensively about the tobacco industry, cigarettes in particular. But there is still no major analysis of the man and his work, while the Duke and American Tobacco papers have not received the critical attention they merit.

Washington Duke, James' father, was born in what is now Durham County, North Carolina, in 1820. He became an independent, small dirt farmer, raising hogs and chickens and growing corn and wheat, with a little tobacco in order to have a cash crop. His first wife died, leaving one son, Brodie, who grew to maturity. Washington remarried, and his second wife, Artelia, gave birth to Mary, Benjamin, and James Buchanan Duke, known as a child as "Buck." She died when Buck was two years old, after which her sister, Elizabeth, moved into the Duke cabin and raised the children while Washington worked in the fields.

Durham was not a wealthy part of the state but it was known for its high quality tobacco, a bright leaf that was milder than the dark that went into much of the plug then consumed. It enjoyed local favor, and some went out into the world as part of plug mixes and as granulated tobacco for pipe smokers. But there was no indication in the 1850s that Durham leaf would achieve any major popularity. Nor was Washington Duke particularly interested in tobacco. As was the case with most of his neighbors, he seemed content with a small farm, and owned only one slave, who worked in the house.

Washington Duke was an opponent of slavery, though not an outspoken one, but certainly no abolitionist. He voted for Abraham Lincoln in 1860, one of the few North Carolinians to do so, and remained a Republican for the rest of his life, also unusual for a North Carolinian. Like most in the state, he opposed secession when the first call to arms went out in February 1861. Two months later, however, the tobacco South divided, with North Carolina joining the cotton South in separation. Washington Duke did not volunteer, and entered the Confederate forces in 1863 only when drafted. For a while he served as a guard, and was never in combat. At the end of the war Washington was taken captive and sent to a Union prison. Shortly thereafter he was released, more than one hundred miles from home.

Brodie Duke volunteered for service and also became a guard. The young children remained at home and were there in 1865 when Union soldiers commanded by William T. Sherman entered Durham in the last skirmish they would face. The town did not suffer much from combat. The Union and Confederate soldiers were weary, and realizing that the war was about to end, fraternized in the fields. Together they broke into tobacco warehouses and corn whiskey distilleries, taking what they found and consuming it while awaiting news of the armistice.[3] Some had smoked and used alcohol before the war, but the fighting resulted in increased consumption, as do all such struggles. The Durham bright leaf was a new experience for most of them. Many liked it, either straight or mixed with the darker leaf, as plug or pipe tobacco. They would carry the taste back home with them.

Washington Duke walked home from prison. According to stories later told by family members, he arrived in Durham a bedraggled man, leading two blind mules, and with

[3]John G. Barrett, *The Civil War in North Carolina* (Chapel Hill, 1963), pp. 386–88.

no funds except a half-dollar piece, for which he had traded
a Confederate five dollar bill with a souvenir-hunting Yankee.

> Better off at that than many of his neighbors, for hun-
> gry, footsore, almost in rags, service in the army had
> not broken his physique or spirit, the head of the
> family accepted conditions as they were and set to
> work to better them.
>
> Gathering his children together, he brought them
> back to the home place. But his farm had been sold on
> credit to a neighbor, the purchaser could not pay for
> it and would not be ousted. Months elapsed before the
> owners regained possession. In the meantime a work-
> ing arrangement was made with the occupant by
> which the Dukes resumed farming, receiving a share
> of the crops and some return for their labor.[4]

Like most of their neighbors, the Dukes seemed destined
to become sharecroppers or, at best, independent small
farmers once more. In any case, survival was the most
important problem for the moment. They found the farm
stripped except for an old wagon, and the land overrun
with weeds. Somehow the soldiers had overlooked a small
quantity of cured bright tobacco. Duke and his sons beat it
out with a grain flail, granulated the leaf, and then packed
it in muslin bags, with the label Pro Bono Publico—For the
Public Good. Washington Duke hitched his two mules to
the wagon, loaded the bags, and set out to sell them, or
barter for food and other goods.

The trip went well; Duke returned home with food and
some money, as well as an understanding that the bright
tobacco business would prosper, and that he would do well
to enter it on a permanent basis.[5] Together with his sons,
Washington Duke built a small log cabin which would

[4]John W. Jenkins, *James B. Duke: Master Builder* (New York, 1927), p. 44.
[5]*Ibid.*, pp. 43–45.

serve as a tobacco workshop. He planted his fields with tobacco, purchased the crops of other farmers, cured and granulated the leaf, packed it, and then went out on the road to sell Pro Bono Publico to all who would take it. In 1866, its first full year of operation, the log factory produced 15,000 pounds of tobacco.[6]

Washington Duke died in 1905, at the age of eighty-five. During the last years of his life he was known as "Buck Duke's daddy," a folksy eccentric who visited American Tobacco plants and offices, chatted with the workers, and loved to talk about the old days in Durham. His sons recalled that he was a good father, a man of integrity, who, for example, spoke out for Negro rights and remained a Republican during Reconstruction, a time when he was trying to sell tobacco products to Confederate veterans, among others. He also must have been a man of no mean intelligence and daring. Other Durham farmers knew that tobacco sales were good, and many had more capital and better facilities than Duke. He was the only farmer in the area to enter the business in 1865, and soon after he left the land completely to devote all his time to the factory. His was the first such business in postwar North Carolina, and as late as 1868, the leading one in that part of the state.

By then other farmers had become interested in production and sales, and some smaller units—many really adjuncts of farms—began to expand. The 1870 census showed that there were 111 tobacco factories in North Carolina, representing an investment of more than $375,000 and producing almost $720,000 worth of snuff, plug, and smoking tobacco. Two years later there were twelve factories in Durham alone, and Washington Duke's was not the largest or best known.[7]

[6] *Ibid.*, p. 45.
[7] Hugh T. Lefler, ed., *North Carolina History Told by Contemporaries* (Chapel Hill, 1934), p. 358.

W.T. Blackwell and Company was a rapidly growing factor in the industry, one that began when distribution-minded individuals took over installations owned by men who understood only production. John Ruffin Green had produced tobacco on his Durham farm before the war, and in 1860 had established a small factory in Durham, where he turned out a local brand of granulated leaf—Best Flavored Eureka Spanish Smoking Tobacco. A fairly large supply was in Green's warehouse when the soldiers descended upon it, each taking as much as he wanted, with no one to stop them. Green must have thought this would be the end of his business, but a few months later—after the war had ended—he received letters from some of the soldiers, asking to buy more of the product. Encouraged, Green reopened his factory and renamed his product Bull Durham, after his town and a bull's head he had seen on a jar of mustard produced in Durham, England.[8] Bull Durham quickly became established as a quality product, while its trademark was known in many parts of the state, and to mail order customers elsewhere.

This was an age of local brands, news of which spread by reputation more than anything else. Each factory produced several brands, hoping one or more would catch the imagination of buyers, and few were sold more than a hundred miles from the factory. Lone Jack and Killikinnick came out of Lynchburg, Virginia, for example, while Honest 7, Brown's Mule, Oliver Twist, World's Choice, and Strawberry were brands out of Winston, North Carolina, factories.[9] Much of the product was shipped to other markets, but this was done through jobbers, most of whom handled dozens of brands from many factories. Before the Civil War, what is now called "brand loyalty" did not exist in plug and smoking tobacco, especially among travelers, for no retail outlet could handle all of the brands.

Green had no intention of making Bull Durham a na-

[8]Joseph C. Robert, *The Story of Tobacco in America* (New York, 1949), p. 123.
[9]Lefler, *North Carolina History*, pp. 358–60.

tional brand. He was an old and sick man, hoping to sell his business before he died. In 1868 he did sell half of the firm to William T. Blackwell and I.R. Day, two tobacco merchants and jobbers, who apparently had such notions. Green died the following year, and in 1870 Julian S. Carr, the son of a Chapel Hill merchant, entered the business, and shortly thereafter he and Blackwell bought out Day's interest.

Blackwell and Carr were merchandisers, not producers. They introduced new machinery into the plant and insisted on maintaining quality, but for the most part delegated production responsibility to others, while they concentrated on advertising and sales. Stewart solicited testimonials from prominent individuals, printed them up, and spread them through the state and beyond. W.T. Blackwell and Company spent over $100,000 a year on advertising in the early 1880s, and in the process made Bull Durham the nation's best-known tobacco product. Imitators appeared—Sitting Bull Durham, Dream Durham, Jersey Bull, Nickel-Plate Durham, and the like—but Blackwell successfully defended his trademark and was the uncrowned king of the brands.[10] He had also demonstrated that in the case of a undifferentiated product like tobacco, advertising and distribution were paramount, far more important than production. The old-time producers either would have to sell out to aggressive promoters like Blackwell or learn distribution and advertising techniques. Otherwise, they could hope for no more than the local markets, if that.

Those who learned the lessons survived. James Thomas, Jr., of Richmond, the head of Thomas C. Williams and Company, created several pipe tobacco brands, among them Lucky Strike, and was the wealthiest man in the city when he died in 1882. J.D. and Adolph Dill created Dill's Best, advertised it nationally, and in the 1880s had world-

[10]Robert, *Story of Tobacco*, pp. 122–24.

wide distribution. The Cameron family, headed by Alexander, ran three firms—Alexander Cameron and Company and Cameron and Cameron in Richmond, and William Cameron and Brothers of Petersburg. The family had a multitude of smoking brands, offices in Europe, and even an Australian factory in the early 1870s. Insofar as production was concerned, Richmond was emerging as the pipe tobacco capital of America.

Winston was coming to occupy the same position in plug. Pleasant H. Hanes produced over a million pounds of plug in the late 1880s, and Missing Link, Greek Slave, and Man's Pride were used nationally. Young Richard J. Reynolds opened his first factory in Winston in 1874. Oronoko and Reynolds' Bright 7 were two of his best-known brands, and Reynolds would create new ones regularly, believing at the time this was necessary to stir the public's interest.[11]

The competition in plug and smoking tobacco was fierce. Advertising and price wars were common, with all the manufacturers dreaming of toppling Bull Durham. None succeeded, however, but they continued to experiment with advertising, brand names, and pricing changes. New companies appeared regularly. They would purchase an old warehouse, buy leaf, and produce either granulated or plug, adding licorice, honey, and other flavorers, each claiming a "secret formula." Then they would try to market the product with a gimmick. Most failed, due to inadequate capitalization and an inability to compete against the more established brands.

Washington Duke and his sons were not major factors in the industry in the late 1860s, even though the company was growing. In 1869 it moved to a new factory in Durham, and in 1872 recorded sales of 125,000 pounds of granulated tobacco.

[11]Lefler, *North Carolina History*, pp. 358–61.

Brodie Duke was the family's driving force in this period. Washington was content to remain a small factor in the industry, but Brodie, still in his teens, wanted the business to expand rapidly. When Washington would not agree to a move to a larger installation, Brodie set up shop on his own, developing new brands—Semper Idem and Duke of Durham—and in the end Washington followed along. Father and son clashed repeatedly over costs and development, and for a while Brodie operated in a separate part of the factory.[12]

Both agreed, however, that Buck and Ben should be taken into the business. Buck already showed interest in tobacco, traveling through the area, talking with farmers, and even selling the Duke brands. After a while he went on business trips too, and was known through much of the tobacco belt.

Apparently Brodie encouraged Buck. If the operations grew as expected, the firm would need a comptroller. Brodie wanted his half-brother to learn bookkeeping, and Washington agreed to send him to the Eastman School of Business at Poughkeepsie, New York. On his return, Buck established double-entry accounts at the plant, and for a while seemed content to work under Brodie.

But the two never got along well together, then or later. Soon after he reached his eighteenth birthday, Buck asked Washington to "emancipate me," meaning to let him go off on his own. At first the father agreed, offering Buck $1,000 to start him in business. Then he changed his mind. "No, Buck. I won't give you that thousand dollars. Instead, I'll take you and Bennie into partnership. Hereafter our sign will read, 'W. Duke and Sons.' "[13] Such was the case, although the actual name of the firm was W. Duke Sons and Company.

[12]The American Tobacco Company, *"Sold American!"—The First Fifty Years* (New York, 1954), p. 19.
[13]John K. Winkler, *Tobacco Tycoon: The Story of James Buchanan Duke* (New York, 1942), p. 39.

Little is known of what happened at Duke Sons from its formation in 1874 through 1878. Sales increased steadily in this period, and Buck spent much of his time in the field, selling the Duke brands throughout the upper South.

The competition was fierce. Hundreds of companies had been formed to take advantage of the tobacco boom after the war. The 1866 crop had been 316 million pounds, with 384,000 acres under cultivation. Eleven years later production peaked at 621 million pounds with 789,000 acres in tobacco. Tobacco was a glut that year, and cutbacks followed, with 1880 production declining to 469 million pounds and acreage to 650,000.[14]

The industry was stabilizing, and weak firms were falling into receivership or merging with larger units. Even Blackwell, the master of Bull Durham, advertised for a buyer, and finding one in 1882, left the tobacco business to open a bank. Washington Duke knew he either had to expand to meet the competition or go out of business. He was reluctant to borrow money or sell a share in the concern, and thus his business declined. Perhaps feeling the end was near, Brodie turned to real estate speculation and became a part-owner in a furniture and funeral supplies store. Buck remained at the plant, and in time talked his father into seeking new capital.[15]

In 1878 the Dukes sold one-fifth interest in their firm to George W. Watts, a Baltimore merchant and investor. Duke Sons and Company was recapitalized at $70,000, and Watts brought $14,000 to the company. Two years later Washington sold his interest to Richard H. Wright, a tobacco manufacturer whose own firm was on the decline because his smoking brand, Orange of Durham, had not met with public favor.[16]

Now Buck Duke became the acknowledged leader at the

[14]United States, Department of Commerce, *Historical Statistics of the United States, Colonial Times to 1957* (Washington, 1960), p. 302.
[15]Winkler, *Tobacco Tycoon*, pp. 45–46.
[16]Jenkins, *James B. Duke*, pp. 59–60.

company. He took charge at the office and factory, while
Ben became secretary, Watts treasurer, and Wright sales
manager. For the time being the company would concentrate on smoking tobacco, although even then Buck
planned to get into plug. But he faced problems in both
areas. Bull Durham still ruled in the granulated field, and
no Duke brand could challenge it effectively. The Winston
companies dominated plug, and cigars were out of the
question, since the local tobaccos were not of the kind that
went into their production. "My company is up against a
stone wall," Buck wrote his lawyer. "It can't compete with
Bull Durham. Something has to be done and that quick. I
am going into the cigarette business."[17]

Cigarettes were almost unknown outside the eastern cities
prior to the Civil War, when most tobacco was sold in the
form of plug. Smoking was an indoor habit for the most
part, an accompaniment to discussion and part of leisure,
not the almost automatic habit it became a century later.
Americans chewed on the job, while in the streets, or working in the fields. There probably were many reasons for
this, most of which are based more on surmise than anything else. One that should be considered is the matter of
lighting the smokes. Before the days of matches, cigars and
pipes were ignited from fires in homes, by taper or live
coal. The first successful matches appeared in France in the
1830s, and improved versions came out of Sweden the following decade. Phosphorus matches, not yet believed dangerous to health, were in use in Europe in the late 1850s, at
a time when all major nations had match factories. The
match became common in America in the 1860s—just in
time for the increased smoking that came with the Civil
War. But cheap "book matches," given free with tobacco
sales, were invented in 1892 by Joshua Pusey, a lawyer. The

[17] *Ibid.*, p. 65.

development of the match might have taken place just as rapidly if tobacco had not existed. But the easy availability of them enabled pipe and cigar smokers to enjoy their habits whenever they felt like it. Still, their costs were high. "Lighting up" a cigar or pipe was still an occasion.

Cigarettes were another matter. At first they were savored, as though miniature cigars. By the 1880s, however, they had progressed to the status of a "quick smoke," and could not have been enjoyed as they were without cheap matches. At the time cigars were sold singly; even then, most cigarettes came in packs of ten, to be carried wherever one went. Buck Duke decided to enter the cigarette business in 1881. That same year, Diamond Match received its charter, and fourteen years later, it purchased the patent for the book match.

Before the Civil War, cigarettes were considered aristocratic European indulgences, somewhat effete, certainly not for the democratic male. Liberated American women experimented with them, and in 1854 a Dr. R.T. Trall, complaining about the use of tobacco in New York, wrote: "Some of the *ladies* of this refined and fashion-forming metropolis are aping the silly ways of some pseudo-accomplished foreigners, in smoking Tobacco through a weaker and more *feminine* article, which has been most delicately denominated *cigarette.*"[18] French and British soldiers who fought in the Crimea in 1856 picked up the habit from the Russians, and smoking the hard-paper tubes of granulated black tobacco became a London and Paris fad.

It is not known when the first cigarettes appeared in the United States, but in 1869 only 1.7 million were produced here, mostly of dark tobacco, and smoked by Europeans and the more venturesome in large eastern cities. These cigarettes were made by hand, usually by east European Jews, and often sold in small, elite tobacco shops. Some were made of domestic tobacco, but at this time most used imported Turkish leaf.

[18]Robert, *Story of Tobacco*, p. 112.

This was the situation in 1881, when Duke decided to turn to cigarettes. He hired ten rollers and their Russian-born foreman, J.M. Siegel, who came to Durham and set to work in a corner of the factory, turning out Duke of Durham and Pinhead cigarettes at the rate of some 20,000 a day.[19] That same year—1881—James A. Bonsack patented the first truly workable cigarette-making machine, one capable of turning out over two hundred cigarettes a minute. For the time being, however, Duke and the few other cigarette makers used hand labor.

Other companies in North Carolina and Virginia entered the cigarette business, but only as a sideline. For example, Blackwell hired J.M. Siegel's brother, David, to produce Bull Durham cigarettes, but he continued to concentrate on smoking tobacco. If cigarettes failed, the others could continue in plug and granulated tobacco. Duke, on the other hand, planned to stake all on cigarettes.

It was a daring move for the small company to make. Cigarettes still were considered exotic and effeminate. Allen and Ginter, a Richmond cigarette firm and one of the largest in the nation, was a marginal operation. Most of the other companies were in New York; none was very profitable. Duke would have to enlarge the market through advertising, hoping to create a brand in cigarettes as popular as Bull Durham in plug. His chances for success were slight. There was no guarantee Americans would take to cigarettes in large numbers, or, if they did, that Duke would be the major beneficiary of the change.

The tax situation posed another problem. In 1864 the federal government levied a tax of $1.00 per thousand cigarettes, and the rate was raised on several occasions, reaching the $5.00 level in 1867. Those who wanted to smoke cigarettes often rolled their own, while ready-made brands suffered. The rate was cut back to $1.50 the following year, but went to $1.75 in 1875, with the likelihood of further raises in the future. Duke Sons, which committed itself to ready-

[19]Jenkins, *James B. Duke*, p. 66.

mades, could be destroyed by a reversion to the 1867 rate.

The technological problem remained. Allen and Ginter offered $75,000 for a practical cigarette-making machine, with many takers but none successful. The Bonsack machine of 1881 seemed only one in a long line of failures at the time. Without an efficient machine, cigarettes could not become a mass smoke. And given their low price, without a mass market, no cigarette company could became a large enterprise.

There were reasons for optimism too, however. Cigarette smoking was on the rise in America, going from 1.8 million in 1869 to 500 million in 1880, with most of the increase coming from brands using the domestic leaf. As America industrialized and urbanized, the desire for a "quick smoke" may have developed too. Cigars were not the answer to this supposed craving, not even the smaller ones that cost two or three cents apiece in those days of the good five-cent cigar. Not many Americans could afford that much for a casual smoke during the day. A box of ten cigarettes, on the other hand, sold for ten cents, while some brands went for as little as five. This price appealed not only to the thrifty but to the urban poor. Smoking a cigar was still something of a ritual. Lighting up a cigarette could be an almost automatic act—if the smoke cost around half a cent. Such smokes might do well overseas as well, in parts of the world where price was a prime consideration, and among people who for one reason or another didn't like plug or pipes.

At first Duke tried to convince retailers who handled his smoking brands to carry Duke of Durham cigarettes. All but two refused. So Duke hired a salesman whose task it would be to place the cigarettes in stores and attract customers to buy them. He selected the right man. Edward Featherstone Small, the dashing son of a prominent southern family, took the job, which required him to travel

throughout the central United States promoting and advertising Duke of Durham, Pinhead, Cyclone, Cameo, Cross
Cut, Pedro, and Town Talk. Small was expert at extracting
testimonials from actresses and political figures, introducing a mild form of sex and politics in the place of the
cigar-store Indian. When St. Louis merchants refused to
see him he hired an attractive woman as a salesperson—a
novelty at the time, and one that got him stories in the local
press. Small set about creating brand loyalties in cigarettes,
and although others had tried before him, he was the first
to succeed. "The essential element in creating trade is a few
grains of common sense, strategy and tact well sharpened,
properly administered and rubbed with a little nigger
luck," wrote Small. "Above all, judicious advertising, especially if the same is novel and astounding in magnitude."

Largely as a result of Small's efforts, Duke was deluged
with orders. The retailers agreed to carry his brands. But
were the cigarettes selling to the public? Duke was concerned, and urged Small on to greater efforts. "The fact
that jobbers are getting calls from retailers is not sufficient
proof that consumers are demanding very many of them,"
he noted. "I want to know how the sales of retailers compare on our Duke with other brands both with the prominent retailers & the smaller ones."[20] Duke was a master of
detail; Small was the innovator in advertising.

Along with other manufacturers, Duke lobbied for lower
cigarette taxes. In 1883 Congress responded by reducing the
tax from $1.75 to $.50 per thousand. Duke promptly reduced
the price of his brands from ten cents to five per package
of ten, provided orders arrived within two months. His
factory was swamped with requests for shipments. Encouraged, Duke announced he would construct a large new
factory in Durham. By then he was one of the largest cigarette manufacturers in the nation.

Having secured the mid-American market, Duke ex-

[20]Winkler, *Tobacco Tycoon*, pp. 48–52.

panded his horizon. First, in order to make certain he could produce sufficient cigarettes for the market and at the same time reduce costs, he installed two new Bonsack machines in his factory, on condition he receive special rebates. Bonsack agreed; this was his first sale. It was also one of the most important moves Duke ever made, for with control of the Bonsacks, he was assured future domination of cigarettes. The machines were altered somewhat by William O'Brien, a Duke machinist, and now Duke's cigarette costs were the lowest in the industry.

Then Duke sent his partner and sales manager, Richard Wright, on an overseas selling trip, one that took him to four continents. Leaving management of the factory to Ben and Washington, who now returned to the business, Buck went to New York, to capture the eastern market.

All these ventures succeeded. Cigarette sales rose, reaching one billion in 1885, and Duke controlled about 10 percent of the market, which was the fasting growing in the industry.[21] In that year too, the company changed from a limited partnership to a corporation, and was capitalized at $250,000. Wright was bought out soon after his return from his foreign travels, and now the Dukes controlled all the important positions in the firm, with Buck—not yet thirty —viewed as the most dynamic and disruptive force in the cigarette industry.

Cigarette sales were increasing rapidly, but Duke Sons was growing even faster. Up to 1885, Buck had been content to develop markets where none existed before, hoping that by so doing, he would dominate the industry. His missionary work had gone well, but other firms were still larger than his. Allen and Ginter, now equipped with a better sales force and soon to install its first Bonsack machines, was the largest factor in cigarettes. Kinney Tobacco of New York was bigger than Duke, as were Goodwin and Company, also of New York, and William S. Kimball and

[21]Nannie M. Tilley, *The Bright Tobacco Industry, 1860–1929* (Chapel Hill, 1948), pp. 534–35, 570.

Company of Rochester. Together these four firms, which worked closely together, had about 80 percent of all sales in 1880. They considered Duke a maverick. The young man still had few of the social graces, appeared far too serious about his work and himself, and "pushed too hard." While in New York, Buck boarded in a cheap rooming house instead of a hotel, and he worked in the field six days a week while planning new operations on the seventh. The other cigarette men, solid middle-class merchants and manufacturers, saw him as an outcast. Duke knew of their feelings but didn't seem to mind. Later he said:

> I have succeeded in business not because I have more natural ability than those who have not succeeded, but because I have applied myself harder and stuck to it longer. I know plenty of people who have failed to succeed in anything who have more brains than I had, but they lacked application and determination.[22]

It was little wonder that the other cigarette manufacturers feared Duke. While they spoke of the virtues of hard work and competition, Duke was a living example of them, and without moderating alloys. He cut prices ruthlessly in 1885, not in seeking new markets, but to drive his competitors to the wall. Duke outspent all of them for advertising and promotion, and plowed his profits back into the firm to pay for additional campaigns. Some of the manufacturers felt the pressure couldn't continue for long. "He will be broke before the year is out," said one. Duke heard of this and replied, "I don't talk, I work."[23]

In 1887 some of the manufacturers approached Duke to determine his goals. He told them he wanted to organize what amounted to a tobacco trust. They could come into

[22]Jenkins, *James B. Duke*, p. 52.
[23]*Ibid.*, p. 86.

Cigarette Sales of Five Major Manufacturers, 1889

Company	Millions of Cigarettes
W. Duke Sons & Co.	834
Allen & Ginter	517
Kinney Tobacco Co.	432
William S. Kimball & Co.	237
Goodwin & Co.	168

SOURCE: U.S. Bureau of Corporations, *Report of the Commissioner of Corporations on the Tobacco Industry* (Washington, 1909–15), II, 96.

the trust on a participation basis, but it would have to be under his domination. Lewis Ginter didn't think much of the idea. "Listen, Duke, you couldn't buy us out to save your neck. You haven't enough money and you couldn't borrow enough. It's a hopeless proposition." Duke disagreed. "I make $400,000 out of my business every year. I'll spend every cent of it on advertising my goods as long as it is necessary. But I'll bring you into line."[24] He spent $800,000 on premiums and advertising in 1889, making cigarette cards ubiquitous and a collector's item. Allen and Ginter responded with a costly campaign of its own, and met Duke's price cuts, to the point of selling below cost. But Duke's production advantage, obtained through the early introduction of the Bonsack machines, could not be overcome. The sales figures for 1889 indicated that Duke not only dominated cigarettes, but that his lead over his rivals was growing rapidly.

Throughout the year Duke and Francis Kinney met to discuss industry problems, and perhaps it was Kinney who first acceded to Duke's overtures. Certainly Lewis Ginter was the last to succumb. In any case, the five companies came together in late 1889, and on January 31, 1890, the first incarnation of the American Tobacco Company was proclaimed. The new firm, capitalized at $25 million, controlled companies that produced over 90 percent of all the

[24] *Ibid.*, p. 87; Richard B. Tennant, *The American Cigarette Industry: A Study in Economic Analysis and Public Policy* (New Haven, 1950), p. 24.

Cigarettes Produced and Taxed in the United States, 1869–1911
(in thousands)

Year	Number
1869	1,750
1870	13,890
1871	18,930
1872	20,691
1873	27,087
1874	28,717
1875	41,297
1876	77,420
1877	149,069
1878	165,189
1879	238,276
1880	408,708
1881	567,386
1882	554,542
1883	640,019
1884	908,090
1885	1,058,748
1886	1,310,960
1887	1,584,504
1888	1,862,726
1889	2,151,515
1890	2,233,254
1891	2,684,538
1892	2,892,982
1893	3,176,698
1894	3,183,582
1895	3,328,476
1896	4,043,798
1897	4,153,251
1898	3,753,695
1899	2,805,130
1900	2,639,899
1901	2,277,069
1902	2,651,617
1903	3,041,572
1904	3,235,102
1905	3,376,632
1906	3,792,758
1907	5,167,021
1908	5,402,336
1909	6,105,255
1910	7,874,239

Source: William W. Young, *The Story of the Cigarette* (New York, 1916), p. 115.

nation's cigarettes. Duke and Allen and Ginter received $7.5 million each of the stock, Kinney got $5 million, and the other two firms, $2.5 million each, in return for which they relinquished their businesses to the trust.

At the time the purported total tangible assets of American Tobacco was $5 million, while an inventory study indicated it was below that. Later on, reformers would claim that American Tobacco was a prime example of stock watering—a process by which the tycoons inflated the value of their holdings in order to make quick and large profits. The stock-watering charge was leveled at other major trusts formed in this period and comes down to us in the present as accepted truth. But in fact there are questions regarding the charge. Tangible assets are only a small part of many companies' value. For example, the trademark "Coke" has no tangible worth in terms of reformist beliefs of the late nineteenth and early twentieth century. But it certainly is worth a considerable amount, as are other brand names, trademarks, goodwill, and management skills. American Tobacco was capitalized at a far higher value than its net worth. The difference between the two figures was more than compensated for by industry position, trademarks, and management. This was amply demonstrated during the next few years when, from 1890 to 1895, American Tobacco earned more than $4 million a year on its $5 million in assets, or, in terms of its capitalization costs and value, showed a return of 20 percent.[25]

Only thirty-five years old, Duke headed the trust. During his first year he attempted to integrate the five different sales forces and distribution networks and rationalize operations. The Goodwin factory was closed, for example, and all cigarette production was concentrated in the Richmond area. Duke signed an agreement with the Bonsack Machine Company guaranteeing American Tobacco sole use of its devices. He cut back on advertising expenses—the wars

[25]Bureau of Corporations, *Tobacco Industry*, I, 65–68; II, 145–48.

against competitors were over—but the price of a pack of
ten cigarettes remained fixed at five cents. Rates to retailers
were lowered however, to assure them higher profits and
secure their loyalty in the continuing effort to make cigarettes the national smoke. Duke clearly was trying to make
one company out of five. But he still would not take the
major step of cutting down on brands. Nor would he ever
do so. Instead, he concentrated on selling all of the old ones,
and even introduced new cigarettes from time to time.

Duke had always considered himself a salesman and advertising innovator. His work at American Tobacco indicated that Brodie Duke had been correct in assessing his
abilities many years before. Duke was an excellent office
manager, his abilities at financial manipulation were being
honed, and he wanted power. Duke realized he was not
bold and imaginative; as he indicated, his penchant was
hard work. No one in the firm labored more than he, and
in its first incarnation, American Tobacco was a success.
Duke had ability, and a goal.

Given time, Duke might have made American Tobacco
into a great cigarette firm. But he refused to take that time,
or limit his horizon to cigarettes. Instead, American Tobacco became a magnet, attracting other tobacco enterprises, who dubbed it an octopus, grasping them against
their wills. In September, 1891 one of the firm's vice presidents said, "The company is organized for the purpose of
curing leaf tobacco, to buy, manufacture and sell tobacco
in all its forms [emphasis added]." In other words, Duke
would not be content to remain a cigarette king, although
the title and glory was his for the taking. Perhaps this was
because cigarettes were growing rapidly but still lagged far
behind other forms of tobacco. "We wished to manufacture
a full variety to make every style of tobacco the public
wanted," he said later on.[26]

Without waiting to fully rationalize the cigarette opera-

[26]Jenkins, *James B. Duke*, pp. 90, 92.

tions, Duke embarked on what would be called "The Plug War." He increased American Tobacco's capitalization to $35 million, using the new stock to exchange for the assets of several plug companies. Pfingst, Doerhoefer and Company, a successful Louisville, Kentucky plug firm whose brands—Piper-Heidsieck, Newsboy, and Battle Ax—were well known, agreed to a takeover, provided the price was right. It was. The firm was reorganized as the National Tobacco Works, and was then sold to American Tobacco for $600,000 in cash and $1.2 million in American Tobacco stock. In the same way, American Tobacco acquired Marburg Brothers, Gail and Ax, and other significant producers of smoking tobacco and snuff, as well as plug. By the end of the year, American Tobacco was one of the major plug firms, and had established strong beachheads in snuff as well.[27]

In 1893 Duke approached the remaining plug companies with a merger proposal, which was rejected. Now he initiated major price cuts and increased advertising expenses. The plug companies—P. Lorillard, Liggett and Myers, Drummond, and Brown among them—responded by making cuts of their own. At one point all the firms were selling plug at below cost. Plug sales rose dramatically, from 20 million pounds in 1895 to 31 million in 1896, but in the latter year, losses on sales exceeded $1.3 million.[28] This was a contest not only of wills but assets. Duke plowed his cigarette and smoking tobacco profits into plug, where they were swallowed up and transformed into losses. Cigarette sales declined for a while, as consumers purchased the cheap plug. Liggett and Myers and Drummond responded by entering the cigarette business, in what amounted to a flanking operation. But their losses were too great to continue—they didn't have the Bonsack machines, and without them could not compete against the Duke brands.

[27] *United States v. American Tobacco Co.* Appeals from the Circuit Court of the United States for the Southern District of New York, 221 U.S. 106, pp. 156–57.
[28] Bureau of Corporations, *Tobacco Industry*, III, 51.

Some of the small companies broke ranks first, giving Duke options to purchase them. Then Brown came over, a small firm but important in that it had some popular brands and valuable patents. Drummond, a much larger concern, was purchased for $3.5 million. Further price cuts convinced most of the others that continued struggle was useless. All but Liggett and Myers granted Duke options to buy.

By this time Duke was well-schooled in most aspects of the tobacco industry, and had learned much about finance. But the restructuring of the plug industry was too complicated for him to handle at the time. In addition, he would have to raise a large amount of money through stock sales in order to finance the options. So he turned to Moore and Schley, a medium-sized investment broker, which handled the restructuring and refinancing operations. As was the case with all the major trusts formed through acquisitions, investment bankers had to be brought in as midwives at the time of this major transformation of many companies into one. At no time did Moore and Schley dominate the tobacco business, but from that time on, it played a significant role in its fortunes.

Together with the partners at Moore and Schley, Duke formed Continental Tobacco Company, which was capitalized at $75 million in 1898, and was soon raised to $97.7 million in order to acquire additional firms. The stock and cash were used to exercise options, which brought P. Lorillard, P.J. Sorg, P.H. Mayo, Daniel Scotten, and other large plug companies under the Continental umbrella. Then American Tobacco sold its plug facilities and brands to Continental for $1.1 million in cash and $15.2 million in stock —a highly inflated price. This made American the largest stockholder in Continental, and Buck Duke was president of both firms.[29]

Without pausing to rationalize plug operations—a repeat

[29] *Ibid.*, I, 101.

of his performance at American Tobacco in 1891—Duke sought other firms to acquire. American Tobacco engulfed thirty firms in 1899 and Continental seven more, with plants from North Carolina to Japan, producing goods ranging from plug to tinfoil and cigar boxes. Clearly both concerns were engaged in vertical and horizontal expansion, seeking to dominate the entire industry.

Not all of the takeovers were complete. In most cases Duke was content to purchase controlling interest in operating companies, and continue to run them as separate entities. This meant that although American and Continental were growing rapidly in terms of assets and industry control, the firms themselves were more like holding companies than operating ones. Duke was no longer a tobacco man, much less a cigarette manufacturer, in 1899. Rather, he was a manager, an acquirer, one who made as much if not more money through financial manipulations and takeovers as through salary and dividends. He was one of a new breed of businessmen, unrecognized for what they were then and not even appreciated at the present time. In effect, Duke was a conglomerateur, a man who no less than the makers of the major conglomerates of the 1960s was in the business of opportunity. The major difference between Duke and others of his generation and James Ling, Harold Geneen, Charles Bluhdorn, and the other conglomerateurs of the present was that he took over companies dealing in one way or another, directly or indirectly, with tobacco, while the later group went further afield. But in most other matters—the use of financing, attitude toward competition, communities of interest—they were more alike than is generally realized even now. Buck Duke and Harold Geneen have far more in common than William McKinley and Richard Nixon.

Duke did face opposition, this time from a group of Wall Street speculators and sometimes businessmen. Thomas Fortune Ryan, P.A.B. Widener, Anthony N. Brady, and William C. Whitney were fresh from triumphs in restructuring trolley operations and other raids on the economy. Now they hoped to make a fortune in tobacco. They knew Duke controlled the only major entity in the industry, but also realized that there were some important independents remaining. These were approached and offered "safety" within a new company, Union Tobacco. National Cigarette and Tobacco accepted, and so did Blackwell's Durham Tobacco, the successor to W.T. Blackwell, which still produced Bull Durham, the leading plug brand.

At this point two new figures appeared. Oliver H. Payne, a Standard Oil millionaire, had been investing in American Tobacco since late in 1897, as had his associate in Wall Street speculation, Herbert L. Terrell. Seeing in Union Tobacco a perfect vehicle with which to take over the Duke interests, Payne and Terrell joined the group and managed to obtain an option on Liggett and Myers, the largest plug manufacturer in America. At the same time, Payne and Terrell began buying American Tobacco stock on the open market through James R. Keene, who made a living conducting bull and bear raids for others. Keene did his work well and assured Payne he had control of American Tobacco. By this time Duke had learned of the operation, and went to see Payne. According to later accounts, Payne told Duke he could remain as operating head of the company but that his group would enter the picture and assume major roles at American Tobacco. Payne wasn't interested in expansion. In the future, he said, American Tobacco would concentrate its attention on rationalizing what it already had, forming a single giant trust around the holdings of American, Continental, and Union, the latter company to be brought into the combination.

Duke rejected this approach. Not only did he intend to continue expansion but insisted on full control of American and Continental. Presumably Payne observed that there were antitrust considerations to be taken into ac-

count; the reformers were making noises, and although no major trust had been destroyed, there was no assurance this situation would continue. This too did not interest Duke. "If you fellows want to do this," he said, "you won't have to turn me out; I'll quit." Payne asked Duke what his plans would be if he left American. "I'll sell every share of my stock and start another company."[30]

Payne backed down. If Duke were to leave, the entire structure could fall, and a new Duke firm might defeat American–Continental–Union. On the surface it seemed a victory for the industrialist over the financier-speculator, expansion over consolidation, and a vindication of "watered stock." As for this last point, Duke was not listed as an asset on the company's books. But Payne realized that his managerial skills were vital to continued prosperity at the trust.

Payne and his friends did not lose, however, and Duke's victory was not complete. Late in 1899 American purchased Union, while Continental obtained control of Liggett and Myers. The group made huge profits on both takeovers. Payne, Brady, Ryan, and Widener joined the board at American Tobacco and had an interest at Continental too. As a group, the financiers had a larger interest than Duke himself. At the same time, the old cigarette crowd that had come into the company at the time of the first merger in 1890 was eased out. In this way, the cigarette company became a tobacco concern, which in turn became a management operation. Buck Duke led at each turn of the wheel. He was now forty-three years old.

The expansion continued. American Snuff Company was organized in March 1900, capitalized at $23 million, with $10 million apiece issued to Continental and American in return for their snuff operations, and the rest to George W. Helme, at the time the largest independent snuff manufacturer. Again, fortunes were made by all involved. Less

[30]Jenkins, *James B. Duke*, pp. 99–102.

than a year later American and Continental organized the American Cigar Company, capitalized at $10 million, with each of the parent firms receiving $3.5 million for their cigar operations.

Meanwhile antitrust sentiment was growing rapidly, but Duke ignored it. Shortly after forming American Cigar, he brought American and Continental together under an all-embracing umbrella trust, the Consolidated Tobacco Company, which was initially capitalized at $30 million. Without pausing, Duke began purchasing controlling interests in foreign tobacco companies, and establishing manufacturing and distributing subsidiaries in Europe and Asia.[31]

Faced with this invasion, the British firms united behind Imperial Tobacco, and now a new tobacco war began, this one for the world. Both sides agreed to a peace in late 1902. Imperial would withdraw from the American market, and Duke would leave the United Kingdom. American and Imperial then formed a new firm, incorporated in London, British-American Tobacco, which would seek to dominate the rest of the world. Duke received two-thirds of the stock, and Imperial the other third. And while restructuring his American interests, forming subsidiaries in cigars and snuff, and fighting a world battle, Duke found time to invade the retail side of the business, acquiring control of the United Cigar Stores.

By 1904 the antitrusters were on the march, having just defeated the Northern Securities combine. In order to bring together their many holdings and at the same time form a company that presented a less inviting target in the light of the Supreme Court decision, Duke and his associates merged American and Continental into a new American Tobacco Company. This firm claimed total assets of $274 million, but the figure might have been higher. The structure was complex, and it was believed Duke alone understood it, and he understated the assets to avoid criti-

[31]For an interesting account of the foreign business, see James A. Thomas, *A Pioneer Tobacco Merchant in the Orient* (Durham, 1928).

Subsidiaries in the "Duke Companies," 1906

American Tobacco

Company	Total Shares Outstanding	Owned by American Tobacco
CIGARETTE COMPANIES		
S. Anargyros	$450,000	$450,000
John Bollman	200,000	102,000
Wells-Whitehead	75,000	75,000
Monopol Tobacco	40,000	40,000
PLUG COMPANIES		
R.J. Reynolds	7,525,000	5,000,000
D.H. Spencer & Sons	800,000	450,000
Liipfert Scales	400,000	266,667
F.R. Penn	262,800	100,200
Nall & Williams	116,800	116,800
Nashville Tobacco	120,000	120,000
SMOKING AND FINE CUT		
P. Lorillard	5,000,000	4,581,300
Blackwell's Durham	1,000,000	1,000,000
R.A. Patterson	150,000	150,000
Spaulding & Merrick	100,000	100,000
F.F. Adams	400,000	400,000
R.P. Richardson	500,000	180,000
John W. Carroll	425,000	200,000
SCRAP TOBACCO		
Luhrman & Wilbern	902,000	902,000
Day & Night	400,000	400,000
Pinkerton	100,000	77,500
COMPANIES IN CONTRIBUTORY ENTERPRISES		
MacAndrews & Forbes	6,758,300	2,961,200
Mengel Box	1,973,200	1,436,000
Columbia Box	150,000	150,000
Tyler Box	25,000	25,000
Golden Belt Mfg.	700,000	652,100
Conley Foil	575,000	345,000
Johnston Tin Foil	400,000	300,000
American Machine & Foundry	100,000	100,000
New Jersey Machine	100,000	100,000
International Cigar Machine	10,000,000	6,286,900
Standard Tobacco Stemmer	1,730,000	1,664,000
Garson Vending Machines	50,000	25,000
Kentucky Tobacco Products	1,000,000	560,000
Kentucky Tobacco Extract	10,000	10,000
Manhattan Briar Pipe	350,000	350,000
Baltimore Briar Pipe	1,000	1,000

Amsterdam Supply	225,000	225,000
Thomas Cusack	250,000	100,000

DISTRIBUTING COMPANIES

Crescent Cigar & Tobacco	20,000	20,000
United Cigar Stores	1,950,000	1,840,000
United Cigar of Illinois	389,800	389,800
Royal Co.	100,000	100,000
United Cigar of Rhode Island	125,000	125,000
Wm. Baeder	5,000	5,000
Moebs Cigar Stores	10,000	10,000
United Merchants' Realty	500,000	500,000

American Snuff

W.E. Garrett & Sons	600,000	600,000
Weyman & Bro.	500,000	500,000
Standard Snuff	281,600	281,600
DeVoe Snuff	50,000	50,000
Skinner & Co.	40,000	40,000
H. Bolander	135,000	135,000

American Cigar Company

MANUFACTURING COMPANIES

American Stogie	11,855,000	7,307,275
American Stogie of Philadelphia	1,250,000	1,250,000
Federal Cigar	250,000	250,000
Havana-American	250,000	250,000
Porto-Rican-American	2,071,538	1,315,438
Havana Tobacco	42,500,000	19,375,000
Havana Commercial	18,500,000	17,943,000
Henry Clay & Bock	2,430,330	1,189,178
Havana Cigar & Tobacco	3,795,870	1,140,756
J.S. Murais y Ca.	1,157,600	1,157,600
H. de Cabanas y Carbajal	1,500,000	1,500,000

LEAF COMPANIES

F. Garcia	10,000	10,000
Cuban Land and Leaf	100,000	100,000
Porto Rican Leaf	500,000	309,500

MISCELLANEOUS COMPANIES

Federal Cigar Real Estate	30,000	30,000
Cuban Tobacco	5,000	5,000
J. & B. Moos	150,000	100,000
M. Blaskower	500,000	375,000
Cliff Weil Cigar	50,000	25,500
Le Compt Dusel & Goodloe	56,100	29,100
Jordan Gibson & Baum	50,000	41,000
Louisiana Tobacco	50,000	37,500

J.J. Goodrum	60,000	47,700
R.D. Burnett Cigar	15,000	7,700
Smokers' Paradise	75,000	53,500

British-American Tobacco Company		
T.C. Williams	400,000	400,000
David Dunlop	450,000	300,000
W.S. Mathews & Sons	500,000	363,700

SOURCE: Bureau of Corporations, *Tobacco Industry*, I, 212–18.

cism. The new firm issued $40 million in common stock, $79 million in preferred, and had $136 million in bonds outstanding.[32]

On the surface it appeared that Duke dominated the industry and could do with it what he wished. Such was not the case. American Tobacco was hated by many farmers, even though it sponsored reforms in bidding for leaf, and tobacco profits rose for a majority of growers.[33] The combine was never truly rationalized. American Tobacco owned controlling interest in many companies but actually operated few of them. The subsidiary firms were not coordinated, and competition between them was not only wasteful but counterproductive. Duke's product mix was unstable, in part due to a large-scale anti-cigarette campaign mounted toward the end of the century. Cigarette production peaked at 4.2 billion in 1897, and then declined to 2.3 billion in 1901 before resuming the upward climb. Duke did not know how to cope with this, and in any case, was no longer as interested in cigarettes as he had been a decade earlier.

Richard Reynolds refused to follow corporation strategy, taking an independent line whenever it suited him, undercutting other trust brands and conducting pointless price wars. Duke wasn't able to control him. Nor did he have a firm grip on his jobbers, and efforts at dominating marketing were half-hearted, even though a move in

[32]Bureau of Corporations, *Tobacco Industry*, I, 11–12.
[33]Tilley, *Bright Tobacco Industry*, pp. 421–45; Robert, *Story of Tobacco*, pp. 152–53.

that direction would have made sense. Duke had a reputation for motivating his staff, but any original idea different from Duke's was quietly but firmly shoved aside.[34]

American Tobacco dominated cigarettes, plug, snuff, and smoking tobacco, but the most prestigious prize of all, cigars, eluded it. Try as he might, Duke never found the key to control there. In part this was because the cigar market was so fractionalized, but so was plug at one time. More important, perhaps, was the lack of efficient cigar-making machinery. Duke made a major effort in cigars in 1904–1905, but failed miserably, and soon after abandoned the attempt. Perhaps the key to Duke's success was not management skills or manipulation, or even advertising, but his almost complete control of the important Bonsack machines, as is the view of one scholar.[35]

Duke was considered a master at wringing profits from the enterprise. The tobacco trust's earnings were excellent and dividends high. Most of the increase came not from economies of scale and internal savings but from the addition of new firms through mergers. There is little evidence that Duke's managerial abilities had been sufficient to increase efficiency in small units he acquired, or raise profit margins substantially above what they had been before the

American Tobacco's Share of the Tobacco Product Market, 1910

Product	Percentage
Cigarettes	86.1
Plug	84.9
Smoking	76.2
Fine Cut	79.2
Snuff	96.4
Little Cigars	91.4
Cigars	14.5

Source: Bureau of Corporations, *Tobacco Industry*, III, 2.

[34]Thomas, *Tobacco Merchant*, pp. 52–61; Glenn Porter and Harold C. Livesay, *Merchants and Manufacturers: Studies in the Changing Structure of Nineteenth Century Marketing* (Baltimore, 1971), pp. 207–13.
[35]Tennant, *American Cigarette Industry*, p. 33.

Sales and Profits for American Tobacco Companies, 1890–1908
(in millions of dollars)

Year	Sales	Total Assets	Earnings		
			AMOUNT	PERCENT OF SALES	PERCENT OF ASSETS
1890	9.6	13.9	2.5	26.1	18.1
1891	15.3	20.7	4.4	28.8	21.3
1892	16.7	22.5	4.7	28.4	21.0
1893	17.7	23.5	4.3	24.5	18.4
1894	18.0	25.3	5.1	28.2	20.0
1895	21.1	26.9	3.8	18.1	14.2
1896	22.2	27.5	3.4	15.3	12.4
1897	23.5	29.1	4.0	17.0	13.7
1898	26.9	29.0	3.6	13.3	12.3
1899	63.0	79.0	6.7	10.6	8.5
1900	74.1	83.4	9.9	13.4	11.9
1901	77.5	86.1	13.8	17.9	16.1
1902	85.2	98.6	18.3	21.2	18.6
1903	91.4	100.8	21.5	23.6	21.4
1904	93.9	99.2	19.8	21.1	20.0
1905	101.8	105.4	23.0	22.6	21.8
1906	111.3	109.2	25.9	23.3	23.7
1907	117.7	113.7	25.7	21.8	22.6
1908	128.6	124.8	28.8	22.4	23.1

SOURCE: Bureau of Corporations, *Tobacco Industry*, II, 242.

constituent companies were taken into the American Tobacco maw.

The stockholders had little reason to complain. If a person had invested $1,000 in 1890 by buying twenty shares of
American Tobacco and held the stock until 1908, he would
have received $4,030 in dividends, while the stock rose from
50 to 340 (adjusting for stock splits).[36]

When under attack by trustbusters, American Tobacco
spokesmen liked to say that the firm had standardized products while lowering costs to consumers, in this way expanding the market for its products. At times they would
compare Duke with John D. Rockefeller, who had done
just that in petroleum. Such was not the case, however.

[36]Bureau of Corporations, *Tobacco Industry*, II, 310–11.

Average Price of American Tobacco Company Products, 1893–1910

Year	Plug (pound)	Smoking Tobacco (pound)	Cigarettes (per thousand)	Cigars (per thousand)	Snuff (per pound)
1893	$0.340	$0.298	$3.52	—	—
1894	0.351	0.293	3.49	—	—
1895	0.215	0.310	3.27	—	—
1896	0.189	0.307	2.96	—	—
1897	0.182	0.297	2.94	—	—
1898	0.252	0.321	3.27	—	—
1899	0.330	0.331	3.51	—	—
1900	0.348	0.348	3.66	—	41.7
1901	0.360	0.343	3.61	31.13	41.4
1902	0.355	0.338	3.86	27.98	40.3
1903	0.354	0.332	4.05	28.08	40.2
1904	0.359	0.346	4.00	26.58	42.6
1905	0.362	0.337	4.09	26.96	43.8
1906	0.360	0.343	4.26	27.69	43.5
1907	0.362	0.346	4.42	26.82	44.2
1908	0.363	0.352	4.49	27.06	44.1
1909	0.357	0.354	4.49	27.06	44.1
1910	0.360	0.364	4.66	27.50	44.8

SOURCE: Bureau of Corporations, *Tobacco Industry*, III, 51 *passim*, and Neil H. Borden, *The Economic Effects of Advertising* (Chicago, 1942), p. 217.

Tobacco products' prices did not decline; instead, they rose, often substantially. Cigarette consumption did not increase as a result of trust activities but instead continued the gradual upswing that began in the 1880s. The trust was unable to halt the gradual decline of chewing tobacco or, for that matter, affect the per capita consumption of most tobacco varieties, even though advertising costs were substantial in this period. All Duke could have done was to use advertising to increase sales of one brand at the expense of others. Perhaps had he cut down on the number of brands he sold he could have effected economies. But he refused to do this, and so had less effect on the industry than otherwise might have been the case.

In sum, the tobacco trust tried to maximize profits, as might have been expected. Duke would lower prices drastically in attempts to destroy competitors, but once this was

Per Capita Consumption of Tobacco Products in the United States,
1900–1910
(pounds)

Year	Large Cigars	Cigarettes	Chewing Tobacco	Smoking Tobacco	Snuff	Total
1900	1.33	0.14	2.39	1.31	0.20	5.37
1901	1.42	0.12	2.38	1.44	0.22	5.58
1902	1.47	0.13	2.28	1.51	0.23	5.62
1903	1.62	0.14	2.29	1.58	0.24	5.87
1904	1.57	0.15	2.22	1.80	0.25	5.99
1905	1.59	0.15	2.09	1.92	0.25	6.00
1906	1.65	0.16	2.16	2.01	0.27	6.25
1907	1.75	0.21	2.16	2.10	0.27	6.49
1908	1.57	0.22	2.06	2.07	0.25	6.17
1909	1.54	0.24	2.15	2.17	0.30	6.40
1910	1.59	0.34	2.17	2.30	0.34	6.74

SOURCE: Borden, *Economic Effects of Advertising*, p. 216.

accomplished he would raise them higher than before. In general, the greater control American Tobacco had over a product, the higher would be its price. Of course, this did not seem wrong to free enterprisers at the time, and could be defended even today. There seems little evidence to indicate that Duke was a master entrepreneur, however. He demonstrated great abilities at bringing small and large firms into his trust, but far less in making them work in harmony with one another, increasing profits and productivity, and creating a better industrial climate. He was not alone in this; few of the major trusts put together through amalgamations worked out as well as had been expected at the time of their births. U.S. Steel, no less than American Tobacco, was an almost unmanageable giant.

The greatest irony may be found in that Duke began his career as an acquisitor hoping to put together a cigarette combine, feeling at the time he had no hope of success in the leading product, plug. Had he stopped his acquisitions after forming the first incarnation of American Tobacco in

1890, and then concentrated on that variety of smoke alone, he would doubtless be considered a far-sighted genius today. Such a firm, large by 1890 standards but medium-sized by those of today, could have been managed effectively by a man of Duke's intelligence, abilities, and drive. In time, through internal growth, and aided by the natural drift of the market, the cigarette company would have become a giant, but one that developed organically, changing its internal structure to meet new demands made upon it. This kind of firm would have resembled John D. Rockefeller's famous American Beauty Rose, that crowded out the other blooms in order to flourish. Such had been the case at Standard Oil. American Tobacco, instead, resembled a fruitcake, rich in nuts, dates, and fruits but rather weak in the binding.

This resulted from Duke's drive to conquer not only plug but every other variety of tobacco product, and to control all operations from factory to retail outlet, controlling all suppliers along the way. Duke was not even content with this; he had to dominate the world market in tobacco, with his brands selling in every country in the world.

But to what end? Power for its own sake? A drive to make cigarettes popular and oust plug is understandable, especially if you are a cigarette manufacturer. This was the goal of American Tobacco in its first incarnation, and Duke's initial dream. In its final form American Tobacco had no other goal but to survive, make profits, and, on occasion, serve as a vehicle for speculators. Buck Duke was a keen opportunist in the 1890s, and he was most successful at the task. Afterward, he became an unguided missile in the business firmament, and his later self-description—in which he said he had no more natural ability than most but only worked harder and stuck to tasks longer—seems fairly accurate.

In retrospect, 1904 seems the pinnacle of Duke's life. Not only was it to mark the formation of the American Tobacco trust but late in the year Duke found time to get married.

Shortly thereafter he brought charges of adultery against his wife and won a divorce. Nor was Buck the only member of the family to face personal difficulties; Brodie Duke became involved in a series of escapades that titillated readers of the scandal sheets.

Attacks on the trust grew. North Carolina editor Josephus Daniels, who had spoken out against Duke in the early 1890s and never let up in the years that followed, wrote that the company was using bullying tactics against its few remaining rivals in the state. The faculty at Trinity College, a North Carolina institution Buck Duke befriended, had several firebrands on the faculty who spoke and wrote against him and the company, and Daniels supported them. All of this saddened Washington Duke, who had never wanted to go into any other business except cigarettes. "I wish Buck had never put us into the company and that we could carry on our business like we used to do it," he confided to Daniels. "We were making lots of money and did not have any criticism."[37] Washington died in 1905, and Buck lost one of the very few people he was close to, a man who sometimes could act as a rudder for his ambitions.

The attacks against Duke and American Tobacco in North Carolina were based not only on the trust's power in the state but on Duke's Republicanism and his family's longtime support of economic improvement for blacks. In the North, Duke was criticized for his policies. "The tobacco trust keeps the price just high enough to tease the grower into continued production, but not high enough to yield him any appreciable profit beyond the bare payment for his labor," charged Ray Stannard Baker, the famous muckraking journalist.[38] "The Tobacco Trust is the Scourge of the South," added *McClure's*, and other reform journals were equally strong in their condemnations.

The trust continued to show fine profits, but like Duke's

[37] Robert, *Story of Tobacco*, pp. 160–61.
[38] *Ibid.*, pp. 162–64.

personal life, seemed out of control. Reynolds went his own way, actually financing some of the reformers in their struggles against American Tobacco.[39] He admitted to Daniels that he wanted the combination destroyed so that he could go his own way. "You will never see the day when Dick Reynolds will eat out of Buck Duke's hand," he boasted. "If any swallowing is to be done, Dick Reynolds will do the swallowing."[40] Reynolds forged ahead on his own, even though American Tobacco owned two-thirds of his company's stock. Duke gave him complete authority over his own operations, and a larger share of the profits than might have been expected. He did the same with Lorillard and a few others, who viewed Duke's concessions as signs of weakness, which perhaps they were. Many of the managers of firms controlled by the trust resented their positions. Under the best of circumstances, Duke could not have brought them into line. If such a situation developed at a conglomerate today, the manager would be fired, or given an employment contract tantamount to dismissal with several years' pay. But this was not done at the turn of the century. And beset by marital problems, shaken by the death of his father, seeing his firm under strong attack and not knowing how to respond, and increasingly turning to drink, Duke merely drifted.

The government settled the matter for him. The first antitrust action against American Tobacco was filed in North Carolina in 1890, and other state suits followed. The New York legislature began an investigation of trusts in 1897, and four years later the United States Industrial Commission did the same. With the handing down of the Northern Securities decision in 1904, and the completion of the gathering of information by state and federal agencies, it seemed only a matter of time before President Theodore Roosevelt ordered an investigation and indictment in federal court.

[39]Tilley, *Bright Tobacco Industry,* pp. 270–71.
[40]Winkler, *Tobacco Tycoon,* pp. 194–95.

This came in 1907, in the Circuit Court for the Southern District of New York. The trust was found guilty of violations of the Sherman Anti-Trust Act, and appealed the verdict to a higher court. The Circuit Court decision went up the judicial ladder, reaching the Supreme Court in 1910. By then American Tobacco and other large trusts had become political footballs in a power struggle between former President Roosevelt and President William Howard Taft. Senator Albert Beveridge and others spoke out strongly against Duke and American Tobacco, and it seemed the case would be decided at least as much on political as on legal grounds.

The Court found American Tobacco in violation of the Sherman Act and ordered its dissolution. Since Duke knew more of the company and its problems than any other man, he was asked to prepare a plan for its division. The task was complicated, but the division itself fairly obvious. Liggett and Myers, Reynolds, and Lorillard had entered the trust against their wills, each had good management teams and had been more or less on their own for several years. Now they were "set loose." In addition several other companies emerged from the trust—American Snuff, American Cigar, American Stogie, MacAndrews and Forbes being the largest. The divestiture was carried out with ease, an indication that the American Tobacco empire had never been a monarchy, but rather was a confederation.

Division of Business under Dissolution Decree, Based on 1910 Output
(percentage of business)

Company	Tobacco Variety					
	CIGARETTES	SMOKING	PLUG	FINE CUT	CIGARS	SNUFF
American Tobacco	37.1	33.1	25.3	9.9	21.5	—
Liggett & Myers	27.8	20.1	33.8	41.6	—	—
Reynolds	—	2.7	18.1	—	—	—
Lorillard	15.3	22.8	3.7	27.5	39.5	—
Others	19.8	21.4	19.0	20.6	86.6	100.0

SOURCE: *U.S. v. American Tobacco Co.*, 191 F. 371, 412, 413 (1911)

Under the divestiture, American Tobacco remained the largest firm in the industry, the leader in cigarettes and pipe tobacco. Liggett and Myers would dominate in plug and fine-cut tobacco, and Lorillard would be the major factor in the still diverse cigar field. American would retain such smoking brands as Lucky Strike and Bull Durham, plugs like Newsboy and Piper Heidsieck, and the popular Sweet Caporal, Hassan, Mecca, and Pall Mall cigarettes. Liggett and Myers had Star, Horseshoe, and Drummond's in plug, while Lorillard had a variety of Egyptian-type cigarettes in its stable. Reynolds received all his old brands, over fifty in plug alone, and now was out of the cigarette and cigar business entirely.

Duke was fifty-five years old in 1911, when the dissolution was arranged. He remained at the head of American Tobacco for a few months, and then resigned in favor of Percival Hill. Duke became chairman of British-American Tobacco, but was required to spend little time at the job. In effect, he was retired. Duke's second wife, Nanaline, was pregnant, and Buck hoped for a boy. But Nanaline gave birth to a girl, Doris, in 1912. Still, Duke enjoyed her childhood, and found time for other activities. He became interested in hydroelectric power, and helped found what became Duke Power and Light. Then he turned his attention to education, and his millions transformed Trinity College into Duke University. These were worthwhile tasks, performed with skill. But like the other tycoons discussed, Duke's last period of life was not on the same level as his earlier one. Still, he had been able to master electricity and even win confidence at the new university; he had not done so well at American Tobacco.

Duke must have been somewhat chagrined at developments in tobacco after he effectively retired. American Tobacco, with which he was still identified, stagnated, while Reynolds, headed by a man he disliked and who despised him, became the innovative leader of the industry, and in a way that resembled Duke's own entry into cigarettes in the late 1880s. Having no brands of his own, and realizing that the other major firms had effective control of the so-called foreign blends, Reynolds experimented with a new mixture, a sweetened burley. He called the new cigarette Camels, to evoke the Turkish brands, and test marketed them in 1913. Camels were sold for ten cents for a pack of twenty, at a time when Turkish-Virginia blends sold for fifteen cents. But Reynolds did not include cigarette cards in the packs, or offer other premiums or discounts. He placed a notice on the package. "Don't look for premiums or coupons as the cost of the tobaccos blended in Camel Cigarettes prohibits the use of them."

Camels was an instant success. Throwing almost his entire cigarette advertising budget behind this one brand, Reynolds created the first major national cigarette, something Duke had not even attempted. Reynolds Tobacco did not produce cigarettes in 1912. By 1914 it had 3 percent of the market. Two years later Reynolds had 26 percent, and in 1918, the year of his death, Camels and the minor Reynolds brands had 40 percent of the market.[41] Nor was this Reynolds' only success. Putting his power in smoking tobacco behind a single brand, Prince Albert, his share of that market rose from 7 percent in 1911 to 23 percent in the year of his death. American, Liggett and Myers, and Lorillard countered with their single brands; Reynolds had become the acknowledged leader in tobacco, forcing others to follow his lead, just as Duke had done with cigarettes in the 1880s and had not been able to do afterward.

Duke died in 1925, having been out of the public limelight for almost a decade and a half, spending much of his time organizing the power company and more of it in setting up Duke University. As so often happens when major if contentious figures die, praises for the man and his accomplish-

[41]William H. Nicholls, *Price Policies in the Cigarette Industry* (Nashville, 1951), p. 36.

ments were published and spoken. What were these accomplishments? The obituaries noted his work in introducing new packaging, promotion, and manufacturing methods in cigarettes, but even his supporters could not find much positive to say in the way of the tobacco trust's work, or indeed why it was formed. Most of the writers spoke glowingly of his work as a "builder of the new South," and his efforts at the university.

The obituaries and speeches were bare of comments on the man himself. Two years later John Jenkins' authorized and sponsored biography of the man appeared. Nowhere in the book is there a word of criticism of Duke, or any indication of flaws in his character or shortness in his vision. Jenkins ended his book by quoting from a statement made by Clinton W. Toms, president of Liggett and Myers, shortly after Duke's death. Clearly he meant this as a definitive statement on Buck Duke.

His power of concentration—his ability to put into any one task his whole power, and then to turn around and do the same thing with another entirely different problem.

His enthusiasm—not the hurrah kind, but the intelligent, forceful expression of a great personality.

His facility of putting emphasis where it belonged, readily discerning between the essential and the nonessential.

His power to inspire men to be something and do something, creating within them a real ambition to succeed. Often by praise and then again by fair and just criticism, even though at times it might be severe, he enabled men to overcome a weakness—and they were grateful to him.

His consideration for men—those who worked under him were always given more than due credit—and his desire that those who tried to do their part should be liberally rewarded.

His big-heartedness—a kind and sympathetic nature.

His love and admiration for his father and mother.

His strong faith—a genuine faith—a firm belief in the Eternal; a strong confidence in the Church and the Christian religion.[42]

These were the qualities of the man, said Toms, who had worked with Duke at American Tobacco. Jenkins appears to have agreed. In other words, Duke's capacity for work in all its forms made him prominent. Ignoring the hyperbole that usually appears in such tributes and reading between the lines, this is what emerges. To his credit, Duke understood this. He could sell tobacco, but not himself.

Duke never made a public speech in his life, and unlike Rockefeller and some of the other tycoons, refused to hire a public relations man to cast him in a better public light. Shortly before his death he explained to a friend what he considered the key to his success, and did so in a way that anticipated Toms' remarks, but was more to the point. "I resolved from the time I was a mere boy to do a big business," he said. "I loved business better than anything else. I worked from early morning until late at night. I was sorry to have to leave off at night and glad when morning came so I could get at it again." "Any young man can succeed if he is willing to apply himself," said Duke on that occasion. "Superior brains are not necessary."[43]

[42]Jenkins, *James B. Duke*, p. 217.
[43]*Ibid.*, pp. 53–54.

VI

Theodore N. Vail:
The Subtle Serendipidist

Few businessmen were as successful as Theodore Vail—
who might properly be considered the founder of American Telephone and Telegraph Company—and fewer still
were able to function as smoothly as he. Yet Vail is a neglected figure, the subject of only one biography, an authorized one written a half century ago. He receives little more
than passing mention in most histories of American business and is ignored in several of the best economic histories
of the United States. Of course, he figures significantly in
the few works on American Telephone that have been
written and published. But the authorized and sponsored
studies fail to discuss some of his more important contributions because of corporate attempts at image-making, while
the others concentrate on the administrator and neglect the
man.

At the time of Vail's death in 1920, American Telephone
had assets of over a billion dollars, and although the firm
was not as large as United States Steel, it had twice the
assets of Standard Oil of New Jersey. Vail was lauded in
obituaries, but his passing was not front-page news, as
would be those of J.P. Morgan, Andrew Carnegie, and John
D. Rockefeller, the men most responsible for the creations
of the other two giant firms.

For most of his business life Vail was an almost anonymous figure, a man who willingly subordinated himself to his creation. He was a businessman who operated in a far more subtle fashion than did Morgan, Rockefeller, Hill, and Duke. All of them saw some of their creations challenged in the courts, and the Standard Oil trust, Northern Securities, and American Tobacco were dissolved, in cases still studied in colleges and law schools. In large part because of Vail's deliberate underplaying of his firm, it survived as a trust, the result of what was known as the "Kingsbury Commitment," a quiet settlement that has never received the attention it merits.

Many European governments operated their own telephone companies during Vail's business career, while others nationalized private lines. Pressure grew in the United States for a similar settlement, and while the nationalizers spoke and wrote of the need for publicly owned utilities, antitrusters demanded the breakup of AT&T. That neither occurred was the result of Vail's activities. He formulated a theory of utility monopoly under private control—one of his successors called AT&T a "publicly owned, privately managed institution"—and convinced political leaders of its soundness. "No government can run a business, and no business can run the government," said Vail in 1912, and he initiated an "educational campaign" to convince the public of the soundness of that principle.

At the time of Vail's first association with telephones, it appeared competing lines might well become the rule. Vail soon developed a concept of a universally interconnected system under single ownership and operation, and sketched a rationale for public utilities that survives to this day. He spoke of the telephone as a "natural monopoly," while in fact the monopoly was contrived, and its development was an accomplishment of major significance that should have earned Vail a more prominent position in business history than he has at present.

Vail's missionary activities were carried on through ad-

dresses, articles, and work with political and financial leaders. He was always prepared to subordinate the means to
the end, and to allow others to lead and take credit when
he might easily have had both. When he left the industry
in 1878 it was not so much due to a frustrated desire for
power but rather because he was not permitted to participate under rules he believed fair and just. He returned to
the firm in 1907, and during the next thirteen years established the quasi-monopoly in such a way that it no longer
is attacked seriously. AT&T is the nation's largest corporation in terms of assets and profits, and second only to General Motors in revenues. The firm's manufacturing subsidiary, Western Electric, has greater sales than either RCA or
Westinghouse and is responsible for more basic research
than both combined. But while antitrusters talk of break-
ing up IBM and General Motors, they barely discuss the
largest trust of them all, one that dominates its market to
a greater extent than either of the other two firms.

Among other things, history is the record of what happened combined with an analysis of the meaning of events.
There are other subjects historians rarely discuss—those
events that *might* have taken place but didn't because of the
work of exceptional individuals. Vail was important for his
work at AT&T—for what he caused to happen. He merits
at least as much credit for what didn't happen in the industry. For example, the telephone company was not destroyed or taken over by a stronger and better-financed
competitor—Western Union—in its early years, and Vail
had a hand in making certain this did not take place. The
company developed long-distance lines through the creation of what amounted to a unitary system, rather than
fitting together many companies as parts of a mosaic, and
this too was a Vail accomplishment. The telephone company survived the end of its patent monopoly. It did not
become a consolidated giant as J.P. Morgan wanted it to be,
in which case it would have become a fine target for antitrusters. Vail cooperated with Morgan and, in fact, was one

of his several satellites. Because he knew how and when to behave himself in regard to the financier, he was given a free hand in AT&T operations, and so created a longer-lived trust than any other, one of the few Morgan creations not brought into the courts under the antitrust acts.

Vail knew when and how to use his power, but more important, when not to. Had he been enamored of expansion for its own sake—as was Duke to a large degree—he might have turned AT&T into a mega-giant. But he prudently refused to enter certain natural expansion areas, and for this he might be criticized as being too cautious. In many things unrelated to AT&T, Vail was a plunger, a man who could not resist investing funds in any invention that caught his eye. Insofar as AT&T was concerned, however, he was cautious. Vail was aware of the limits of his powers under existing laws and customs and accomplished his tasks as noiselessly as possible. Perhaps this is why he has not attracted the attention of more biographers and historians.

In some important ways—and in some trivial ones as well—Vail was a mirror image of Buck Duke, and possessed qualities the tobacco king lacked. Vail was outgoing and open, where Duke was withdrawn and secretive. AT&T was very much an organization and Vail an organization man. American Tobacco was a one-man operation, with all other managers clearly subordinate to the leader. From the beginning, Vail planned what he wanted to accomplish, and he rarely deviated from the pursuit of his goal, as did Duke. Vail understood instinctively how to "get around" people; Duke's style was to plow right through the opposition. Where Duke was brutal in corporate dealings, Vail was sophisticated. Duke would ignore the government; Vail worked well with political leaders, even those who openly stated their intention to destroy AT&T.

Duke spent most of his business life in the tobacco business, turning to electric power and education only after his trust was dismembered. Vail had a checkered career, coming late to telephones, and then leaving the field in 1887 in order to engage in other activities that took him to Latin America and Europe. After that chance and fortune—two forces men like Duke tended to ignore, or tried to control —made it possible for him to re-enter the telephone business. In 1907, Vail returned to AT&T as its president— under Morgan's domination—and he spent the rest of his career with the company. Vail enjoyed life; he hosted many large parties and was a convivial storyteller. Duke was not a social animal, being completely at ease only in corporate headquarters or in the field.

Despite obvious management talents, Duke often lacked the ability to differentiate between important and unimportant issues, considering all problems worthy of his attention. Vail was altogether different. He moved smoothly through corporation headquarters, delegating authority and power, insisting on having a major role in setting strategy, but leaving the tactics to others, men he had carefully trained for such tasks. In writing of Vail's management abilities in 1924, his successor, Harry Thayer, noted that "because Mr. Vail had arranged for the election of a president when he was supposed to be well and vigorous, there was hardly a ripple of anxiety about the administration of the business when he died." Vail molded the presidency of AT&T so that it didn't require superhuman powers and abilities to fill. In this way, Vail made certain he was replaceable, a thought Duke couldn't entertain.

As much as any businessman of his time, Vail created the modern corporation executive style and stance. The line from him to the men in the gray flannel suits of the 1950s and the often anonymous corporation executives of today is clear. Tycoons like Hill, Harriman, Rockefeller, and Duke left no descendants; the makers of conglomerate giants in the 1950s and 1960s were of quite a different stripe, even though there were some surface similarities. The companies they created are headed today by men in the Vail tradition. Hill and Duke strode like lions through the corporate jungles of the early twentieth century. Vail recognized that government was taming the jungle, and adapted to the change. The lions would be extinct when this happened. The Vails of his world would survive.

Vail was born in 1845, near the small Ohio town of Minerva. His family was well-to-do, making its living from a New Jersey iron works the Vails had owned since the early part of the century. Davis Vail, Theodore's father, had taken the family to Ohio shortly before his son was born, and there tried to establish an iron facility of his own. The venture failed, due in part to Davis' lack of business acumen and his easygoing way in selling his wares. He had a large family —Theodore was one of seven children who survived infancy—and enjoyed playing with the children more than working in the foundry.

When Theodore was two years old, Davis returned to New Jersey to manage the family's operation there. From the only account available on Vail's childhood, it would appear he grew to manhood in New Jersey, enjoying his life enormously, resembling his father in most ways. Theodore's grandfather once complained to Davis that the young man was always whistling, and perhaps wasn't as serious about life as he might have been. Davis responded that his son probably wouldn't amount to much—that he would have to support him for the rest of his life. But given Davis' temperament, the fact might not have bothered him too much.[1]

[1] Material regarding Vail's private life may be found in Albert Bigelow Paine, *In One Man's Life* (New York, 1921). This is the only biography of Vail ever written. Fortunately, Paine knew Vail well, and spent many hours interviewing him, both for his own enjoyment and in order to write his book. Paine was a well-known biographer in his day, the author of several popular studies of Mark Twain. He clearly admired and liked Vail, and was not particularly interested in his business career, although it is discussed in his book.

According to his biographer, Vail liked to read, and especially enjoyed the rags-to-riches stories in vogue at the time. He also thought of a career. The iron foundry didn't attract him, while farming appeared boring. At different times in his youth Vail considered the ministry, medicine, and law. Vail toyed with the idea of becoming a scientist, even though he was poor in mathematics, and a wanderlust he shared with his father made him think of exploring as a career. But when he finished high school, Vail found a job as clerk in a drugstore not far from his home.

By chance Vail's job was in a store that also housed a telegraph. The instrument interested him not only for its mechanical intricacy but as an outlet to the rest of the world. Vail later told his biographer that he learned how to send and receive messages, and even constructed one or two instruments of his own. A diary he kept in this period does not mention his interest in telegraphy, however. Instead, it contains entries about his social life, discusses local baseball games—he was an enthusiastic player—and at times his reflections on the Civil War then raging. On several occasions the young Vail set down his resolution to spend his time more profitably. "We must discourage all wastefull slothfull untidy Base Wicked thoughts and actions in ourselves," he wrote. "We must examine ourselves and see if we have lived up to our markings out—if not we must examine wherever we have come amiss and then strive to cease entirely all such."[2] Perhaps Vail saw these flaws in his own character and determined to change. But repeated entries such as these indicate that his determination was not very strong at the time.

At the age of nineteen Vail decided to leave his home. Writing to a relative who worked for the Western Union, he asked for help in getting a job in telegraphy in New York. Whether Vail wanted the job to pursue an interest in that field or just to see the big city is unknown. In any

[2] *Ibid.*, p. 19.

case, he got a job in a telegraph office and moved to the city before his twentieth birthday.

Vail later recalled enjoying his life in New York, working at the telegraph office during the days, going to the saloons and billiard parlors at night with his friends. "Staying up late of nights playing Billiards and drinking lager is not what young men should be doing, and for one I am determined to stop it," he wrote in his diary. "Yes, But how many times have you said the same before and are you stopping it now."[3]

Because he was generally sloppy at his work, Vail was transferred to another office. His career—if it could be called that—was foundering. Actually, Vail was without strong ambition in those days. His chief desire at the time was to own a sable coat and a ruby ring, and not to become an important and successful businessman. So when he learned that his family planned to buy a farm in Waterloo, Iowa, he joined them.

Now Vail tried being a farmer, and although he was strong and good at his tasks, they didn't interest him. So he looked for other work. For a while he preached at prayer meetings, and it appeared Vail would wind up in the ministry after all. He also became a regular at the local pool hall, and threw himself into baseball once spring arrived. Afterward he tried his hand at teaching school. Then he examined the McCormick reaper and thought he could improve upon it and turn out a self-binding harvester. Clearly he was not meant for the farm at that time. "I have had all of that dam' farm I want," he told a friend. "I am going where I can make some money."[4]

In 1868 Vail obtained a job as telegrapher for the Union Pacific at Pinebluff, Wyoming, and he set out for what was then a wild Indian frontier. Now he had a job he liked, but he did not intend to remain there for long. While in the East he had met Emma Righter, and their separation con-

[3] *Ibid.*, p. 22.
[4] *Ibid.*, p. 36.

vinced him they should be married. Not wanting to bring her to the frontier, Vail decided to get a job in a more settled area and then send for her. Once again he wrote to friends of his desire, and they helped him obtain a new position, that of mail clerk in Omaha, Nebraska. Vail traveled east to get married, and then returned to take up his duties.

Vail was fairly happy in his work, but marriage and, later, the birth of a son made him more ambitious. He began studying law at night with a friend, William Connell. Soon after, Connell was elected prosecuting attorney in Omaha. Vail congratulated him, saying, "When you get through with that job, if I can get elected to it, I'll be the happiest man in the world."[5]

Meanwhile, Vail became interested in some aspects of his work. In particular, it seemed to him that the method of delivering and sorting mail was irrational. Each clerk on the railroad would sort through all the mail in the bags, taking those for his line and returning the rest, with the process being repeated at each mail drop. Vail began separating the mail according to drops, and after studying the route carefully, worked out a system by which the mail could be delivered more rapidly and with less effort than was then the case. His work was approved by the superintendent of the railway mail service, and he gave Vail a new job, one with more authority and higher pay. Soon Vail was chief clerk of the Union Pacific division of the mail service, and in February 1873 he was called to Washington as assistant to George Bangs, the new head of the service. Within a year Vail was named assistant general superintendent, and had earned wide recognition within the service for his knowledge of the lines and reform ideas. Vail was now twenty-eight years old, earning $1,600 per year with a liberal traveling allowance. Foreign governments sought his assistance, and he was a rising star in the bureacracy,

[5] *Ibid.*, p. 50.

one clearly destined to head the service within a few years.

Vail was happy and content. He enjoyed family life, lived in a large house, and had a convivial circle of friends. And he spent money lavishly, not only on food and wine but in investments in new inventions, most of which never worked. Vail was constantly in debt, borrowing from one friend at interest rates of from 12 to 18 percent to pay off old debts, and then renegotiating once more. He had little trouble borrowing money; Vail always paid on time or at least was able to renew his obligations, clearly was a man of his word, and one who quickly put people at their ease and earned their confidence.[6] His circle of friends widened; Vail's ambitions grew as his appetite for spending was whetted. For a while he spoke of running for governor of Nebraska, and there was some talk of his becoming postmaster general, even though that office was usually a political plum reserved for influential party backers. He did become general superintendent of the mail service in 1876, with an increase in salary (and expenses) and a chance to put his ideas into practice and deal with important national figures.

Vail served in his post for two years, hardly long enough to remake the service in his own image but sufficient to make an impression on Washington political leaders and eastern businessmen. He had hoped to create an integrated, effective mail service, one in which the mail would travel swiftly from sender to receiver, without too much concern on whose railroad it traveled. But the railroad managers were interested in this, and throughout this period Vail fought them bitterly, especially W.H. Vanderbilt of the New York Central. When Vail entered into a contract with the rival Pennsylvania Railroad, Vanderbilt objected, and warned that he would "throw off every sack of mail from our trains" unless the contract was altered. In the end this and similar clashes were resolved, but in the process Vail

[6] *Ibid.*, p. 70.

came to understand that the nation had railroads, but not a railroad system. It would have been far more sensible, he thought, to have a single line operating all the tracks, so that goods could be shipped more effectively and cheaply than was the case at the time.

He also learned that in order to negotiate with government and business officials, it was sometimes necessary to grease a few palms. At one point he met with a senator concerned with a bill to provide funds for the department. "Mr. Vail, I have every reason to believe I can get that bill of yours through, and I shall be glad to do so, increasing the amount somewhat if the railroads will agree to allow me a ten per cent commission on the sum available." Vail knew such kickbacks were common during that corrupt period. As he told his biographer, he believed the needs of the mail service were more important than the questionable ethics of entering such an arrangement. Vail agreed to relay the offer to the railroads. The bill went through.[7]

Vail was thirty-three years old in 1878, and could consider himself a success by most standards. He had gone from job to job in a rapid fashion, always rising as he went. Now he was considered the nation's leading expert on mail delivery, but it was also a dead-end position; there seemed no chance of rising higher in the department or, for that matter, in the federal bureaucracy. "I am not going to stay in the postal service," he told a friend. "I shall keep an eye open for something there is more to than anything in a government department." He had much to offer a private concern. Vail had established himself as a generalist who through work and intelligence could become a specialist in a short period of time. He had a variety of interests but was most concerned with communication and transportation. Vail understood how the federal bureaucracy—the largest in the nation—operated. He understood the many ways used to get things done, and was pliable in his operations.

[7] *Ibid.*, pp. 85–86.

In his personal life Vail clearly liked money, and knew how to borrow when necessary; he could do the same for a business needing capital. His mail experience had convinced him national systems were needed in transportation and communication. All of these qualities were needed at the Bell Telephone Company.

The telephone industry had barely started when Vail became associated with it. Alexander Graham Bell had filed an application for a telephone patent on February 14, 1876, and almost immediately was embroiled in conflicting claims and law suits. Even today it is not certain that Bell's device was the first telephone. Experiments with inventions similar to his had been going on for years. Some said that Daniel Drawbaugh, an American, transmitted sound over a "variable resistance device" as early as 1860. Three years before, Philipp Reis, a German inventor, wrote about his successful experiments with a telephone. Antonio Mucci had his defenders, who claimed that while in Havana in 1849 or 1850 he demonstrated a telephone-like device. On the same day that Bell filed for his patent, the noted American inventor Elisha Gray filed a "caveat" at the Patent Office claiming he had developed "a new art of transmitting vocal sounds telegraphically." And there were others.[8]

Bell, a teacher of the deaf, spent a good deal of his time during the next few years demonstrating his invention and arguing with rival claimants while still teaching in Boston. Some of his rivals challenged Bell to dual displays, somewhat in the fashion of the reaper field trials of pre-Civil War days. Gray, his most serious competitor, conceded that Bell was the first to demonstrate a machine, but insisted that he had perfected a laboratory model earlier. The law-

[8]Silvanus P. Thompson, *Philipp Reis: Inventor of the Telephone* (London, 1883); Warren J. Harder, *Daniel Drawbaugh, the Edison of the Cumberland Valley* (Philadelphia, 1960); Frederick L. Rhodes, *Beginnings of Telephony* (New York, 1929), pp. 49–75.

suits and squabbles regarding patents were among the most important concerns of the "Bell interests" at the time.

The other was the organization of a firm to exploit the new invention, and this was the contribution of two of Bell's associates. While working on his invention in 1874, Bell met Thomas Sanders, a prosperous leather merchant whose son was one of Bell's students. Sanders agreed to provide the inventor with funds in return for which he would receive a share in the patents if and when they were granted. About this time Bell took on another pupil, Mabel Hubbard, whose father, Gardiner G. Hubbard, was a wealthy lawyer. Hubbard had brought gas lines to Boston and later on helped develop the water and trolley utilities for the city. Hubbard had many interests—he dabbled in politics, was a regent of the Smithsonian Institution and founder of the National Geographic Society. He was also intrigued by the telegraph, and during a period in which he spent time in Washington explored the possibility of entering the field, perhaps in competition with the Western Union Telegraph Company. On learning of Bell's work, Hubbard began to meet with the inventor. Soon after, he too helped finance the experiments, and organized an informal firm known as the Bell Patent Association. Bell married Mabel Hubbard in 1877, by which time Gardiner Hubbard had become the *de facto* spokesman for the Association.

Hubbard helped stage Bell's demonstrations, hoping they would stimulate interest in the invention. At the time, however, neither he nor Bell appeared to have a clear idea of how they would be sold, and for what purpose. Both men were convinced the telephone was superior to the telegraph. It didn't require a skilled operator, few telegraphers could relay messages as rapidly as the human voice could speak, and the Bell telephone was less expensive than the telegraphs, since it didn't require batteries or costly machinery.

How would the service operate? The telephone pioneers

had a model in Western Union. Telegraphers were situated in stations, to which customers went to send messages. These would be received on the other end of the wire, and then were carried by messenger to the recipient. Whether or not Bell or Hubbard considered the establishment of telephone offices of this kind is unknown, but such a model would have made sense. At the time, Western Union was capitalized at $40 million, and even this amount seemed astronomical to the Association. With such money a start toward the station development could have been made. Bell had other ideas, which reflected his lack of financial knowledge as well as his poor understanding of management problems. He spoke in 1878 of telephone lines, either buried or overhead, that would enter into every home and place of business in the nation. The local lines would be gathered at local offices, and these interconnected through main cables to other locals. In this way, any two people in the nation could speak with one another whenever they wished. Bell later wrote of all Americans talking on telephones at the same time, singing songs in unison, and the like.[9]

Hubbard was interested in practical matters. For example, would the telephones be sold or rented? Hubbard had been an attorney for a shoe machine company that rented its machines and collected royalties for every pair of shoes turned out. He would bring that same principle to the telephone. Hubbard also knew from his studies of Western Union of the vast amount of capital required to establish a system, and realized he could not possibly hope to raise that much—even if the Bell patents held. So he formulated a more modest strategy, one that would require a smaller amount of money than the grandiose Bell scheme. Hubbard wanted to sell franchises to local telephone companies, which would use the Bell patents and pay royalties to the Association and its successors. These locally owned

[9]Horace Coon, *American Tel & Tel: The Story of a Great Monopoly* (New York, 1939), p. 32.

companies would raise capital on their own and, hopefully, purchase equipment from the mother company too. At the same time, Hubbard would develop business in his own part of the country, renting as many telephones as he could and then forming a separate company to sell stock to friends and subscribers, with the pledge of liberal dividends. In effect, Hubbard wanted to go in two directions simultaneously, and there seemed no reason why this could not be done. Hubbard cared little for interconnections between companies and the national system; he wanted to survive, and this required a beginning somewhere. In fact, even this modest plan almost was abandoned. With Bell's agreement, Hubbard offered to sell the Bell patents to Western Union for a reported $100,000. The offer was refused.[10]

In April 1877, Charles Williams, Jr., of Massachusetts, contracted for a line from his Boston factory to his home in Somerville. Other, similar, lines followed, and within a year there were almost 800 in operation, all of which were two-party connections. E.T. Holmes, the son of the inventor of the burglar alarm, linked several banks to his office by telephone in what was more a party line than a true exchange, but this was an exception to the rule. The telephone was still a curiosity more than anything else. Bell's associate and member of the group, Thomas A. Watson, put together the devices and hired men to string wire. In early 1878 he supervised the establishment of a public exchange in New Haven, Connecticut, and others were on order.[11]

In July 1877, Hubbard organized the Bell Telephone Company, with all its shares in the hands of the founders or their relatives. Then, in February 1878, he formed the New England Telephone Company, which was to concen-

[10]N.R. Danielian, *A.T. & T.: The Story of Industrial Conquest* (New York, 1939), p. 10.

[11]J. Warren Stehman, *The Financial History of the American Telephone and Telegraph Company* (New York, 1925), pp. 7–8.

trate on developing the business in that part of the country. Five months later the Bell Telephone Company received a new charter, and shares were sold to a group of interested investors, most of whom were Boston aristocrats and some the descendants of men who had worked with Francis Cabot Lowell almost a century before.

Just before the restructuring was completed, Western Union entered the picture. Its subsidiary, the Gold and Stock Telegraph Company, was losing business to the telephone. At the same time, Hubbard had sold some franchises, and new telephone companies were developing throughout the East and Midwest. Deciding the telephone was more than a toy and in order both to protect itself and dominate a new area, Western Union organized the American Speaking Telephone Company as a subsidiary of Gold and Stock. The new firm obtained the Gray patents as well as several owned by Amos E. Dolbear. Then it commissioned Thomas Alva Edison to develop a new device, one superior to any then in use. Speaking Telephone, backed by Western Union's financial power and organization, established rival exchanges in territories sold by Bell to franchisees and went into areas Bell hadn't yet developed. It appeared Bell would soon fall to its larger rival. Thomas Sanders was now convinced the end was near. Writing in February 1878, he lamented:

> How on earth can we make our position better by fighting when we have nothing to fight with? . . . The W.U. has frightened everyone connected with us, directly or indirectly. My business has suffered, that is, my notes have been thrust onto the market at a high rate from the feeling that I am largely interested in a shaky concern, and it will require all the money advanced to the Bell Tel. Co. to take care of the business to which it belongs.

Sanders noted that the company was close to insolvency. "I must stop the manufacture of telephones if some arrangement is not made by which we can pay for them." He told Hubbard that the failure was through no fault of his. "No doubt you have done the best that you could, but I do not think you fitted by your education and training for the work required."[12]

Hubbard responded that he had confidence in the company. He advised Sanders to sell his leather business and put all his funds into Bell Telephone, a suggestion he gave to others. But Hubbard was a poor administrator and, fortunately for the company, he knew it. He had done a poor job with the franchisees, awarding territories to men and syndicates that lacked experience, ability, and sufficient funds. Bell Telephone needed a manager who could supervise the entire operation and at the same time lead a counterattack against Western Union. Hubbard had shown he could not do the first, and he didn't know how to handle the second. He felt Vail was the man for both tasks.

Hubbard had met Vail in Washington a few years before. At the time he showed the Superintendent a pair of telephones, and Vail was taken by them, as he was with so many mechanical devices. Later on, Vail had telephones installed in his Washington home, and he invested in Bell and urged his friends to do the same. This was not unusual; Vail put his money and borrowed funds into several chancy ventures during this period. Hubbard and Vail became close friends. They shared interests and ideas, and clearly could work together.

Bell Telephone needed a manager, while Vail was seeking a way out of what he believed to be a dead-end job. In addition, he was angered when Congress seemed about to

[12]Paine, *One Man's Life*, pp. 104–5.

cut down on his expense allowance. After Vail met with others at the company, he was offered the job of general manager at a salary of $3,500 a year, $1,500 less than what the government was paying him. He accepted, to the chagrin of his congressional friends. In his rather stilted letter of acceptance, he said: "My faith in the success of the enterprise is such that I am willing to trust to it, and I have confidence that we shall establish the harmony and cooperation that is essential to the success of an enterprise of this kind."[13]

The initiation of the negotiations with Vail was one of Hubbard's last duties as president. Even before Vail arrived to take his post, the Boston interests reunited New England Telephone and Bell Telephone to form a new company, National Bell Telephone, which was capitalized at $850,000, with 8,500 shares at $10 par value each. The old stockholders received 6,500 of these shares, while the rest were to be sold to any who would buy them. In recognition of the need for new money and the growing power of the Boston financiers, one of their number, William Murray Forbes, was elected president in Hubbard's place. The Forbeses were one of the most distinguished families in Boston, if not among the wealthiest at that time. The family had interests in shipping, railroads, and banking. Some of Forbes' closest friends ran Lee, Higginson and Company, one of Boston's most aggressive and respected investment banks, and Forbes had other friends at R.L. Day and Company, Estabrook and Company, and Kidder, Peabody. National Bell would need money for its expansion plans and to finance its struggle against rivals in the field. The Boston investment banks would provide this capital, but only if one of their number were in charge. The replacement of Hubbard by Forbes was accomplished smoothly, but in late 1879 it was evident that the investment banks, and not the old Bell-Hubbard

[13]Herbert N. Casson, *The History of the Telephone* (Chicago, 1910), pp. 61–62.

family alliance, controlled the administration.[14]

Vail was supposed to take office on July 1, 1879, but during the previous week he met with Hubbard, Forbes, and other Boston figures to discuss strategy. He then went to New York to talk with officers of the Bell Telephone Company franchise there. These two meetings convinced him the New York operation, a key one to the company, had to be revamped. Vail also understood the meaning of Forbes's election. Even then he had ambitions to run the company, and not remain as general manager. To do this he would need financial backers. Forbes already had the Boston group, and at the time Boston was the leading marketer of industrial securities in the nation, with New York in second place. By taking charge of New York Telephone, and situating himself close to Wall Street, Vail may have been seeking financial support there to buttress any future attempt at independence he may have had in mind.

The struggle against Western Union was more important at the moment, however, for if that company became the leader in telephonic communication, power at National Bell—short of cash and dispirited as the firm was at the time—would have been worthless. Vail went to Menlo Park to meet with Edison. He returned with the inventor's assurance that he accepted Bell as the inventor of the telephone. But he also learned that Edison was perfecting a superior model for use at the Speaking Telephone Company.[15] That firm's parent, Western Union, had pushed ahead vigorously in the field, seeking to destroy the Bell interests. In September 1878, Bell sued Western Union for patent infringements, and at the time it appeared the larger company might win the case and so disarm its young rival.

In May 1879, however, a struggle in the telegraph industry eclipsed the telephone fight, working to Bell's advantage. Jay Gould, fresh from successes on Wall Street, decided to either replace Western Union or take it over from

[14]Arthur S. Pier, *Forbes: Telephone Pioneer* (New York, 1953), pp. 199 ff.
[15]Paine, *One Man's Life*, pp. 115–16.

the Vanderbilts, who then controlled the firm. He organized the American Union Telegraph Company to attack Western Union in the field, and at the same time began purchases of shares in Bell telephone companies, indicating he would merge them into American Union in time to create a broad-based communications firm. This placed National Bell in a strange position, between two of the major business forces in the land, each with an interest in obtaining its goodwill. What Gould tried to accomplish through stock purchases, the Vanderbilts did by approaching National Bell with a settlement offer, which was accepted in November 1879. Under the terms of an agreement worked out by Forbes, Hubbard, and Vail, Western Union agreed to withdraw from the telephone business and sell its properties in that area to National Bell. In return, Western Union would receive 20 percent of Bell's license fees. It would pay 20 percent of the costs of developing new Bell patents as well, and Bell promised not to enter the telegraph business, a clear blow to Gould.[16]

News of the settlement caused the price of National Bell stock to rise to over $1,000 a share. Now the company had clear sailing in the telephone field, and in addition had added the 56,000 Western Union telephones in fifty-five cities to its holdings.[17] But the agreement seemed minor at the time, a sideline to the greater Vanderbilt–Gould struggle for telegraphs, one that Gould won in 1880 when he took control of the Western Union.

Vail helped direct strategy against Western Union during his first months in office, but he spent even more time restructuring field operations. Anticipating a Western Union victory, several franchisees and employees adopted a conservative policy regarding expansion, and a few talked of withdrawing from the company. Vail attempted to revive their spirits. In letters to franchisees he noted that Western Union, though a large firm, had an inferior posi-

[16]Danielian, *A.T. & T.*, pp. 42–43.
[17]Coon, *American Tel & Tel*, p. 59.

tion in telephones. National Bell owned most of the significant patents and had a larger field force. "If it [Western Union] was all massed in your one city you might well fear it; but it is represented there by one man only, and he has probably as much as he can attend to outside of the telephone." In words that might have been drawn from the novels he read as a boy, Vail concluded: "We must organize companies with sufficient vitality to carry on a fight, as it is simply useless to get a company started that will succumb to the first bit of opposition it may encounter."[18]

The settlement of the Western Union suit, together with the revamping of field operations and the company's clear intention to expand rapidly, made it easy for National Bell to sell stock. In order to broaden its base, the firm underwent still another transformation in April 1880, when it received a charter to become the American Bell Telephone Company and was authorized to issue $10 million in stock. National Bell's stockholders received six shares of the new issue for each one they held, which accounted for $5,950,000 of the capitalization.[19] The rest of the stock was to be sold to the public through the underwriters associated with Forbes and his group. Forbes remained president, while Vail continued on as general manager. In effect, Forbes set policy and made important decisions, while Vail was supposed to carry them out.

The two men had quite different personalities. Forbes was quiet, somewhat withdrawn, and a brahmin to the core, while Vail was aggressive and clearly plebian. Forbes considered himself a spokesman for his group, one that didn't include Vail, whom he tended to consider as an important employee, but not a member of management. Vail recognized this and must have resented his exclusion from the inner circle, where men who understood telephones less

[18]Paine, *One Man's Life*, p. 126.
[19]Stehman, *Financial History*, pp. 20–21.

216

than he did had the power. For the time being, he said nothing to contradict the Forbes policies, perhaps hoping to become accepted into the inner circle, or awaiting the time when he could mount a challenge to it.

In practice, Forbes and Vail shared many convictions regarding the future of the company. Both men realized that, for the present at least, American Bell's power rested with its patents. These would run out in time, and they prepared for the period when the company's earnings would come from other sources. Forbes issued licenses to local business groups, which in effect were five-year contracts allowing them to use Bell patents and purchase Bell equipment on the understanding they would develop their areas and, in return, issue from 30 to 50 percent of their stock to the parent company and pay fees. Forbes thought that "By pursuing this plan the company will gradually acquire a large permanent interest in the telephone business throughout the country, so that [it] will not be dependent upon royalties when the patents shall have expired."[20] In other words, Forbes tended to view American Bell as a firm that would exchange its patents for equity in operating companies, which would be managed for the most part by franchisees. Both Forbes and Vail hoped that, in time, several or perhaps most of these firms would come under the control of American Bell.

They differed on how this might come about. Forbes insisted the operating companies pay large dividends, much of which would go to American Bell. That firm then could initiate a liberal dividend policy of its own, which would reward the Bostonians who had invested in its shares. The rest of the money would be used for research and to purchase additional shares of operating companies, to the point where these would be dominated by the parent firm. Forbes would not replace local managers—he believed they should remain in order to maintain goodwill in

[20]Coon, *American Tel & Tel*, pp. 62–63.

HISTORICAL CHART OF THE PARENT
ORGANIZATIONS OF THE BELL SYSTEM

BELL PATENT ASSOCIATION
(Feb. 27, 1875—July 9, 1877)

BELL TELEPHONE COMPANY
(Massachusetts Association)
Articles Signed—July 9, 1877

Active Existence	Stock Outstanding
July 1877	5,000 Shares
July 1878	5,000 Shares

NEW ENGLAND TELEPHONE COMPANY		BELL TELEPHONE COMPANY	
(Massachusetts Corporation)		(Massachusetts Corporation)	
Incorporated—February 12, 1878		Incorporated—July 30, 1878	
Active Existence	Stock Outstanding	Active Existence	Stock Outstanding
Feb. 1878	2,000 Shares	July 1878	4,500 Shares
Mar. 1879	2,000 Shares	Mar. 1879	4,500 Shares

NATIONAL BELL TELEPHONE COMPANY
(Massachusetts Corporation)
Incorporated—March 13, 1879

Active Existence	Stock Outstanding
Mar. 1879	7,250 Shares
May 1880	8,500 Shares

AMERICAN BELL TELEPHONE COMPANY
(Massachusetts Corporation)
Incorporated—April 17, 1880

Active Existence	Stock Outstanding
May 1880	73,500 Shares*
May 1900	258,863 Shares

AMERICAN TELEPHONE AND TELEGRAPH COMPANY
(New York Corporation)
Incorporated—March 3, 1885
Subsidiary of American Bell Telephone Company 1885–1899
Acquired Assets of American Bell Telephone Company Dec. 30, 1899
Publicly Owned, 1900 to Date

Stock Outstanding	Dec. 31, 1900	569,901 Shares
	Dec. 31, 1935	18,662,275 Shares

Legend: Transfer of Assets
            Licensee Company

Note: All stock is $100 par.
    *Includes 14,000 shares of trustee stock held by National Bell Telephone Company

SOURCE: United States, Federal Communications Commission, Proposed Report: Telephone Investigation (Pursuant to Public Resolution No. 8, 74th Congress) (Washington, 1938), p. 6

the communities served by operating firms. Rather, he would coordinate affairs from Boston, administering what amounted to a confederated corporation.

Vail had a different, more ambitious, program, which looked to federation or unitary control. He would maintain equity positions in the operating companies but encourage them to pay small dividends, retaining most of their earnings for expansion. By the time the patents ran out, he said, the Bell companies should be so large and powerful that no rival would dare oppose them in their territories. American Bell should concentrate on connections between the systems and create long-distance services without which the local firms could not grow beyond a certain point. Then the parent firm would charge the locals for the service and, in this way, dominate them even though not owning controlling interest in their operations.

The two men were in substantial agreement on most other matters. Both supported research in order to produce better instruments and obtain new patents. Forbes and Vail agreed that it would be best to place telephone cables underground, among other reasons so that the public would not become too aware of American Bell's power by seeing masses of wires overhead. Vail supported Forbes' 1882 agreement with Western Electric Company, a cross-licensing arrangement under which each company could use each other's patents at cost. Western Electric, which had been formed in 1869 by Elisha Gray and others, was a major supplier of telephones and other equipment to both the telegraph and telephone industries. Forbes would have been content with the agreement as it stood. But Vail, ever the expansionist, pursuaded him to approve the purchase of Western Electric stock as well, and for $1 million American Bell obtained a controlling interest in the firm.

American Bell was a successful company by any measure of performance. Total assets reached $60 million in 1885 and

[21]Stehman, *Financial History*, pp. 20–29.

revenues that year were $10 million, with 330,000 tele-
phones in operation and an average of 755,000 conversations
daily.[22] Dividends from franchisees, only $11,000 in 1881,
rose to $597,000 by 1885. As Forbes dictated, American Bell
paid liberal dividends. An initial payment of $3.50 a share
was made in 1880 and was raised in each of the next five
years, reaching $16.00 in 1885.[23] And all the while, Vail
complained the firm was short of expansion capital.

Under the terms of the 1880 reorganization, New York
Telephone became part of the parent firm. Vail had to
move to Boston, where he was close to but not part of the
firm's inner circle. He received salary increases and his
dividends made him a moderately wealthy man. Vail lived
well, purchasing a large house and entertaining lavishly.
But he lacked power, as the Forbes group either ignored
him or refused to allow him added responsibilities.

Since the Bostonians were not particularly interested in
long-distance operations, Vail concentrated on this aspect
of the business, where he had a free hand. In 1884 he completed a line from Boston to New York which proved
profitable, and he planned new connections between Bell
systems. Now the firm decided to establish a separate company to handle that part of the business, with Vail as its
president. This gave him the authority he so clearly
wanted, but at the same time divorced him from American
Bell affairs. The long-distance company, called American
Telephone and Telegraph, was incorporated in New York
in 1885. Its entire initial capital was $100,000, owned by
American Bell. Vail had to resign from the mother company to accept the assignment. As American Bell put it,
"Mr. Vail, feeling that a due regard for his health required
relief from the arduous duties of General Manager, resigned that position." He was replaced by John E. Hudson,
American Bell's attorney, a classics scholar, and a man
whose ancestors had settled in Massachusetts in the eigh-

[22]Danielian, *A.T. & T.*, p. 15; Stehman, *Financial History*, p. 72.
[23]Stehman, *Financial History*, p. 70.

teenth century. Vail would head his own organization from New York, far from the seat of power, almost as though in exile. His company was small, but the Bostonians, perhaps writing in the tradition of New England humor, gave AT&T a charge that was impossible of realization given its capital and the technology of the times. According to Vail's instructions, his firm was:

> To connect one or more points in each and every city, town, or place in the State of New York, with one or more points in each and every other city, town, or place in said State, and in each and every other of the United States, and in Canada, and Mexico; and each and every of said cities, towns, and places is to be connected with each and every other city, town, or place in said States and countries, and also by cable and other appropriate means with the rest of the known world.[24a]

During the next two years Vail did extend service to Albany and several other places in the region, but the long-distance program was never well capitalized and did not have a high priority with American Bell's management. Vail also worked to replace New York City's telephone poles with underground cables, and this task occupied more of his working time than any other. In fact, given the firm's capital, Vail had little to do except direct a handful of associates in their tasks. He spent an increasing amount of time at his Vermont home in Lyndonville, and sought out other businesses in which to invest, doing so by telephone from the front porch at Speedwell Farms. Vail may have tired of the telephone business at this time; certainly he must have realized he had no real hope of advancement within the organization, while AT&T would never fulfill its mandate without proper financing. He and Forbes got

[24a]Casson, *History of the Telephone,* pp. 174–75.

along well enough, and in fact one of Forbes' horses provided stud service for a Vail mare. But Forbes gave no indication that Vail would be called back to Boston for a higher position.

On July 8, 1887, Forbes wrote to R.B. Minturn, one of his American Bell associates: "I am about retiring from the presidency of the American Bell Telephone Company, as I have given as many years to it as I am willing to. It is proposed to put Howard Stockton in my place." Shortly thereafter Forbes submitted his resignation and Stockton, a man who had little to do with the company and was president of the First National Bank of Boston, succeeded him. This change in management must have discouraged Vail; it was proof he would forever be in the background at American Bell. He resigned from AT&T in September and, as expected, his place there was taken by Hudson, who two years earlier had succeeded Vail as general manager.[24b]

Vail did not leave AT&T without business plans. Since 1886 he had been involved in a scheme to create an underground steam facility for Boston. He had invested $150,000 in the Boston Heating Company, and shortly after leaving AT&T added another $100,000 worth of stock to his holdings. In the spring of 1888 Vail went to London to sell shares there, and he traveled through Europe, combining work and vacation. But the Boston Heating venture failed, due for the most part to technological deficiencies, and Vail lost his investment. Vail's venture in an ostrich farm—typical of the imaginative though harebrained schemes he sometimes became involved in—also failed, and according to one story, all Vail got from it was one dinner with friends, in which they ate an ostrich egg.

By 1880 the once-substantial Vail fortune had shrunken considerably. Vail sold his yacht and his house in Boston, as well as several valuable paintings. He went to Vermont to live, expanding Speedwell Farms and acting the role of

[24b]Pier, *Forbes*, p. 181; Paine, *In One Man's Life*, p. 181.

a country squire. He still had dividends from American Bell stock to tide him over, and an investment in the Consolidated Subway System paid a decent dividend. Then the Pelican and Dives mine, a defunct operation Vail had once invested in, reopened, and Vail's net worth increased. Fairly wealthy once more, Vail added to his land holdings in Lyndonville, renovated his house, began breeding livestock, and for the first time seemed serious about retirement. He was not yet fifty, and despite several illnesses was a vigorous man. Vail thought of spending summers in Vermont and winters in Europe. He had more than enough money for such a life. And he pursued it for almost four years.

In the summer of 1894 Walter Davis, an American astronomer who worked in the Argentine, visited Speedwell Farms. He told Vail of the economic growth of that nation, and of an option he owned on the water and electrical concessions in the city of Cordoba. Davis was in the United States seeking capital. He had learned of Vail's interest in investments and hoped to bring him into the plan.

Vail was intrigued. Soon after, he sailed for Buenos Aires to investigate the Davis proposal. Within days he became enthusiastic about developing power for the Cordoba region, and also a transportation system for Buenos Aires. Vail put most of his money in these investments, and both proved successful. He spent summers in Vermont during the next few years and in September would set out for the Argentine to spend winters (summers in that part of the world) in Buenos Aires. It was not only a pleasant way to live, but a profitable one.

Vail retained his shares in American Bell throughout this period and showed an interest in the company's fortunes. The company continued to expand and prosper and, as the ruling Bostonians insisted upon, paid large dividends. Stockton continued the Forbes policies, and when he resigned in 1889 and was replaced by Hudson the situation remained the same. By 1895 American Bell had assets of over $120 million and revenues of $24 million. Dividends from franchised companies rose to well over $2.5 million that year. Clearly the company was a financial and operating success.[25]

But it did have problems, those that Vail anticipated before he left the firm and which Forbes had ignored. In the first place, it was chronically short of capital for expansion and had to sell additional equity in order to obtain it. Some of this money might have come from retained earnings, had the Bostonians been willing to forgo dividends, which they were not. These peaked at $18.00 in 1888, and then declined to $15.00 in steps to 1894. American Bell stock sold in a range of 163–208¼ that year, so the return to investors was over 9 percent for those who bought in at the low, and over 7 percent for those who purchased stock at the high.[26] This return was comparable to that obtainable in industrial stocks, and it may have been that the directors felt this should be the case. In addition, a liberal dividend might have been considered necessary in order to assure bondholders of the company's solvency. But the state of Massachusetts, in which American Bell was incorporated, took another view of the situation, and refused to allow American Bell to increase its capital stock to $50 million from $20 million and then sell it in order to obtain additional funds. The state took the position that the company was in a public service area and intimated that it was not behaving as such a corporation should. In addition, American Bell was accused by some legislators of engaging in stock watering.

By using loopholes in the law, the company managed to increase its capitalization to almost $26 million and sell the additional stock. But troubles with the legislature persisted, and in 1899 the company resolved them by merging American Bell into American Telephone and Telegraph, which was incorporated in New York, and operating

[25]Stehman, *Financial History*, p. 28; Danielian, *A.T. &T.*, p. 15.
[26]Stehman, *Financial History*, pp. 72–73.

through that firm instead, even though the management remained in Boston.[27]

The expiration of the company's basic patents in 1894 represented an even more serious problem. Vail had hoped that by then the franchisees would be so strong and well entrenched that they could withstand competition. Some were in this position, but most were not. While they enjoyed a monopoly status the franchisees prospered, but they did not improve service significantly or reduce charges so as to attract all potential clients in their areas. Nor were the companies as close to their customers as Forbes had hoped they would be. Public relations deteriorated under Hubbard, so that in addition to attacks by antitrusters, American Bell was criticized by local newspapers as being an alien influence in the communities served by the franchisees.

As a result, independent telephone companies were formed to compete with the Bell operations, and in some communities mutual firms made appearances, the latter being viewed as a first step in the direction of public ownership. In 1894 there were only seven mutuals; there were 295 in operation by 1902.[28]

The mutuals and independents realized that cooperation between them was necessary not only to present a united front against American Bell but to provide long-distance services between their stations. They held a convention in Fort Wayne in 1897, and formed the National Association of Independent Telephone Exchanges, considered by some the first step in the establishment of a rival to American Bell itself. Of course, most of the independents and mutuals were poorly capitalized and used inferior equipment. But given sufficient backing, they could pose a serious threat to the older organization. The independents were

27 *Ibid.*, pp. 59–61.
28 *Ibid.*, p. 54.

particularly successful in the Midwest, and in fact the further one got from Boston, the greater was their power.[29]

The obvious success of telephony also attracted major capitalists to the field, with plans either to replace American Bell as the major force in the industry or take it over. P.A.B. Widener and others of the group that was then in the process of challenging James Duke at American Tobacco decided to take on American Bell. In November 1899, the group formed the Telephone, Telegraph and Cable Company of America, capitalized at $30 million and controlled by Widener and his friends. George Brady and William C. Whitney, the New York traction kings associated with J.P. Morgan, were in the syndicate, along with Thomas Dolan and H.E. Gawtry, who were on the periphery of the Rockefeller constellation. The new firm held a controlling block of shares in the Erie Telegraph and Telephone Company, a major property with a dominant position in seven states. Erie had expanded rapidly, and as a result was chronically short of capital. The syndicate planned to use Erie as a base, acquire other telephone companies in similar situations, and rapidly make Telephone, Telegraph and Cable a major concern.

Less than a month later Widener and his circle withdrew from the new company. All the plans were now forgotten, and the new company's activities were suspended. At first the collapse was a mystery. Then it was learned that Widener withdrew after learning that Whitney planned to leave the syndicate. This was a sign that Morgan was prepared to enter the communications picture, and would do so on his own, and not through a firm that included Widener and had strong Rockefeller participation.

Morgan believed that the consolidation of American industry into large trusts was natural and beneficial to all. Competition brought waste and disruptions, not progress and order, and he saw the choice in that light. He had done

[29]Coon, *American Tel & Tel*, pp. 85–87.

what he could to "harmonize" the nation's railroads, and was about to bring order to the steel industry through the creation of United States Steel. Morgan also proposed to create a large communications company, one that would end the bickering between rivals that he felt was harmful to the business community.

There were four large forces in private communications: AT&T, the independent telephone companies, Western Union, and the Postal Telegraph Company, a holding operation that was second only to Western Union in size. Western Union was still under the control of the Goulds, and Morgan meant to ignore it for the time being. He would not attempt to consolidate and take over the independents, an unwieldy task to say the least. Rather, Morgan hoped to unite AT&T and Postal Telegraph to create a communications giant that would crush the independent telephone companies and then take over the Western Union.

The first step would be to seize AT&T from the Boston group. Morgan felt the firm had been badly mismanaged, and that it would not be a difficult task.[30] The company had poor public relations, was in constant need of additional capital, and as a result of dilutions, the Bostonians controlled only 5 percent of the common stock.

Hudson died in 1900, and the AT&T board sought a new leader while Alexander Cochrane, one of its number, served as interim president. A measure of the group's fears regarding a Morgan takeover may be seen in its overtures to Vail, who, had he so desired, could have had the presidency that year. He showed no interest in the feelers from Boston, however. Vail said he was too busy with his Argentine ventures to undertake a new assignment, but he must have considered that if he returned under these circumstances, he would not have a free hand. Besides, the Bostonians still clung to the Forbes pattern of high dividends and confederation.

[30]Danielian, *A.T. & T.*, pp. 47–48.

Vail's views of the future of the company were more in line with Morgan's. He knew Morgan from his days at the old American Telephone and Telegraph Company, and they respected one another. Sometime in this period the two men must have met, with Morgan offering Vail the AT&T presidency if and when he took command at the firm. In any case, Vail became a Morgan man in 1900. That year Vail met with John Mackay, the mining tycoon who also controlled Postal Telegraph, and spoke of the desirability of closer relations between that firm and AT&T sometime in the future. John Waterbury, the president of the Manhattan Trust Company and another Morgan satellite, also met with Mackay on the matter, and it appears some kind of arrangement was about to be worked out at the time of Mackay's death in 1902, at which time his son, Clarence, took over at Postal Telegraph.

Cochrane stepped down from the AT&T presidency in 1901, and was succeeded by Frederick Perry Fish, a brahmin like the others. Fish was affiliated with Lee, Higginson and had friends at Kidder, Peabody, the company's two largest investment bankers. Both were fearful of losing underwritings if and when Morgan took command, and so they backed Fish in the hope he would be able to secure the business for them. With their support, the new president attempted to improve public relations and set the company's financial affairs in order. AT&T continued to expand, a sign of success, but one that indicated difficulties in raising capital were looming. To further complicate matters, Fish acquired the assets of the short-lived Telephone, Telegraph and Cable Company in 1901, and with it the equity position in Erie Telegraph. That company was in even more desperate need of new capital than AT&T, and the Boston investment bankers couldn't handle the job.

T. Jefferson Coolidge offered help at this time, not only in the financing but in serving as a bridge between the New York and Boston groups. Coolidge was president of the Old Colony Trust Company of Boston, an institution close to

AT&T, which had Fish on its board. He was an old Morgan ally as well. With Morgan's support, Coolidge began purchasing Erie Telegraph shares on the open market. Then he approached Fish with an offer to take up some of that firm's obligations if AT&T agreed. The brahmins realized they were facing insolvency; the telephone operations could no longer be financed entirely in the Boston market. Help would be needed, even if this meant the Bostonians had to concede leadership to New York. The details of what followed are unknown, but the settlement became evident in the next few months and years. Old Colony helped reorganize Erie Telegraph through Kidder, Peabody, and in the end Erie Telegraph became a wholly owned subsidiary of AT&T. Soon after, George F. Baker, head of the First National Bank and a major Morgan ally, purchased a block of 50,000 shares of AT&T. Then he and Waterbury were named to the company's board. That same year Theodore Vail also joined the board, a sign that the transfer of power from Boston to New York had begun. In the future Morgan would lead the underwritings for AT&T securities, but the Bostonians would remain on the board, while Kidder, Peabody and Lee, Higginson would handle distributions for the syndicate in New England. In this way, the AT&T world was resliced, a prelude—so it was believed—to the merger with Postal Telegraph.

Vail believed himself in line for the presidency of the new communications giant, if and when it was formed. He had the support of Coolidge and Waterbury, and was close to others in the Morgan group. But he had a rival. Clarence Mackay, now the president of Postal Telegraph, agreed to the merger in the belief that his company would take over AT&T, with himself as president of the combined communications firm. Finally, the Bostonians were not yet prepared to bow. Fish remained president of AT&T and insisted on the right to veto any plan the other two forces agreed upon. The telephone company continued to expand under his leadership even while the struggle for power and organization raged.

Although always informed of events in New York and Boston, Vail remained far from the scene, content to allow Waterbury and Coolidge to represent his interests. His work in Buenos Aires went well and Vail also traveled to Europe frequently, not only making contacts for his Argentine operations but renewing contacts with those bankers there interested in AT&T securities. His wife died in 1905, and his only child the following year. Vail was devoted to both, and for a while withdrew from business entirely, allowing his South American partners to handle the work. He sought new interests, and some friends suggested he might consider a political career, running for senator or governor of Vermont. Vail rejected these suggestions and spent a good deal of time on his farm, brooding over the future.

As he did this, the communications war continued. Mackay and Coolidge had a falling out, one that culminated in Mackay's refusal to participate in an AT&T underwriting. Coolidge and Waterbury resigned as trustees of several Mackay companies in 1903 and turned their attention to Western Union, hoping to merge that firm with AT&T. Fish opposed the plan, which in any case was not acceptable to the Gould interests. He realized that the Bostonians would be squeezed out if any merger transpired.

While this maneuvering went on, Morgan formed a syndicate to market a $150 million bond issue for AT&T. This was a very large offering at the time, and would have been difficult to sell in the best of circumstances. The problems were compounded by a tight money situation, and the syndicate was obliged to hold on to many of the bonds, not completing the distribution until 1909. But by holding them, the Morgan syndicate had effective control of AT&T, since it retained all rights inherent in the paper while it was in its hands.

Mackay understood the meaning of the flotation, but prepared to reenter the picture. He began purchasing AT&T stock on the open market until he owned some 5 percent of the equity and was the largest single stockholder. Mackay approached Fish in March 1906, asking for representation on the board. Now Fish found himself between the giant forces of the Morgan interests and Mackay, having little leverage with either. Mackay demanded Vail step down and be replaced with one of his nominees. Vail refused, saying he owned shares of his own, and in any case represented all the stockholders and no single one in particular. Mackay persisted, and his attitude served to solidify the Coolidge–Waterbury–Vail alliance and move it to action.

In January 1907, Waterbury traveled to Boston to meet with Fish. He suggested that AT&T was in need of restructuring, and that the executive committee should appoint a special committee to prepare for changes. Fish knew what this meant but could do nothing to prevent it. The committee was named, and included Waterbury, Coolidge, Baker, W. Murray Crane, and Vail—all Morgan men. The business of the company went on, with Fish reelected president on March 26. Then the special committee recommended its work be taken over by a refashioned executive committee. Fish did what he had to. Cochrane and C.W. Amory—Bostonians—resigned from the board, with Vail and Waterbury taking their places. Two weeks later Fish resigned, effective May 1, 1907. Then the executive committee selected Vail as his replacement.[31]

Years later Vail indicated that he really didn't want the job. When he spoke with his sister of the AT&T offer, she urged him to reject it. "No, I must take it," was his supposed reply. "I refused it six years ago; I am in a position to take it now. Besides, now they need me." Like so many other of the Vail statements, this echoed the Horatio Alger

[31] *Ibid.*, pp. 57–66; Coon, *American Tel & Tel*, pp. 93–99.

hero. On the other hand, Vail prepared for the offer by selling his Argentine interests to a European syndicate for $3 million, after several months of negotiations.[32]

Vail's return was hailed by the press. He was called one of the telephone industry's pioneers, but in terms that made him appear more a relic than a viable businessman. Vail was sixty-two years old in 1907, sometimes sick, and absent from participation in American affairs for years. It was generally assumed Vail would be Morgan's man at the company, accepting dictates from Wall Street, while carrying on the day-by-day operations at the firm. In other words, Vail was general manager once more, with the Morgan bankers acting as Forbes did a generation earlier.

This was not the case, or at least is a gross exaggeration and misunderstanding of Vail, Morgan, and the development of American business since Vail had been at AT&T's predecessor in 1887. Vail had left American Bell when his direct attempt at winning the presidency failed. Twenty years later his more subtle approach, as part of a team, succeeded. The difference between these two paths is significant. In the first instance, Vail acted as any capitalist might have in the age of the entrepreneur in industrial America, when the company was viewed as an extension of the man. This had changed by 1907, by which time the man served the company, especially in the giant corporations. Vail knew that Morgan had many interests, and would not interfere with him at AT&T. In addition, it was clear that he and Morgan agreed on fundamentals; if this were not so, Morgan would not have supported him for as long as he did. The investment banker would place his men on the AT&T board and would have a major say in financing. Both Vail and Morgan understood this, and they had few differences in the years that followed. That their ideas were

[32]Paine, *One Man's Life*, pp. 221, 230.

similar was evident in Vail's 1907 report to stockholders, in which he echoed Morgan's ideas regarding order and efficiency:

> The strength of the Bell System lies in its universality. It affords facilities to the public beyond those possible on other lines. It carries with it also the obligation to occupy and develop the whole field. . . . Two exchange systems in the same community, each serving the same members, cannot be conceived of as a permanency, nor can the service in either be furnished at any material reduction because of competition, if return on investment and proper maintenance be taken into account. Duplication of plant is a waste to the investor. Duplication of charges is a waste to the user.[33]

Vail had a single objective in all he did as president of AT&T, although his tactics took different forms. He wanted to transform the firm into the only significant force in telephone and telegraph communications in America. This giant firm would be on good terms with its customers, offering them better service and lower rates than its competitors. In other words, it would not behave like a monopoly even though it would become one. Vail constantly pressed to lower charges and did all in his power, including subsidizing historians to write favorable studies of the company, to maintain public goodwill. His monopoly would be self-sufficient, not only providing communications but producing equipment. His would be a vertical as well as horizontal monopoly.

This program required huge sums of money, and Vail realized that he would have to work closely with Morgan in order to get it. At the same time, he intended to maintain the old dividend policy. In fact, in 1907 he raised the payout

[33] *Annual Report, 1907.*

from 1906's $7.75 a share to $8.00. But he would go no further; the dividend remained stable as long as Vail was president. Vail felt that a steady dividend policy, in bad as well
as good years, would attract investors. He believed that
many small stockholders and people who had never owned
shares before would purchase American Telephone shares
and retain them for lifetimes, even handing them down to
their children as though heirlooms. Broad ownership
would protect AT&T against corporate raiders. It would
also support his publicity program geared to make the telephone company appear a good neighbor; each stockholder
would be a *de facto* AT&T publicity person in his locality.
Broad ownership would also assist the company in with-
standing the government antitrusters, who by 1907 appeared to be gaining power.

Shortly after Vail took command he received a communication from Morgan and Company. "We consider it
of vital consequence to the financial welfare of the Company that no expenditures should be entered upon in the
near future, except such as are absolutely necessary, no
matter what the prospective profits on other expenditures
may be—the credit of the Company being of paramount
importance."[34] Vail responded by firing 12,000 employees
at Western Electric and reorganizing that company so as to
make it more efficient. Centralized control was introduced
in the manufacturing area, and Western Electric was permitted to sell equipment to independent lines for the first
time. After the period of financial stringency passed in
1909, however, Vail began to move ahead with his expansion plans. That year AT&T purchased a large block of
Western Union shares, enough to give it a 30 percent interest in the company and working control. In 1915 Western
Electric was recapitalized and reincorporated, with AT&T
controlling almost all the stock. Vail also had the company
purchase all of Mackay's stock when it came on the market

[34]Danielian, *A.T. & T.*, p. 72.

in 1909. Then he enbarked on a program to take over the independents.

This campaign, one that Vail continued throughout his presidency, was carried on in several ways, all of them indirect. By improving service and lowering costs, he discouraged new independents from entering Bell territories. Whenever possible he would purchase shares of independent firms, consolidating his power over them in this fashion. Through Morgan, Vail was able to discourage the New York investment community from underwriting stock and bond issues for the independents. AT&T tried to prevent independent companies from obtaining linkages with its wires, in this way making their services less attractive to customers. When state agencies stepped in to prevent such actions, AT&T moved slowly to make connections, and even more so to repair breaks in services. The corporation prevented the Peoples Telephone Company from using subways for wiring underground cables, and employed similar tactics elsewhere.

The most common device against the independents was lower rates and better service. Given the choice between AT&T-affiliate low rates and good service on the one hand, and the independents' higher rates and often indifferent service on the other, most subscribers chose AT&T.

The campaign showed results. From 1902 to 1907, the number of independent telephones in operation rose from 1 million to almost 3 million, a more rapid increase than AT&T's 1.3 million to 3 million. Then, in the first five years of Vail's leadership, AT&T subscribers and stations rose to over 5 million, while the independents went to only 3.6 million.[35]

Although Vail could be ruthless in campaigns to eliminate the opposition, he rarely insisted upon unconditional surrender or complete victory. When a company conceded defeat, he would either purchase controlling interest in the

[35]Stehman, *Financial History*, p. 127.

AT&T Operating Affiliates on January 1, 1910, and Amounts Pledged
to Secure Bonds

Name of Company.	Stock Outstanding. $	Owned by American Tel. & Tel. Co. $	P. C. Owned.	Amount Pledged. $
Bell Telephone Co. of Canada, Ltd.	12,500,000	4,822,400	39	986,000
Bell Telephone Co. of Missouri	8,788,000	5,831,800	65	5,826,600
*Bell Telephone Co. of Pennsylvania	41,550,000	28,647,700	69	28,647,700
*Central District & Printing Teleg. Co.	13,000,000	8,694,500	67	8,694,500
Central Union Telephone Co.	5,450,927.50	4,375,173.33	80	
Chicago Telephone Co.	27,000,000	14,049,600	52	
Cincinnati & Suburban Bell Telep. Co.	7,058,050	2,118,000	30	2,029,550
Cleveland Telephone Co.	3,100,000	700,000	23	697,000
Colorado Telephone Co.	8,500,000	4,363,900	49	4,361,100
Cumberland Telephone & Telegraph Co.	19,680,150	10,508,400	53	
Iowa Telephone Co., Preferred	932,450	932,225	100	
Iowa Telephone Co., Common	1,263,625	321,770	26	
Missouri & Kansas Telephone Co.	3,627,700	1,944,200	54	1,939,500
Nebraska Telephone Co.	4,637,200	3,330,616.67	72	3,323,100
New England Telephone & Telegraph Co.	39,161,500	22,888,700	58	20,803,700
New York Telephone Co.	85,672,800	85,672,800	100	
Northwestern Telephone Exchange Co.	6,000,000	1,074,800	18	1,069,800
Pacific Telephone & Telegraph Co., Preferred	18,000,000	9,027,200	50	
Pacific Telephone & Telegraph Co., Common	18,000,000	9,027,200	50	
Pioneer Telephone & Telegraph Co.	4,522,700	4,094,400	91	
Providence Telephone Co.	3,000,000	900,000	30	899,250
Rocky Mountain Bell Telephone Co.	2,369,500	1,205,400	51	1,171,300

Southern Bell Telephone & Telegraph Co.	21,400,000	21,394,300	100	13,815,000
Southern New England Telephone Co.	7,693,700	2,554,900	32	2,553,100
Southwestern Telephone & Telegraph Co.	14,000,000	2,296,300	16	2,292,800
Western Electric Co.	15,000,000	12,047,700	80	
Western Electric Telephone System	1,000,000	510,000	51	
Western Telephone & Telegraph Co., Preferred	16,000,000	12,187,600	76	
Western Telephone & Telegraph Co., Common	16,000,000	9,143,500	57	
Wisconsin Telephone Co.	9,012,000	1,515,300	17	1,511,600
Miscellaneous		354,400		

SOURCE: *Moody's Industrial Manual, 1911*, p. 1008.

firm at a price above current market quotations, or offer to exchange AT&T shares for those of the subdued competitor. To placate community leaders, he would agree to give local governments a portion of the affiliate's operating profits, in this way making certain the political authorities had a stake in the company's future. Often the old management remained; few individuals lost jobs when AT&T took over. It was through actions such as these that Vail believed the universal communications empire would be realized.

Vail's successes in eliminating competitors and acquiring control of operating independents led to demands that AT&T be broken up under the terms of the Sherman Anti-Trust Act. Some reformers began to speak seriously of nationalizing the entire telephone and telegraph industry. This was the case in most of Europe, and in 1912 Great Britain nationalized its system. Vail met these challenges by slowing down his acquisitions program. At the same time, he became an advocate of public service commissions, realizing that an oblique approach—one in which AT&T came out in favor of regulation—would be more effective than outright opposition to all government interference.

Addressing AT&T's stockholders in the 1913 annual report, Vail said, "We are opposed to government ownership because we know that no government-owned system in the world is giving as cheap and efficient service as the American public is getting from all its telephone companies. We do not believe our government would be any exception to the rule."[36] This was true only insofar as long-distance rates were concerned, however, for at that time most Europeans paid less per local call than most Americans.[37] In an article in the *Atlantic Monthly* in March 1913, Vail argued that competition in telephones would result in higher costs for the subscriber because low charges were only possible if the system contained all potential users. As had become his practice, Vail was conciliatory toward his opponents, and refrained from using old Social Darwinist slogans and arguments as did other trust magnates of the period. "All utilities are dependent not only upon the public for support," he wrote, "but upon the public good-will and favor, in that, from the public or its representatives, they must have franchises or permits under which they can operate." Nor can this permit be absolute. "It must be admitted that regulation and control by commission has become a permanent feature of our economic policy, particularly as to utilities. That being so, it is essential for the well-being of the community that such regulation and control should be effective, equitable, acceptable to the public, and final."[38] Vail spoke out for a "regulated monopoly" in telephones and telegraphs. He was praised by some as a far-sighted, enlightened businessman. Such individuals might not have considered that, given the political climate of the times, the only alternative to regulation was dissolution or nationalization.

[36] Coon, *American Tel & Tel*, p. 139.
[37] A.N. Holcombe, *Public Ownership of Telephones on the Continent of Europe* (Cambridge, 1911) esp. p. 412 ff.
[38] Theodore N. Vail, "Public Utilities and Public Policy," *Atlantic Monthly* (Vol. III, March, 1913), pp. 309–11.

AT&T: Selected Financial Statistics, 1885–1920

Year ended Dec. 31	Revenues	Net earnings	Net income	Dividends paid	Undis- tributed net income
1885	$10,033,600	$4,909,300	$4,881,600	$3,107,200	$1,774,400
1890	16,212,100	7,144,500	6,865,800	4,101,300	2,764,500
1895	24,197,200	8,708,800	8,053,300	5,066,900	2,986,400
1900	46,385,600	15,753,200	13,363,600	7,893,500	5,470,100
1905	97,500,100	31,310,700	25,474,400	15,817,500	9,656,900
1910	165,612,881	50,994,408	39,437,544	25,160,786	14,276,758
1915	239,909,649	66,181,757	48,086,114	32,897,065	15,189,049
1920	458,140,556	79,509,168	47,785,065	39,999,579	7,785,486

SOURCE: *FCC: Telephone Investigation*, p. 49.

AT&T: Statistics of Growth, 1885–1920

As of Dec. 31	Total Bell-owned stations	Total miles of wire	Total cen- tral offices	Total num- ber of em- ployees	Total pay- roll	Average daily total conversations
1885	155,751	155,791	1,165	5,766	—	755,742
1890	227,857	331,642	1,241	8,740	—	1,444,161
1895	309,502	675,415	1,613	14,699	—	2,402,543
1900	835,911	1,961,801	2,775	37,067	—	5,817,514
1905	2,284,587	5,779,918	4,532	89,661	—	13,911,551
1910	3,933,056	11,642,212	4,933	121,310	—	22,284,010
1915	5,968,110	18,505,545	5,300	156,294	$99,454,302	26,002,829
1920	8,333,979	25,377,404	5,702	231,316	263,729,030	33,162,600

As of Dec. 31	Total assets	Telephone plant	Long-term debt	Surplus and reserves
1885	$60,081,500	$38,618,600	$367,400	$18,866,000
1890	84,102,200	58,512,400	7,796,100	29,212,200
1895	120,385,000	87,858,500	12,074,100	44,710,200
1900	230,225,900	180,699,800	51,137,900	35,497,800
1905	452,716,100	368,065,300	128,079,500	63,698,000
1910	753,323,720	610,999,964	267,358,639	119,598,526
1915	1,057,907,703	880,068,520	355,641,384	223,401,663
1920	1,634,249,533	1,363,826,327	595,924,216	444,039,203

SOURCE: *FCC: Telephone Investigation*, pp. 49, 53.

AT&T: Financial Statistics, 1900–1920

Year	Average number of shares outstanding	Recorded net income	Bell Telephone System net income available (Per share)	Dividends paid (Per share)
1900	543,813	$8.82	$12.30	$7.50
1901	673,337	9.68	12.84	7.50
1902	877,921	9.80	12.55	7.50
1903	1,149,220	9.90	11.81	7.50
1904	1,306,549	8.18	10.42	7.50
1905	1,315,514	9.43	12.20	7.50
1906	1,315,514	9.52	11.94	7.75
1907	1,367,956	11.16	14.00	8.00
1908	1,557,395	10.99	13.55	8.00
1909	2,129,535	10.38	13.39	8.00
1910	2,597,103	9.90	12.48	8.00
1911	2,771,181	9.56	11.63	8.00
1912	3,251,948	9.86	12.13	8.00
1913	3,431,755	9.59	11.29	8.00
1914	3,446,584	9.38	10.88	8.00
1915	3,637,574	9.52	12.07	8.00
1916	3,890,273	9.77	13.46	8.00
1917	4,060,202	9.48	11.28	8.00
1918	4,403,712	9.97	9.50	8.00
1919	4,419,542	10.05	9.25	8.00
1920	4,422,099	11.72	9.32	8.00

SOURCE: *FCC: Telephone Investigation*, p. 601.

The public clamor against the company continued. The independents pressed President William Howard Taft's Attorney General, George Wickersham, to initiate antitrust actions, and were joined by Clarence Mackay, who claimed AT&T was destroying his Postal Telegraph Company. Taft lost the 1912 Presidential election to Woodrow Wilson, known for his anti-big-business pronouncements. On January 3, 1913, two months before Taft would leave office, Wickersham indicated that AT&T might indeed be in violation of antitrust laws in regard to certain of its acquisitions. But he did not begin a prosecution, feeling perhaps that this should be the task of his successor.

Vail did not wait. He ordered one of his vice presidents, N.C. Kingsbury, to meet with Wickersham to work out a settlement, one that would avoid an antitrust action. This settlement, released in December and called the "Kingsbury Commitment," stated that AT&T would dispose of its holdings in Western Union, restrict its acquisition of independent telephone companies that competed with its licensees, and cooperate with independents in connecting them to Bell lines. The Western Union divestiture took place three months later, and resulted in a loss of $7.5 million for AT&T. In addition, the company ended plans to take over several midwestern telephone operations, compensating Morgan and Company almost $2.5 million for its work in handling the acquisitions. AT&T did not say it would cease acquiring noncompeting lines, and this work continued.[39]

The Kingsbury settlement was hailed by businessmen as a sign that AT&T was a responsible corporate citizen, and that Vail had proven himself an enlightened entrepreneur. Skeptics noted that the settlement headed off an antitrust suit, one that AT&T would almost certainly have lost, in which case the company might have suffered the fate of American Tobacco or Standard Oil. Nor did the Kingsbury Commitment mention Western Electric, a far more valuable and profitable property than Western Union, and one that dominated its field. In effect, Vail had sacrificed a calf to save the herd, once again proving his sophistication in the ways of business and government, his subtlety and calculated caution. "I saw the moon over my right shoulder once, with a beautiful star in it, making a perfect star and crescent. Perhaps that was good luck," Vail once confided to his biographer. He was not a superstitious man, but wasn't taking chances. "I don't believe in ghosts, but I am afraid of them."[40]

Talk of nationalization continued, however. Maryland

[39]F.C.C., *Telephone Investigation*, pp. 115–17.
[40]Paine, *One Man's Life*, p. 302.

Congressman David Lewis became the leader of the movement, and Wilson's Postmaster General, Albert Burleson, came to agree with him. Late in 1913 Burleson noted that the Constitution provided for federal control of the postal system, and from this he deduced that if telephones had existed in the late eighteenth century, the founding fathers might have added that means of communication as well. Vail responded forcefully against such arguments, charging as he had in the past that government control would destroy what he considered the finest telephone system in the world. Besides, what would be gained by nationalization? The telephone companies were quasi-public as it was, since "all surplus is returned to the public in reduction of rates or is set aside for depreciation."[41] The AT&T dividend, stable since 1907, buttressed Vail's argument. The company's stockholders had not benefited from increased earnings, he noted, but instead the public had received better service and ever lower costs.

AT&T was a natural target for antitrusters. Vail's successes in taking over Western Union, draining business from Postal Telegraph, and engulfing the independents made that corporation more powerful than it had ever been. Furthermore, he did this during a period when the antitrust movement was at its apogee—the Taft administration brought forty-four indictments under the Sherman Anti-Trust Act, including several directed against Morgan-dominated firms. Even with the Kingsbury Commitment, AT&T might well have been indicted had not President Wilson's attentions been diverted from domestic affairs by the coming of war in Europe. After 1914, there were few federal indictments under the Sherman and Clayton acts.

At first Wilson was determined that the United States should remain neutral in the war. The Morgans felt other-

41Coon, *American Tel & Tel*, p. 144.

wise, supporting the Allied cause and leading a large Wall Street contingent which felt as they did. Morgan and Company was particularly interested in floating British loans in the United States, and informed presidents of companies it dominated that they would be expected to use corporate funds to purchase the bonds. Henry Davison, a senior Morgan partner, wrote to Vail in August 1916. "Aside from being very gratifying to us, it also would be very helpful to the general cause if you could see your way clear to buy say $5,000,000 of the new British Two Year Loan." Vail tried to stall, but on November 2 he received a note from Thomas W. Lamont, whose position at Morgan's was higher even than Davison's, saying a decision would be needed soon. More than a generation before, when Vail was at the postal service, he had been told by a congressman that his bill would pass if a kickback was arranged. The Davison and Lamont letters were different, but the principle was similar. Vail continued to put the matter off, but in the end, Morgan floated a $80 million bond issue for AT&T, and $20 million of this went into the British bonds.[42]

There was talk of America's entering the war in early 1917. Prior to that time, those who favored nationalization argued that all utilities should be owned and managed by government for the public good and not private profits. Such individuals were among the more extreme elements of the reform movement, and Vail had little trouble marshaling support against them. The situation was different in 1917. If war came, so the argument went, the entire nation would have to be mobilized in the effort, and this would require government operation of the telephones. Those railroaders who protested were branded unpatriotic, and Vail had no intention of joining with them. Government controls might be necessary, he thought, but he would make certain the men who ran the firm prior to war would continue to do so if the nation entered

[42]Danielian, *A.T. & T.*, pp. 77–80.

the struggle, even if they wore uniforms.

Vail offered his cooperation to the Council of National Defense in March. "These are emergency times and it has been a great pleasure for me to be of service in bringing together the telegraph and telephone interests of the nation to serve the government's needs," he said. "We are all co-operating with the Council of National Defense to the best of our ability and myself and my associates on this commit-tee stand ready to do anything and everything that the army and navy or any other government departments may require of us."[43]

The company was prepared, then, when in July 1918 Post-master General Burleson—still an advocate of government ownership of telephone companies—took over at AT&T. The financial and business press protested, viewing the action as a prelude to nationalization. Vail remained calm, and offered Burleson his full cooperation. Burleson ac-cepted, and throughout the war the government-AT&T partnership worked well, usually to the benefit of the com-pany. The government set the rates but underwrote all deficits and at the same time allowed the company to raise charges when necessary. As one historian put it, "The gov-ernment was left with a deficit whereas the Bell System derived benefit in increased rates."[44]

Vail was seventy-three years old in 1918, still president of the company but prepared to turn operations over to a successor. There were several men ambitious for the post, but two were obvious candidates: Harry B. Thayer, for eleven years head of Western Electric; and Union N. Be-thell, the first vice-president of AT&T, who had been the company's prime contact with Burleson during the war. Both were close to Vail and shared his beliefs; each could be counted upon to continue his policies. But Bethell was more aggressive than Thayer, whose interests were more in technology than management.

Vail favored Thayer, and as a result he was named to the

[43]Paine, *One Man's Life*, p. 310.
[44]Coon, *American Tel & Tel*, p. 154.

presidency in June 1919, with Vail becoming chairman of the board. Bethell, now in a position similar to that of Vail in the 1880s, requested retirement, which was granted in 1920.

Vail may have wanted Thayer as president because he knew he wouldn't occupy the post for long and would turn it over to another Vail man. For several years Vail had been close to Walter S. Gifford, who had joined the company in 1904 at the age of eighteen, after graduating from Harvard in three years. Gifford moved up the corporate ladder rapidly, and during the war he served as executive director of the Council of National Defense. He returned to AT&T in November 1918 and was named comptroller of the company. Gifford was only thirty-three years old in 1919 and fresh from government service. He needed time to convince the other executives that he could handle the presidency and at the same time develop better relations at J.P. Morgan and Company. It went according to plan. Gifford became a director of AT&T in February 1922 and the following year was named executive vice-president. On January 20, 1925, Thayer moved into the chairmanship, with Gifford becoming president.[45] In this way, Vail assured a continuity at the company, something Duke, Hill, and other tycoons had either failed to do or accomplished not as well. Gifford was his surrogate son, and when Vail died on April 16, 1920, Gifford was well on the road to the presidency.

The nation's newspapers praised Vail in their obituaries. Bell had invented the telephone, they said, but Vail had made it a practical success. "He brought near the era and the scheme under which any individual in any place may consider himself at the center of nation-wide communication," wrote the *Boston News Bureau*. The *Boston Transcript*

[45]Danielian, *A.T. & T.*, pp. 80–83.

called him "a living, breathing, acting, and thinking expression of 'Yankee Gumption.' " "The telegraph and telephone needed a Vail as they needed a Morse, a Bell," said the *New York Times.*[46]

In terms of his proclaimed goals, Vail was an undoubted success. At the time of his death AT&T was a thriving concern, a quasi-monopoly which had come to terms with both the government and the public. Vail had not succeeded in creating a unitary communications monopoly, but, in practice, the nation was well on the way to realizing one. The independents would remain, and in time AT&T would work in harmony with them, in much the same fashion as the whale lives with smaller animals in the sea. Western Union was on its own, but clearly would be no threat to AT&T in the field of communications.

Of course, Vail had to pay a price for this achievement. One was the alliance with Morgan, and later on with other investment bankers. More important, however, was prudence in expansion, the willingness to throttle down the company, a sophisticated caution, which Duke and other major tycoons could not or would not master, and which in the end led to the dissolutions of their trusts. Vail realized that AT&T would have to refrain from entering some fields, and he made certain this was so. Finally, he inculcated the idea in those in management positions at the firm. Thayer accepted it, and so did Gifford, who remained the major power at AT&T until his death in 1966.

This prudence must have come hard to a person of such wide-ranging interests as Vail. The man who invested large sums of money in strange, out-of-the-way inventions, stuck to his strategy at AT&T throughout his tenure in office. It bore results, to be sure, but it also meant the firm would have to forego opportunities in new technology areas not directly related to telephones in order to maintain a low profile for the Justice Department's Anti-Trust Division.

[46]"Theodore N. Vail: Whose Folly Is His Monument," *Literary Digest* (Vol. 65, May 15, 1920), pp. 76–87.

Nowhere was this more obvious than at Western Electric. Vail had endorsed the takeover of that company so as to have a captive source of telephone and related equipment. By the time of his death, however, Western Electric was not only a giant in its own right but one of the most advanced if not the major research company in the nation. In 1924 Western Electric spun off Bell Telephone Laboratories, and together and separately these two operations, both controlled by AT&T, developed basic inventions in the fields of radio, motion pictures, television, computers, and other advanced technology areas. AT&T did not enter these fields, leaving them for others to exploit, and this usually through licenses to use Bell inventions. At one time or another AT&T might have become the dominant force in all of these industries, and on each occasion, it held back, leaving the field to RCA, IBM, and General Electric, among others. This too was the price to be paid for a quasi-monopoly in telephones. Vail's successors were willing to forgo adventures to retain what they had. Whether Vail the serendipidist would have done the same is another matter.

VII

Marcus Loew:
An Artist in Spite of Himself

Despite their legendary restlessness and the myth of the western magnet, most Americans of the 1880s traveled little more than thirty or forty miles from their places of birth. Their horizons were being broadened, however, for if they did not move into the larger world, technology and commerce would bring that world to them. In addition to their economic functions, this was a major result of the introduction of the railroad and the telephone.

From the first, the railroad was more a carrier of goods than people, a corporate and commercial vehicle rather than one for personal use. Similarly, the first telephones were instruments for businessmen and curiosities installed by the fairly well-to-do. It took decades before the long-distance trains were proletarianized, for even though they were used to carry immigrants from the eastern seaports to their places of employment, settled Americans didn't use them for long-distance travel until later on. The telephone, which didn't require its user to relocate, became a fixture more rapidly. In 1896 there were fewer than six per thousand population; by 1914 there was more than one telephone for every ten Americans. Both inventions and industries had major impacts on the lives of the general population; the telephone's was more obvious in everyday life, while the railroad's was indirect for the most part.

The pace of industrial development and change quickened in the twentieth century, an era of proletarian technology and sociological upheaval. In 1890, for example, almost twice as many Americans lived in rural as in urban areas. John Wanamaker was postmaster general and Theodore Vail lived in semiretirement, dabbling in ostrich farms, steam generation, and new inventions. James Hill's Great Northern Railway and Buck Duke's American Tobacco trust were formed that year. John C. Frémont, who in 1856 had been the first Republican Presidential nominee, died in New York at the age of seventy-seven in July. Dwight Eisenhower, the last American President to be born in the nineteenth century, arrived three months later in Denison, Texas, and would live to the age of seventy-nine.

Together the lives of Frémont and Eisenhower span a period from 1813 to 1969. Francis Cabot Lowell's Boston Manufacturing Company was incorporated in the year of Frémont's birth. Space travel was a reality at the time of Eisenhower's death.

The nation industrialized during Frémont's lifetime, with the pace quickening toward its end. Industrialization affected the lives of most Americans, to be sure, but in rural places and small towns the changes were more quantitative than qualitative. Technology may have begun to transform the general environment, but it had less of an impact on the specific. News traveled more rapidly in 1890 than in 1813, though newspapers carried the same kinds of stories. Home illumination was better, but there was still little to do in the evenings in the way of amusement. People went to bed early. Church socials were major events. Communication and transportation between distant places were better than at any previous time in history, but most Americans did little communicating with any but their immediate neighbors. The national horizon had expanded; the personal horizon was widening slowly, if at all.[1]

[1] The impact of the quickened pace on one town can be found in Michael Lesy, *Wisconsin Death Trip* (New York, 1973).

The situation was changing, and in a qualitative fashion. The pace of urbanization quickened, with the population of the cities increasing at four times the rate of the countryside. Children of farmers, and the farmers themselves, relocated to cities, where there were greater economic opportunities than in rural America. An uprooting process was at work in the 1890s and after. By 1910 one out of every four native-born Americans lived in a state other than that in which he had been born. Ten years later the census showed that, for the first time in the national history, more Americans lived in urban than in rural areas.

Not all of these urban Americans were native-born. Indeed, many cities resembled foreign enclaves. In 1890 some 455,000 immigrants arrived in America, and most remained in eastern cities. Over 1.2 million arrived in 1907, the peak year for the New Immigration. The 1910 census showed that 13.5 million of the 92 million Americans had been born in other lands. One could cross Manhattan Island from river to river, or from the Battery to Thirty-fourth Street, without hearing a word of English. Half of Manhattan's population was foreign born, a statistic matched by Boston, Buffalo, Cleveland, Chicago, and Detroit. Fall River, Holyoke, and Lawrence, Massachusetts, had over 60 percent foreign-born residents.

Some claimed that America's future would be found in the cities. And these were populated by uprooted native born Americans and the non-English speakers from central and southern Europe. The prospect frightened many. William Allen White, considered an enlightened moderate, wrote *The Old Order Changeth* in 1910, in which he said, "We are separated by two oceans from the inferior races," and hoped the oceans would be able to keep most of the potential newcomers where they were. Theodore Roosevelt worried about the dilution of Anglo-Saxon blood; Robert LaFollette saw immorality in the cities and blamed it on the newcomers and the effects of the squalid living conditions of native-born relocated farmers. Prohibitionists said the foreigners were drunkards; businessmen clearly would not accept the exotics into their ranks.

Urbanization, the New Immigration, the quickening of technological progress, developments in business organization—these were some of the forces at work in the world Frémont left and into which Eisenhower had been born. The vitality and momentum of nineteenth-century business would be combined with these newer forces and the mixture would radically alter the daily lives of most Americans in the twentieth century, and above all, change their ideas about themselves and their world. Eisenhower would witness the coming of aviation and space travel, the atomic bomb and the computer. More important, he lived at a time when the inexpensive automobile enabled Americans to travel long distances on their own, when the telephone became ubiquitous, and he was alive at the birth of motion pictures, radio, and television. Societal change and technological developments made these new industries possible. Immigrants in large cities, especially those ambitious for success but unable to enter the established industries and professions, were drawn to the new ones. Prejudice combined with the American Dream enabled the immigrants to take command of the communications and information industries of the twentieth century at the time of their creations. Ironically, in an age of communications and information, the means for both—and the industries that control them—came under the domination of immigrants, people despised by many native-born Americans, who feared they would change the national character. This they would do, but in the process they would try to reinforce the old ethics, not destroy them.

The motion picture industry predated radio and television. It helped create the mass market for radio and provided it with technical and artistic talent and assistance. Later on, despite the opposition of industry leaders, motion pictures did the same for television. In this respect, motion pictures and the industry itself were the progenitors of twentieth-century mass entertainment and communication.

Yet the men who created the industry have never received the kind of serious attention they merit, a situation that is in striking contrast to that other great twentieth-century industry, automobiles. There are more scholarly works available on Henry Ford and his company than on all the movie magnates combined.

Part of the reason for this is the unavailability of material, much of which has been destroyed or simply lost. Also, the motion picture industry is not particularly proud of its founders, of their ethics, standards, and moralities. Thomas Alva Edison, the man credited with developing motion picture technology, is a hero; others who turned that technology into the basis for a giant industry are treated in a frivolous manner, ignored, or subjected to exposés rather than scholarly respect.

There are other reasons for this neglect. The movies were business, but also—and perhaps to most more importantly—art. It was the art that interested the public, not the work behind the scenes, especially in the front offices. And the same has been true of writers on the subject, who have concentrated on actors and actresses, producers and directors, and appeared to have considered the movie tycoons as necessary evils and even philistines. This is understandable, perhaps. After all, we have many biographies of great novelists, but few of their publishers.

The development of the industry proceeded rapidly, and after early attempts at creating a giant motion picture trust failed, it fractured into several fields—with production, technology, and distribution separate at first, and each in the hands of many different competitors. No single individual emerged to dominate the entire industry, as Carnegie did in steel, Rockefeller in petroleum, and Ford in automobiles. Marcus Loew and Adolph Zukor created major entertainment empires, and either man might have served as a symbol for the industry. Yet neither has been the subject of a serious full-scale biography. In other words, the motion picture business does not have a single human symbol, one that has been admired or attacked, or even seriously debated.

Instead we have a composite of several men, and as a result a caricature, one with elements of truth but much exaggeration. To outsiders, the movie moguls seemed carbon copies of one another. Most had been born in central or eastern Europe, or in American ghettos soon after their parents arrived. Almost all were uneducated Jews, who, if they didn't have accents, spoke with Yiddish cadences. As a group they were short and stocky, wore flashy clothes, and smoked large cigars. Many had begun their business careers as marginal salesmen. Because of brains, ability, and opportunity, they became wealthy, powerful public figures, living in a world of glamour, and at times this made them belligerent or defensive.

They were opportunists, businessmen trying to succeed in a new industry that still had no form or rules. They understood their previous businesses and tried to apply lessons learned in furs, textiles, and junk to the new one. They would have to determine the nature of the market, the kind of product to be sold, and the way it should be packaged, advertised, and finally exhibited for the public. At first they called themselves film manufacturers, not producers, and spoke in the language of the garment industry rather than that of the stage or vaudeville. They were interested in product and profit, not art.

They succeeded. In the process they—not the artists—created the industry, and in so doing demonstrated at least as much creativity as any other single group in motion pictures.

But such is not the stuff from which Americans create symbols, and they suffered too since they operated in a context where artists tended to overshadow businessmen in the public eye. David Wark Griffith, Charlie Chaplin, Rudolph Valentino, Mary Pickford—these are the symbols of the silent screen, and not Marcus Loew or Adolph Zukor. As a result, the motion picture *business* remains virtually a virgin field for scholars.

As with the telephone, the industry began with inventors, not businessmen. Shortly after the development of photography, experiments with motion pictures were conducted in England, France, and Germany. The first viable motion picture camera was developed by Edison, who in 1888 filed a caveat at the Patent Office. "I am experimenting upon an instrument which does for the eye what the phonograph does for the ear, which is the recording and reproduction of things in motion, and in such a form as to be both cheap, practical and convenient. This apparatus I call a Kinetoscope."[2]

Actually, the camera produced pictures upon film and was later called a Kinetograph. Other experiments and improvements followed, and all the while Edison considered motion pictures an adjunct to the phonograph. Almost deaf himself, Edison, like Bell, was concerned more with the ear than the eye. But he continued to work on the device. In 1889 he began using George Eastman's new, improved film, and that same year he invented a mechanism for advancing the film at a given rate of speed. Edison finally developed the Kinetoscope, a large box which contained the device, with an eyehole through which the viewer could see the "show." At the time, he thought phonograph music would be played to accompany the performance, but he had no conception of the film as a story-telling vehicle.

Years later, Edison said he had hoped the Kinetoscope would become an educational tool. "I figured that after the novelty wore off the camera would either be taken up by the big educators and pushed as a new agency in the schools —or that it would be developed mostly along straight

[2]Matthew Josephson, *Edison: A Biography* (New York, 1959), p. 386.

amusement lines for entertainment and commercial purposes. I guess up to date the entertainment and commercial
purposes have won."[3]

In 1894, however, Edison was primarily interested in the
profitability of the new invention, which he still considered little more than a curiosity. He produced Kineto-
scopes for sale and set up facilities to "manufacture" films
for use in his boxes. He did not proceed in a forceful manner, however, as his attention was taken up by other inventions. Rival firms, seeing great potential in the machine,
produced models of their own. American Mutoscope and
Biograph—later known as Biograph—was formed by a college professor, Henry Marvin, and several associates, including one who had worked on the Kinetoscope. The
Lambda Company put out the Pantopticon. In London,
Robert Paul produced a similar machine, while in Paris
Auguste Lumière called his device the Cinematograph. All
these firms had similar ideas as how best to profit from their
devices. They would sell them to storefront operators who
would place the rows of machines in sight of passersby.
The potential customer would see an "advertisement" for
the show above the box. Then, if he wanted to view it, he
would insert a coin in the side and then look through a hole
in the box to see some fifty feet of film. The first of these
"peep shows" opened on Broadway in New York in April
1894 and was an instant success. Others followed, there and
in other large cities in the East, and then spread to other
urban locations.

The companies that produced the machines also produced the films. Money could be made on both, and each
depended upon the other, for the films of one manufacturer
usually could be used only on machines put out by the same
company. Although Edison attempted to win patent violation suits against his rivals, he had little success with them.
In fact, his own company was eclipsed by Biograph, for

[3]Dagobert D. Runes, ed., *The Diary and Sundry Observations of Thomas Alva Edison*
(New York, 1948), p. 63.

although that firm's machines were inferior to Edison's, its films were in greater demand. While the famous inventor dreamed of showing scenes from grand opera, accompanied by phonograph recordings of the actual singing, Biograph concentrated on more popular fare. One of its early films, for example, was *The Pretty Stenographer: or Caught in the Act*, while another was *How Bridget Served the Salad Undressed*. The actual films were not as risqué as the titles, but they drew customers.[4]

What was Biograph's business? Was it a machine company that produced films in order to sell the projectors? Or was it a motion picture production firm that marketed projectors in order to make the films more desirable? Later on Biograph purchased several store front operations, thus placing the firm in the theater and distribution ends of the industry as well. None of these questions appear to have been asked at the time. The industry was still small and evolving rapidly, so that one company could be in all three areas and not give the matter much consideration. From the start, however, these three areas existed, and over the years they would become more sharply defined.

Almost as soon as the storefront theaters appeared, some spoke of projecting the moving pictures on a screen, perhaps in a theater, and charging admissions. Then, instead of a reel being run a hundred times for as many viewers, one show could take care of them all. Frank R. Gammon and Norman C. Raff, two of Edison's associates, urged the inventor to turn his talents in that direction. Edison rejected the idea. Not that many people would want to see a show, he thought. Edison preferred to remain in the Kinetoscope machine and film business, selling both to distributors. He did not believe the invention would progress much beyond that stage.

Thomas Armat and C. Francis Jenkins, both of Washington, D.C., were interested in projection. At first they

[4]Terry Ramsaye, *A Million and One Nights: A History of the Motion Picture* (New York, 1926), p. 399.

worked independently of one another, and then they joined forces in 1895 to produce the Vitascope. This was a simple device—actually little more than a combination slide projector/Kinetoscope—and it didn't work very well. The two men sought financial support, but without success. Then they quarreled, and Armat went off on his own.

Meanwhile, others worked on motion picture projectors. Woodville Latham demonstrated his version, while the Lambda Company claimed to be on the verge of perfecting a superior projector. Fearful of being left behind, Gammon and Raff convinced Edison to either work on the projector himself or hire Armat to do the job. Armat was taken on; the new "Edison Vitascope" resulted and was given its first public demonstration at Koster and Bial's Music Hall in New York on April 20, 1896.

The debut was a success; the Vitascope was hailed as a marvel. But the *Boston Herald* concluded that "there is not the slightest chance that any universal use . . . will be made of the invention."[5] In other words, it was still just a curiosity, a device not to be taken seriously by serious men. Other demonstrations were held, and these too were well attended and enthusiastically received. But they were just that—demonstrations, not performances. Customers came because they were curious, not to be entertained. These early films portrayed ships at sea, dances, and brief skits. Exhibitors could draw customers for a while, but after the novelty wore off, more interesting fare would have to be provided.

Motion pictures and peep shows did not attract big businessmen and investment bankers. There was no major firm in the field, with the exception of the Edison organization, and motion pictures took only a small fraction of the inventor's time and money. The way was clear for small entre-

[5] *Ibid.*, p. 266.

preneurs, even outsiders, to enter the industry, either as producers or exhibitors, and then move from their base to the other area as well. Such men could develop and exploit motion pictures, and in the process give the industry form and content, both of which were lacking in the late 1890s.

Peep shows and projected demonstrations were urban phenomena, suitable only for places with large populations. Without a plentiful supply of potential customers, the shows could not operate profitably. Even then, the peep show operators constantly demanded new films, for although some customers would see the same one several times, there seemed a limit to their interest. New York was the largest city in the nation, and so it was a natural place for the industry to become located.

The city's immigrant population took to the peep shows and motion picture houses. This was a time when the immigrant stage was at its zenith, with the Yiddish theater in particular in full bloom. Most of the popular plays either were classics or reflections of old-country experiences and values. The rapidly Americanizing immigrants were interested in native entertainment, and could not find it in the American theater, since their English was still halting. They were attracted to vaudeville shows, the most plebian public entertainment of the day, but here too the language problem created difficulties. The films, being silent, suited their needs. One did not have to know English to understand the pantomime of the film actors, something the immigrants came to appreciate. Interestingly enough, the silent films of this period were perhaps more successful than "talkies" would have been.

Films had a greater impact on immigrant areas than on those inhabited by native-born Americans. In the latter the peep shows were curiosities, while in the former they were windows on the American experience. Ambitious and intelligent native-born Americans could find jobs and "work their ways up the ladder," especially during the economic boom that developed in the late 1890s. Their immigrant counterparts faced obstacles; their ladders had only a few rungs. Seeking opportunity, they went into the peep show and film operations, and many in New York were run by foreign-born citizens, especially Jews. In this period the production of both equipment and films was controlled by the native-born, but the display and exhibition sides of the industry were coming under the control of the foreign-born.

Given the capital requirements of the times, this division seemed natural. The establishment of studios to film and process vignettes required a fairly large amount of money, perhaps running into the tens of thousands of dollars. Similarly, the invention and manufacture of cameras, projectors, and related equipment demanded substantial capital, as well as experienced personnel. But far less money was required for a peep show. Still, a ten-machine operation in a decent urban location could not be opened for less than $1,000. Motion picture theaters were the least expensive method of getting into the industry. In 1926 Adolph Zukor spoke of the situation three decades before.

> The main business of the Edison Company . . . was to make these machines. Naturally, they all concentrated on the mechanical end of the business. That was very necessary and very important for this reason: In those days you could buy a projection machine for $75 or $95. People with money or with a substantial business would never think of opening a little store show, but as long as it did not take more than $300 or $400 to open up a theatre, a good many small investors took a chance, and that helped develop the business. . . . The great number of these store shows created a market for the moving picture producers and gave them an opportunity to develop.[6]

---

[6]Joseph P. Kennedy, ed., *The Story of the Films* (Chicago, 1927), pp. 57–58.

The cost factor favored the motion picture theater and hurt the peep shows. Furthermore, the potential return on investment was larger for projected shows, since many people would see the show at the same time. This meant that the theater owners needed films that would attract paying customers—they had to know their market. In turn, the owners put pressure on film producers for "attractive products." The public grew tired of displays of technical skill; in order to lure customers, story films were needed.

In 1903 James White and Edwin S. Porter of Edison's "Kinetograph Department" put together a five-hundred-foot film entitled *The Life of an American Fireman*, which was followed by *The Great Train Robbery*. Both were "hits," and the theater owners demanded more of the same. Thus, a symbiosis developed between the production and display ends of the industry, with each affecting the other. By the early twentieth century, however, audience demand—as interpreted by owners of theaters that charged five cents to enter, and so were called nickelodeons—was the most important single factor in determining the nature of the film product. This gave the nickelodeon owners a great deal of power, but they held it only because of their success in interpreting public tastes. Carnegie, Rockefeller, and Morgan need not concern themselves with such matters. Even Buck Duke thought of the public as a undifferentiated mass. William Vanderbilt could proclaim, "The public be damned," and other tycoons might nod their agreement. Motion pictures was a different kind of industry and required a wholly different view of the public. Without mass acceptance, the nickelodeon operators would have quickly shut down, followed in turn by the producers. This meant that Zukor and others like him had to become experts in public tastes, and in time concern themselves with a national market. The individuals who performed this task in the early twentieth century were, for the most part, immigrants with knowledge only of urban America.

Zukor was typical of the immigrants who entered the

business in this period, though he was the industry's tower-
ing figure in the silent days. He was a Hungarian Jew, born
in 1873, who immigrated to the United States in 1889. Zukor
became a furrier's apprentice in New York and then
opened his own business in Chicago. He enjoyed the theater and vaudeville, but seemed intent on making a fortune
in furs. In 1903, however, Zukor and his partner, Morris
Kohn, loaned $3,000 to Max Goldstein, who wanted to open
a peep show arcade. Zukor found the business interesting
and he invested directly in it. After moving to New York
he opened several nickelodeons and theaters, and his Crystal Palace on Fourteenth Street was the most magnificent
in the city in 1904. Later on, Zukor entered the production
end of the industry and for a while abandoned exhibition.
In 1912 he organized the Engadine Corporation, which purchased rights to Sarah Bernhardt's *Queen Elizabeth*. Out of
this came Famous Players Corporation, followed by Famous Players-Lasky, Paramount-Famous-Lasky, and
finally, Paramount Pictures Corporation. Then Zukor
moved back into theaters, intent on creating a unified trust,
one that would dominate all aspects of the industry. More
than any other motion picture figure in the early days,
Zukor came closest to forming a quasi monopoly. But his
actions stirred others to follow his example, and by the end
of the 1920s Paramount had lost its chance at industry control.[7]

Jesse Lasky was also Jewish, but native-born in San Francisco in 1880.[8] As a boy he studied music, and quit school
to become a cornetist in a local orchestra. For a while Lasky
played the vaudeville circuits. Then he became a producer
of vaudeville acts, hoping to expand his operations to cover
the nation. He made his major attempt at being an impre-
sario in 1912, when he opened the Folies Bergères, a music

[7]Will Irwin, *The House That Shadows Built: The Story of Adolph Zukor and His Circle* (Garden City, 1928); Norman Zierold, *The Hollywood Tycoons* (London, 1969), pp. 157–87.
[8]Jesse L. Lasky with Don Weldon, *I Blow My Own Horn* (New York, 1957).

hall, in New York. The venture failed, leaving Lasky penniless. Now he reentered vaudeville production, but became increasingly interested in motion pictures. His brother-in-law, Samuel Goldfish, was a glove manufacturer whose operations were crippled when the United States eliminated the leather tariff in 1913. Goldfish shared Lasky's enthusiasms regarding films and, in addition, was seeking a new area of opportunity. Together they joined with Cecil B. De Mille and Arthur Friend to form Jesse Lasky Feature Plays, a production company which was one of the first to move to Hollywood. Within a year the company became the most successful in the industry, at which time it merged with Zukor's Famous Players.

Samuel Goldfish was born in Warsaw in 1882, ran away from home at the age of eleven, went to England, and then to America in 1897.[9] He became an apprentice in a glove factory and then opened his own shop. Chance led him into the partnership with Lasky. Three years later, in 1916, he left Famous Players-Lasky to join with the Selwyn Brothers in forming Goldwyn Picture Corporation. Clashes with the brothers followed almost immediately, and Goldfish broke with them in 1919. He retained the name, however, and changed his to Samuel Goldwyn. Using his contacts and experience, Goldwyn became an independent producer, one of the most important in the industry.

The other major tycoons began in much the same ways and had similar backgrounds. As such, they must have appeared alien to the manufacturers of films and equipment, almost all of whom were native Americans. On January 1, 1909, the producers announced the formation of the Motion Picture Patents Company, comprising seven domestic and two French firms, including Edison, Biograph, Vitagraph, and Melies. The Patents Company was a major attempt at forming a motion picture trust. All the participants would pool their patents and each would receive a license to pro-

[9]Samuel Goldwyn, *Behind the Screen* (New York, 1923); Alva Johnston, *The Great Goldwyn* (New York, 1937).

duce films and equipment. The member firms would act in unison against the exhibitors. Had the trust been successful, the motion picture industry would have been under the control of businessmen, scientists, and artists; the exhibitors would have been mere adjuncts, tolerated but no more than that.

All but two of the major distributors bowed to the trust. One of the two was William Fox, a Hungarian Jew who had come to America in 1880 when only a few months old. After a brief career in the garment district, Fox opened a penny arcade and then a chain of nickelodeons. Fox also owned the Greater New York Rental Company, which distributed films to his own and other theaters. When the trust refused to supply him with films, Fox attacked in two ways. He sued the Patents Company, charging it with violations of the Sherman Anti-Trust Act, and in time won his suit. Fox also entered production directly, turning out his first film in 1912, and three years later forming the Fox Film Company, the predecessor of Twentieth-Century Fox. Like Zukor, Fox moved from exhibition to production, creating an integrated organization which produced, distributed, and exhibited motion pictures.[10]

Carl Laemmle also defied the trust. He was the son of a German Jewish estate agent who arrived in America in 1884, at the age of seventeen. At first Laemmle tried to become a merchant prince and failed. Then he turned to nickelodeons, opening one in Chicago in 1906, with others following soon after. Then came the Laemmle Film Service, a distribution organization. Like Fox, Laemmle fought the trust, organizing the Independent Motion Picture Company (IMP), which in 1912 became Universal Pictures. Laemmle hoped to control all aspects of his operations, from film to theater, though in time he concentrated on production.[11]

Laemmle had an assistant by the name of Jack Cohn, who

[10]Upton Sinclair, *Upton Sinclair Presents William Fox* (Los Angeles, 1933).
[11]John Drinkwater, *The Life and Times of Carl Laemmle* (New York, 1931).

in 1918 asked for a job for his brother, Harry. At the time Harry Cohn was twenty-seven years old, and had worked as a trolley car conductor and song plugger, with little success. Laemmle agreed, and Harry Cohn joined the company as his secretary. After learning the rudiments of the industry, Cohn went off on his own, forming the CBC Sales Company in 1920. Four years later Cohn restructured the firm as Columbia Pictures, with himself as its president.[12]

Sam Katz, born in Chicago of immigrant parents, entered show business as a piano player in Laemmle's first nickelodeon. Shortly thereafter he opened three of his own. Together with Barney Balaban, who became his partner, Katz became one of the major exhibitors in the Midwest. He too was interested in forming a firm that would participate in all aspects of the industry. In 1925 Katz and Balaban joined Paramount-Famous-Lasky, making that firm one of the two industry giants.

Louis B. Mayer, born in Russia in 1885, came to America via Nova Scotia. His first job was that of a junk dealer. In 1907 Mayer purchased a nickelodeon in Haverhill, Massachusetts, the first in a string of them that made him a major exhibitor in the East. Mayer turned to production in 1917, and seven years later became head of production at Metro-Goldwyn-Mayer.[13]

Ben Warner arrived in America in 1883, having left Poland with his wife and son Harry, then two years old. During the next nine years Albert, Sam, and Jack were born. The family traveled while Ben looked for employment. The boys worked in a variety of jobs, most of which were connected in one way or another with sales. In 1904 they pooled their resources and purchased a projector, giving traveling shows throughout the Midwest. Then they purchased a nickelodeon, opened a distribution center which they sold to the Patents Company, and went back

[12]Bob Thomas, *King Cohn: The Life and Times of Harry Cohn* (New York, 1967).
[13]Bosley Crowther, *Hollywood Rajah: The Life and Times of Louis B. Mayer* (New York, 1960).

into road shows. The boys went into production in 1912, but failed. After the war they tried again, and this time did better. In 1923 they organized the Warner Brothers Company, which concentrated on production, but owned theaters as well.[14]

A pattern may be seen in the careers of these men. The pioneers—Zukor, Fox, Laemmle, Cohn, Katz, Mayer, and the Warners—all began as exhibitors and then went into filmmaking—they took the path from commerce to art. Even Lasky made his start in theaters. These men were the founders of Paramount, Goldwyn Pictures, Twentieth-Century Fox, Universal, Columbia, and Metro-Goldwyn-Mayer, most of the major studios during the golden age of motion pictures in the 1930s and 1940s. All were significant business and artistic forces, and with the exception of Katz, all are the subjects of anecdotal and often self-serving biographies, written for the general public.

There is no biography of Marcus Loew, one of the most important of this early group, whose career was typical of the rest.[15] There are good reasons for this, in addition to the ones already mentioned. Loew was not a colorful character, given to dramatic gestures and malapropisms. He died in 1927, before the golden age, and although his work continued, he was not a strong enough personality to stamp his mark on the industry. Loew was not the kind of man to hire a writer to do a hack biography. Nor would he ask the publicity men at his organization to get his name into the newspapers. Still, he was a major force in motion pictures, the creator of a giant operation, with only Paramount able to challenge it in size and scope in the 1920s. He was not an artist, and never pretended to be one, even when thrust

[14]Ted Sennett, *Warner Brothers Presents* (New Rochelle, 1971).
[15]There is, however, a fine popular history of Loews, Inc. and Metro-Goldwyn-Mayer. See Bosley Crowther, *The Lion's Share: The Story of an Entertainment Empire* (New York, 1957).

into positions where he had to make artistic judgments. Loew was a businessman, an artist in spite of himself, who left the scene an undoubted success, with a personal fortune and the goodwill of the industry and public, neither of which knew him very well, however.

Loew was born on Manhattan's Lower East Side in 1870. His father was a waiter, and Marcus was his third child. Two others followed. The family was both large and poor, and so Marcus went to work at the age of six, selling newspapers after school. At the age of ten he and an older boy began a neighborhood newspaper, with Loew selling advertisements. The newspaper was short-lived, and Loew next went to work as a messenger boy/clerk/stock handler for a small clothing store. Having saved a little capital, he went into the fur business, failed, and at the age of nineteen declared bankruptcy. Loew tried again and this time left his shop just before it was foreclosed. Now married and with responsibilities, he took a job as salesman for another furrier, Herman Baehr. The Baehr firm was also shaky, with boom times alternating with periods of near collapse. The uncertain nature of the business bothered Loew, who was basically a cautious, prudent individual. He would adjust to the situation, for he was ambitious. More than anything else, however, he wanted security, a comfortable home, a steady income, independence, and time to enjoy the theater and vaudeville, his only two pastimes.[16]

Real estate offered the promise of such a life. He pooled his savings with Baehr's and together they purchased a small tenement on 111th Street. Now Loew was a landlord, a magic word to the Lower East Side Jews. He hoped in time to purchase additional houses and then manage them for a living.

Later on, Loew would tell of the time he stood in front of his tenement and saw a man looking at an apartment house down the street. Loew thought the stranger a real

[16] *Ibid.*, pp. 19–23.

estate agent, and walked over for a chat. He quickly recognized him as David Warfield, a fairly successful actor. The two men struck up a friendship, and they would meet to discuss the theater and real estate quite often.

On one of his selling trips in the Midwest Loew met Adolph Zukor and Morris Kohn, still in the fur business and planning to move to New York. Loew helped Zukor find an apartment in the city, not far from his, and the two men became close friends. When Zukor opened his first nickelodeon in New York in 1903, and the Crystal Hall the following year, Loew's interest in the ventures and industry developed. He invested some money in the Zukor nickelodeons, but decided it would be more prudent to enter the industry directly, in charge of his own operation.

Loew spoke with Warfield and Baehr of his plans to form a new company, which would explore the possibilities of show business, beginning with a peep show. The cautious Loew was not convinced films were more than a fad, however, so when the three men pooled their assets he named the firm People's Vaudeville Company. Since both films and vaudeville were considered plebian art forms, Warfield insisted that he remain a silent partner—news of his participation might harm his stage career.[17]

Loew rented a storefront on Twenty-third Street, purchased peep show equipment, and opened for business in late 1904. The venture was an immediate success. Loew managed the arcade for a small salary plus a percentage of profits, but still held on to his job as fur salesman, just in case the company failed. Even while on the road for his firm, he thought of improvements for his New York emporium. While in Covington, Kentucky, a friend took him to see a projected movie. In 1927 Loew recalled it. "I never got such a thrill in my life." He told his friend, "This is the most remarkable thing I have ever seen." It was not the film

[17]Mae D. Huttig, *Economic Control of the Motion Picture Industry: A Study in Industrial Organization* (Philadelphia, 1944), p. 10.

that excited him. Rather, the audience struck him almost speechless.

> The place was packed to suffocation. We wired at once for machines and started that Sunday in our arcade on the second floor. We took thirty feet of space and hired chairs. The first day we played I believe there were seven or eight people short of five thousand and we did not advertise at all. The people simply poured into the arcade. That showed me the great possibilities of this new form of entertainment.[18]

Loew began to acquire new locations as quickly as he could, turning them into small theaters. He looked for bargains, and found them in out of the way places, often in old buildings that had low rents. Profits from these places would be used to open theaters in better parts of town, and eventually Loew hoped to construct his own entertainment palaces. "I started after theatres, and the only kind of theatre I could get was the one that they thought was gone forever and no good for anything else," he claimed. "It was the best thing I could do, so I would take them and develop them until I finally got the theatres on such a high plane that they were not only looked up to but were patronized by the very best people."[19]

Loew was not referring to the wealthy upper classes but rather to the respectable middle-class family trade—people like himself. He had a keen instinct for what these people wanted and how rapidly they would move and accept the new art form. Such individuals had been raised on vaudeville; in time they might come to accept films, but the time was not the early years of the twentieth century. Still, films were clearly growing in popularity. In 1907 there were some 2,000 vaudeville houses in the United States. That year the number of nickelodeons—really double-nickelodeons, since

[18]Kennedy, *Story of the Films*, pp. 286–87.
[19]*Ibid.*, p. 288.

the price had recently been raised to ten cents—was estimated at between 4,000 and 5,000.[20] It was a time when admission to vaudeville houses cost a quarter, however, and price had a good deal to do with popularity. Indeed, some vaudeville houses were showing films in place of some of the live acts, in order to lower costs as much as provide an alternate form of entertainment. In retrospect, it would appear the movie houses were destined to replace vaudeville theaters in time. Loew was not the kind of man who looked too far into the future, however, and he was not of the stuff pioneers are made of. Rather, he preferred to live in the present, and when he entered the business, vaudeville was still king. So he combined live and filmed entertainment in his theaters. Of course, he could not afford expensive acts, and his vaudeville operation was small, a fraction of the size of such major operations as Keith, Albee, Klaw and Erlanger, Martin Beck, and the Shuberts. So at first he concentrated on obtaining low-priced acts that had failed to make good on the major circuits.

> We started with vaudeville and pictures and then went back in some places to the straight pictures, because we found that the class of vaudeville we were then playing did not appeal to the very highest type of people and we wanted all classes. So when we got to a neighborhood where they wanted the very high type we gave them pictures only and left the vaudeville out. Where we found the masses attending the theatre we gave them vaudeville and pictures.[21]

In other words, Loew tried to exhibit quality pictures instead of quality vaudeville in order to attract middle-class audiences, and for the "masses" provided cheap vaudeville with lower-priced films.

[20] Abel Green and Joe Laurie, Jr., *Show Biz from Vaude to Video* (New York, 1951), p. 50.
[21] Kennedy, *Story of Films*, pp. 288–89.

Loew was also a victim of pressures that often forced him to move more rapidly than he might have preferred. In 1908 he opened the Royal, a large new theater that cost $400,000 to construct. The Royal was a success and Loew began to see his future with such operations. At this point he might have considered turning most of his attention to vaudeville, for he began to acquire higher-priced acts. The Shuberts noted his success, and asked Loew to manage several of their New York operations, a request that he gladly accepted, for it indicated he was being viewed as an equal by one of the major forces in vaudeville.

That same year Mayor George McClellan initiated a campaign against the nickelodeons, which he claimed were fire traps and vermin-infested holes for the most part. Loew objected, but he did close down some of his early theaters, moving more directly into vaudeville, while retaining films as fillers in the quality houses and using them for shows in the more run-down, smaller locations. In this way he switched their roles in his operations of only a few years earlier. When McClellan forced 550 nickelodeons to close down completely, imposed a ban on Sunday performances, and obliged the remaining operators to sign a pledge not to show films tending "to degrade the morals of the community," Loew moved even more closely into an alliance with the vaudeville interests.[22]

By now Loew was intent on creating an entertainment empire. He moved to deepen his organizational structure by adding new executives, always men with his own kind of background. In the summer of 1909, for example, he leased film concessions at Paradise Park, an amusement area at the north tip of Manhattan, from Joe and Nick Schenck. A third brother, George, became manager of one of the Loew nickelodeons, while Joe and Nick, together with their amusement interests, joined People's Vaudeville. Loew also cooperated with Zukor on some joint ven-

[22]Green and Laurie, *Show Biz*, p. 50.

tures, including one in "Humanova," an early attempt at talking pictures. In February 1910, these men organized Loew's Consolidated Enterprises, which acquired the assets of People's Vaudeville and issued an additional $200,-000 worth of stock, which the Shuberts took. Loew was the president of the new firm, with Zukor treasurer and Nick Schenck secretary.[23]

For the first time in his business career Loew had sufficient capital with which to operate, and he used it to expand his nickelodeon and vaudeville enterprises. In October he opened the National Theater in the Bronx and then took over control of the lucrative Harlem Casino. In 1911 Loew purchased the William Morris circuit of vaudeville theaters, a move which placed him among the major leaders in that industry. Once again he restructured his holdings, forming Loew's Theatrical Enterprises, which was capitalized at $5 million, and took over control of Loew's Consolidated. Loew moved his offices to the American Music Hall, the pearl of the Morris chain, and from his Forty-second Street windows viewed the theatrical world he now hoped to dominate.

Thus, while Fox, Laemmle, and others were fighting the Motion Picture Patents Company, Loew was at work creating a vaudeville-film exhibition corporation. The People's Film Exchange cooperated with the trust and followed its dictates; Loew was no crusader, and in any case, he was not yet committed that deeply to motion pictures. Nor did Loew show much interest in the organization of new production companies or the moves they made to California and Florida. Rather, he entered into a consolidation with Sullivan and Considine, a large booking agency that specialized in second-rate acts in the Midwest and Far West. This gave him a coast-to-coast network, so that by 1912, Loew's Theatrical Enterprises was the largest force in the backwoods and second-line business.[24] He achieved his po-

[23]Crowther, *The Lion's Share*, p. 32.
[24]*Ibid.*, pp. 32–33.

sition when this branch of vaudeville was being challenged by films, which by that time were already developing into a serious art form. Loew walked out of a screening of the Italian-made two-hour version of *Quo Vadis?* He was the only exhibitor to do so; Loew argued that the public would not sit through so long a show.

Quo Vadis? was a major artistic and business triumph. The public rushed to pay the dollar admission price. American producers realized that a bonanza awaited them and began turning out longer dramas and comedies, though not ignoring the two-reelers that had already proven themselves. Zukor, De Mille, Goldfish, and others, now in Hollywood, began contracting for such epics; David Wark Griffith and several new directors worked to turn them out.[25]

Still, Loew was not overly impressed. He would show the films, but in sections, several reels a week, as a second feature for his vaudeville acts. He did contract with some film "stars" to appear at his theaters when their pictures were playing, as an added attraction, and in search of profitable gimmicks, rented Ebbetts Field in Brooklyn as a showplace for vaudeville and outdoor films. More important, perhaps, was Loew's continuing drive to acquire and build theaters. Land was solid, substantial, and would not vanish like entertainment. A film could fail, and a vaudeville act could sour. But a solid building on good property was an investment. Such acquisitions enabled Loew to straddle the fence, too. He would concentrate on vaudeville, but if films displaced that medium, switching to films would be a simple matter.

Had Loew been less of an opportunist and pragmatist, he might have remained wedded to second-line vaudeville and so be remembered today as one of the last impresarios, and not a significant or original one at that. Fortunately for him, Loew did not see the interplay between films and

[25]Ramsaye, *A Million and One Nights*, p. 607.

vaudeville as a struggle of art forms; nor was he a sentimentalist. At one point he said he was in business "for the money there is in it."[26] This attitude enabled him to survive while other vaudeville booking houses remained staunch defenders of their part of the industry, taking a brave but losing position and defending it to the end.

As Loew edged toward film, Zukor moved rapidly. Fresh from his success in exhibiting *Queen Elizabeth,* he combined forces with Broadway producer Daniel Frohman to form Famous Artists in 1913. Zukor hoped to develop his own stars and stories—he won Mary Pickford, the leading film personality of the time, for Famous Artists—but he would begin by persuading leading actors and actresses to perform in film versions of their plays, and so bring them to a vast audience. Zukor brought John Barrymore, Elsie Janis, Lenore Ulric, Douglas Fairbanks, Ina Claire, and H.B. Warner from Broadway to Hollywood, and became the major link between the films and the legitimate stage.

As part of his battle against the trust, Zukor sought a distribution firm to complement his production unit. Together with Jesse Lasky Feature Players, Zukor's Famous Players provided almost all the business for Paramount Pictures, a distributor then controlled by William Hodkinson, which had been organized with Zukor's aid. Zukor approached Lasky and Hodkinson with a proposal that the three merge. Hodkinson objected; he wanted to maintain a separate organization. After Zukor threatened to take his pictures elsewhere, Hodkinson was deposed, and in 1916 the merger went through, forming Famous Players-Lasky.

With distribution in hand, Zukor moved to control production and exhibition. He refinanced his firm and used the proceeds to purchase theaters. In 1926, Zukor recalled his actions at that time:

[26] Green and Laurie, *Show Biz,* p. 143.

I approached several different bankers and tried to sell them the idea of big profits in the motion picture business. They were very glad and wished me good luck and hoped I would succeed, but they did not see their way clear to participate in this lucrative business until one day I met Mr. Otto Kahn, of Kuhn, Loeb and Company. I thought that on account of his connection with the Metropolitan Opera House and his interest in theatres and artists I could refer to the possibilities of the picture business and perhaps he would be interested. I talked to him a bit and he told me that he was much interested.

Soon after, Kahn invited Zukor to lunch in order to discuss the matter more fully. Jacob Schiff, head of Kuhn, Loeb, opposed the financing, but others prevailed. "It was romantic. It had a future. After a few days negotiation they gave me $10,000,000."

I did not think the whole industry was worth $10,000,000. Coming back from Wall Street I said to myself, "Ten million dollars! What a responsibility!" . . . I realized now that having the management of the Famous Players meant something more than getting your photograph in the trade papers every day and now and again in the daily papers.[27]

Zukor first moved to control production. Within two years he had almost three-quarters of the leading stars under contracts, doing so by raiding other studios, in some cases putting them out of business as a result. Together with Lewis Selznick, Zukor formed Select Pictures, in this way acquiring the Selznick stars—the Talmadge sisters, Nazimova, and Clara Kimball Young. By 1917 Zukor was handling some two hundred films a year. He dominated

[27]Kennedy, *Story of Films*, pp. 73–74.

production, and began to flex his muscles. Prices to exhibitors went up. Zukor insisted on the practice of "block booking," which meant that exhibitors had to purchase several Zukor films in order to get the one or two they wanted.

The exhibitors—or at least some of the leading ones—retaliated. The First National Exhibitors Circuit, formed in 1917 by twenty-seven leading showmen, entered into contracts with independent production outfits and was particularly close to Warner Brothers. First National also produced films on its own, to free members of dependence upon the producers. Thus, as Zukor built a production empire, First National moved toward becoming a trust, integrating operations from exhibition to distribution to production.

Nor was this Zukor's only problem, or the only alternative to his formula for the industry. Ben Schulberg formed United Artists Company, a distribution firm controlled by the stars themselves, people "too expensive for any single company to maintain on a permanent payroll." Mary Pickford, Douglas Fairbanks, Chaplin, and D.W. Griffith were the "big four" of United Artists, but such producers and directors as Mack Sennett and King Vidor were associated with the firm. United Artists posed the possibility that the artists themselves might control the industry. In time U.A. could create a distribution network, and even purchase theaters, although this might not have been necessary, for the threat of withholding the stars' pictures would have sufficed to keep the exhibitors in line.

Facing threats from both the exhibitors and stars, Zukor decided in 1919 to enter the theater business in a major way. He hoped to destroy First National and with added profits lure the stars from United Artists. With the backing of Kuhn, Loeb, Zukor embarked on a massive acquisitions program; by 1921 he owned more than three hundred theaters. At that time too, the Federal Trade Commission began an action against Famous Players-Lasky, charging the firm and its affiliates with violation of the antitrust laws.[28]

[28]Green and Laurie, *Show Biz*, pp. 162–63.

Marcus Loew remained on the sidelines in this fight. His long friendship with Zukor, in addition to his self-interest, dictated an alliance with Famous Players-Lasky, and Loew was considered a "captive chain" by the First National leaders. On the other hand, he seemed content to remain where he was, adding to his vaudeville-film houses in a steady fashion. This is not to suggest that Loew was a mere satellite or an inconsequential figure, but rather that he instinctively remained aloof from great controversy. He was named codefendant in the FTC suit, but only as a matter of form, and emerged from the action unscathed. As early as 1916, however, he was recognized as a major force in vaudeville; George M. Cohan called him "the Henry Ford of show business," a bit of hyperbole, but an indication nonetheless of his having "arrived."[29] Loew spent over $8 million in 1917 to open ten theaters in eight cities. By 1919 he had theaters in cities from Montreal to New Orleans, blanketing the East. The Marcus Loew Booking Agency not only controlled hundreds of acts but ran theaters on its own, and in addition to his eastern interest, Loew had a majority of the stock of the California Hippodrome, the Fresno Hippodrome, and similar major theaters in Sacramento and San Jose.

In mid-1919 Loew announced his intention of consolidating his holdings in a new company, Loew's, Inc., which acquired the assets of all the other Loew enterprises. The new corporation was capitalized at $17.5 million. Such impressive figures as William C. Durant of General Motors and Harvey Gibson of the Liberty National Bank were on its board, along with Charles B. Danforth, head of the firm of Van Emburgh and Atterbury, which handled the underwriting. Interestingly enough, Danforth was one of the financial district's leading plungers, while his firm was known for its manipulations of issues it brought to the public. Durant and Gibson, while substantial businessmen, were also gamblers, risk-takers who liked to "play the mar-

[29] *Ibid., loc. cit.*

ket." Thus, Loew's, Inc. came out under rather racy sponsorship, quite unlike Zukor's. This was strange company for a man like Marcus Loew.[30]

The reason for their interest, and perhaps the reason Loew sought out the company of such men, was that he was preparing to expand his operations in new directions. Both Zukor and First National were attempting to become trusts, while independent producing companies like United Artists had the potential to revolutionize the industry. Loew was still interested in exhibition, but had come to realize that if either of the two giants succeeded, he would be at their mercy, having to pay high prices for films. Too, by 1919 he understood that although vaudeville would survive, films would increasingly replace live acts. In the past Loew had been reluctant to enter production. He knew very little of that side of the business and cared less. Loew had hoped to become a showman, in the Frohman tradition. But the age of men like Frohman was passing, and that of Zukor was at hand. It was necessary to imitate Zukor in order to survive. Loew meant to survive. And so he would acquire a production unit. The refinancing and establishment of Loew's, Inc., had been for that purpose.

Late in 1919, Loew made overtures in the direction of the Metro Pictures Corporation. He would not start a fresh operation. Rather, he would try to acquire a going concern at a bargain price. It was a recession year, and Loew had money. The possibilities were excellent.

Metro rose out of the failure of another company, Alco Film Corporation, which in turn emerged from an attempt on the part of several distributors and exhibitors to bypass the studios—Zukor in particular—and produce their own films. Al Lichtman, who in his time had been a waiter, actor, and then one of Zukor's salesmen, founded Alco in 1914. The company could draw on the talents of other ex-

[30]Crowther, *The Lion's Roar*, p. 42; Robert Sobel, *Amex: A History of the American Stock Market* (New York, 1973), pp. 84, 89.

Components of Loew's, Inc., 1919

Company	Common Stock Auth.	Issued
Loew's Consolidated Enterprises	$1,000,000	$100,000
People's Vaudeville Co.	150,000	107,700
Loew Amusement Co.	25,000	12,000
20th Century Amusement Co.	7,500	7,500
International Vaudeville Co.	50,000	30,000
Humanova Producing Co.	50,000	16,000
Marcus Loew, Inc.	50,000	10,000
Mascot Amusement Co.	50,000	10,000
Lorraine Amusement Co.	25,000	20,000
Newark Heights Theatre Corp.	10,000	1,000
Mostern Amusement Co.	10,000	1,000
Normandy Amusement Corp.	5,000	1,000
Midvale Amusement Corp.	10,000	5,000
Loew's Syracuse Theatre Corp.	5,000	1,000
Loew's Atlanta Theatre Co.	10,000	10,000
Brevoort Holding Co., Inc.	200,000	200,000
Cedric Amusement Corp.	10,000	1,000
Donnelly & Timmons Amusement Co.	20,000	20,000
McGee Amusement Co.	2,000	2,000
Marcus Loew Booking Agency	1,000	1,000
Monarch Amusement Co.	5,000	1,000
Loew's Theatres Co.	2,000,000	1,370,000
Borough Theatre Co.	3,600sh.	3,600sh.
Greeley Square Amusement Co.	250,000	250,000
Delancey Amusement Co.	150,000	136,000
Natoma Amusement Co.	200,000	200,000
Warwick Amusement Corp.	10,000	10,000
Brookside Amusement Corp.	10,000	10,000
Marloew Amusement Corp.	50,000	50,000
New Columbia Co.	250,000	225,000
Tennessee Theatre Corp.	10,000	10,000
Gates Theatre Corp.	250,000	60,000
Loew's Enterprises of Tennessee	300,000	—
Diamond Amusement Co.	50,000	10,000
Putnam Theatrical Corp.	2,500sh.	2,500sh.
Anchor Theatrical Co.	300,000	300,000
Birmingham Amusement Co.	10,000	10,000
Loew's Central Theatre Corp.	30,000	15,000
Midas Amusement Corp.	100,000	65,000
Loew's Memphis Theatre Co.	250,000	—
Loew's Metropolitan Theatre Co.	250,000	—
State Theatre Co.	500,000	500,000
St. James Amusement Co.	5,000	5,000
Globe Vaudeville Co.	5,000	5,000

SOURCE: *Moody's Industrials, 1920*, p. 2736

hibitor-controlled production units, which had contracts with such artists as Ethel Barrymore, Francis X. Bushman, and William Faversham. It was an intriguing idea, but the company failed. Lichtman then tried to interest some of the exhibitors in forming a new firm along the same lines, which he would call Metro. J. Robert Rubin, a New York lawyer who had been named by the courts to handle Alco's affairs, cooperated with Lichtman in the search, which was successful. Richard Rowland, a Pittsburgh exhibitor, became Metro's president, while Louis B. Mayer, the owner of a small eastern string of theaters, was its secretary. Maxwell Karger, who had once been a violinist with the Metropolitan Opera, was soon named to head production.

At first, Mayer was satisfied to handle distribution of Metro's films. But as he became more involved with studio affairs, production began to interest him. He acquired New England rights for *Birth of a Nation,* helped produce a Francis X. Bushman serial, and in 1917 lured Anita Stewart, one of the reigning queens of the movies, to Metro by forming a separate production unit for her. The success caused complications, as Vitagraph, which had a contract with the actress, threatened to sue. Fearful that Metro would go the way of Alco, Rowland agreed not to distribute her films. He and Mayer argued, and in the end Mayer left the firm to produce films on his own.[31]

Mayer had been the brains of the company and responsible for whatever success it had. After he left, the firm foundered. Karger proved an imaginative but incompetent producer, while Rowland wasn't able to handle front office matters and at the same time take care of his Pittsburgh interests. In the summer of 1919 Rowland and Rubin tried to sell Metro to Zukor, who wasn't interested in the company. Soon after, Loew, who was in search of a studio, made inquiries through third parties as to price. He then met with Rowland and Rubin, and in January 1920 he acquired Metro. The net price was $3.1 million, but $1.5 mil-

[31]Bosley Crowther, *Hollywood Rajah: The Life and Times of Louis B. Mayer* (New York, 1960), pp. 42–66.

lion came in the form of newly issued Loew's stock—then selling for below par, and soon to be offered to patrons of Loew's theaters through handbills—while the rest was to be paid through profits on the sale of Metro pictures overseas. In effect, Loew acquired a potentially valuable property for two packages of paper and promises.[32]

The acquisition of Metro committed Loew to motion pictures, and for the rest of his life he concentrated on films, with vaudeville taking up less of his time and energies. Exhibition was still his prime interest, however, and the opening of the Loew's State Theater in New York in 1921, a large prestige house, was one of his high points. Others followed, as Loew went on a building spree in the early 1920s. Part of the reason for this was a suspicion that Zukor, still an old friend and occasional ally, would squeeze him out. By 1924, Loew had one hundred theaters, most of which were either new or recently renovated. He added forty-four in the next three years, and was considered the dominant force in such places as Cleveland, New Orleans, and Pittsburgh, and a contender in New York. But Famous Players-Lasky owned or controlled over two hundred theaters and was expanding at only a slightly less rapid pace than Loew.[33]

By then, Zukor had evolved a strategy and an organization to enable him to accomplish his goals. He hoped to become the largest single factor in production and used his theaters to show his pictures along with those of others who cooperated with him. Independent exhibitors and smaller chains could show Zukor's films, but only on a block-booking basis. Since Zukor believed he could obtain what amounted to a corner on talent, the non-Famous Players houses would be forced to accept his terms or go out of business.

Zukor's logic was inescapable, but his understanding of public tastes and motion picture art was flawed. Like most of the early film tycoons, he felt that he was dealing in

[32]Crowther, *The Lion's Share*, pp. 50–53.
[33]*Ibid.*, pp. 124–26.

"product," not art. If films were products, then each would be only slightly different from the rest; if they indeed were art, than each film was unique, and would attract different audiences, striking different chords in each viewer. At the time—and later too—films were both. There were and are "formula pictures," such as the early westerns, in which each film was similar to the others. But the better pictures —and, in the early 1920s, these did draw large audiences, for the public was more sophisticated than any of the tycoons realized—were art as well. Famous Players-Lasky had more than its share of such quality films— such as *Beau Geste* and *The Covered Wagon* and many others—but the studio's rulers still used intuition to select subjects, writers, and artists, and their intuition was trained in the ghetto, in the fur business, in the junk business, and not in the arts. "I would go to a theatre, take the first row or sit in a box and there study the audience and see what effect the picture had on them," said Zukor in 1926. "So I was pretty certain in my mind after the experience I had had in watching audiences that I could use a subject and not go very far wrong."[34] Zukor would watch the audience, not the film, in judging its success. At one point, Lasky decided to produce *An American Tragedy*, not because it was a major American novel, or even good literature. "I saw in that a picture that ought to teach a great moral lesson," he said. "The book contains things that every American boy ought to know." Considering Lasky's own views on public matters, it is doubtful he understood the book, or realized that Theodore Dreiser's message was opposed to the ethic of men like him. Lasky went on: "That book contains eight or nine hundred pages. It is something you could not even skim in less than four or five hours. Producing it would mean handing it to a scenario writer and saying, 'Make nine thousand feet; tell it in an hour and twenty-five minutes.' "[35]

[34]Kennedy, *Story of the Films*, p. 61.
[35]*Ibid.*, pp. 118–19.

If film production truly was what Zukor and Lasky believed it to be, then a quasi-monopoly might have been possible. At the turn of the century, when people went to nickelodeons to witness the phenomenon and not see a story, this was the case. By the 1920s, however, the artistic element had become more important. Audiences were captured by motion picture stars, and not by the movie house. Script writers and directors who could turn out money-making films were more important than the managers of successful motion picture palaces. The industry had begun with stress on equipment. Then it moved to distribution and exhibition. By the early 1920s, production had come into its own. The nature of the industry and the evolution of the public taste militated against Zukor's strategy and its fulfillment. Zukor realized this himself, and began to stress production more than before. Had he not done so, his fortunes might have declined.

Loew lacked a strategy at this time; in general, he went along with Zukor. As far as he was concerned, for example, there was nothing wrong with block-booking. Loew thought films were pretty much alike. When a friend protested and came out in favor of the sales of individual films, Loew responded, "Such a practice would be analogous to ... a plum salesman ... selling one plum at a time."[36] Had Loew retained this attitude—and in practice as well as words he indicated that this indeed was his belief—he probably would have declined as an industry figure.

But he was in production already with Metro, and in order to obtain product for his theaters, he would add to his holdings. In 1924, Goldwyn Pictures, headed by Frank Godsol, was in financial difficulties. The firm had a large production facility in Culver City, California, a good reputation, leading artists, and several affiliated theater chains. It owned the Capitol in New York, a house Loew admired. Godsol tried to sell his company for two years, without

[36]Crowther, *The Lion's Share*, p. 131.

success, and each time he failed, the price would drop. Now it was at the point where Loew was interested.

By 1924 Loew had become more deeply involved in the artistic end of the industry than he had expected. Often against his inclinations, he had been required to pass on Metro's plans, even to the point of authorizing the purchase of scripts and the hiring of artists. This sort of thing did not interest him; Loew would fidget during such meetings and leave as soon as possible.

Metro was profitable but was still a small part of the Loew empire, certainly not as significant as theaters or even the vaudeville booking agency. Now Loew had the opportunity to acquire Goldwyn, but that studio's production chief, Abe Lehr, was a weak reed and responsible in part for the company's decline. Lehr would have to be replaced before Loew would make a move in the Goldwyn direction.

The situation was further complicated when Loew acquired a radio station, WHN, in New York, in 1923. At first it had seemed a good idea. The station was to be used to advertise Loew theaters and Metro pictures. But now Loew had to learn more about yet another field, and this taxed his physical resources. Shortly thereafter, he suffered a heart attack and wanted to withdraw from active business. The following year he was asked how he managed to accomplish all he had done and still remain alive. Loew replied, "I make somebody else do it. Let the other fellow go crazy."[37]

Rubin thought that Louis Mayer would be the perfect "other fellow" to handle Loew's motion picture enterprises. Loew agreed to permit Rubin to discuss the matter with the former Metro executive, who at the time was a successful independent producer and in a strong bargain-

[37] *Ibid., loc. cit.*

ing position. After several meetings, Mayer agreed to come into the company on condition that he be granted a free hand in his own sphere. Loew was more than willing to accede.

The merger was announced in April 1924. Goldwyn was taken over by Loew's through an exchange of stock and then merged with Metro to form Metro-Goldwyn Pictures. Immediately thereafter the Mayer interests were brought in. The understanding was that the new production chief would have his choice of credits. His films either would be "Produced by Louis B. Mayer for Metro-Goldwyn Corporation" or "Produced by Metro-Goldwyn-Mayer." The latter designation was selected. Metro-Goldwyn-Mayer was thus formed.[38]

Mayer proved one of the industry's most talented leaders. His first major film, *Ben Hur*, was a financial success and it was followed by *He Who Gets Slapped* and *The Big Parade*, which were among the best silents ever made. The studio had a roster of leading players, including John Gilbert, Greta Garbo, Lillian Gish, and Buster Keaton. Irving Thalberg, who had been Mayer's assistant prior to the merger, became the industry's leading producer. Within a few years, M-G-M was the most prestigious company in Hollywood—and the most profitable. In 1923, Loew's, Inc. was a major theater chain, known primarily for its "family

Loew's, Inc.: Gross Income and Earnings Per Share, 1920–1927

Year	Gross Income (millions)	Earnings Per Share
1922	$19.6	$2.14
1923	19.6	2.28
1924	42.9	2.78
1925	56.3	4.44
1926	62.2	6.02
1927	79.6	6.35

SOURCE: *Moody's Industrials, 1928*, p. 2948.

[38]Crowther, *Hollywood Rajah*, pp. 95–99.

houses" and second-rate vaudeville, while Loew lived in the shadow of Adolph Zukor insofar as the industry was concerned. By 1927, M-G-M was providing the major part of the corporation's profits.

The theater business languished and fell behind as the more aggressive chains expanded rapidly. Fearing antitrust prosecution in 1925, Zukor spun off his theaters and merged them with the Balaban and Katz Chicago operations to form Paramount-Publix, which was two-thirds owned by Famous Players-Lasky. This new giant had well over five hundred theaters, twice the number owned by Loew's. By the end of the decade Fox and Warner Brothers either owned or were affiliated with more theaters, while Loew's was a distant fourth, soon to be passed by Radio-Keith-Orpheum as well. Marcus Loew had entered production in a half-hearted fashion, more to provide films for his beloved theaters than anything else. By the time of his death the tail was wagging the dog. The period in which exhibition and distribution predominated was drawing to a close, to be replaced by one noted for production and integrated operations.

Zukor was one of the few who were able to move with the times. He shifted into production and helped make Paramount a major studio. Later he went into radio as well, in an attempt to create a major communications-entertainment trust. Were it not for antitrust actions, he would have succeeded. As it was, he evolved into the most imaginative and creative executive in motion picture history.

Loew remained in the East, controlling his empire from Manhattan even while making forays to California from time to time to visit the studio. He was like an interloper on the grounds, however; this was Mayer's territory, and both men agreed to that in a friendly fashion. Loew knew his limitations and would not interfere with artistic decisions except in the financial area. As his health deteriorated, even money ceased to concern him.

Loew also remained on good terms with Zukor. They would play tennis whenever a match could be arranged, with Loew usually winning. Zukor's daughter married Loew's son, and the two men were friendly rivals. They would raid one another for talent and bid against each other for theaters and scripts, but this did not affect their friendship. Furthermore, each man's theater chain had preferential distribution rights to the products of the other's studio, a practice that continued for long after Loew's death. Later this practice was pointed to as evidence of violations of antitrust acts and an attempt to create a community of interest. This was not collusion in the ordinary sense of the term but rather courtesies paid one friend by the other, and then returned.

The public knew little of Loew or Zukor. An increasingly movie-mad nation saw the stars and their pictures, read of studio heads in gossip columns and often on front pages, and followed their activities avidly. Motion pictures became an American art form, and the major one, in the first three decades of the twentieth century. Furthermore, it involved the vast majority of the public, not just a small elite. One might have expected some recognition of the work of the tycoons, but none was forthcoming.

If the industry leaders remained in the background, their power was intact. Hollywood, not the lower East Side, was the industry's symbol, and the tycoons may have reflected that this was all for the good, for motion pictures could not have become as popular as they did if the immigrant Jewish influence had been more pronounced and evident. Still, many of the silent stars were immigrants too—Charlie Chaplin, Rudolph Valentino, and Garbo, among others, came to America from Europe. They did well in the silents, for the audiences could not hear their accents. The coming of the "talkies" ruined many careers, but the tycoons were able to survive, since they were as silent in the 1930s as they had been in the 1920s.

The unlettered immigrants helped shape the industry, and did so as a result of pragmatic decisions. Whether through accident or design, the industry came to have several similarities with the garment and fur businesses from which many of the motion picture pioneers emerged. Had the tycoons remained in these fields, they would have competed with one another in terms of style, price, and display. Designers would have been stolen, salesmen would have been lured by one firm from another. But the leaders would have coexisted and their sons and daughters intermarried.

Loew went into semi-retirement after his heart attack, and his son, Arthur, became more powerful at the New York headquarters. Marcus lived on an impressive estate in Glen Cove, Long Island, and owned a large yacht, the *Caroline*, named for his wife. Within the industry he was hailed as a pioneer, but Loew didn't take such talk seriously. Even then the art of films was of little interest to him. Loew was more concerned with theaters—with *real* estate in its literal meaning—and not with what he deemed to be ephemeral shadows on screens. Yet in retirement he saw M-G-M rise brilliantly while his theater empire went into slow decline.

In 1926 Joseph Kennedy, then president of F.B.O. Pictures, organized a symposium at Harvard around the motion picture industry. Zukor, Lasky, De Mille, Fox, and Harry Warner attended, and Loew, then near death, made the trip to deliver his thoughts to the students. "I cannot begin to tell you how much it impresses me, coming to a great college such as this to deliver a lecture, when I have never even seen the inside of one before," he said.[39] Others spoke of the artistic and production problems involved in film making. Loew's topic was "The Motion Pictures and Vaudeville," since he held on to his vaudeville interests longer than the others and still was among the nation's leading impresarios. Loew said little about films but he spent a good deal of time on theater management, one of

[39]Kennedy, *Story of the Films*. p. 285.

his favorite subjects. This was also one of the very few times he conceded that he believed himself a major showman as well.

Although it is absolutely essential in conducting and operating theatres that you have experience, that alone does not make for successful operation. You have to have the showman's instinct with it. That is something undefinable, something that I really cannot explain. It is something that comes to you if it is in you, and if it is not in you you will never succeed no matter how much experience you have had in that particular branch. Experience, however, will help you a good long way toward bringing out that something that otherwise, perhaps, you might never have known was there.[40]

At the time other showmen, Fox in particular, were eyeing the Loew empire, preparing for a raid on it once the founder died, for it was evident he would not last much longer. The theaters were desirable, but the real prize was M-G-M. Mayer and Thalberg, not Marcus Loew or his son, Arthur, were the most familiar names at the company by then. In any case, they were correct regarding Loew's health. He died in September 1927 at the age of fifty-seven. The following week, Loew's, Inc. announced that during the previous fiscal year, sales had been $79.6 million, and profits, $8.5 million. At the time of the formation of Metro-Goldwyn-Mayer, Loew's common stock sold for 15. Just prior to Marcus Loew's death, the price was 62. In this same period the Dow-Jones Industrial Average rose from 93 to 191, doubling while Loew's common quadrupled in value. The Loew family controlled some 230,000 shares of common. Estimates as to Loew's personal fortune varied, but it was generally agreed to be in the neighborhood of $30

[40] *Ibid.*, pp. 290–91.

million. It had been founded on theaters, but the quantum jump had come through production.

The Loew funeral was well-publicized, with his old friends from the industry in attendance. Eulogies stressed that Loew had no enemies and was universally loved. This was hyperbole, to be sure, but the man who remained aloof from the major industry struggles and entered new areas gingerly, after others had tested the waters, did have more friends and fewer enemies than most of his peers.

All people are products of their times and places, but some act to alter them and, if they succeed, are considered shapers and movers of their eras. Marcus Loew was not one of these but instead was an opportunist in the finest sense of the term, in that he made the most of the few opportunities presented individuals such as he at the turn of the century in urban America. After he died, humorist Will Rogers said of him, "He would have been successful in a legitimate business."[41] Of course, this was meant as a wry comment on the man and the industry, but Loew might not have appreciated the humor. For him show business was legitimate, since the business always took precedence over the show.

---

[41]Crowther, *The Lion's Share*, p. 134.

VIII

Donald Douglas:
The Fortunes of War

Of the many new industries that flowered in the twentieth century, four have been considered more glamorous than the others. Two of them—motion pictures and radio-television—are in communications, while the other two—automobiles and aviation—are concerned with transportation. The first three had direct impacts on the daily lives of most Americans. Aviation has always been more mysterious, more dramatic, and somehow removed from the humdrum existences most people have. There have been many poets of the skies and space, but few for movies, cars, and radio. These are commonplace items and services, while the airplane is relatively unusual, even today. According to some estimates, less than a quarter of all American adults have flown even once, while a far smaller fraction use air facilities with any regularity. There are fewer than 200,000 airplanes of various kinds in operation today, a figure that includes military craft. The United States has never produced more than 17,000 civilian planes a year. In contrast, the automobile industry turns out over 10 million units each year and has little trouble selling them.

Less than 10 percent of all travelers employ airplanes for interurban travel, while almost 90 percent utilize private autos; the car, not the plane, killed the passenger railroad. The coming of transoceanic flights on a scheduled basis did contribute to the demise of the ocean liner, but only recently. As late as 1953, fewer than 8,000 people per week left America for Europe by air at the height of the tourist season.[1] Even now, air travel is a departure from the norm for most Americans, an adventure that is somewhat romantic. For them, the airplane's major impact has been on the imagination.

Aviation did revolutionize warfare, however. Classic cavalry tactics could be adapted to the automobile and even to the tank and other armored vehicles. The airplane and later the missile, however, caused military and naval strategists to rethink all their old axioms. Debates over the uses of air power began in the 1920s and intensified in the 1930s. During World War II, the airplane came to be viewed as the key weapon in war; with the explosion of the atomic bomb, some military thinkers concluded that armies and navies were obsolete and only control of the air mattered. Because of this, central governments deemed it important to foster the development of aviation, and the national interest dictated its growth. The same could hardly be said of radio, television, motion pictures, and automobiles.

There are some surface similarities between these new industries, however, and in particular between motion pictures and aviation. In both a small group of pioneers came to dominate the field in its early days and did so by taking command of one branch of the industry—exhibition in the case of motion pictures, production in aviation. The pioneers in both industries knew one another well, engaged in joint ventures, and some began their careers working for their future rivals. Loew worked with Zukor and Mayer, while Lasky and Schenck were involved with several other movie moguls. Similarly, Lawrence Bell and Donald Douglas worked for Glenn Martin, and John Northrop's com-

[1]Lloyd Morris and Kendall Smith, *Ceiling Unlimited: The Story of American Aviation from Kitty Hawk to Supersonics* (New York, 1953), p. 380.

pany began as a subsidiary of Douglas Aviation. These men and others of their generation knew each other well and shared a bond of friendship even when competing for orders.

In the cases of motion pictures and aviation, the public idolized "performers," people who were both celebrities and heroes, while often overlooking those responsible for organizing the industries. Films had Mary Pickford and Greta Garbo. In aviation there were Jacqueline Cochran and Amelia Earhart. Charles Lindbergh achieved a status unmatched by any other twentieth-century American. World War I aviators like René Fonck, Raoul Lufbery, and Eddie Rickenbacker became romantic figures, and afterward, other military aviators and then the astronauts captured the public imagination. But most people knew little of those responsible for producing the machines these individuals flew, just as the producers and studio owners of Hollywood were shadowy figures outside the industry.

There are significant differences between aviation and films, however. In the case of the latter, a handful of companies and, in time, a few giants tried to dominate the industry—to become "the General Motors of the Movies." This was not the experience in aviation. Only for a brief period in the late 1920s did the creation of such a giant appear possible, and even then it was more the result of Wall Street dreams than practical business. During the depression that followed, capital requirements and the small size of the market militated against such an effort. Instead, some firms concentrated on design and production, others on engines, a third on group airlines, and so forth. Then, during and after World War II, aviation became a major business. At that time the prices of individual planes could be well over $2 million, with military and airline contracts running as high as a billion dollars and more. The stakes were such that only large companies could afford to play. The rewards were enticing, but the price of failure could be near bankruptcy. Few motion picture companies had ever found themselves in such a position. The movies had a large, complex audience. Aviation producers had only one class of consumer outside the small, private plane market.

From the first, government was the major factor in the industry and helped shape it and dictate its direction. Not only was the federal government a purchaser of planes, but without its support and assistance the second-largest purchaser and user, the airlines, could not have survived and flourished, while federal help of various kinds has always been extended to and used by private flyers.

Movie-makers and exhibitors like Zukor and Loew had to concern themselves with mass marketing, and like others of their generation struggled against artists who insisted on producing films for specialized audiences. The opposite situation prevailed in aviation. Airplane manufacturers such as Douglas and Boeing produced vehicles that were almost handcrafted; even during World War II, mass production techniques such as those of the automobile industry could not be fully employed, while several attempts on the part of automobile firms to enter and dominate mainframe construction failed badly. A successful automobile model would have several million "copies" each year, selling at a price middle-class consumers might afford. Its counterpart in airliners would be considered a great success if two hundred were sold, in various configurations, with improvements added as the line progressed. So the aviation firms were concerned with a special market—the federal government and the airlines—and although some were intrigued by the idea of the "family plane," it is still far from realization. Those who understand the nature of the industry and the problems of flight believe it will not happen in this century, and perhaps never.[2]

[2]The manufacturers of small private planes would differ with this judgment. Such firms as Taylor, Bellanca, Beech, and Piper concentrated their efforts in this market. In 1936, for example, the Taylor Cub sold for $1,325 and was marginally profitable. On the other hand, most of those who flew this and similar models did so for enjoyment of flight and not for transportation, as was the case with the auto. After World War II there was a brief bonanza in the private plane market,

From the first, the aviation pioneers had to be at least as concerned with marketing as they were with engineering and manufacture. Only the most daring of them would produce a prototype without first assessing the chances of selling it to the military or the airlines. As the industry grew, the large manufacturers would try to do both—they would produce a prototype for the military designed in such a way as to be adaptable, with modifications, for the civilian market. Similarly, several passenger planes of the 1930s proved out as troop carriers and bombers in altered form during World War II. Such large planes were purchased by military and naval officers, backed by civilians in the federal government, or by airline executives who by the nature of their work maintained close relations with such individuals. In one way or another, directly and indirectly, the government was involved closely with the aviation industry, and changes in attitude on Capitol Hill and the White House were watched closely by industry leaders, who were not above attempting to influence votes and appropriations. The right contract could mean bonanza profits for a company and prosperity for the region in which its factories were located. The loss of a contract could mean bankruptcy for even a major firm, and its region could suffer the effect of unemployment. The federal government's power over the aircraft and, later, aerospace industry was countered by political pressures the companies brought to bear upon the politicians.

In 1961, President Eisenhower talked of the "military-industrial complex," and throughout the next decade many critics argued that business and government worked far too closely together. This kind of criticism was not new. The Wright Brothers and Glenn Curtiss were accused of lobbying for financial support. After World War I congressional

which has since subsided. In more recent years the demands for helicopters and corporate planes has grown, but in terms of gross sales, these still represent a small part of the total market. Devon Francis, *Mr. Piper and His Cubs* (Ames, Iowa, 1973).

critics argued that excess profits were the rule in aircraft procurement. The Nye and Black committees of the early 1930s were harsh on the munitions industry in general, the aviation companies included. During World War II the Truman Committee found evidence of chicanery in relations between the government and selected aviation companies. Other committees followed, so that by the time of the Eisenhower statement the relationship was fairly well known and recognized.

Defenders of the services often denied the very existence of a military-industrial complex, while attackers claimed it was a conspiracy whose power and goals were dangerous to democracy. Few noted that given the nature of the aviation industry some kind of nexus between it and the federal government was inevitable. Only those manufacturers who understood this, and could function well in the monopsonistic markets the industry dictates, could survive and help their companies flourish.

It was not surprising, then, that the founders of major aviation firms were cut from the same cloth as their counterparts in the armed services and federal government. Most were engineer-businessmen with outgoing personalities and an enthusiasm for flight, not only as a business but as an art. Many were midwestern Protestants. All had close friends in the armed services, while attendance at one of the service academies was a decided plus. The path from the army and navy into the aviation industry began in the 1920s and continues to this day. This was not necessarily sinister, but to be expected. Men who spent years in administration, especially those charged with dealing with aviation manufacturers, were natural choices to head departments in those firms later on. Qualities that made excellent commanding officers were similar to those of successful businessmen and executives.

The origins of manned flight were not in the need for better war-making capacity or the drive for business profits but rather the work of scientists and romantics. The yearning to fly was evident in the ancient world, where legends of Icarus and other would-be aviators abounded. Medieval thinkers considered flight too, for secular as well as religious reasons. Nineteenth-century novelists wrote of the possibilities of air travel, and balloonists succeeded in leaving the earth. Publicists proclaimed that manned flight was not only possible but inevitable. Little attention was paid the commercial aspects of aviation, although some lip service was given the military factors. Poets and scientists wanted to fly for its own sake, a sentiment that was reflected, in part at least, in the later desire to conquer space. People such as these often became businessmen; the early flyers headed some of the major firms when the industry was being born. In addition, only those Annapolis and West Point graduates enthusiastic about flight would seek commissions in that branch of the army or navy, since flying was considered a dead-end career. Thus was born the romantic-scientist-businessman-soldier, the kind of person who dominated aviation and, later on, aerospace. Charles Lindbergh was one of many such individuals, as was Donald Douglas.

The Wright Brothers were romantics and scientists; their bicycle business and limited formal education supported the legend of two inspired tinkerers, but their papers reveal men who understood aerodynamic principles and how to apply them. One of the nation's leading aviation experts, Octave Chanute, who also was president of the Western Society of Engineers, was one of their closest friends and advisors and always showed respect for their learning.[3] Chanute was also close to the Cabots of Boston, businessmen and social leaders who traced their descent to and through Francis Cabot Lowell. Godfrey Lowell Cabot had backed several aviation ventures in the past in the hope

[3]See the Wrights-Chanute correspondence in Marvin M. McFarland, ed., *The Papers of Wilbur and Orville Wright, Including the Chanute-Wright Letters and Other Papers of Octave canute.* 2 vols. (New York, 1953).

that one of them would prove commercially viable. Shortly after the Wrights' first flight he wrote to ask if they thought freight could be carried economically by air. The brothers' response satisfied him that it could, and so Cabot offered to finance additional experiments. He also wrote to his cousin, Senator Henry Cabot Lodge, and told him of the flights less than a month after they took place. "It has occurred to me that it would be eminently desirable for the United States Government to interest itself in this invention," he said.[4] Lodge sent the letter to the War Department, where it was promptly forgotten. But Chanute told the Wrights that he could obtain support for their work from others governments, including Britain and Japan, if they would agree to travel and work abroad.

From the first, then, there were those who recognized the possibility of a scientific-business-government alliance in flight. For the moment, however, the United States Government was not interested.

The Wrights were disappointed. They felt that government was the logical supporter of flight, since it had the money and need for weapons. Although foreign governments did purchase planes from the Wrights and others, the United States did not enter the field until 1907, and then in a small way, taking bids from forty-one manufacturers and would-be manufacturers for a single airplane. Private investors like the Cabots, on the other hand, were eager to support commercial aviation, expecting it to be in operation in a matter of a few years. In December 1905, for example, Chanute wrote to Wilbur:

> When in Boston last April, I told Mr. S. Cabot that you had offered your machine to the U.S., and had been turned down. A week or so ago he wrote to ask whether you needed financial assistance. I answered that you did not but had talked of organizing a joint

[4]Morris and Smith, *Ceiling Unlimited*, pp. 46–47.

stock co. He now writes that this may be floated by Lee Higginson & Co. of Boston, and suggests that you and I should come on for an interview, and a consultation with a patent expert. I have answered that I would submit the question to you, but doubted your readiness to make talk at present. What do you say?[5]

The Wrights said, "No." They and other scientist-manufacturers continued to develop new craft, selling to European governments, participating in air shows, and even races sponsored by scientific and sporting societies. Airplanes seemed to be developing into a war and sports industry in Europe and solely sports in America. Cortlandt Bishop, president of the Aero Club of America, predicted in 1914 that "Soon we shall have the best people in the world interested in flying machines."[6]

War came later that year, and with it a new interest, even mania, for military aviation. But the country hadn't much of a military aircraft industry upon which to build. In 1913 France spent $7.4 million on war planes, and Germany and Russia $5 million each. Even Mexico spent $400,000. The United States expended $125,000. In 1914, France had 260 war planes and 171 pilots, and was far ahead of all other nations. The United States had 6 war planes—Japan had 14 —and 14 trained pilots. Italy had 39.[7]

The government embarked on a crash program. In July 1917, Congress approved the largest single appropriation for a specific purpose to that time: $640 million for military aviation. Yet at the time, the government had no organization capable of allocating these funds intelligently. The job was done in a haphazard fashion, with a great deal of waste. At war's end, the United States owned 14,000 airplanes and 42,000 engines. It had trained 800 pilots. Most of the engines

[5] *Wright Papers*, I, 531.
[6] Morris and Smith, *Ceiling Unlimited*, p. 145.
[7] I.B. Holley, Jr., *Ideas and Weapons: Exploitation of the Aerial Weapon by the United States During World War I* (New Haven, 1953), p. 29.

could not fit existing planes—even had there been sufficient planes to accommodate them. Almost all the planes were copies of European models. No American-designed and -produced airplane participated in combat during the war.

The aircraft industry was small and shaky in 1914. Curtiss Aeroplane and Motor, Glenn Martin, and Dayton-Wright were its leaders, and together with a handful of smaller firms they turned out two hundred craft a year, almost all upon receipt of orders and down payments. The automobile industry, on the other hand, was large and expanding rapidly. More than a half million units were sold in 1914, and the number tripled in the next two years. That industry's leaders had designs on aviation, seeing little difference in the construction of a flivver and a biplane; both had engines and both were transportation vehicles. Some auto men had good relations with the Wilson Administration, and as a result, they dominated aircraft procurement. Howard Coffin of Hudson Motor Car, who had an interest in Dayton-Wright, became head of the Aircraft Production Board. Later on he was succeeded by Edward A. Deeds of Dayton Engineering (Delco), an auto man who earlier had worked for National Cash Register. They favored their own industry in awarding contracts and tried to shut out the aviation firms. Of the 9,742 airplanes produced by the aviation companies, Curtiss turned out 4,014 and Dayton-Wright, 3,506. Both firms were owned, in part, by automobile firms. In contrast Fisher, a leading manufacturer of automobile bodies, produced 2,000 airplanes during the war period, even though it had no previous experience.[8]

The automobile companies concentrated on engines. General Motors, Packard, Lincoln, Ford, and Willys-Overland dominated the field. Of the established aircraft operations, only Wright-Martin received substantial contracts, and it had close connections with auto industry leaders through a merger with Simplex.

[8]John B. Rae, *Climb to Greatness: The American Aircraft Industry, 1920–1960* (Cambridge, 1968), pp. 221–23.

After the war, the House Select Committee on Expenditures in the War Department investigated the procurement process. It learned that Coffin, Deeds, and others had botched their jobs and exhibited favoritism to select firms when awarding contracts. For example, the most important American design of the war, the Liberty engine, was a product of collaboration between engineers from Hall-Scott Motor Car Company and Packard. At first they tried to design an eight-cylinder engine—one that could be used in cars as well as airplanes—and failed. Then they developed a twelve-cylinder water-cooled model, and 32,000 of these were produced, almost all by the auto companies. To help his own firm, Deeds insisted they use Delco parts in construction.

The Liberty was a fine engine, but no existing plane could contain it. For the next eight years aircraft designers would construct planes around that engine, while work on alternate models was crippled due to the overhang of cheap, durable Liberties on the market.

The government spent $1.2 billion on aviation during the war, so that each of the 9,742 aircraft cost approximately $120,000. By 1920, many could be had as surplus for less than $1,000. According to one aircraft engineer, only $5 million of the total investment was salvaged and usable by 1920.[9]

Aircraft production dropped sharply after the Armistice, going from 14,000 to 263 from 1918 to 1923.[10] Not many firms could survive in this kind of an atmosphere, one in which hope was at a premium. Such companies required businessmen who understood engineering and science, and not scientists who had entered business as an afterthought.

The Wright Brothers—romantic scientists and mechanics —were archetypes for the prewar and wartime manufacturers. Glenn Curtiss and Glenn Martin were tinkerers,

[9] *Ibid.*, p. 2.
[10] *Ibid.*, p. 3.

interested in kites, balloons, engines, flight theory, air-planes, and all other aspects of aviation. William Boeing was a graduate of Yale who majored in science, while Grover Loening was the first Columbia student to special-ize in aeronautics. All headed companies bearing their names, and each made important contributions to aviation, but none could be described as an imaginative or efficient businessman, and none even demonstrated much of a ca-pacity or willingness to learn. Instead, they either faltered when engaged in management functions or associated themselves with others who specialized in that part of oper-ations.

Donald Douglas was the most prominent of the second generation of aviation leaders in America: businessmen who understood the military ways while at the same time empathizing with the scientist-tinkerers.[11] He was born into a middle-class family in Brooklyn in 1892. According to his later recollections, Douglas's parents spent a great deal of time with their children, sailing on weekends, and reading tales of Scots history in the evenings. William Douglas, the father, worked in a bank and made a comfort-able living. Donald and his older brother, Harold, were free to explore the neighborhood after school and write poetry. Donald was particularly interested in poetry and would remain so for the rest of his life, even publishing in the field.[12]

The weekend sailings led Douglas to believe he might be happy in the navy. He attended the Trinity Chapel School and after graduation, a preparatory school for Annapolis. Harold had made the same decision and was already en-rolled at the Naval Academy. Donald Douglas was an im-

[11]The only biography of Douglas is Frank Cunningham, *Sky Master: The Story of Donald Douglas* (Philadelphia, 1943). It is marked by inaccuracies and exaggera-tions and is of limited use.

[12]Interview with Donald Douglas in March 1959 for Aviation History Project, Oral History Research Office, Columbia University.

pressionable young man, and as he recalled, he drifted toward the sea, which he loved, but felt no vocation for it.

In 1908, after a visit to Annapolis, Donald went to Fort Myer, Virginia, to witness a demonstration of the newly acquired Wright airplane. He soon became interested in flight, abandoning sailing and concentrating on the construction of model airplanes. For a while Douglas thought he would enlist in the army and then try to get assigned to the newly formed air squadron rather than take the Naval Academy examination.

Douglas entered Annapolis in 1909, more the result of closeness with his brother and sheer inertia than anything else. He spent a good deal of time there engaging in athletics—especially boxing and lacrosse—and in constructing model planes. Douglas's grades were better than average but he was an indifferent student. He did well on his midshipman cruise to Europe, and with Harold's moral support remained in school. Harold graduated in 1911, however, and Donald, now interested only in airplanes, decided to leave as well. The Massachusetts Institute of Technology offered a new program in aeronautical engineering, for which he applied and was accepted. Douglas left Annapolis for M.I.T. in 1912.

He did well at M.I.T., graduating with distinction in 1914. After another year at the school as a graduate assistant in aeronautical engineering, Douglas took a job at the Connecticut Aircraft Company, then at work constructing dirigibles for the navy. Soon after, he was given major design responsibilities there.

Less than six years after witnessing his first flight, and at the age of twenty-three, Douglas was considered one of the nation's major aeronautical talents. This was not because he was a prodigy but rather was a reflection of the nature of the industry and its size on the eve of America's entry into World War I. At the time, Douglas was one of the few men with an academic background in flight theory, a strong background in aerodynamics, and a working knowledge of plant operation. Such was the nature of this second generation of aircraft leaders that with all of this he did not take his first flight until 1915. But he knew aviation as did few others. As such, his talents were in demand, as the American aircraft producers received orders from abroad for planes and lacked trained personnel to produce them.

At the time, Glenn Martin was one of the most famous aircraft pioneers. He had conducted experiments with kites as a boy in Kansas and then entered the automobile business. Martin explored the possibilities of gliders and constructed airplanes, teaching himself all the engineering he would need for the task. From 1910 to 1912 he flew demonstrations, experimented with air mail, and even performed in motion pictures in Los Angeles, appearing in a Mary Pickford epic, among others. In 1912 he formed the Glenn L. Martin Company of Los Angeles, a part-time operation hoping to sell planes to the government. At first it languished. Then, in 1915, Martin received a contract from the French government to produce 450 aircraft engines, as well as several smaller contracts from the War Department. Martin had to turn his full attention to the company and in particular needed engineering help. He had heard of Douglas and offered him a job. The offer was accepted and Douglas joined Martin in 1915.

The Martin factory was a handicraft operation at the time, run by self-taught mechanics who learned by trial-and-error. Douglas's predecessor, Charles Day, was an engineer who came to flight by way of motorcycles. Douglas was one of the few men in the industry whose engineering work had been exclusively on airplanes. Lawrence Dale Bell, Martin's superintendent and later head of his own firm, had made his first airplane in 1910, but before that worked on automobiles, and the same was true for most of the other technical and managerial personnel. Douglas introduced the use of blueprints and pretest planning on a regular basis at Martin—which soon after his arrival became Wright-Martin through a merger with Simplex Automobile Company and the Wright Company. As the firm became more involved with engines than with mainframes, and as the federal government became increasingly interested in flight, Douglas was both disenchanted with his job and attracted to new opportunities. In November 1916, he was offered the post of chief civilian aeronautical engineer for the Signal Corps, which at the time was charged with the army's air potential.

Douglas's responsibilities included the design of aircraft that might be used if the United States became involved militarily in the war. He did not understand the politics of the situation, however. The automobile industry wanted to produce the Liberty engine. The army preferred British and French planes to American and insisted any plane it used be based on the foreign designs. Douglas's task was to please both groups—to place the Liberty engine in a British fighter plane, the Bristol. This was a well-designed pursuit, which in its British configuration was powered by a 200-horsepower engine. The 400-horsepower Liberty would rip it apart, and Douglas said so to his superiors. For a while he tried to redesign the plane, and the army objected. Then Douglas attempted to convince his colleagues to allow him to develop an air-cooled engine for the Bristol, and this displeased the Coffin-Deeds group. In his stay at the military installation, Douglas was unable to get a single one of his designs accepted.[13] In time he and other industry leaders would learn to cooperate with the government in such matters. In both the military and airlines areas, aviation was structured as a buyer's market. Douglas received his first important lesson in this in 1916–1917.

Glenn Martin was also unhappy about the way aviation was developing in the wartime atmosphere. Wright-Martin was in full swing in 1917, producing American copies of British and French planes at a time when Martin was convinced his own designs were superior but could not get a

[13]Rae, *Climb To Greatness*, pp. 8–9; Cunningham, *Sky Master*, p. 88.

hearing. The company produced a plane a day at a time when Henry Ford claimed he could turn out several thousand a year, and the automobile men on the Aircraft Production Board demanded Martin commit himself to three a day. Martin said this was impossible, and a deadlock was reached. In anger and disgust, he left the company and sought backing for a new one. A group of Cleveland industrialists learned of his situation and, eager to counter the thrusts of Detroit and Dayton groups into aviation, offered to support him in the creation of Glenn L. Martin Co., which was supposed to produce planes of such a superior design that the government would be obliged to purchase them. Martin needed a staff, and knowing of Douglas's difficulties with the Liberty, asked him to join the new firm as chief designer. The offer was accepted. Douglas resigned his government post in early 1918 and went to Martin, with Bell as his assistant.

Douglas applied the lessons learned in government at his new post. Asked to design a two-engine bomber, he made certain the airframe would support the Liberty engines. The Martin MB bomber was ready for testing in August 1918 and at the time was considered far ahead of European rivals in performance and design. The total cost for the prototype was less than $50,000. Over time, this method of production and sales would become prohibitively expensive, but in 1918 it could be done this way.

The MB was developed too late for war service, but the government ordered models, enough to keep Martin in business in the early 1920s. Martin and Douglas hoped civilian orders would take up the slack. Most importantly, Douglas believed the MB could be adapted for civilian use, either as a mail plane or a passenger carrier. The MB was significant in several ways, one of which was its usability in either market. No less than the auto makers, the aviation companies hoped to utilize their military experience in the production of civilian goods. Later on, Douglas would become the master at this, teaching other aviation firms how it was to be done. In 1920, however, all Martin could do was to speak of the possibility of using converted MBs on the New York to Philadelphia run, with "ten to twelve passenger machines leaving in both cities every half hour."[14]

Martin, Douglas, and others in aviation had few illusions regarding the postwar markets. The government canceled all outstanding contracts when the Armistice was confirmed, and given the growing antiwar sentiment in the nation, there seemed little likelihood that new aviation appropriations would be forthcoming for several years at the very least. Interest in aviation had grown during the war, and there might be a market for pleasure or sports planes. Finally, there was commercial aviation—the fulfillment of the Cabots' expectations. Airmail contracts were a possibility, with scheduled flights further in the future. All of these would increase the demand for aircraft and might provide a stimulus for the industry.

The overhang of surplus warplanes was one of the major blocks in the path of expansion in production. Unlike automobiles, airplanes did not "wear out." Instead, parts were replaced when needed, so that a well-serviced plane could last for decades. Replacements would be needed for those that crashed or if expansion in services took place, but the surplus planes might take care of both.

The airplane producers had to turn out new planes that would make the World War I models obsolete, and do so in different ways for their three markets. Insofar as sports and pleasure planes were concerned, they would enter sponsored races, hoping to win prizes that would turn into orders for their products. This was a small market, however, and not very profitable, though racing was glamorous and exciting in the 1920s.

Government orders were far more important. The aircraft producers would have to convince politicians, admirals, and generals that air power was a significant new

[14] *Ibid.*, pp. 96–97.

development the United States could not afford to ignore, and having done that, demonstrate that ever-newer models would be needed—that war planes should not wear out in peacetime but be replaced regularly as technology advanced.

The Post Office Department would have to be sold on the idea of air transport, and here there was not only great promise but actual experimentation. But given a period of peace, the greatest expansion of all could be in commercial flight, in the carrying of freight and passengers. If the nation became "air-minded," then it would need hundreds, eventually thousands, of passenger and freight planes, as well as many airports and other ground-support stations. Could the passenger plane compete with the railroad? Perhaps it could in terms of traveling time, but not in cost. The same was true for cargo. Planes might be used to carry special shipments when speed was of the essence, but for most other traffic, railroads and trucks seemed more suitable. In 1920, the industry had no plane capable of operating successfully in the commercial field. Furthermore, it didn't seem likely the manufacturers would create one for a market that did not as yet exist. In this area too, government aid was believed necessary, on a scale not unlike that of military aviation during the war. Without major subsidies it did not appear likely that passenger flight could even begin.

No aircraft manufacturer could afford to ignore any of these markets. Most would construct planes to compete in the various "cup races," hoping to attract wealthy sponsors who might order sports planes or private craft. The setting of new speed, altitude, and endurance records engaged not only pilots but companies, for such notoriety might well be translated into sales and profits. The most famous flight in history, that of Charles Lindbergh from Long Island to Paris in 1927, was in response to a $25,000 prize offered by French restaurant and hotel owner Raymond Orteig, and others beside Lindbergh were prepared to make the flight.

The Spirit of St. Louis was a Ryan monoplane powered by an air-cooled Wright engine. The success of the flight made Lindbergh a hero and provided impetus for the aviation industry, but it also boosted the fortunes of the Ryan and Wright organizations. Before and after the flight, other manufacturers besides Ryan were interested in such competitions, though none of them—Ryan included—ever derived much more than a share of the prize money for their efforts. The manufacturers recognized this but continued in the private field in order to test their new designs and in the hope that victories and performance records would attract military buyers and even those few interested in civilian commercial flight.

The Post Office was the only other potential customer. Experimental postal flights had been made as early as 1911, and in 1918 a more regular service was initiated. The Post Office purchased the necessary planes, but these were flown by civilians, usually on an irregular basis due to weather and mechanical complications. The Army Air Service also carried mail and, like the Post Office, did so at a net loss. There was no significant public or commercial demand for airmail, and the planes were too small and the charges inadequate for even full loads to show profits. Still, airmail did provide a potential market for airplanes, though a small and questionable one.

Like other survivors of the postwar slump, Martin hoped to make significant sales in all markets. But cash was short and orders slow in 1919, a year when even the giant (by aviation standards) Curtiss operation almost closed down. Martin had the MB bomber, recognized as a superior machine and adaptable to airmail and passenger service. He decided to make a major effort to sell the plane to the army while at the same time adapting it to civilian uses. Meanwhile, Douglas and Bell were to design airplanes for the future.

At the time Douglas received a salary of $10,000, excellent by industry standards. At the age of twenty-eight he was recognized as a major designer, and he could have had a place at any of the major firms of the period. But like others in similar positions, Douglas wanted to head his own operation. Furthermore, he was not certain the Martin strategy was wise. Douglas thought military and naval aviation would be barren; attempts to sell the MB would fail. Later on, the services might ask for designs for special planes for specific purposes, and at such moments a prudent businessman might give the assignment to his design staff. For the time being, whatever future there was in aviation lay in the sport and commercial fields, and the MB was not salable, thought Douglas, to such buyers. Instead, Martin should produce an entirely new plane, one that not only would fill the needs of existing markets but also help create additional ones by its capabilities. Lawrence Bell agreed, and favored the construction of fast, maneuverable, high-powered craft for the sports market. Douglas disagreed and designed slower but larger and safer planes that might be used for commercial flight. Martin would not construct either model, but favored Bell's approach, since the sport model might be salable to the army after proper alterations were made.[15]

For these reasons, Douglas decided to leave Martin and start his own company. During the previous year he had become interested in California as a base of operations. The weather there was such that flying was possible most of the year. There was only one firm on the West Coast—Boeing, in Seattle—so that a new firm could capture whatever local capital and markets existed. Also, Douglas had a friend in Los Angeles, Bill Henry, who had worked for Martin and then became a sports writer for the *Times*. Henry urged Douglas to move to Los Angeles, saying that he knew several people who might give him construction contracts.

Shortly after Douglas made the move, Henry introduced him to David Davis, a wealthy sportsman interested in

[15]Richard G. Hubler, *Big Eight: A Biography of an Airplane* (New York, 1960), p. 22.

flight. Davis wanted to be the first man to fly nonstop from Los Angeles to New York and asked Douglas to build him a plane for such a trip. Douglas agreed and took a small advance from Davis. With it he set up operations in the back of a local barbershop and wired several of his associates at Martin to join him. They came, on the basis of the one-plane order. They then incorporated as Davis-Douglas Airplane Company and set about producing a plane that was known as the *Cloudster*, which was powered by a Liberty engine and technically capable of making the flight.

Davis invested $40,000 in the plane, which was ready for flight in early 1921. It crashed on its trial, however, and before it could be repaired and readied once more, two army pilots made the trans-continental flight in a converted wartime plane. Disgusted, Davis withdrew his support, leaving Douglas with debts and no other orders.

But the *Cloudster* had attracted attention in Washington. The plane broke several records in test flights, including one for altitude. The navy was interested in the plane and wanted to know if it could be adapted in such a way as to make it a torpedo bomber. Douglas submitted plans for what was to be called the DT–1. He received a contract for three planes, at $40,000 each, on the basis of the plans, with the understanding that the first payment would be made after work had begun.

Broke and in debt, Douglas could not begin. He appealed to Henry for help, and the reporter set up an appointment for him with Harry Chandler, publisher of *The Los Angeles Times*. Douglas offered to exchange 49 percent of Davis-Douglas stock for Chandler's guarantee of a $15,000 bank loan. Chandler refused but said he would underwrite the loan for nothing if Douglas could get other cosigners. This was accomplished, again with Henry's help. Douglas got his loan, and the plane was produced. The navy order yielded a profit of $40,000. Davis-Douglas was solvent for the time being. Other military orders followed, and Douglas was able to move his firm to larger quarters, the motion picture studio of a defunct Santa Monica firm, Herrman Film Corporation.

One of the reasons Douglas had left Martin was his belief in the future of commercial aviation. But as would usually be the case in the industry, the market determined his course of action. In late 1922, Douglas was a significant factor in military aviation, without much hope of a commercial sale.[16] His was not too different from other firms seeking military contracts. Douglas would receive a small private or military order, create a new plane to specifications, and if it were successful, hope for additional sales.

In 1923, Douglas received an army order for four planes, which were to make an around-the-world flight. He accepted and produced the *World Cruiser,* which was powered by the Liberty and could fly for eighteen hours before refueling. The *World Cruiser* was larger than World War I fighter planes but not very different in appearance. The four planes set out in April 1924. Two of them completed the trip in less than five months, but only fifteen flying days. It was one of the most publicized aviation feats to that time, although three years later the Lindbergh flight would eclipse it. The circumnavigation was a major accomplish-

War Department Aircraft Acceptances, 1920–1930

Year	Pursuit Planes	Bombers	Observation Planes
1920	112	20	1,000
1921	200	85	270
1922	60	25	200
1923	0	0	180
1924	35	0	124
1925	18	2	126
1926	83	1	176
1927	49	9	56
1928	69	34	151
1929	78	22	185
1930	108	30	122

SOURCE: Holley, *Ideas and Weapons,* p. 172.

[16]Cunningham, *Sky Master,* pp. 141–45.

ment for the army too, and even more so for Douglas. The contract had been awarded in 1923, a year during which the military had received not a single new bomber or pursuit plane, and the army hoped that favorable publicity would lead to new congressional appropriations for airplanes. Douglas, of course, hoped to get orders. He knew, however, that these would be few.

On the other hand, the services continued to purchase small, inexpensive observation planes. While working on the *World Cruisers,* Douglas designed the XO observation plane, which he entered in a competition. He received a handful of orders—both foreign and American—for *World Cruisers,* but in 1924 the army awarded him a $750,000 order for fifty XOs, one of the largest in terms of numbers since the Armistice.[17]

That year American manufacturers produced 317 warplanes, over half of which were sold to foreign governments; the industry produced only 60 civilian airplanes. Clearly, the only large market for aircraft was the military. So Douglas and the other manufacturers allied themselves with air power advocates in the armed forces. Admiral William Moffett of the navy's Bureau of Aeronautics and General William "Billy" Mitchell of the army were two of the more prominent air power advocates. Moffett did his work through channels. The flamboyant and outspoken Mitchell often used the press as a vehicle for his ideas and criticisms. In 1925 he exploded against the army's neglect of aircraft, and this led to his famous court martial that year.[18]

More important, however, was the renewed interest in aviation created by the combination of the around-the-world flight and the Mitchell trial. Because of it, Congress passed the Kelly Air Mail Act of 1925, which provided for the transfer of airmail lines from the Post Office to private carriers. This not only would stimulate the growth of air-

[17] *Ibid.,* pp. 163–64.
[18] Edward Arpee, *From Frigates to Flat-Tops* (Lake Forest, Ill., 1953), Morris and Smith, *Ceiling Unlimited,* pp. 197–212.

lines but also help the manufacturers, since the lines would need aircraft to operate. Then President Coolidge appointed a commission—the President's Aircraft Board—under the chairmanship of Dwight Morrow (later to be Lindbergh's father-in-law as well as a major figure in his own right)—to make a study "of the best means of developing and applying aircraft in national defense." The Morrow Board issued a report favorable to military aircraft, but also made several recommendations in the area of civilian flight. One of these resulted in passage of the Air Commerce Act of 1926, which established the Bureau of Air Commerce in the Commerce Department. This body was to help establish air routes, set up safety regulations, encourage the construction of airports, and in general assist in the development of private commercial aviation. In addition, Congress authorized further expenditures in the area of military aviation.[19]

All of this boosted the industry's expectations and sales. Demand for airplanes increased, and after the Lindbergh flight, so did that for aircraft stock on Wall Street. In the late 1920s, investment bankers set about creating industry giants—United Aircraft and Transport, Curtiss-Wright, North American, AVCO, and Detroit Aircraft—and floating their securities for an eager public to take. These firms attempted to blanket the industry and through stock deals took in producing and operating firms in the airframe, engine, maintenance, and airlines fields. United, for example, brought together Boeing (airframes and airlines), Chance Vought (airframes), Pratt and Whitney (engines), Hamilton Aircraft (propellers), Standard Steel Propeller (propellers), Stearman Aircraft (private planes), Sikorsky Aviation (airframes), Avion Corporation (experimental planes), and three airlines affiliated with Boeing—Varney, Stout, and National. Frederick Rentschler, one of the most knowledgeable men in aviation, headed United, and he

[19] *Ibid.*, pp. 211–13.

brought in an excellent staff from the industry. In addition, he pursuaded Eugene Wilson, who was Admiral Moffett's closest friend, to resign his naval commission to work for his company. Later, Wilson convinced Raymond Walsh, a major who had served in the Office of Chief of Air Corps, and other military and naval officers to join United, in this way cementing a close alliance between the company and the War Department.[20]

The formation of the giants marked the reentry of the automobile companies into aviation. General Motors held a major interest in North American, while executives from that company, along with others from Ford, Hudson, and Reo, were involved in the formation of Detroit Aviation. The industry had become a major glamour area, at the tail end of the great bull market on Wall Street in 1928–1929.

Douglas was approached by several investment bankers who hoped to use his firm as the nucleus for another giant. He rejected these overtures, since it would mean that he would lose power either to other executives or to the bankers. But he did agree to sell stock in Douglas Aircraft (the name was changed in 1926). In November 1928, 300,000 shares were floated and in 1929 their price reached a bull market high of 45½, giving the company's outstanding stock a paper value of $13.5 million and making Douglas a paper millionaire.

The firm was still small. Douglas sold $1.9 million worth of airplanes in 1928 and $2.6 million in 1929 and showed profits of $400,000 in each year. In 1931 he invested in another company for the first time, taking a majority interest in Northrop, which was to experiment with new kinds of planes and engines. Douglas made another attempt to crack the civilian market with the *Ambassador,* one of his few failures in production models. Afterward, he turned fully to military sales, both foreign and American. All this while he behaved conservatively, keeping his firm as liquid as

[20]Rae, *Climb To Greatness*, pp. 39–48; Eugene E. Wilson, *Slipstream: The Autobiography of an Air Craftsman* (New York, 1950), p. 168.

possible and not contracting debts he might have difficulty in paying later on. It was as though Douglas remembered the experience of getting into aviation more than he considered the dreams of 1928–1929.

As a result, his was one of the better prepared companies for the depression that followed. Aircraft production plummeted, as it had after World War I. Detroit Aircraft went bankrupt, Lockheed went into receivership, North American and AVCO, both of which were overcapitalized, barely escaped failure, and even United was in difficulties. Douglas Aircraft suffered. By 1932, that company and Northrop had a working force of 135, and together the two firms produced only seventy airplanes, with profits of $100,-000. In mid-year, Douglas's common stock sold for 5.

On the other hand, the firm was never in danger of failure. It was not an overblown, unconsolidated and poorly financed giant. Nor did Douglas resemble any of the dozens of small firms that specialized in two-seaters for the civilian market. Douglas barely entered that greatly oversold part of the industry and so did not suffer when it collapsed. At no time during the depression did Douglas Aircraft report an annual deficit, although it came close to one in 1933 and 1934.[21]

As had been the case in the early 1920s, the market for

American Aircraft Production, 1926–1933

Year	Military	Civil	Total
1926	532	654	1,186
1927	621	1,374	1,995
1928	1,219	3,127	4,346
1929	677	5,516	6,193
1930	747	2,690	3,437
1931	812	1,988	2,800
1932	593	803	1,396
1933	466	858	1,324

SOURCE: Rae, *Climb to Greatness*, p. 49.

[21]Cunningham, *Sky Master*, pp. 198–99.

planes declined after the depression began, just as it had overexpanded during the previous boom period. But the comparison did not go beyond this. The Liberty engine, low in price, helped dictate the shape of the industry until late in the 1920s. There was no hope of a major commercial boom in that decade, while the role of aviation in war was still being debated. During the Great Depression, the military and civilian markets for airplanes expanded, and the technology of the 1920s, as well as the machines of that decade, were inadequate for the needs of both. As the Europeans and Asians prepared for a new war, they demanded new airplanes, many of which were produced in the United States, and eventually America too began its war preparations. The growth of airmail, and then air transport, both aided by the government, expanded the market for commercial airplane manufacturers, especially those able to meet the specifications set down by the airlines. Only several firms could, and of these, Douglas Aircraft performed best. In 1931, just before the bottom fell from the aviation market, Douglas Aircraft sold $4.7 million worth of planes and had a profit of $500,000. In 1935, sales were $7.4 million and profits, $1.3 million. That year Douglas common stock earned $2.70 a share and sold for 58, and in all respects performed better than the company had in the so-called bonanza years. In 1937, a depression year when the economy slipped badly, Douglas's sales were $21.4 million and headed upward.

A large part of this success derived from Douglas's ability to maintain his share of the military market. Although civilian planes outsold military throughout the 1920s and well into the 1930s, the latter craft cost more per unit. For example, the United States Government purchased 466 airplanes in 1937, valued at $9 million. That same year, civilian sales were 591 units, which cost $6 million. Furthermore, military contracts provided manufacturers with security. The company might produce a prototype, submit plans, or enter a competition. Over 90 percent of all government contracts, however, were let without competitive bids, and so having friends and influence in the armed forces was extremely important for all the major firms. Once the contract was granted, be it for one or one hundred planes, the firm would tool up for production and be paid as progress and deliveries were made. The profits were great; a return of over 30 percent on sales was not unusual in the military sector.[22] The situation was quite different in the civilian market, where the manufacturer had to produce his airplane and then try to sell it, thus being forced to keep a large part of his capital in inventory. In addition, profits as a percentage of sales were far lower for civil aviation products.

Douglas had an excellent reputation for military airplanes. He also had good connections with foreign governments. During the 1920s and 1930s, Douglas Aircraft sold planes to the Japanese, Chinese, South American governments, and the Germans, as well as anyone else who placed orders. Douglas granted licenses to the Nakajima Aircraft Company of Japan and permitted its representatives to visit Douglas factories even when the American government did not favor such actions. In the mid-1930s, Douglas at-

American Aircraft Production, 1932–1939

Year	Military	Civil	Total
1932	593	803	1,396
1933	466	858	1,324
1934	437	1,178	1,615
1935	459	1,281	1,710
1936	1,141	1,869	3,010
1937	949	2,824	3,773
1938	1,800	1,823	3,623
1939	2,195	3,661	5,856

SOURCE: Rae, *Climb to Greatness*, p. 81

[22]Irving Brinton Holley, Jr., *United States Army in World War II: Buying Aircraft: Matériel Procurement for the Army Air Forces* (Washington, 1964), p. 10; Elsbeth H. Freudenthal, *The Aviation Business: From Kitty Hawk to Wall Street* (New York, 1940), pp. 122–25.

tempted to sell aircraft to the Hitler government, with no success. On the other hand, the sale of technical information presented opportunities that Douglas was able to capitalize upon.[23] Given the company's abilities in the military sector, it might have appeared prudent for it to have concentrated on that lucrative part of the market. Orders from the War Department were scarce during the early years of the depression, but they picked up sharply in 1936, when federal expenditures for military aviation were $44 million. The figure reached $58 million in 1937 and $67 million in 1938.[24] As for foreign governments, these took some 10 percent of American production in 1929, or $8.8 million worth of airplanes. In 1934 the figures were 40 percent and $17.7 million, with Douglas accounting for more than 15 percent of sales in both years.[25] Some 90 percent of all Douglas sales were to governments—both the American and foreign—and most were warplanes of one kind or another, products with high profit margins, the kind that enabled Douglas to show fine profits in the 1930s.

With such a secure industry position, Donald Douglas might have been expected to remain wedded to the military and foreign markets. While he did continue to seek government orders in the 1930s, he also made a major move in the civilian market, in this way hedging his bets somewhat. In part this was due to a desire to utilize the talents at Northrop fully. That company, still more or less a Douglas subsidiary, possessed an excellent design staff that was proficient in military craft. Northrop would design the planes, and Douglas would produce them. The Douglas designers and engineers would work on other military airplanes, but at the same time, Douglas was able to indulge his continuing interest in commercial aviation by scouting for orders in that segment of the market. There seemed little chance of success.

[23] *Ibid.*, pp. 284–89.
[24] Rea, *Climb to Greatness*, p. 103.
[25] Freudenthal, *Aviation Business*, p. 295.

In 1932 most of the airlines and airmail carriers were controlled or owned outright by aircraft producers. These firms either used their own planes or those of companies with whom they had close relationships. General Motors, then a major factor in aviation, still had an interest in North American, which owned Trans World Airlines. General Motors also owned Fokker, whose 10-A Trimotor was used by Trans American. Similarly, the Boeing 80-A was used by United Air Lines, which was owned by United Aircraft, the parent of Boeing. The Ford Trimotor appeared on several routes, usually those with close connections with Ford Motor Car. Douglas lacked these connections. Even had he been able to produce a superior plane, it is doubtful major sales could have been made.

This situation changed as a result of events during the early years of the New Deal. In 1933, Senator Hugo Black of Alabama charged several aircraft companies with violations of the antitrust acts, citing as evidence the fact that United, North American, and AVCO had received most of the airmail contracts then outstanding. The firms denied the charge, replying that the industry had been structured the way it was by federal actions. But Black persisted, and as a result of his efforts, President Roosevelt canceled all outstanding contracts with private firms and turned the airmail business over to the Army Air Corps. The change proved disastrous. Several fatal crashes later, Congress passed the Air Mail Act of 1934, which returned the mails to the private carriers, but at the same time provided for the separation of the air lines from their parents. United Air Lines was spun off from United Aircraft, North American sold Trans World to the Atlas Corporation, while AVCO divested itself of American Air Lines. Other divestitures followed; the Air Mail Act was a major step in the creation of an independent airline industry.

Now Douglas was free to compete in the field, and he meant to do so. Federal subsidies for mail carrying continued, though at a somewhat reduced rate, while the use of airmail increased throughout the 1930s.[26] The airlines needed new planes capable not only of dependable flight but economical as well. Douglas understood this, as did other manufacturers. All of them cultivated airline executives at the unaffiliated lines and, after passage of the Air Mail Act of 1934, tried to cover the field. Douglas was one of these, and in time he would join the board of directors at Pan American Air Lines and serve on committees with executives of other lines.

Although he had prepared designs for commercial planes prior to 1932, Douglas's first major project was in response to an invitation by Jack Frye of Transcontinental and Western Airline that year. This carrier, unaffiliated with a manufacturer, competed with National Air Transport on part of its route. National was owned by United Aircraft, and another United company, Boeing, had just produced a new carrier, the 247D, which Boeing President P.G. Johnson called "the best commercial plane in the nation." National took twenty of the bimotors, which had a peak speed of 155 miles per hour and carried ten passengers. Later on, United Air Lines—of which Johnson was the president too —took additional planes. Although the 247D could not operate profitably on passenger revenue alone, it did show a decent return when airmail subsidies were added. Furthermore, Boeing hoped to sell a version of the plane to the army.

General Aviation and Sikorsky responded to the Frye invitation with trimotors. Douglas realized that Frye wanted a plane similar to the 247D but better in every respect. In effect, his designers produced such a plane. The DC-1 was powered by two engines and traveled at a peak speed of 160 mph. It carried twelve passengers and a larger mail cargo than did the 247D. Frye accepted the model and ordered twelve of them at a price of $65,000 each, with the

[26] *Ibid.*, pp. 305–12.

understanding that alterations would be made. Douglas agreed, and the result was the DC-2, which carried fourteen passengers and had a peak speed of 170 mph. The first of these planes was delivered to Transcontinental and Western in May 1934. By then, Douglas had considered further the implications of the Air Mail Act and was even more strongly drawn to the commercial market.[27]

Douglas Aircraft was still primarily a maker of warplanes, and although the commercial sales were profitable, the returns on sales were lower than those for bombers, pursuits, and observation planes. At the time Douglas was planning the DC-2, however, the Senate Special Subcommittee Investigating the Munitions Industry, headed by Gerald Nye of North Dakota, was in session. This body held a far-ranging series of inquiries, most of them dealing with relations between businessmen and government figures. Although the subcommittee proved little, it left the impression that arms manufacturers—"merchants of death" as they were termed by the press—worked with political allies to foment wars, from which they derived profits. Some senators included the aircraft manufacturers in this number, although the primary attack was against bankers and chemical manufacturers. Still, in 1934 it appeared as though future arms budgets would be cut, with aircraft suffering more than most industries as a result of antiwar feelings. As it happened, this did not occur. But the Nye hearings, together with passage of the Air Mail Act and the initial success of the DC-2, impelled Douglas further in the direction of commercial flight.

The logical next step was an improved version of the DC-2, one that could capture additional markets from Boeing and other carriers. Douglas had greater ambitions than that, however. Even the DC-2 could not carry passengers economically, having to rely upon airmail to make up defi-

[27]Donald J. Ingells, *The Plane That Changed the World: A Biography of the DC-3* (Fallbrook, California, 1966), pp. 68–76 ff.

cits in charges. Douglas believed it possible to alter the DC-2 in such a way as to make it the first commercially viable passenger plane.

Three assumptions played a role in his thinking at the time. First of all, airmail charges had been lowered, as were government subsidies. It was incumbent upon the airlines to adjust their thinking, to realize that their planes of the future need not be mail carriers that occasionally took on passengers but passenger planes that carried the mail. This, he believed, would soon occur in airline boardrooms. Douglas also believed the public would come to realize that flying need not be hazardous. The DC-2 was an extremely safe plane, constructed with margins of error unusual in commercial designs. If the craft had a good safety record, the public would be put at ease. Passenger flights would become more common, in which case additional planes would be needed. Airlines would prefer those passenger planes that carried the most people at one time, and so Douglas set about to produce such a carrier. Finally, he assumed that any successful commercial plane would have military uses as well. The combination of sales would make the new plane one of the most profitable ever produced.

Douglas sold 190 DC-2s in the next two years, a period he used to prepare his new model. In contrast, only 75 Boeing 247s were sold for its run. The DC-3 was unveiled in 1936, after only a year and a half of preparation. It featured powerful engines and even greater safety margins than the DC-2. It could carry twenty-one passengers, and more if necessary. The DC-3 also had the power to lift almost twice the load of the Boeing 247D.[28]

The plane was an immediate success. Within two years Douglas had sold over 800 of them, and the DC-3 carried 95 percent of the nation's commercial air traffic.[29] Before the plane was replaced, some 13,000 DC-3s were delivered, an

[28]Peter W. Brooks, *The Modern Airliner: Its Origins and Development* (London, 1961), pp. 71 ff.
[29]Hubler, *Big Eight*, pp. 44–45.

all-time commercial record. By 1937, the company's backlog was so great that the airlines had to wait at least a year before delivery could be made.

Safety and comfort were major factors in the plane's success, but still more important was economy. The DC-3 could show a profit even without airmail. Cyrus Smith of American Airlines said, "It was uneconomical and unsightly to have a system full of mismated aircraft. What was needed was one attractive type capable of carrying a sizeable load a good distance in jig time and at a low cost. The DC-3 . . . we considered the perfect airplane." Orville Wright inspected the plane. "The body is big enough to carry a sizeable payload and this is important," he said. "There is plenty of room and the seats are comfortable. They tell me, too, that it is so sound-proof that the passengers can talk to each other without shouting. This is a wonderful improvement. Noise is something that we always knew would have to be eliminated in order to get people to fly. . . . Somehow it is associated with fear."[30]

The DC-3 was soon called "the Model T of Aviation" and awarded other, similar titles. Even today hundreds of them are in service, and pilots talk of the plane with measured reverence. But in fact, the way for the change had been prepared by federal legislation, since Douglas and others in the industry had been obliged to seek commercial orders when it appeared the military markets might decline. And it was the DC-2, not its successor, that ushered in the new era in aviation, one the DC-3 was produced to capitalize upon.

The new plane, fully equipped, cost around $100,000, while passenger planes of the previous generation cost a third of that amount. The airlines had to strain their finances to purchase the new craft. Those that hoped to survive had to take them, for after a while, passengers refused to fly in any but the DC-3s except in emergency

[30]Ingells, *Plane That Changed the World,* pp. 101–2.

situations. It was one of the two times in aviation history where the aircraft manufacturers dictated a technological change to the airlines—the other being the advent of the pure jets in the late 1950s. On the first occasion, Douglas emerged as the leader in civilian aviation.

The DC-3 carried more passengers than the planes it replaced, and so fewer planes were needed to carry the passenger loads for most airlines. But to do this, the lines would have had to cut down on schedules, and none were willing to do so. As a result, the DC-3s flew half-filled or less at first, as though awaiting the time when demand for seats would catch up with supply. At first it didn't. Revenue miles flown rose from 64 million to 68 million in 1936–1938, hardly sufficient to justify the turnover of planes, and much less than anticipated. At the same time as the airlines had to pay for their DC-3s they expanded airport facilities and supports to accommodate the new generation of airliners. Because of these factors, most of the major airlines showed increased deficits in this period.

The DC-3 proved a commercial passenger plane could be profitable if flown fully loaded. This was not the case at first. It was not until the great expansion of airline use that came with the war that the DC-3 returned large profits to its buyers and earned its reputation as a money-maker. Revenue miles flown jumped to 83 million in 1939, and by 1945, the last year of the war, stood at 209 million.[31]

With the DC-3, Douglas became the leader of the commercial aviation manufacturing field. For the next two decades the company's passenger planes would evolve from the DC-3. Douglas would react to new technology and design but would create neither. The other firms took the lead there—Boeing in particular—in the hope that in this way they could topple the standard-bearer.

Douglas's laggard status might have been expected. Given the magnitude of his accomplishment, which may

[31]Holley, *Buying Aircraft*, pp. 16–17; *Historical Statistics*, pp. 467–68.

have exhausted his and the company's genius, along with his always cautious attitude toward change, Douglas seemed to coast. The DC-3 was his major creation. All that followed was imitation. There are few encores for American business tycoons.

Douglas Aircraft now had a commercial market to go with the military. In 1937 Douglas acted to acquire control of Northrop, merging its fine design division into his own, at least in practice. Sales and profits rose, largely the result of orders for DC-3s. But military demand was also on the rise. In 1936, the company produced the prototype for a new bomber, the B-18, which was based on the DC-3, soon to become the C-47 in its military incarnation, a leading transport.

The airlines were not so fortunate. In 1938, when it appeared the DC-3 was about to return handsome profits, Boeing and Douglas announced their intentions of producing a four-engine passenger plane.

Boeing had a head start in that it possessed a basic design. Three years earlier it had flown a prototype of its new Army Air Force bomber, the B-17, the first four-engine, all-metal, low-wing monoplane for the services. Its new plane, the 307 *Stratoliner*, was based on the B-17, and seemed a major advance over the DC-3. On the basis of plans and the one prototype, Boeing was able to get several advance orders.

Douglas lagged a trifle, and then produced drawings for its DC-4, which looked like a blown-up, stretched-out DC-3. The company's expansion into the military field had left it short of funds, and in order to get needed capital, Douglas approached the presidents of Pan American, Trans World, Eastern, and American and obtained advance orders as well as deposits of $100,000 each for the plane. TWA and Pan American also purchased Boeings under the same conditions, and there were indications the other companies would do the same. Boeing got into production and made deliveries before Douglas, and several airlines switched from the DC-4 to the 307 in 1938. In desperation, Douglas revamped his plans and turned out a new prototype, one more powerful and larger than either the original DC-4 or the 307. Had it not been for the intervention of the war, the 307 would have outsold the DC-4, in which case Boeing would have emerged as the industry's leader. As it was, the war intervened and, in effect, saved Douglas Aircraft from humiliation and a recognition of its flaws and Boeing's assets.[32]

The two companies had different strategies, even then. After the 247D had been bested by the DC-2, Boeing concentrated on military planes, attempting to draw passenger designs from its experiences in that field. For its part, Douglas hoped to develop a family of passenger planes from the DC-2, and would do so for the next two decades. In retrospect, it appears the Boeing concept was the more sensible, at least in an economy based to a large extent on war. The Douglas strategy would work only if arms expenditures remained low and aircraft procurement budgets shriveled. Both firms would prosper in World War II, but in the cold war atmosphere, Boeing had a decided advantage over its rival.

Douglas received an influx of military orders in 1939. Company facilities were converted from civilian to military production, and double shifts were put into effect to meet a 100 plane order for the A-20 *Havoc* bomber placed by the French government. Britain also ordered *Havocs*, and the United States followed. Douglas Aircraft had sales of $28.4 million in 1938. Six years later, as a result of wartime orders, sales went beyond the billion-dollar mark.

The company was the nation's leading producer of aircraft during World War II, delivering 29,385 planes to the armed forces. Of these, 10,124 were C-47s (the military version of the DC-3) and another 1,162, C-54s (a military version of the DC-4). The firm leased facilities from the govern-

[32]Hubler, *Big Eight*, pp. 145–46; Brooks, *Modern Airliner*, pp. 93–97.

Douglas Aircraft Co., Selected Statistics, 1939–1944

Year	Revenue	Income	Earnings	Dividends	Price Range Common Stock	
	(millions of dollars)		(per share)		High	Low
1939	28.0	2.9	$4.81	$3.00	87 3/4	55
1940	61.1	10.8	18.05	5.00	94 7/8	65 1/8
1941	181.4	18.2	30.29	5.00	79 1/4	59 1/4
1942	501.8	11.1	15.38	5.00	70 3/4	51
1943	987.7	6.0	9.92	5.00	72 1/2	47

SOURCE: *Moody's Manual*, 1942, 1945

ment in Tulsa, Oklahoma City, Chicago, and Long Beach and operated its own plants in Long Beach and Santa Monica. Business boomed, and Douglas's profits, as those of other firms in the manufacturing business, soared. On the other hand, the manufacturers knew what they could look forward to after the war; they remembered their experiences after the World War I Armistice. As Douglas put it, "After the war we can lock the doors and throw away the keys."

The early 1920s had been noted as a period when surplus aircraft were easily obtainable at low costs, and when aircraft technology was crippled by the presence of low-cost engines and airframes. Some economists expected a repetition of this after World War II. And for a while it appeared this might happen. Surplus C-54s were purchased for as low as $10,000 by nonscheduled airlines; when new the plane cost in excess of $200,000. The DC-4 clearly could not be produced economically under such a situation. Douglas was forced to close down his wartime plants, in the process firing 90,000 employees in one week, and attempt to retool for the civilian market, while awaiting cold war developments in regard to the military. His counterparts at Boeing, United Aircraft, Curtiss-Wright, Lockheed, and the other warplane manufacturers had the same problem.

Douglas Aircraft was in sounder shape than most. In early 1946 its backlog for both military and civilian planes was $170 million, placing it third in the industry behind Consolidated-Vultee and Lockheed. It was still the industry's leader in net sales, although Lockheed was closing in quickly. In the military area, Douglas had a large order for *Sky-Raiders.* In addition, the army had ordered fourteen *Globemasters,* huge four-engine planes that clearly derived inspiration from the DC-4s. Analysts thought Douglas would have deficits, but there seemed little doubt that it would remain a leading force in aviation.[33] It was not clear, however, how Donald Douglas would view the postwar markets and what his strategy would be.

Douglas was once described as "A man with his head in the clouds, his feet on the ground, and his hand in his pocket, counting the pennies."[34] From his first days in aviation, Douglas encouraged people to believe he was a practical man with vision and, most important, one who could make his company profitable. The nature of the industry was such that at times gambles were necessary for survival and prosperity. The DC-1 represented a risk and, in retrospect, was Douglas's greatest moment of daring. Yet had the plane not been acceptable, the company would have gone on making military planes at good profits. The DC-3, of course, made Douglas's reputation as the Henry Ford of aviation as well as being a money-maker for the firm. During the war, Douglas produced a variety of aircraft, but most of them were multi-engine transports and bombers, and those that Douglas designed bore strong family resemblances to the DC-3.

The postwar strategy was a continuation of the old, an attempt to dominate the industry while not offering startling leadership in design or creation. From all indications, it seemed the airline business would do well, and that civil

[33]George Bryant Woods, *The Aircraft Manufacturing Industry, Present and Future Prospects* (New York, 1946), pp. 69–72.
[34]Hubler, *Big Eight,* p. 61.

aviation would boom, especially in the area of private planes. At the same time, international tensions were such that the government would require new warplanes. The United States emerged from the war the strongest military power in the world, with sole possession of the atomic bomb and the means of its delivery. Air power advocates were on the ascendent in Washington, and this boded well for the industry.[35] In addition, there was the hope of foreign sales. If the United States was to be "the leader of the free world," it would have to supply craft for its allies or at least encourage them to rearm.

Douglas seemed to understand this, for although he did not speak or write on the subject, Douglas Aircraft's strategy was geared to meet these realities. The company was by far the dominant force in passenger planes and would concentrate on that part of the industry, producing larger and better versions of the DC-3 and DC-4. In addition, it would seek government contracts for bombers and transports, multi-engine planes that would be designed in somewhat similar configurations as the civilian planes. The company would experiment with jet planes, pursuits, and other craft, and in addition seek a position in the missile, and later the space, program. As before, Douglas planned to all but ignore private aviation.

This was both an understandable and sensible strategy, and events bore out the essential wisdom of Douglas Aircraft's approach. The number of passengers carried by the airlines went from 6.5 million in 1945 to 15 million in 1946, and in the same period revenue miles flown on domestic flights rose from 209 million to 352 million, while the figures for international flights increased from 33 million to 105 million.[36] The number of civil aircraft in the United States, which stood at 37,789 in 1945, rose spectacularly. A record 35,000 were produced in 1946, and although this pace could

[35]Woods, *Aircraft Manufacturing Industry*, p. 33.
[36]United States, Department of Commerce, *Historical Statistics of the United States, Colonial Times to 1957* (Washington, 1960), pp. 467–69; Rae, *Climb to Greatness*, p. 202.

not be sustained, by 1949 there were 92,622 private and commercial planes in the country.[37] Douglas remained aloof from the private market but took command in passenger planes. In 1958, more than 53 percent of all such craft were Douglas-built.[38]

The DC-6, first produced in 1946 and based in part on wartime experience and designs, was the key plane for the company. It cruised at over 300 mph and could carry as many as seventy passengers along with their baggage, mail, and other cargo. The DC-6 made the New York–Santa Barbara trip in less than seven hours and with greater passenger comfort than had been offered by airlines in the past. Douglas had also beaten his rivals—Boeing, Lockheed, and Consolidated in particular—to the market with the first postwar passenger liner. The company had little difficulty obtaining orders. Within the next ten years, forty-four airlines had over six hundred DC-6s in operation. And, as had been the case since 1935, it was part of the "Douglas family," an outgrowth of DC-4 design. Similarly, the C-64, which appeared in 1947, and the C-124, first manufactured in 1949, derived inspiration from DC-6.

Once again, Douglas appeared to have achieved the proper blend of military and civilian business, but the company's major stress in the late 1940s was on the civilian side of the industry. This is not to say that Douglas did not compete for military contracts but rather that the winning or losing of one would not cripple the company. Its AD-1, F3D, and F4D fighters sold well, as did other Douglas military craft, and the company engaged in work for the National Aviation and Space Agency as well. Increasingly, however, Douglas became identified as the one company in the aircraft industry with balance—a firm that would survive "if peace broke out." It was an enviable position, one that other firms hoped to emulate. The only way they could do this, of course, would be to

---

[37] *Historical Statistics*, p. 469.
[38] Hubler, *Big Eight*, p. 19.

grab part of Douglas's commercial business.

In the early 1950s, Douglas set to work on a plane to replace the DC-6, which naturally would be called the DC-7. American Airlines gave the company an advance order for an airliner that could carry as many as ninety-five passengers and would fly over 400 mph. The plane made its appearance in November 1953, by which time Douglas had more than enough orders to assure its financial success and to keep his plants busy for several years. This was deemed important, for the Korean War had just ended, and with it, the beginning of a decline in military procurement. The other aircraft companies suffered; Douglas was thriving.

Though well-received, the DC-7 was not an advanced plane. Clearly, it was more akin to the DC-6 than that model was to the DC-4. As one Douglas engineer put it, "We stretched the DC-4 again—eight feet and from 70,000 to 140,000 pounds. We got us a new work horse."[39] Within industry circles it seemed that Douglas was running short on imagination and creative energies.

On the surface these doubts appeared unjustified. Doug-

American Aircraft Production, 1946–1957

Year	Military	Civil	Total
1946	1,417	35,001	36,418
1947	2,122	15,617	17,739
1948	2,536	7,302	9,838
1949	2,592	3,545	6,137
1950	2,680	3,520	6,200
1951	5,055	2,477	7,532
1952	7,131	3,509	10,640
1953	8,978	4,134	13,112
1954	8,089	3,389	11,478
1955	6,664	4,820	11,484
1956	5,203	7,205	12,408
1957	5,198	6,745	11,493

SOURCE: Rae, *Climb to Greatness*, p. 202.

[39] *Ibid.*, p. 64.

las's supporters responded that he had found the right formula and would apply it as long as it worked, after which changes would be considered. They did not seem necessary in mid-decade. In 1954, the company surveyed the field and learned that Douglas airliners not only had achieved domination of the field but that its used planes were commanding premium prices. It was a sellers' market, with Douglas as the leader of the pack. As always, Donald Douglas was well attuned to the market, but it may have been that he didn't feel the need for major innovations yet.

Costs had a good deal to do with it. The DC-3 sold for less than $100,000, while the DC-6B went for well over $1.5 million. The costs of designing such craft were high, while production could not take place until firm orders were received. Similarly, the airlines at one point could make a commitment for a single plane which, if it proved acceptable, would be the prelude to other orders. By the 1950s, the airlines had to commit hundreds of millions of dollars for new models. In 1954 alone, for example, Douglas received orders for 123 DC-7 airliners, worth in excess of $200 million. That same year it released the DC-7C—the *Seven Seas* —an improved version of the basic plane. If the manufacturers continued to develop new planes at an ever more rapid pace, and the public demanded they be put into service, the airlines would find themselves in an impossible financial situation. Ordinarily a new airliner did not "break into the black" until its fourth year of service. Even as the DC-7 was hailed as a fine plane, it appeared questionable that it would be a money-maker.

By 1954, it was evident that the airlines would no longer accept changes unless they were basic. Many of the lines suffered losses that year and were fearful that they could not afford to service their debts. The next new airliner they accepted would have to be quite different from those that went before. One model demanded was a jumbo liner, that could carry many more passengers than existing planes, and so offer the lines a higher return on each flight. Another and more significant demand was for a jet liner, one that would carry more passengers by virtue of faster and more economical flights.

The future clearly was with jets. The only questions were when the new planes would be produced, and how the market for them would be when it came time for orders. In addition, jet technology would enable Douglas's rivals—especially Boeing and Lockheed—to compete on a more equal basis with Douglas. Other manufacturers might also enter the field. Those with experience in the production of military jets, such as North American Aviation and the Convair division of General Dynamics, indicated an interest in passenger planes, although they did little in the piston field.

The other manufacturers had more experience than Douglas in the manufacture of military jets. Lockheed was the prime contractor for the B-47 bomber, and Convair produced the B-58. North American had extensive experience in jet fighters, and company executives spoke of developing a new four-engine bomber. Boeing had the KC-135 refueling tanker, as well as other planes that made it the firm most committed to jet aviation in the transport field. Its B-52 bomber was one of several Boeings on duty with the air force. It was also a larger company than Douglas in terms of total sales.

Of all the firms in the field, Boeing was best equipped for the challenge. In the KC-135 it had a proven plane with the basic configurations of a passenger carrier. Major modifications would be needed, of course, but in essence both a military and civilian version were possible. In May 1954, the plane was tested. The four-engine jet flew at 646 mph and appeared to justify Boeing's investment of over $15 million in the plane. The air force announced it would purchase the military version, and Boeing's engineers were given the task of reshaping it into the 707.[40]

Donald Douglas and his staff understood what this meant. Ever since 1943 the company had been interested in jet propulsion, and in 1952 a special projects team was established in the company to work on the idea. By then, however, Boeing had a head start in the field and was on better terms with the military than was Douglas. And Douglas Aircraft wasn't eager to close the gap. In its annual report for 1952, the company stated:

Operational experience and cost data on the use and maintenance of engines of the size required for jet transports of the future are meager or nonexistent. These cost figures will play a deciding part in the desire or ability of the airlines to absorb the jet transport into the existing traffic patterns of their individual operations and earn sufficient additional income to pay for the new equipment.[41]

Donald Douglas wasn't at all certain that jets would be economically feasible. Aircraft engineers were divided on the issue. Some believed turboprops were a sensible compromise, while others, admitting the jet could offer speed and even comfort, thought it would result in higher unit costs, which customers would be unwilling to pay. In any case, the pioneer would have to take major risks, and for the moment at least, Douglas was unwilling to assume them. He would not compete with Boeing for the first sales in the commercial jet field, at least not until it could be shown that the venture would be profitable. Douglas Aircraft entered the competition for the jet tanker and lost out to Boeing there. That meant Boeing would be able to design

[40] Aircraft Industries Association of America, *The Aircraft Year Book, 1954* (Washington, 1954), pp. 86–87.
[41] Rae, *Climb to Greatness*, p. 206.

its passenger plane with the aid of the government in the form of a military contract for $100 million worth of planes. If Douglas were to produce a jet passenger plane, it would have to do so on its own. Donald Douglas said, "There may be some distinction in being the first to build a jet transport. It is our ambition at Douglas to build the best and most successful."[42] There was no doubt, however, that the company would have to make its move into the jet field. A generation earlier, it was possible to conceive, design, and produce a passenger plane in a year and at a cost of around $100,000. By 1955, the time between conception and realization was more than three years, and could involve hundreds of millions of dollars in investments. When Donald Douglas realized Boeing would go ahead with the 707, he set into operation plans for his own jet passenger plane, the DC-8. "We had to go into the building of the DC-8 as a jet transport or else give up building airplanes," said a Douglas executive later on. "Our hand had been forced."[43]

Boeing had a lead on Douglas technologically, as well as having the military contract and the advantage of a running start on the 707. Douglas put all its resources behind the DC-8 and, like Boeing, sold aggressively from plans. This was the most serious and significant civilian competition in aviation history to that time. Both firms banked heavily on success; defeat not only would mean a financial loss but a loss of prestige as well. Industry leadership, both real and symbolic, was at stake.

Douglas directed the sales effort himself, visiting many airline executives and drawing upon old friendships. This worked in the 1930s but had little effect in the 1950s, when hundreds of millions of dollars worth of orders were at stake and an error could mean bankruptcy. The DC-8 was to be a wholly new plane, not merely a stretched-out version of the DC-7C. Some industry executives began to

[42] *Ibid.*, p. 207.
[43] Hubler, *Big Eight*, p. 148.

doubt Douglas's ability to make the change. For years there had been talk that the DC-3 had been the work of John Northrop, who had left Douglas in 1938 to form his own company. Ever since then, so the saying went, the company had been living off Northrop's ideas. The new passenger plane came from an experienced engineering team, but one that was at least as untested as the Boeing group. Whether or not this was so is impossible to say, but the rumors may have had their effects and hurt Douglas's chances.

Douglas's age militated against him, even though he was vigorous and even youthful-appearing. On many occasions Douglas had indicated his intention to remain in the industry until he died. But he was also grooming his son, Donald Douglas, Jr., to take his place. Another rumor was to the effect that after production on the DC-8 began, Douglas Sr. would step down, and turn power over to his son. Although a capable and experienced aviation man, Douglas Jr. was still an untested quality in top management, while several airline executives who knew him doubted he had the abilities of his father.

The airlines had been impressed with the DC-7 as a technological feat, but at the time of their purchases, they assumed jet travel was at least a decade off. Some had ordered Lockheed's *Electra* turboprop as an "intermediary" between propeller and jet planes, but most waited on the sidelines, expecting to reap large profits from their DC-7 fleets before having to enter the jet race. The 707 changed this, and so it appeared the DC-7s would not be major money-makers after all. In large part, this was the result of short-sightedness at the airlines, which never should have made such a major investment in what was a revamped DC-6. Nevertheless, they blamed Douglas for having foisted an obsolete plane on them and so had negative thoughts regarding the company and its president.

Finally, there were the planes themselves. In order to catch up with Boeing, Douglas took the daring step of going into production immediately, without a prototype.

The gamble paid off, but at the time it was feared that the new plane might develop bugs and so prove inferior to the 707. Furthermore, although the two planes were similar in design and performance, the Boeing cost some $500,000 less than the DC-8. In addition, Boeing conducted a more aggressive sales campaign than Douglas and was more willing to alter its airliners to customers' requirements.

Douglas won the first order. National Airlines, a medium-size operation on the New York to Florida run, announced it would convert to 100 percent jet service through purchases of the DC-8. Pan American hesitated. It wanted to be the first international carrier to use jets, but the 707's range was too small. For a while it appeared the company would await performance tests on the DC-8. Then, when it learned that British Overseas Airways was planning to use a British-made *Comet*, it placed orders for twenty-five DC-8s and twenty 707s, with the understanding that additional 707s would be ordered if the range were increased. United Air Lines selected Douglas after Boeing refused to absorb special charges for major alterations. "We didn't want to lose twenty-one years of Douglas experience with us and ours with Douglas," said President W.A. Patterson. Douglas made the alterations and kept its price down, but as a result showed only a small profit from the United order. It had absorbed the charges in order to show momentum in its struggle with Boeing and to convince other airlines to follow suit. The gamble didn't work. American Airlines—which had been considered the one most loyal to Douglas—announced soon after it would purchase thirty 707s. With this, the balance tilted in Boeing's favor.

In the foreign area, SAS and Trans Canada took the DC-8, and Air France and Air India ordered the 707. Then Boeing announced it was preparing the 720, a smaller, short-range version of the 707, with additional variants to come in the future. By the fall of 1956, Boeing had eleven airlines and a backlog of 134 planes, while Douglas had twelve airlines and a backlog of 118. A year later, Boeing had an advantage of three to one.[44]

Other manufacturers entered the field, with the Convair Division of General Dynamics making a concerted though inept effort. It produced the 880 and, later on, the 990. Both planes flopped, with the company losing nearly a half billion dollars and almost going out of business. Such were the stakes and punishments in the race. Lockheed, which opted to stand pat with its *Electra,* never caught up, and its decline began at this point. As for Douglas, the company was no longer unbeatable. The relative failure of the DC-8 was the turning point in the firm's history. It had repulsed the Boeing challenge in the late 1930s and was saved from possible defeat then by the coming of World War II. It would not be saved a second time. By the early 1960s, Boeing had replaced Douglas as the nation's major supplier of commercial planes. The 707 was to the jet age what the DC-3 had been to the propeller era—a symbol as well as a plane.

The Boeing 707 went into airline service in 1958, with the DC-8 arriving the following year and the Convair 880 in 1960. Although Boeing did not dominate the subsonic jet age to the degree that Douglas had that of the propeller commercial plane, it was the clear industry leader, both in design and production.

American Airliners in Service on World Airlines, 1958–1962
(Pure Jets Only)

Plane	Year				
	1958	1959	1960	1961	1962
Boeing 707	5	76	143	150	209
Boeing 720	–	–	23	40	51
Convair 880	–	–	9	40	44
Convair 990	–	–	–	–	21
Douglas DC-8	–	21	110	149	167

SOURCE: Aerospace Industries, Assoc., *Aerospace Facts and Figures, 1964,* p. 104

[44] *Ibid.,* pp. 162–66; Charles J. Kelly, Jr., *The Sky's the Limit: The History of the Airlines* (New York, 1963), pp. 187–98.

There was a squeeze on airline profits in 1957, as earnings dropped and funded debt soared. This gave Boeing's lower-priced plane an ever greater advantage as new orders continued to come in. At this point, having lost the first round with a bleak outlook for the others, Donald Douglas, Sr., stepped down as president, at the age of sixty-five, and was replaced by his son. The following year, Douglas had record sales. Then, as the Boeing lead increased and Douglas lost several significant military contract competitions, sales and profits declined. In 1958, Douglas Aircraft had working capital of $187 million. As the decline continued, its liquidity fell. By 1966, Douglas had only $34 million in working capital. The following year it was taken over by McDonnell Company, a large manufacturer of military aircraft that wanted to diversify into the passenger business. At the time, Donald Douglas, Sr., was still chairman of Douglas, and he saw his firm become the junior partner in the new McDonnell-Douglas Corporation.

All the aviation pioneers had major failures, and in the end their companies fell into the hands of others. Curtiss, Martin, the Wrights, Boeing, the Lockheeds, and Douglas, the last to fall, saw their creations merged into more vigorous and successful firms or stepped down to be replaced by fresh leaders. Some did not succeed in business because they were not good at it. Others, and Douglas was one of them, went from engineering and flying to management without too much trouble and did well in both fields. The nature of the industry was such, however, that one major mistake could cause disaster. At first, when the companies were small, a shift in government policy could accomplish this. Later on, when aviation was a mature and giant enterprise, the loss of a military contract or, as was the case with Douglas, a late decision to enter a new field, could result in failure, for the stakes at that point were quite high.

In terms of sheer survival, Douglas led the rest. At the

Douglas Aircraft Co., Selected Statistics, 1956–1966

Year	Revenue	Income	Earnings	Dividends	Price Range Common Stock High	Low
	(millions of dollars)		(per share)			
1956	1,073.5	33.2	$7.08	$3.16	75 5/8	57 1/4
1957	1,091.4	30.7	6.54	3.16	72	40
1958	1,209.9	16.8	3.59	1.99	59 1/8	43 1/8
1959	883.9	(33.8)	d7.21	.81	48 5/8	30 1/8
1960	1,174.0	(19.4)	d4.15	0	34 5/8	22
1961	791.3	6.0	1.27	0	34 5/8	22 7/8
1962	749.9	10.2	2.18	stock	30 1/2	14 5/8
1963	698.3	11.8	2.52	stock	25	18 1/8
1964	650.1	13.7	2.92	stock	30 5/8	18 3/4
1965	766.8	14.6	3.06	.58	81 3/8	22 1/8
1966	1,048.0	(27.6)	d5.23	.74	108 5/8	30

SOURCE: *Moody's Manual*, 1967

time of the merger, he was the only one of the men who put their names on a major aviation company to remain in the field; the others were either dead or retired. He had been one of many pioneers in the 1920s, and then, in the 1930s, he developed one of the most important vehicles twentieth-century man has known, the DC-3, which tilted the aviation business away from the military for a brief moment and toward the civilian sector. He managed to hold on to this lead during and after the World War by putting together "sets" of planes, each emerging from its predecessor. This not only provided military and civil aviation with sensible evolution but held down costs. The large monopsonistic markets of military and civil aviation in the 1950s and 1960s were treacherous. In the end, Douglas Aviation fell because it failed to win the contract for the C-5A transport, a huge plane that represented a billion-dollar commitment by the military. Lockheed won the competition, and because it could not fulfill its obligations at a profit, almost went bankrupt.[45] Such was the nature of the market when Donald Douglas was chairman of the board, and his son ran

[45]Berkeley Rice, *The C-5A Scandal: An Inside Story of the Military-Industrial Complex* (Boston, 1971), pp. 5–10.

the company. The wonder was not that Douglas saw his company fall in the end but that it survived as long as it did. Too, it was ironic that Douglas became a merger candidate when it did, in 1967, at the climax of the great mergermania of that decade, when combinations far more complex than McDonnell-Douglas were being assembled by investment houses and conglomerate executives. Douglas was one of the few major aircraft firms to survive the last such movement, that of the late 1920s. It failed to do the same four decades later. When news of the merger was first announced, Douglas common stock soared to 108⅝, an all time high. At the height of its success, the company's stock sold for below 80. Now that it was about to pass out of individual existence, Douglas became a Wall Street favorite. Such was the nature of the mergermania of the conglomerate era.

IX

Royal Little:
The Spider and His Webs

In 1966, its last year of independent existence, Douglas Aircraft reported sales of $1,048 million and a loss of $27.6 million. The company might have survived on its own but would have needed a credit line of $400 million to carry it through the coming year. Such funds were available, but not for Douglas, which had fallen behind in a race where there could be only one winner, and that was Boeing.

Several aerospace firms were interested in acquiring Douglas, all of which were capable of extending sufficient credits and absorbing future losses, if any. After reviewing a field of six would-be partners, Donald Douglas and his son selected McDonnell, a major corporation with annual sales of $1,060 million.

Douglas was a giant corporation but ranked only seventy-third among American manufacturing companies, with McDonnell, Grumman, Lockheed, North American, and Boeing reporting larger sales in 1966. But even these were not in the inner circle. With revenues of $2,357 million, Boeing ranked only twenty-third that year. In 1967, the new McDonnell Douglas Corporation, revived and strong, grossed close to $3 billion. Yet there were fifteen other manufacturing concerns with higher sales that year.[1]

Francis Lowell died in 1817, and at the time was considered a major industrialist, a man whose words could move senators and representatives, the voice of the New England textile interests. Boston Manufacturing was flourishing, the leading mill of its kind in the land. That year, it reported sales of $34,000.

It goes without saying that in almost all respects, the worlds of Francis Lowell and Donald Douglas were strikingly dissimilar. Comparisons between these two men, their careers and accomplishments, would not be very fruitful. In both quantitative and qualitative terms, the two businessmen operated in different contexts, with contrasting horizons and ambitions. Nevertheless, both men depended upon the federal government for assistance, Lowell in the form of a tariff, Douglas in subsidies and aid for airlines and contracts for military and space vehicles. However, the role and function of government was quite different in 1966 from what it had been during and after the War of 1812. Each man had problems raising money, but Douglas thought in terms of hundreds of millions of dollars, while Lowell's capital needs were taken care of through subscriptions from friends and relatives. Lowell had no recourse to stock exchanges and investment bankers, for these were in their infancies in America at the time; Douglas and other aircraft manufacturers were the vehicles for the descendants of J.P. Morgan. Management was an art to Lowell, a talent that could be transferred from one phase of business to another, in his case from foreign trade to manufacturing. Douglas was raised in aviation, and although the industry was noted for its swift technological change, he was an aviation (and, perhaps, aerospace) man to the end of his career, during a period in which executives spoke of management as a science.

At first blush, the line from Lowell to Douglas seems

[1]T.A. Wise, "How McDonnell Won Douglas," *Fortune* (Vol. LXXV, No. 3, March, 1967), pp. 155-56, 214-34.

clear enough. It runs from the small to the big, from the diversified to the specialized, from the dabbler to the professional, and some might say from the chameleon to the dinosaur. During World War II, when defense firms such as Douglas were in their glory, and even in the post-war period, after a successful conversion to a war-peace economy, the line appeared extendable. It was generally assumed that large corporations would try to become larger, through absorption of rivals and successful forays into their fields. Indeed, this had occurred in the Douglas-Boeing contest, with the McDonnell merger its capstone. The government's role would be to make certain the competition was fair and within the law and to preserve competition through enforcement, and possibly a revamping of, the antitrust laws. It would be a world in which men like Douglas could function. Corporations might be structured like Duke's American Tobacco and be staffed by the kind of executives nourished by Vail at AT&T—faceless "men in gray flannel suits." Progress seemed to mean a still further development away from the kind of management and business philosophy exemplified by Francis Lowell and his associates.

It didn't happen. Instead, a different kind of business form and businessman emerged in the post–World War II period, whose roots were as much in the milieu of Lowell as that of Donald Douglas. The conglomerate corporation, headed by a "new breed" of manager, shook the foundations of the American business scene—and indeed those of other countries as well—in the quarter century following the end of the war. They were headed not by Vail's anonymous executives but by bold, forceful individuals who seemed to thrive on publicity—such as James Ling, Harold Geneen, and Charles Bluhdorn, men who placed their stamps on their creations in much the same ways as had McCormick, Wanamaker, and Duke. They were empire-builders in the tradition of Hill, and opportunists like Marcus Loew. Their creations resembled not the highly specialized corporations confidently predicted in the 1920s, or even the giant trusts so feared throughout the twentieth century. Rather, they were highly diversified, mobile, ever-shifting, and flexible. Each conglomerateur developed his own philosophy of management, usually a rationalization after the fact. But all were alike in that they attempted to spread their risks, utilize their capital effectively, manipulate governments, and stress flexibility. In this, they resembled Francis Lowell far more than Donald Douglas. The conglomerateurs were not only the next stage in the history of American entrepreneurship but a recapitulation of all the others.

Conglomerate corporations were known to and analyzed by businessmen and economists in the 1950s, and they became familiar to readers of business pages in the early 1960s and the front pages of newspapers later in the decade. Even then, there was no universal agreement as to what constituted a conglomerate. The crudest definition was a firm engaged in several nonrelated enterprises at the same time. But that would include General Motors (automobiles, household appliances, locomotives, and defense work), RCA (television, electronics, carpeting, publishing, computers, land development), and American Brands (tobacco, liquor, pet foods, snack foods) as well as such recognized conglomerates as Litton, City Investing, and Indian Head. In terms of the government's standard industrial classifications (S.I.C.s), Allied Chemical, Armour, Bendix, Firestone, and Rexall, not usually classified as conglomerates, were in more businesses than Gulf and Western, often cited as a prime example of that form, while General Electric, with fourteen S.I.C.s, was more diversified than International Telephone and Telegraph, with thirteen.[2] Clearly

[2] *Fortune* (Vol. LXXV, No. 6, June, 1967), p. 177.

diversification alone was not the hallmark of a conglomerate.

For a while in the 1960s conglomerates were defined as firms whose major growth occurred through acquisitions, and it was charged that through complicated exchanges of financial paper, earnings would be exaggerated in an attempt to boost the price of the company's stock, which would then be used for further acquisitions. But mergers alone do not make conglomerates. In some respects the mergermania of the 1960s was less intense than that of the 1920s, a period in which Zukor, Loew, and others created their entertainment empires, and Alfred Sloan brought such companies as Fisher Body, Buick, Olds, Oakland, Cadillac, and many others into General Motors.[3] Also, there seems no consistency among conglomerates as to their use of paper to acquire firms. Gulf and Western usually took on new companies with higher price-earnings ratios than itself, while Litton did the opposite. As a result, G&W's earnings per share often fell as a result of its mergers, while Litton's usually rose after one of its takeovers. Yet both were adjudged conglomerates, while the term was not in use in the 1920s and certainly wasn't applied to General Motors, Paramount, or Loew's.

For a while government and academic economists clung to the notion of vertical and horizontal growth, the former to develop sources of supply and marketing facilities, the latter to become a more dominant force in a field by expanding product lines. Whatever growth or acquisitions that took place outside of these parameters appeared temporary, even frivolous. A Theodore Vail, purchasing suppliers and taking on new operating telephone companies, was understandable, as was a James Duke, who after conquering the cigarette went on to dominate plug and pipe tobacco. But what was one to make of a company like American Home Products? Founded in 1926, it was

[3]Samuel R. Reid, *Mergers, Managers, and the Economy* (New York, 1968), pp. 55–57.

primarily interested in household supplies for its first twelve years of operation. Then, in the 1940–1948 period, the company acquired thirty-two operating firms through mergers, so that it produced ethical and proprietary drugs, coffee, Italian foods, petroleum products, and beauty preparations, among others. There seemed little relationship between these businesses, which only then began to attract some attention.

In 1948 the Federal Trade Commission issued a report on the merger movement that seemed to be reviving in the aftermath of World War II. Most of the report dealt with vertical and horizontal mergers, with "all others" and "unrelated" mergers taking little space and thought. By then such mergers had been given their name—conglomerate. The FTC believed the motives behind them included "desires to spread risks, to invest large sums of idle liquid capital, to add products which can be handled with existing sales and distribution personnel, to increase the number of products which can be grouped together in the company's advertisements, etc." This was not all, however. "There is present in most conglomerate acquisitions a simple drive to obtain greater economic power." Looking to the future, the FTC noted:

> With the economic power which it secures through its operations in many diverse fields, the giant conglomerate corporation may attain an almost impregnable economic position. Threatened with competition in any one of its various activities, it may sell below cost in that field, offsetting its losses through profits made in its other lines—a practice which is frequently explained as one of meeting competition. The conglomerate corporation is thus in a position to strike out with great force against smaller business in a variety of different industries.[4]

[4]United States, Federal Trade Commission, *Report of the Federal Trade Commission on the Merger Movement: A Summary Report* (Washington, 1948), p. 59.

What was true for conglomerates under this charge also held for conventional large enterprises, however, such as those in foods, automobiles, and even aviation. The FTC report concluded that "there are few greater dangers to small business than the continued growth of the conglomerate corporation." Yet here and throughout the FTC and other government publications of the time the term "big business" could be substituted for "conglomerate" with the same impact being made. The vocabulary of the 1950s and 1960s was being created, but the meanings were still those of the great prewar antitrust crusade.

So, for that matter, was the mood among some congressional reformers. Fearful of the revived power of big business, several of them, led by Congressman, and later Senator, Estes Kefauver of Tennessee, worked for a stronger antitrust law. One was written and passed in 1950—the Celler-Kefauver Act—which "put teeth" into the old Clayton Anti-Trust Act. Under the previous legislation, the government acted against corporations whose activities tended to restrain trade *after* the fact. The Celler-Kefauver Act placed restraints on growth *prior* to a corporation's expansion, assuming, of course, such expansion or acquisition tended "substantially to lessen competition, or to tend to create a monopoly."

Enforcement of such a law would have halted Duke and other turn-of-the-century trust managers in their tracks. Clearly American Tobacco lessened competition in its industry, and this could have been discerned even prior to the major mergers Duke had transacted. The law assumed, of course, that an industry could be isolated and defined, and that large firms would—in the future—expand as they had in the past. Kefauver and his colleagues did not have conglomerates in mind when they drafted their measure. They should not be faulted for this. Two decades later, Justice Department lawyers still wrestled with the definition of such terms as "industry," "control," and "domination," to little avail. Even then, they could not define a conglomerate satisfactorily. Many yearned to write laws controlling conglomerate growth, but how could this be done until the term was isolated?

Part of the reason for this failure lay in the fact that conglomerates—also known as "free form corporations"— are by their very nature indefinable. It was as though a person were asked to describe the shape of an amorphous mass, when by definition the mass had none. Roy Ash, president of Litton, once said that his firm was "in the business of opportunity." In other words, Litton would enter a field if its leaders thought they could do well in it, but might abandon the business if conditions changed. Such an attitude would have been alien to Wanamaker, Duke, and Vail. Francis Lowell would have understood, for he too was in the business of opportunity.

In his time, Lowell speculated and engaged in commercial ventures, land, construction, insurance, banking, and manufacturing. Like others of his generation, Lowell was a one-man conglomerate. Men like him diversified their investments. If one failed, the others would carry them through. No one industry or occupation seemed strong enough at the time to be worth the risk of a complete investment, and all enterprises were subject to fluctuations. In a time of risk, diversify. Such was the situation in the days of Francis Lowell. A somewhat similar condition existed in the last days of Douglas Aircraft.

The locus of business in Lowell's day was the entrepreneur, a stable quality, and not his vehicles, which were transitory. In time, the businessmen would concentrate their attentions on single enterprises in clearly defined industries—steel, petroleum, meat packing, tobacco, etc. But along with the movement toward greater specialization was that of economic and social growth, offering opportunities for expansion aggressive businessmen could not overlook. So they would secure a firm base in one industry and then expand to take in other, related ones, in vertical and horizontal moves. McCormick became king of reapers and then entered other farm equipment areas. Wanamaker fortified his position in ready-to-wear clothing in Philadelphia prior to committing himself to other kinds of stores in nearby cities. Hill was a railroader before becoming an empire builder; Duke went from cigarettes to all of tobacco. Loew drifted into theaters, and then to vaudeville, and finally to film production, as opportunities led him from place to place. The shape of the aircraft and later aerospace industry dictated the form of Donald Douglas's ambitions as well as their scope.

As the economy developed and became more complex, the creation often appeared to overshadow the creator. American Telephone and Telegraph and Theodore Vail are good examples of this. While it was true that early twentieth-century antitrusters attacked men—Morgan, Rockefeller, and Duke among them—the corporations themselves took on personal identities. The faceless manager emerged, at the head of a powerful enterprise, one larger than him, that would survive his brief period of stewardship. During the age of the hero-businessman, politicians and scholars concentrated their attention on the entrepreneur. In the age of giant corporations, interest was focused on the enterprise.

This gradual change in focus was in large part responsible for the problems of identification and definition in the 1950s and 1960s. The FTC and other governmental agencies concentrated their interests on corporations and industries, attempting to study, understand, and control creations without first doing the same for creators. James Ling, Harold Geneen, Charles Bluhdorn, and other conglomerateurs were subjected to the kind of treatment in the press and magazines previously reserved for motion picture and television stars. Popular, often sensationalist books and articles appeared, offering surface analyses of their actions and activities, their authors more interested in "life-styles" than in career lines. Those few serious scholars who attempted to delve into the nature of the modern businessman tended to seek quantifiable results, available through computer read-outs, rather than explorations into values, practices, and pressures. As a result, there is a large literature on conglomerates, much of which is in the popular press, but little of a high quality. That on the conglomerateurs is much smaller; most of the work here is of a journalistic nature. Of the major leaders, only James Ling has been treated in a biography, and that admittedly an exploration into the subject rather than a definitive work. Bluhdorn, Thornton of Litton, and others have received far less. There is a popular history of ITT that contains material on Geneen, but it is uncritical of sources and is marred by errors and exaggerations.

One might argue that it is too soon to expect scholarly and definitive works on the conglomerateurs. Most are still active, and almost all have been closed-lipped, an understandable position considering their treatment in the press. But Royal Little, who might justly lay claim to having been the originator of the movement and was its first symbol, has never been subjected to a full-scale treatment, either in books or magazines. His major creation, Textron, is one of the few "mature conglomerates," and indeed, appears almost stodgy when set beside a LTV or ITT. Yet there is no definitive work on that company. Little is no longer active on a day-to-day basis, while Textron has "settled down" into a corporate groove. Studies of present leaders in the movement might still be deferred; a beginning toward understanding the founders is long overdue.

At the height of his career, during the 1950s and early 1960s, Royal Little was a favorite of several writers, especially those who worked for magazines read by businessmen. Little seemed to enjoy talking of his ideas and did so freely, with a boldness and zest unusual at a time when so many corporation presidents and chairmen appeared guarded and circumspect. Little had a fine sense of humor and mixed jokes with observations on business practices at his own company and at others. He was slightly eccentric, a man who enjoyed camera safaris to Africa, admitted that his love of golf led him to unwise investments in that field, and scoffed at the regalia of corporate life, preferring instead a small staff and a less than impressive office. Before such practices were popular, Little encouraged minority business, insisted his managers speak their minds openly in conferences, even to the point of opposing his pet projects, and tried to bring young people into his firm at the managerial level. Too, Little hired women as managers and executives, not because it was the thing to do—it wasn't in the 1950s—but because they had the ability and intelligence for their jobs. He always gave the impression of working because he enjoyed it and not because management was some kind of higher calling, with loyalty to the firm uppermost. He seemed easygoing, but at the same time worked hard at creating a major corporation.

Little later claimed to have drawn attention to himself only as president of his company, and not as an individual. He avoided photographers, so most of the articles dealing with his ideas either were without portraits or included candid shots of Little, often at play, usually smiling, in an informal setting. In what he later characterized as a moment of weakness, Little provided a short biography—six lines—for *Who's Who*, one that told of date and place of birth, his year at Harvard, marriage and divorce, children, and companies headed—no more. Later he tried, unsuccessfully, to have the publication delete it in future editions —saying so in interviews read by many more people than ever consulted *Who's Who*. Little would tell reporters almost anything they wanted to know of his operations, his interests and avocations. But his early life is a blank.

This was not due to fears of revelations regarding family secrets or scandals. Rather, Little guarded his privacy even while functioning in an arena where publicity served his purposes. He deliberately created an image for himself—of a bold, imaginative, daring entrepreneur who was easy to get along with. He was said to be a financial whiz who, while enriching himself, brought rewards to those who joined with him. This was necessary, for it helped convince potential merger candidates of the wisdom of coming under Little's umbrella. His company, Textron, may not have paid as much for companies it took over as did other conglomerates, but Little treated them better than did men like Bluhdorn and Ling. This kind of reputation enabled Little to acquire companies at rock-bottom prices, and indeed several major firms sought out Textron bids in order to stave off others from the more feared conglomerates. Little often spoke of "the Textron strategy," which he made appear sensible and bold, imaginative and conservative, and all at the same time. In fact, he more often than not went on fishing expeditions in the corporate seas, not certain what his net would bring in.

Those conglomerateurs who followed Little often confused the style with the substance, perhaps not realizing that under the hyperbole, Little really was a conservative businessman, obliged by circumstances over which he had little control to change course several times in mid-career, trying to make the best of difficult conditions. He used his fine knowledge of poorly drafted tax laws to his advantage on several occasions to create a misshapen textile giant. Then he adopted and refined the conglomerate philosophy to rid himself of his textile holdings, all the while making it appear that it was part of a master plan, when in fact it was a desperate salvage operation. When necessary, Little would operate at variance with his own dictates and later on amend the "holy writ" in a new interview. Little managed to combine the image of the go-go swinger with the substance of a New England Yankee, stressing one or another when circumstances demanded, and always doing so with panache.

Royal Little was born in Wakefield, Massachusetts, in 1896. His father died when he was two years old, and his mother remarried and the family moved to California, where he spent his youth. When he was fifteen years old, Little returned east, to live with his uncle, Arthur D. Little, one of the nation's leading chemists and founder of the Cambridge industrial research firm that bears his name. Arthur Little hoped Royal would enter a good prep school, go on to Harvard to major in science, and then take graduate work at M.I.T. Afterward, the two would become partners. But Royal was an indifferent student and showed no interest in science. After a year at Harvard he dropped out to join the army and served as an officer in France.

Little returned to Massachusetts after the war and told his uncle he wouldn't return to school. Rather, he would attempt to find employment in some kind of business—preferably a small firm in an area of advanced technology. Arthur Little had been one of the chemists who had developed rayon, the miracle fabric of the day. This so-called artificial silk appeared capable of reviving the moribund New England textile industry, perhaps by placing it on a new base. He spoke of these ideas, and Royal seemed impressed.

Royal apprenticed himself without pay to the Cheney Brothers Silk Company, where he learned silk manufacture. Then he took a sales position at Lustron Corporation, a small rayon producer, and invested all his capital —$2,500—with the firm. Lustron was underfinanced, the fabric met with resistance, and the company was not well managed. On top of this, it was hit hard by the postwar recession. Lustron failed and was sold to Celanese at a bargain price.[5]

Broke but still interested in fabrics, Little sought new

[5] *The Royal Little Story* (Boston, 1966), pp. 5 ff. This privately printed pamphlet is the only source for biographical material on Little's life outside of newspaper and magazine articles. Little apparently liked the Lustron name. Later on, he asked the advertising firm of J. Walter Thompson to pick a new name for his company—"something that says textile products made of synthetics"—and Thompson came up with Textron. "Textron, Inc.," *Fortune* (Vol. LV, No. 5, May 1947), pp. 160–61.

opportunity in that field. With the help of some friends, he borrowed $10,000, which he used to purchase the corporate shell of a defunct firm, the Chemical Products Corporation, and he activated and used its Special Yarns Division, now renamed Special Yarns Corporation. The remainder of the money was used for equipment and operating expenses.

Little's instincts regarding textiles were sound. Slightly more than 10 million pounds of packaged rayon and acetate were produced in America in 1920; the figure crossed the 100 million mark ten years later. But the industry was dominated by giant chemical firms—Du Pont, Celanese, and the like—while the old-line textile operations fought for scraps. Not much business was left for marginal operations like Special Yarns. Seeking power through size, Little merged his company with Franklin Rayon Dyeing in 1928 to form the Franklin Rayon Corporation. Then he tried to interest several investment bankers in underwriting a stock issue. It was at the height of the great bull market, but even then, Franklin was too chancy. No investment banker would touch it.

Rayon consumption increased sharply in the 1930s, even while the nation suffered through the depression. Franklin survived. Little acquired several small mills in this period, following accepted practice during such depressions; when small units went under, they were gobbled up by the survivors. Franklin almost went bankrupt toward the end of the 1930s, immediately after the recession of 1937. At a time when Little's creditors were about to foreclose on him, he managed to work out a merger with a "cash rich" company and then use its liquid assets to pay them off. These assets were $10,000.[6]

Franklin merged with several other firms in 1938, and the following year the company was refashioned and given a new name, Atlantic Rayon Corporation. This was on the eve of World War II. Like so many other small companies,

[6] *Royal Little Story*, p. 8.

Atlantic was saved from gradual bankruptcy by war-related events. Workers in defense industries now had regular and large paychecks, and they came to market for new clothes. More important were government orders for uniforms, tenting, and the like. Mill owners went to Washington seeking contracts and returned home with larger orders than they could handle. The war enabled successful manufacturers to do well, and proved a bonanza for those who had struggled through the depression with excess capacity, now a major asset.

Little was one of these. He obtained contracts for the production of parachutes, put on extra shifts, and sought old, abandoned factories to acquire. In 1943 he took over Suncook Mills, a New Hampshire competitor, for $1,750,000, as part of his plan to become the nation's leading producer of parachutes. The war was going badly at the time, and it appeared the production boom at home would continue for the foreseeable future. That year, Atlantic had a book value of $2 million and working capital of slightly below $1 million, while sales were $23.8 million. Only four years earlier, the company's future existence had been in doubt.

Late in 1943, the government canceled one of Little's parachute orders, indicating that in some fields, at least, overproduction had become a problem. Atlantic's sales rose slightly in 1944, to $26.2 million, while its profits and net worth began to top out. If the company had peaked prior to the end of the war, what would peace and an end to government orders bring? The question was uppermost in the minds of New England textile producers in 1944, and Little, like the others, began formulating plans for peace. Some mill owners, flush with profits for the first time in their lives, hoped to sell out before a new slump hit the industry. Little planned to take advantage of the situation by buying them out and forming a textile giant that would dominate the industry and even challenge the chemical companies that had taken the leadership in textiles.

The tax laws of the time supported such a strategy. Atlantic had reported excess profits during the war, and these would be all but confiscated by the government unless they were somehow disposed of by the company. One way to do this would be to shift Atlantic's profits into operations that were losing money, in this way showing a smaller profit, or even none at all, for the merged company. The law encouraged Little and others like him to explore new avenues, to seek loss situations that might be turned around. If they succeeded, they would have a larger operation, paid for by money the government would have taken anyway. Failure would be unfortunate, but after all, the money lost would have been paid in taxes in any event. "It's the only time in my lifetime that I'll ever have a situation like that," said Little. "You have to have a war that makes marginal operations profit-heavy, a tax situation plus large family holders who want to get out. And you have an insurance policy from the government if you're wrong."[7]

To indicate his new direction, Little changed the name of his company to Textron, Inc., in 1944. Then he sought merger partners, doing so with his customary verve, but without much in the way of foresight.

Little's problem, which he apparently did not recognize as one at the time, was that his two objectives did not mesh. One the one hand, he was seeking firms that would "fit" with one another, companies that would interact both vertically and horizontally. Textron was supposed to convert synthetic yarns to cloth, finish it, produce clothing and other items, and then merchandise the finished product. Clearly, Little should have been seeking firms that would augment Textron's 1944 operations. But he didn't do this— at least, this was not his primary interest. Little would come across a company with a large tax loss on its books,

[7] *Ibid.*, p. 133.

its stock selling for a low price, and whose managers were eager to join with Textron. Such a firm might be purchased through a bank loan, and then part of its operations disposed of through resales, these often enough to pay off much of the loan. On the other hand, the company's products or services might not have a place in Little's plans for Textron. He was put in the position of either rejecting a bargain or abandoning his original plans for an integrated firm. In other words, Little would wind up with a textile giant or a conglomerate, and the choice would be his to make. This was his major decision in the 1944–1948 period, although it was not recognized as such at the time.

In 1944, Little organized a new firm, American Associates, which would serve as a vehicle in his merger plans. Then he began negotiations for the acquisition of Manville-Jenckes, a run-down manufacturer of greige (unfinished) cloth, with a book value of $6.5 million and a long string of deficits. Little paid $5.5 million for the company in 1945, financing the purchase through the First National Bank of Boston and American Associates. Then he sold off several facilities for $2.2 million, and this sum, together with M-J's liquid assets and tax benefits, came to more than the original purchase price. In other words, Little had acquired an operating company, one he believed capable of earning $1 million a year, for nothing. It had been a fine deal, with only one flaw: there was no connection between Textron's main business and that of Manville-Jenckes. M-J had its own line of customers, while Textron's plants did not utilize greige. From the first, Little sacrificed his desire to create a textile giant to that for profits and sensible tax deals.

Later that year, Little acquired the Lonsdale Company, a manufacturer of fine cottons whose line did complement Textron's, and this was followed by a merger with Nashua Manufacturing, whose products didn't. Nashua, which cost $10.5 million, was considered a chancy operation. Its plants were antiquated, its product line poorly considered, and its management shoddy. But, like Lonsdale, it had assets that could be disposed of, and tax benefits. Then Little united his acquisitions under Nashua and proceeded to purchase another company, Gossett Mills, for $12 million, reshaping it into a new holding company called Textron Southern. As a result of these transactions, Textron had two major subdivisions—and a debt of $17 million owed to several banks, along with a $6 million commitment to Textron Southern. Little satisfied these debts by selling off Nashua assets and then transferring the cash and other assets to Textron Southern, after which the banks were paid off. This financial byplay resulted in Nashua being relieved of $9.5 million—only $1 million less than its purchase price—and emerging a stronger firm than before. Textron—the mother company—reported sales of $113 million in 1946, and after adjustments for special items, showed earnings of $17 million, or $6.16 a share.

Textron appeared a success, and Little a financial genius. His manipulations worried investors, however. The company's common stock declined to below 10 in mid-year, at which point it was selling for less than one and a half times earnings. Later on, Little would try to use Textron stock instead of cash for acquisitions, but this could not be done until its price rose. In order to help the stock along, Little started to speak more openly with reporters, and articles on Textron began appearing in the business press, with the stock recommended by investment services. This was to little avail, for Textron would not command a premium position until it had settled down into a fairly conventional mold.

This was one of the prices paid for Little's unconventional approach to business. There were others. Textron was supposed to become a textile giant. At least, that had been what Little had said all along. Instead, he had created a collection of unrelated or barely related companies, almost all of which were saddled with antiquated facilities badly in need of modernization. One mill would overproduce, while another would be forced to the open market for purchases. Little hadn't acquired or developed retail outlets or even clothing production facilities. The reason was obvious: there were no bargain companies in these areas, and Little had concentrated more on bargains and seeking loopholes in the tax laws than on constructing a viable firm.

At the same time, the textile industry was struck by a selective glut, and most of the oversupply was in areas Textron had become committed to. In 1948 it appeared that those who had sold out to Textron, usually at high prices, had outfoxed Little. That year, sales declined to $98.8 million and profits to $6.9 million, and in 1949, sales fell to $67.9 million and profits were replaced by a deficit of almost $1 million. The bottom had fallen out of the textile market, and it appeared Textron might be sucked down the drain. It would survive, but certainly not as a major factor in the industry. Rather, Little would be obliged to revamp his plans, lowering his expectations. The Textron of 1948 seemed well on the road to shrinkage, until the firm approximated the old Atlantic Rayon.

The experience had taught Little two major lessons. First of all, textiles would remain a highly cyclical market. He still meant to master it but now recognized the difficulties along the way better than he had earlier. More important, however, he felt that the mergers had been successful, even though the companies acquired might have been the wrong ones to have pursued. In the future he would continue to seek merger candidates, but not necessarily in textiles. Rather, whenever the situation called for it, Little would separate goals from tactics. On the one hand, he would build Textron into a corporate giant in textiles, and this would be supported by an acquisitions program in diverse areas, one that would earn money, much of which would be plowed into textiles. Thus, one branch of the firm would feed and enhance the other. Furthermore, this diversification would serve to dampen the boom-and-bust problem in textiles, offering counter-cyclical influences within the company a chance to flatten the firm's future ups and downs. Finally, Little would not use his earnings in good years to overexpand his facilities, a practice that had plagued American industry, textiles in particular, for more than a century. Rather, excess capital would be used to acquire ongoing operations at bargain prices. Most of these would be firms that either were in declining industries or had been mismanaged. Textron would move in, sell off part of the operation, and restructure the rest. It had worked well at Manville-Jenckes and subsequent textile acquisitions, although there were troubles at Nashua. Given continued tax breaks, this seemed the wisest way to expand.[8]

Little was well on his way to developing the conglomerate concept, and the ideas for it did not emerge from philosophical speculation. Nor did it derive from the quickening antitrust movement, although this would prove significant later on, not only for Textron but other conglomerates as well. Rather, the movement began as a result of problems peculiar to the textile industry, the nature of the tax laws, difficulties connected with conversion to a peacetime economy after the war, and Little's own abilities at negotiation and financial manipulation.

The change began in 1948 with two unrelated developments. The first was the closing of Textron's mills at Nashua, with a loss of 3,500 jobs. This appeared to signal at least a temporary shelving of Little's strategy designed to make Textron a textile giant. The company's executive vice-president, Charles Dyson, conceded as much, but he added that the cash thrown off as a result of the merger, together with tax savings, had made Nashua a profitable acquisition—even though the operating facilities hadn't worked out as expected. "If we hadn't had Nashua we wouldn't have Textron as it is today," he said.[9]

While preparing to shut down operations at Nashua,

[8]"Royal Little Looks At Conglomerates," *Dun's Review*, May, 1968, p. 27.
[9]"Whose Mistake At Nashua?" *Fortune* (Vol. LVI, No. 11, November, 1948), p. 98.

Little completed the acquisition of the Cleveland Pneumatic Tool Company, the nation's leading manufacturer of aircraft landing struts. The company, controlled by the Schott brothers, was in a curious position. It had prospered during the war, and then suffered deficits in 1945–1946, when government orders were canceled. This was serious, but not too costly, since the losses were eaten up by part of Cleveland Pneumatic's excess war profits from 1942–1945. Then the nation was hit by the 1948 recession, one that had only slight impact on Cleveland Pneumatic, since military appropriations increased as a result of the cold war. Operations were profitable once again, and the Schotts's lawyers and accountants told them that unless they showed large deficits, and soon, the tax credits would run out. In addition, the company would have to pay out a special dividend of $1.5 million to its stockholders, or become subject to an undistributed profits tax. Harold Schott, Cleveland Pneumatic's president, was irate. It appeared that due to the way the tax laws operated, his firm could succeed only by losing money, while profits were a source of worry. "To hell with that!" he was supposed to have said. "I'm going to sell the business!"[10]

The company could not be disposed of that easily. Other aircraft companies either were fearful of antitrust violations or didn't require additional capacity. Nor were they eager to merge with a company like Cleveland Pneumatic if it meant dealing with Schott, known as a man unwilling to give up power, and not easy to get along with.

Textron was interested, but under the terms of its charter, the firm could not purchase a company outside of the textile field. The more Little investigated the tax situation at Cleveland Pneumatic, the more he became convinced he could turn a large profit by owning it. Schott wasn't that much of a problem. Little found he could work with him, offering Schott a large amount of independence

[10]Royal Little, "Why Companies Sell Out," *Fortune* (Vol. LXII, No. 2, February, 1956), p. 117.

in day-to-day operations in return for a measure of financial control. In other words, no attempt would be made to integrate Cleveland Pneumatic with other Textron operations, unless Schott acquiesced.

In the end, Little and Schott agreed to the acquisition. In order to get around the provisions of the Textron charter, Cleveland Pneumatic was purchased by the Sixty Trust, the corporation's pension fund, for a price of $6.8 million. In 1950 the Trust purchased Pathe Industries, Inc., a newsreel and real estate operation that owned some of the Van Sweringen interests in Cleveland. In this way, Textron began its career as a conglomerate.[11]

Little's group of textile companies fared poorly in 1952, a year when sales reached a plateau and the company reported a deficit of $3.5 million, the largest in its history. He realized the textile operations would have to be rationalized, and at the same time he wanted to prepare the company to receive its biggest acquisition, American Woolen Corporation. As a first step in that direction, Little liquidated several small, peripheral, and profitless firms in late 1952. Atlantic Parachute, Manville Fabrics, Nashua Manufacturing, Posees, Textron of Delaware, Textron of New Hampshire, Textron Mills, Textron Southern, and Textron Mississippi—all were written off. The liquidation of Textron Southern was particularly touching, since at one time it was meant to be the nucleus of the corporation. In February 1953, Little spun off Indian Head Mills by distributing its stock to the Textron stockholders.

When the divestitures and spin off were completed, Textron was a much smaller firm. Sales declined from $98.7 million in 1952 to $71 million in 1953, which was a bad year for textiles in any event. But by acting ruthlessly and disregarding sentiment, Little managed to cut Textron's deficit to $200,000, and this was to be the last year the company reported a loss. Then, as though to signal the coming of the

[11]Lawrence W. Brown, "Textron," in Charles Gilbert, ed., *The Making of a Conglomerate* (Hempstead, N.Y., 1972), p. 491.

company's new era, he changed the firm's charter so as to enable it to take control of Cleveland Pneumatic and Pathe.

The charter revision was an important step in Textron's transformation into a conglomerate. Within the next few months Little acquired Dalmo-Victor, a manufacturer of radar equipment, and F. Burkart, a minor factor in the seats and padding business. There was talk of other nonrelated mergers. In fact, Little was still interested in forming his textile giant, and viewed the nontextile operations as subsidiary to his main goal. The 1948 strategy held, masked in part by the acquisitions outside the textile field.

American Woolen was the key to Little's plans, a firm that would take the place of Nashua and Textron Southern as the foundation of the company. Once called "the wool trust," American Woolen had been organized in 1899 through a combination of twenty-seven mills, and for a while dominated the industry. But the amalgamation didn't work out well; the parts didn't mesh, almost as a preview of Little's early empire. American Woolen prospered for most of its existence, and during World War II and the postwar period demand for product masked management errors. Still, profits remained high through the Korean conflict. Then the company suffered a major deficit in the 1953 recession, losing nearly one-quarter of its working capital. Once a large and profitable firm, American Woolen now was only large, a bloated giant that captured Little's imagination. The firm had some $26 million in cash and equivalents, and a tax loss carry forward of $30 million. Its outmoded facilities might be renovated and some sold off for cash. In Little's view, its major liability was Francis White, American Woolen president, who had done a poor job even when factors beyond his control were taken into account.

Little's plan was simple. He would obtain control of the company through open market purchases and then a tender offer for the rest of the stock. At the same time he would acquire Bachmann-Uxbridge, a small firm headed by Harold Walter, considered an excellent manager by people in the industry. Then he would combine the three companies —Textron's textile operations, American Woolen, and Bachmann-Uxbridge—with the B-U management team, headed by Walter, in charge. Walter would run the company on a day-to-day basis, while Little would concentrate on acquiring additional textile companies as well as firms in other areas.

As expected, White opposed the plan, and in late 1953 he promulgated an alternate strategy. White tried to use American Woolen's assets to gain control of companies in related fields, in this way attempting to form a major firm of his own. Little realized what was happening and responded with a new tender offer. White counter-attacked by winning Bachmann-Uxbridge to his banner. The battle was on and lasted more than a year. In the process, Little and White shook New England's textile interests, with the major mills obliged to come out for one or the other. In the end, Little won control of the company, even though White refused to step down and had to be ejected.

By that time too a new force, Robbins Mills, was on the scene. Robbins was a medium-sized firm with a fine management. The company was controlled by J.P. Stevens, one of the leaders in textiles, and concentrated on synthetics and blends. Its factories, all in the South, were considered among the most modern in the industry. Like many other textile firms, Robbins had suffered during the industrywide glut in 1952–1953, and was close to bankruptcy. Little knew he could get the company for a reasonable price. He took control from Stevens in 1954 for $5 million, and the following year purchased the rest of its stock with Textron convertible preferred and common shares. Then he set about uniting the three firms.[12]

The result was a new company—Textron American—which received its form and name in February 1955. This

[12]"Can Three Losers Make a Winner?" *Business Week*, December 4, 1954, p. 86.

was the giant Little had planned for since the end of the war. The company had a large debt, and there seemed some question as to whether Little would be able to coordinate the three constituent textile operations, located as they were in different parts of the country, producing different items. Did Little restructure his operations in 1952–1953, only to return two years later to the same situation that had made rationalization necessary? Little seemed to have learned from his earlier lesson. He formed a management operation, known as Amerotron, which also engaged in sales and purchasing, whose task it would become to coordinate Textron's textile units.[13]

It was a major assignment, for the company was now large and still amorphous. In 1954, Textron reported sales of less than $100 million. In 1955, after the merger, sales almost doubled, and more than 80 percent of the total came from textiles. It was as Little said it would be: Textron American was a textile company with several unrelated and subordinate operations in the van.

Up to and including the American Woolen merger and the creation of Textron American, Little's operations had been financially convoluted but strategically simple. He would acquire a company—call it ABC—that had tax credits, cash, and salable assets, for a low price. Then he would pare off some of the assets and sell them and try to turn the rest of the company into a money-maker. If he succeeded in so doing, he would be left with a profitable operation and a bundle of cash, often as much as the original purchase price. Failure carried little risk. In either case, he would use the money to purchase XYZ, a firm that resembled ABC prior to the merger, and repeat the process. Because of tax credits, Textron was able to retain much of its earnings, and so the revamped, slimmed-down operations appeared extraordinarily profitable. This procedure was combined with such things as sales-and-leasebacks and tax-free stock

[13] *The New York Times*, February 18, 1955.

offerings and other perfectly legal and legitimate methods of avoiding taxes and maximizing profits.

This was considered adventuresome in 1955, but was mild when compared with conglomerate accounting procedures used by other firms in the next decade. Little maintained good relations with executives of acquired firms—American Woolen was the one major exception—and had a reputation for fairness. He was not a "raider," a title that would haunt future conglomerateurs. When the Textron name was affixed to an ongoing concern, it did not cause alarm in the community. With the exception of the Nashua shutdowns, Textron created more jobs and opportunities than it eliminated, and even at Nashua the company stayed and helped the community recover. All this was done in the hope of creating a textile empire. Little had one in 1955.

But it would not jell, and even while he signed the final papers Little seemed to understand this. If Textron American were to become a viable operation, Little would have to acquire well-run, profitable firms, and these were expensive. Or he would have to cut down his firm once again, as he had in 1953, and then initiate another rebuilding program. Neither proposition appeared attractive, and in any case, Little hadn't shown special talents in management or extraordinary abilities in wooing ongoing operations.

Clearly, Little's greatest successes were not in textiles. The need for restructuring in 1952–1953, the anguish of the American Woolen merger, bad feelings at Nashua, and Textron American's inability to overcome the industry's boom-and-bust pattern, were signs of this. The struggles of 1954–1955 may have soured him on textiles. Was the merger worth it? Now he would have to put together his companies and coordinate their activities; the prospect was not inviting. How much simpler it would be to leave them apart, to have intercompany sales, but retain separate management in each firm. In other words, run the operation without the intercession of an Amerotron.

Little had proven himself remarkably adept at acquiring new firms at low prices, and in some cases at turning moribund properties into money-makers. In effect, Textron was a fine management company, but one saddled with textile operations that were undigested, with prospects that were mediocre at best.

Sometime late in the American Woolen contest, Little may have considered his assets and liabilities in this fashion. He had attempted to create a major textile company with himself as its operating head. This was in the tradition of Theodore Vail. But Little wasn't like Vail, and textiles hadn't the growth characteristics of telephones. The opportunities that existed in America in the late 1950s and afterward, as well as his own talents, led Little in a different direction. Instead of making money as a result of acquisitions and then losing it in textiles, he would concentrate on mergers and, in time, get out of textiles completely. After having won his prize, Little seemed to have decided it wasn't worth the effort. Textron American would not become a leading force in textiles after all, but rather a reflection of the particular talents and personality of Royal Little. He would create a company in his own image, and not one that was wedded to a single industry. Units in diverse fields would be acquired and managed, without attempting to integrate them with other units, and if some of them did not turn out well, they would be spun off or sold. Whether such a company could outlast its founder was a moot point. In 1955, Little was fifty-nine years old, so it seemed he would have barely enough time to get the firm into operation before reaching the conventional retirement age. In addition, he had been in textiles for thirty-five years, and relinquishing his dream was difficult. It was a turning point somewhat similar to Lowell's in deciding to leave commerce and enter manufacturing.

Little developed this new set of goals and a new strategy to go along with them. His company would become transformed into a conglomerate, larger and more profitable than any textile firm, so he hoped. It would use up whatever tax credits remained by acquiring other firms, profitable ones in nontextile areas. Little would not make new acquisitions on the basis of their tax situations; the future viability of the firm, not its past failures, would be the prime criterion for mergers. Textron American would seek independent operating companies that were doing well but for one reason or another preferred the umbrella of a conglomerate existence. There would be no additional American Woolen–style mergers. Rather, the pattern would be that set down in the Cleveland Pneumatic takeover.

There were signs that Little would take off on a new tack during the last phases of the American Woolen negotiations. "If Textron American's textile operations do not show striking progress within a year or two," wrote *Fortune* in April 1955, "he will change his direction further toward nontextile operations." Little indicated that no matter how the textile business developed, he hoped that Textron's nontextile business would gross $150 million in 1956, an increase of at least $90 million over 1955, and one that would require major acquisitions.

> That is where Little's heart really lies today—in acquiring, both for profitability and diversification, companies outside the textile field; for there his incredible talents as a deal maker can be exercised to the fullest. The greatest uncertainties about Little's prognosis is in textiles, where the rewards are apt to go to more patient men.[14]

Textron American went on a "merger rampage" in 1955 and 1956, one that set the pattern for future conglomerates. Even prior to the completion of the American Woolen merger, Little released news that MB Manufacturing and

[14]D. Saunders, "Stormiest Merger Yet—Textron-Robbins-American Woolen Merger," *Fortune* (Vol. LXI, No. 4, April, 1955), p. 171.

Newmarket Manufacturing, the former in test equipment, the latter in heavy machinery, were acquired. After the formation of Textron American, Little obtained Ryan Industries (electro-mechanical equipment), Homelite (chain saws), Coquille Plywood, and Camcar Screw. Then came Kordite (plastics), General Cement, Benada Aluminum, and in April 1956, Myrtle Point Veneer. These and other, minor additions, cost Textron American $20,900,000 in cash as well as common and preferred stock. Little claimed they would bring in $9,260,000 before taxes, a figure that proved too optimistic, but one that would indicate a return of well over 40 percent on his cash and stock investment.[15] Then, without stopping to pause, he added Bandon Veneer, Carolina Bagging, Hall Mack, Federal Leather, and Campbell, Wyant and Cannon in the next eight months. Little even purchased the S.S. *LaGuardia*, a passenger ship, from the government, and had it re-outfitted for the Hawaii tourist run as the S.S. *Leinani*. Then, as though to signal the end of his textile ambitions, Little renamed his company Textron, Inc., in May, and diverted assets to the nontextile areas more readily than before.

Textron's sales and earnings soared, but not the price of its stock. Still dubious about the viability of this new corpo-

Selected Statistics for Textron, Inc., 1954–1962

Year	Sales	Earnings
	(millions of dollars)	
1954	99.7	1.3
1955	191.6	9.5
1956	245.8	6.5
1957	254.6	8.7
1958	244.2	10.8
1959	308.2	16.6
1960	383.2	14.2
1961	473.1	10.5
1962	549.5	14.8

SOURCE: *Moody's Handbook of Common Stocks*, 1963 ed.

[15] *The New York Times*, April 13, 1956.

rate form, and not certain Little would be able to carry off his ambitions, investors and speculators shied from it. Because of this, Textron was obliged to make most of its mergers for cash and cash equivalents, and could not use its stock in exchanges of paper for assets, a practice for which conglomerates would be criticized.

The prices for fast-growing companies rose rapidly in the late 1950s and 1960s. Given its situation, Textron could not afford to acquire firms whose stocks carried high price-earnings ratios. Instead, Little sought out firms whose stocks carried low ratios but also showed promise as well as profits. Some were in settled and even stagnant industries, while others were in need of new financing, and a few came out of fear that others might seek to acquire them, and they preferred Textron. Little sought firms that were privately owned, for these were the easiest to acquire. Lacking that, he looked for companies whose stock was in a relatively few hands. He wanted merger partners to have pretax earnings of over $1 million a year, a broad product line, and long-range potential. But he would not acquire a firm just because it would make his year-end report appear impressive. Rather, he wanted operations which could be "turned around" in a few years. Their managements should either be old and ready to step down, or young and aggressive, seeking better opportunities.[16] Later on, Little would say that "all I ever did as a businessman was to bring men and money together. I was just extremely fortunate in some of the men I picked."[17]

From 1955 to 1962, at which time he retired from Textron, Little concentrated on four objectives. First of all, he created a corporate structure to handle Textron's operations. He kept the management team small and his office staff modest. Presidents of operating companies were given

[16]"Closing a Deal," *Business Week*, November 5, 1955, p. 140.
[17]"As They See It," *Forbes*, December 15, 1970, p. 41.

a great deal of leeway; Little was a believer in the adage that one picked the right manager and then gave him freedom. But the headquarters group retained financial control, and all major decisions in this area were made from Little's executive suite in Providence. Always a master at finance, Little increased Textron's debt from $4 million in 1954 to $92.2 million in 1961, using the funds so obtained for expansion and related operations.[18]

Next, Little continued his acquisitions program, adding

Major Textron Acquisitions, 1957–1962

	Company	Business
1957	California Technical Industries	Electronic Test Equipment
	Accessory Products Company	Pneumatic and Fuel Handling Components
	Fanner Manufacturing	Foundry Devices
1958	Waterbury Farrel	Metal Working Machinery
	Shuron Optical	Optical Products
	Precision Methods	Mill Components
	American Microphone	Microphones
	Nemco	Machinery
1959	Nuclear Metals	Metallurgical Research
	Townsend	Metal Fasteners
	Pittsburgh Steel	Steel Castings
	Randall	Automobile Trim
	Ansler	Basic Steel Furnaces
	Terry Industries	Homelite Products
1960	Albert Weinbrenner Co.	Footwear
	Dorset Plastics	Plastics
	E-Z-Go Car	Golf Cars
	Bell Aircraft	Helicopters, Airplanes
1961	Spencer Kellogg	Agrochemicals
	Modern Optics	Lenses
	Sprague Meter	Lenses
	M.B. Skinner	Clamps and Fittings
	Tabular Rivet and Stub	Rivets and Rivet Machinery
1962	American Screw	Screws
	Vita-Var Corp.	Paints
	Geraldine's Ltd.	Oceanographic Research
	Continental Optical	Optical Supplies

SOURCE: Gilbert, *Making of a Conglomerate*, pp. 539–40.

[18] *Textron Annual Report, 1962.*

firms at the rate of one every two months, and seemingly trying for at least one major acquisition every half year or so.

In time, the Textron companies would be organized into four groups: Aerospace, Consumer Products, Metal Products, and Industrial Products, each with a divisional leader, but within each group the heads of large operations, such as Spencer Kellogg; Campbell, Wyant and Cannon; and Bell, would be given a great amount of latitude. These large operations would be further broken down. For example, Bell included Bell Aerosystems, Bell Helicopter, and Hydraulic Research. As the company grew, Little sought firms that might complement already existing units, but this was a primary interest in only a few significant acquisitions.

Little's third objective was to create a semi-independent "glamour company" that in time might be able to attract firms in advanced fields with high price-earnings ratios. This company, Textron Electronics, was formed in 1959, and began with MB Electronics, GC Electronics, and Schafer Custom Engineering, all of which came from the mother company in a stock-transfer operation. Later on, Textron Electronics acquired Globe Electronics as well, also from Textron.

It was a sound idea, but came at the wrong time. The stock market slumped soon after, and then came a recession. Textron Electronics was not afforded a high multiple by investors. Nor did it perform as well as anticipated. Perhaps this was due to one of Little's failings. The man who was excellent at reviving established companies in recognized industries showed less talent at the time for pioneering in new ones. Little was past sixty, close to retirement, and the Textron Electronics failure was viewed by some as a sign that he was no longer capable of growth. Little railed at this, and later on would obtain a measure of satisfaction by starting a new career in the field of technological innovation.

Little's final objective was to liquidate Textron's marginal and unprofitable operations, either by closing them or selling them to others. There were not many of these, since he had taken great care in pre-merger investigations. He did dispose of his plywood companies when unable to develop timber reserves, and small units, unable to meet his performance standards—20 percent pre-tax return on investment—either were sold or reorganized.

In 1962, just before his retirement, Little helped start negotiations for the biggest divestiture of them all. The following year—after Little had left the company—Textron sold Amerotron to Deering-Milliken for $45 million, thus taking the company out of the textile business.

Little stepped down as chairman and chief operating officer in 1960, to assume the presidency of the executive committee. Rupert C. Thompson, Jr., his chosen successor, took his place. Little had been used to managing all of Textron's activities; now the firm was being run by committees, and he was part of that structure. On January 1, 1962, at the age of sixty-six, he retired. Thompson noted that Little "never was much for committees and meetings. The minute he wasn't going to run it alone, he left."[19] Under Thompson, Textron continued to seek mergers, some of them larger than any Little had engineered. The firm settled down as well and within a few years was considered "conventional." It was Little, not Textron, that spearheaded the conglomerate movement, and Textron indeed had become a reflection of the founder. Little had done his work well, and made certain Textron would survive his leaving, even though its direction would change. In 1963, the company was the ninety-fifth largest American industrial firm, bigger than such conglomerates as Litton, Ling-Temco-Vought, and Gulf and Western. Even then, Little was being overshadowed by the second generation of con-

[19]Stanley H. Brown, "How to Manage a Conglomerate," *Fortune* (Vol. LXVIII, No. 4, April, 1964), p. 157.

glomerateurs, men who headed these companies—Tex
Thornton, James Ling, and Charles Bluhdorn.

At first it appeared Little would settle down to retirement.
He went on several camera safaris to Africa, played golf,
served on local charitable and educational committees, and
retained his position as chairman of the board at Indian
Head Mills, a job that required less work than its title
indicated. He remained a director of Arthur D. Little, Inc.,
and a trustee for the Textron pension fund. His most important position was that of chairman of the board of Narragansett Capital Corporation, a small business investment
company. At first, it seemed something designed to keep
him active rather than a major undertaking.[20] "Unless a
man can serve some useful purpose, he loses all interest in
life. Those who just play golf die off," he said.[21]

Narragansett took an increasing amount of Little's time
in the 1960s. This was one of the wildest decades in the
history of American business speculation, one during
which the wheelers and dealers of the conglomerate movement dominated the industrial and financial landscape.
Textron expanded and prospered in this period. But the
real growth and glamour was in small companies in "developing new technologies," the kinds of firms Textron had
always avoided. Indeed, a decade later, Textron would
merge with American Research and Development, an investment company somewhat like Narragansett, which
had helped several small firms begin, and had made almost
a half-billion dollars profit, most of it from the stock of
Digital Equipment.

Under Little's direction, Narragansett invested in several newly formed and struggling companies. By 1971, the
SBIC had provided seed money for thirty of them, includ-

[20]Herbert Solow, "Royal Little's Remarkable Retirement," *Fortune* (Vol. LXVI,
No. 4, October, 1962), pp. 124–26, 207–8.
[21]"The World of Royal Little," *Dun's Review*, February, 1970, p. 39.

ing firms in fashions and others in computer operations. One of these, American Television and Communications, became the third-largest factor in the cable television industry. Amtel, an auto supplies, jewelry, and aircraft conglomerate, with sales of $125 million in 1970, was the largest of the new firms spawned through Little's post-retirement efforts. All American Beverages, a fast-growing bottler, was another. And while he directed efforts at Narragansett, Little joined with a former Textron colleague to form Little and Casler, a financial consulting firm.

In 1973, Little was on the boards of directors of some thirty firms, headed an urban renewal program in Rhode Island, led a business group that helped blacks enter the entrepreneurial ranks, and still went on safaris and engaged in other hobbies. At the age of seventy-five, he showed no sign of letting up. Nor did he ever seem happier.

Little's business career in the 1960s was an extension of his conglomerating activities of the previous decade, even though the context was different. He was, by nature, a man who was happiest when involved in several operations at the same time. Once it was believed that Little had failed to create his textile empire because of an inability to concentrate on a single goal for a long period, and that he was too frivolous to be taken seriously. Later he was seen as an innovative and imaginative entrepreneur. Certainly the nature of the textile industry at the time militated against success, while on occasion—the American Woolen struggle, for example—Little proved capable of intense, concentrated, effort.

He wasn't that good at it, and what was more, Little understood his strengths and weaknesses, and so was able to capitalize on them. Most major businessmen in the nineteenth and early twentieth centuries were like spiders spinning the webs that were to remain their main claims to fame. This was not Little's way. Rather, he wanted several webs, and was interested in each for a relatively short period of time. His was not the style of a Duke or a Wanamaker. Rather, he was closest to his fellow New Englander —a man who did make it big in textiles—Francis Lowell. American business history began with the sedentary merchant, and today we are in the age of the conglomerateur, and the resemblance between the two is striking.

All the businessmen discussed in this work were engaged in opportunistic ventures in the best sense of the term. At each turn of the wheel, the opportunities were different. In the late twentieth century, the wheel has turned full around.

Conclusion

Royal Little assembled the first modern conglomerate, though not through design. Rather, conditions in the textile industry and government attitudes toward business, neither of which he could control, obliged him either to innovate or challenge the "system." He innovated, but on an *ad hoc* basis initially. Only after he had assembled the bare bones of Textron did the concept emerge in a form that could be pursued. As with most businessmen, in Little's case the action preceded the thought. Theory was the response to conditions and pragmatic selection; content dictated form. Once the idea had taken shape, an appropriate strategy could be devised, but even then, constant change would be the rule. Innovate or die might well be the motto of the American entrepreneur, and it has been that way since the nation's founding.

Little concentrated on the erection of a major diversified corporation, and he succeeded admirably. Other conglomerates would follow, and many were larger and more powerful than Textron, while their leaders were hailed as innovators and business heroes. James Ling, Charles Bluhdorn, Tex Thornton, Harold Geneen, and Henry Singleton have had their times of trouble as well, and in each case, it was near fatal. LTV, Gulf and Western, Litton, ITT, and Teledyne are still considered "racy," and somewhat frivolous. Textron managed to achieve a solidity of reputation while retaining much of its adventuresome spirit during Little's last years with the company. Under his successor, Rupert C. Thompson, the company tended to concentrate on internal growth and enhancing its reputation, and this too was a reaction to external events—the attacks on conglomerates by government and the media, and the stock market decline of 1969–1970. Thompson was followed by G. William Miller, and by the mid-1970s, the company seemed little different from other established firms, such as General Electric and Westinghouse, with a faceless executive following established policies when appropriate, and adjusting or changing them when necessary.

Douglas Aircraft was in an industry where significant alterations in strategy were extremely difficult to make, if not impossible. With only two major sets of customers—governments and airlines—aviation and aerospace firms were faced with the choice of cutthroat competition or cooperation. They could struggle against one another for contracts, in which case a few firms would survive and the rest decline or even leave the business, or they could work together in obtaining contracts, share information, and agree to subcontract to one another no matter which firm won. Both strategies made sense; both represented violations of antitrust statutes. When Donald Douglas entered aviation, the industry seemed romantic, growing, and potentially profitable. It is still exciting, and growth appears assured. But profits were hard to come by, except in time of war, and even then a future bust appeared possible.

Douglas took a major gamble with the DC-2, one that seemed to have paid off handsomely with the DC-3. It was typical for the industry that these passenger planes led both to success and failure for the company. The success was almost immediate, as Douglas became the leading airframe manufacturer in the country and remained so for two decades. Had it not been for the cold war—had a truly peacetime economy developed after World War II—Douglas might still occupy its preeminent position. In effect, Donald Douglas gambled on peace and did not make a strong enough effort to win military contracts, especially those for advanced jets. Boeing did, and while Douglas clung to its old designs, Boeing developed new ones while working on military planes and applying the lessons in the creation of the 707. This plane defeated the DC-8. Douglas Aircraft could not regain its lead, not when billions of dollars were needed to play the game.

Another firm, McDonnell Aircraft, began operations in World War II, and in 1943, its first year of existence, had $10.5 million in sales. That year Douglas Aircraft posted sales of $987.7 million. McDonnell concentrated on military contracts after the war, developing some of the most profitable and popular fighter planes the industry would ever know. The company's founder, J.S. McDonnell, had excellent relations with the military and was able to deal effectively with political leaders. Meanwhile, Donald Douglas, Jr., who succeeded his father, could neither meet the Boeing challenge nor obtain sufficient military contracts to keep his firm solvent. In 1966, both companies had sales slightly in excess of a billion dollars, but Douglas had working capital of $34.4 million, and McDonnell, $119.2 million. The two firms began merger talks. Douglas Aircraft could not survive without massive influxes of capital and additional work, while McDonnell saw in Douglas a relatively inexpensive way of entering the civilian market at a time when antiwar activists were growing increasingly loud in America. In April 1967, Douglas was merged into McDonnell to form McDonnell-Douglas Corporation, with the McDonnell management in command, even though Douglas and his staff retained nominal control of that division. Douglas Aircraft was not viable in an industry where even a billion dollars in sales would not assure success.

Loew's, Inc. prospered after Marcus Loew died, becoming the leading force in production and remaining a major one in exhibition. The company made the transition from vaudeville to silents, and from silents to talkies, in a smooth and profitable fashion. Then, after World War II, the challenge of television presented itself, and for a while Loew's and other motion picture companies did not know how to meet it. For a while they tried to fight the new entertainment medium, and then attempted to take command of production of television films. Motion picture attendance dropped steadily in the 1950s, harming both exhibitors and producers. One alternative seemed to be the "blockbuster film," a high-cost lavish production quite different from anything viewers could see on television. While these made money if successful, failure would put a serious crimp in company finances.

In February 1952, the question of profitability became academic. After a long series of hearings, trials, and negotiations, the courts, under terms of the antitrust laws, ordered Loew's to divest itself of all theater properties.

The divestiture proved more complicated than imagined, while at the same time factions within the company jockeyed for power, position, and assets. The segregation became final in March 1959 with the creation of two new companies. Metro-Goldwyn-Mayer took the studios, while Loew's Theaters, Inc., was to have the exhibition part of the business. At the time it seemed to signify the separation of art and commerce. Loew's went on to become a conglomerate, as well as a major investor and speculator in the securities of other companies. As for the theaters, most were either sold off or razed, with hotels constructed on the sites. As far as the general public was concerned, the Loew name signified land and luxury hotels. Marcus Loew would have been pleased. His name was associated with real estate once more.

Metro-Goldwyn-Mayer did not do as well. It made the transition to television film operations, but also produced motion pictures for theaters. A period of concentration on blockbusters was followed by one in which low-budget films were produced. The company sold off much of its property, as well as studio assets, in a vain struggle for survival. Finally, in 1973, it announced that, for all intents and purposes, Metro-Goldwyn-Mayer would no longer produce films for theaters. Instead, it would concentrate on television. But the venture the company relied upon to restore it to solvency was a magnificent new hotel in Las Vegas. Like Loew's, M-G-M's future seemed to be in real estate. Marcus Loew would have felt vindicated.

Vindication but not renown would come for Theodore Vail as well. American Telephone and Telegraph remains one of the best-managed and most powerful entities in the world. Vail's mark is still on the firm, and the major challenge remains relations with governments and the creation of a favorable public opinion. AT&T's size and power assure difficulties, but its survivability is a tribute to Vail, one of the most successful businessmen the nation ever produced, and one wise enough to realize his best method of operation would be from the shadows. This is still the case at company headquarters. AT&T has assets of $61 billion and sales of $21 billion, while ITT has little more than one-sixth the assets and less than half the sales. Yet Harold Geneen of ITT is perhaps the most famous businessman in the nation, while John D. DeButts, head of AT&T, is as faceless as his predecessors. Neither Geneen or DeButts would have it any other way.

American Tobacco, the chief legatee of the Duke empire, proved unable to maintain leadership within the tobacco industry, and bowed to Reynolds. Duke had created a tobacco conglomerate—known as a trust, to be sure—only to see it dissolved by government action. His successors at American, faced with anti-cigarette crusades, returned to the conglomerate idea in the 1950s and 1960s. Today, American *Brands* sells liquor, biscuits, and pet foods as well as tobacco products, and in fact less than half its sales come from the business started by Buck Duke.

In 1970, the Great Northern was merged with the Northern Pacific and the Burlington line to form the Burlington Northern. More than a half century earlier, the federal government had attacked James Hill and E.H. Harriman, preventing the creation and maintenance of Northern

Securities, because the resulting firm was deemed too powerful. At the time, Hill warned that unless combination of this kind were permitted, and even encouraged, railroading would become a sick industry. Events vindicated his judgment, for the Burlington Northern was a re-creation of Northern Securities, and one entered into with more than a little government prodding.

Wanamaker, the eminent American Victorian, would be pleased by his stores today. They remain genteel, carry quality goods at reasonable prices, and have a devoted following. But if Wanamaker's hasn't changed, the country and world has. John Wanamaker was successful in meeting the challenges of a century ago, but neither he nor those who came after him at company headquarters could adjust to the new kind of society emerging from the cocoon of the old. After World War II, Wanamaker's made a feeble attempt to do so in the form of new stores in suburbia, but by then it was too late. Given Wanamaker's attitude toward business and life, perhaps this was fitting. There are some things a man like him could not compromise on. Moralists have a low success quotient in the business world, especially those like Wanamaker who actually practiced what they preached.

Cyrus McCormick had a more impressive monument. After his death the litigations and industry wars continued, with no farm equipment manufacturer able to shake McCormick's leadership, and that firm unable to crush its rivals. J.P. Morgan viewed the scene with growing irritation. In 1901 he and other Wall Street houses brought together most of the companies in the field to form the International Harvester Company, a giant trust that dominated the industry. Despite recurrent threats of antitrust actions and a case during the Wilson Administration, the company survived and prospered, remaining one of the world's leading farm equipment manufacturers.

All of these firms left descendants, and some remain in the form their founders left them. Not so with Francis

Lowell's Boston Manufacturing. Soon after his death, the company became part of the Saco-Lowell operation, which specialized in the manufacture of textile machinery. Saco-Lowell was a long-lived company, a major factor in its field. It was headed by able men, but none with the imagination of a Francis Lowell. Instead of expanding by seeking new challenges, Saco-Lowell remained content to stick to its last. With the advent of the post–World War II merger movement, it appeared a prime candidate for a takeover. In 1960 it became part of the Maremont Corporation, then a small conglomerate with a special interest in the replacement automotive parts industry. Saco-Lowell continued profitable until the late 1960s, when the textile industry became intrigued with double-knit fabrics. Some of the company's rivals acted swiftly to meet the new demand. Saco-Lowell did not, and so it declined.

In 1972, Maremont began to search for a potential buyer for its ailing division. The company that had descended from Boston Manufacturing, which itself had its start when Francis Lowell smuggled textile machine secrets out of England, was sold in 1973 to Stone-Latt Industries of Great Britain. One hundred and sixty years after the founding of Boston Manufacturing, control of Saco-Lowell crossed the Atlantic to the country from which the American entrepreneurial spirit originated.

Bibliography

Chapter I. *Francis Cabot Lowell: The Patrician as Factory Master*

Adams, James T. *New England in the Republic, 1776–1850.* New York, 1926.

Appleton, Nathan. *Introduction of the Power Loom and Origin of Lowell.* Lowell, 1858.

Bagnall, William R. *The Textile Industries of the United States.* Vol. 1. Cambridge, 1893.

Baines, Edward. *History of the Cotton Manufacture in Great Britain.* London, 1835.

Batchelder, Samuel. *Introduction and Early Progress of the Cotton Manufacture in the United States.* Boston, 1863.

Bishop, J. Leander. *A History of American Manufactures from 1608 to 1860.* 2 vols. Philadelphia, 1864.

Bolles, Albert S. *Industrial History of the United States.* New York, 1881.

Bowden, Witt. *The Industrial History of the United States.* New York, 1930.

————. *Industrial Society in England Toward the End of the Eighteenth Century.* New York, 1925.

Cameron, E.H. *Samuel Slater: Father of American Manufactures.* New York, 1960.

Cartwright, Edmund. *A Memoir of Edmund Cartwright.* (reprint) New York, 1971.

Cary, Thomas C. *Profits on Manufactures at Lowell.* Boston, 1845.

Chapman, Stanley D. *The Early Factory Masters: The Transition to the Factory System in the Midlands Textile Industry.* London, 1967.

Clark, Victor S. *History of Manufactures in the United States, 1607–1860.* Washington, 1916.

Coats, A.W. and Robertson, Ross M., eds. *Essays in American Economic History.* New York, 1969.

Cole, Arthur H., ed. *Industrial and Commercial Correspondence of Alexander Hamilton.* New York, 1928.

Copeland, Melvin T. *The Cotton Manufacturing Industry of the United States.* Cambridge, 1923.

Coxe, Tench. *A View of the United States of America, in a Series of Papers Written at Various Times, in the Years Between 1787 and 1794.* (reprint) New York, 1965.

Crawford, Mary Caroline. *Famous Families of Massachusetts.* 2 vols. Boston, 1930.

Dulles, Foster Rhea. *The Old China Trade.* Boston, 1930.

Fisher, Marvin. *Workshops in the Wilderness.* New York, 1967.

Fitton, R.S. and Wadsworth, A.P. *The Strutts and the Arkwrights, 1758–1830: A Study of the Early Factory System.* Manchester, 1958.

Gibb, George S. *The Saco-Lowell Shops: Textile Machinery Building in New England, 1813–1949.* Cambridge, 1950.

Greenslet, Ferris. *The Lowells and Their Seven Worlds.* Boston, 1946.

Handlin, Oscar and Handlin, Mary F. *Commonwealth: A Study of the Role of Government in the American Economy: Massachusetts, 1774–1861.* New York, 1947.

Head, Goerge. *A Home Tour Through the Manufacturing Districts of England in the Summer of 1835.* (reprint) New York, 1968.

Hedges, James B. *The Browns of Providence Plantations: The Nineteenth Century.* Providence, 1968.

Hills, Richard L. *Power in the Industrial Revolution.* Manchester, 1970.

Jahar, Frederic C., ed. *The Age of Industrialism in America.* New York, 1968.

Josephson, Hannah. *The Golden Threads: New England's Mill Girls and Magnates.* New York, 1949.

McGouldrick, Paul F. *New England Textiles in the Nineteenth Century: Profits and Investment.* Cambridge, 1968.

Marx, Leo. *The Machine in the Garden: Technology and the Pastoral Ideal in America.* New York, 1964.

Montgomery, James. *A Practical Detail of the Cotton Manufacture of the United States of America . . .* Glasgow, 1840.

Morison, Samuel Eliot. *Harrison Gray Otis.* 2 vols. Boston, 1913.

———. *The Maritime History of Massachusetts, 1783–1860.* Boston, 1921.

Navin, Thomas R. *The Whitin Machine Works Since 1831: A Textile Machinery Company in an Industrial Village.* Cambridge, 1950.

Pitkin, Timothy. *A Statistical View of the Commerce of the United States.* (reprint) New York, 1967.

Porter, Kenneth Wiggins. *The Jacksons and the Lees: Two Generations of Massachusetts Merchants, 1765–1844.* 2 vols. Cambridge, 1937.

Stanwood, Edward. *American Tariff Controversies in the Nineteenth Century.* 2 vols. Boston, 1903.

Tryon, Rolla M. *Household Manufactures in the United States, 1640– 1860.* New York, 1917.

Walton, Perry. *The Story of Textiles.* Boston, 1912.

Ware, Caroline F. *The Early New England Cotton Manufacture: A Study in Industrial Beginnings.* New York, 1931.

Webber, Samuel. *Manual of Power, with the History of Cotton Manufacture in the United States.* New York, 1879.

Weeden, William B. *Economic and Social History of New England, 1620–1789.* 2 vols. Boston, 1890.

Weisberger, Bernard A. *The New Industrial Society.* New York, 1969.

White, George S. *Memoir of Samuel Slater, The Father of American Manufactures.* (reprint) New York, 1967.

Wiltse, Charles M. *John C. Calhoun, Nationalist, 1782–1828.* New York, 1944.

Chapter II. Cyrus Hall McCormick: From Farm Boy to Tycoon

Bidwell, Percy W. and Falconer, John I. *History of Agriculture in the Northern United States, 1620–1860.* Washington, 1941.

Casson, Herbert N. *Cyrus Hall McCormick: His Life and Work.* Chicago, 1909.

———. *Romance of the Reaper.* New York, 1908.

Dies, Edward J. *Titans of the Soil: Great Builders of Agriculture.* Chapel Hill, 1949.

Davidson, J.B. and Chase, L.W. *Farm Machinery and Farm Motors.* New York, 1909.

Fussell, G.E. *The Farmer's Tools, 1500–1900: The History of British*

Farm Implements, Tools and Machinery Before the Tractor Came. London, 1952.

Gates, Paul W. *Agriculture and the Civil War.* New York, 1965.

————. *The Farmer's Age: Agriculture, 1815–1860.* New York, 1960.

Gras, N.S.B. *A History of Agriculture in Europe and America.* New York, 1940.

Greeno, Follet L. *Obed Hussey.* Rochester, 1912.

Holbrook, Stewart H. *Machines of Plenty: Pioneering in American Agriculture.* New York, 1955.

Hutchinson, William T. *Cyrus Hall McCormick, Vol. I, Seed-Time, 1809–1856.* New York, 1930.

————. *Cyrus Hall McCormick, Vol. II, Harvest, 1856–1884.* New York, 1935.

Jennings, Walter W. *Twenty Giants of American Business: Biographical Sketches in Economic History.* New York, 1953.

Krooss, Herman and Gilbert, Charles. *American Business History.* Englewood Cliffs, 1972.

MacDonald, William. *Makers of Modern Agriculture.* London, 1913.

McCormick, Cyrus. *The Century of the Reaper.* New York, 1931.

North, Douglass C. *The Economic Growth of the United States, 1790–1860.* New York, 1966.

Miller, Marritt F. *The Evolution of the Reaping Machines.* Washington, 1902.

Resneck, Samuel. *Business Depressions and Financial Panics.* Westport, 1968.

Rogin, Leo. *The Introduction of Farm Machinery in its Relation to the Productivity of Labor in the Agriculture of the United States During the Nineteenth Century.* Berkeley, 1931.

Seligman, Ben B. *Business and Businessmen in American History.* New York, 1971.

Thwaites, Reuben G. *Cyrus Hall McCormick and the Reaper.* Madison, 1909.

Tocqueville, Alexis de. *Democracy in America.* 1969 ed. New York, 1969.

Walker, James B. *The Epic of American Industry.* New York, 1949.

Williams, William Appleton. *The Roots of the Modern American Empire.* New York, 1969.

Woodcroft, Bennet, comp. *Specifications of English Patents for Reaping Machines.* London, 1853.

Chapter III. John Wanamaker: The Triumph of Content Over Form

Appel, Joseph H. *The Business Biography of John Wanamaker: Founder and Builder.* New York, 1930.

Beasley, Norman. *Main Street Merchant: The Story of the J.C. Penney Company.* New York, 1948.

Beckman, Theodore, and Nolen, Herman. *The Chain Store Problem.* New York, 1938.

Borsodi, Ralph. *The Distribution Age: A Study of the Economy of Modern Distribution.* New York, 1927.

Converse, Paul D. *Selling Policies.* New York, 1907.

Conwell, Russell. *The Romantic Rise of a Great American.* New York, 1924.

Ferry, John W. *A History of the Department Store.* New York, 1960.

Filene, Edward A. *Next Steps Forward in Retailing.* Boston, 1937.

Gibbons, Herbert A. *John Wanamaker.* 2 vols. New York, 1926.

Gras, N.S.B. and Larson, Henrietta M. *Casebook in American Business History.* New York, 1939.

Harriman, Margaret C. *And the Price is Right.* New York, 1958.

Hower, Ralph M. *History of Macy's of New York, 1858–1919.* Cambridge, 1946.

Hubbard, Elbert. *Little Journeys to the Homes of Great Business Men.* East Aurora, New York, 1939.

John Wanamaker Company. *Golden Book of the Wanamaker Stores.* Philadelphia, 1911.

Lambert, Richard. *The Universal Provider.* London, 1938.

Mahoney, Tom and Sloane, Leonard. *The Great Merchants.* New York, 1966.

Marden, Orison S. *Little Visits with Great Americans.* New York, 1905.

———. *Pushing to the Front.* 2 vols. Petersburg, New York, 1911.

Mayfield, Frank M. *The Department Store Story.* New York, 1949.

Moore, Truman E. *The Traveling Man: The Story of the American Traveling Salesman.* New York, 1972.

Morgan, John J.B. and Webb, Ewing T. *Making the Most of Your Life.* New York, 1932.

Pasdermadjian, Hrant. *The Department Store.* London, 1954.

Twyman, Robert W. *History of Marshall Field & Co., 1852–1906.* Philadelphia, 1954.

Wendt, Lloyd and Kogan, Herman. *Give the Lady What She Wants!* Chicago, 1952.

Chapter IV. James J. Hill: The Business of Empire

American Guide Series. *North Dakota: A Guide to the Northern Prairie State.* 1950 ed. New York, 1950.

Beal, Merrill D. *Intermountain Railroads: Standard and Narrow Gauge.* Caldwell, Idaho, 1962.

Belcher, Wyatt W. *The Economic Rivalry Between St. Louis and Chicago, 1850–1880.* New York, 1947.

Berton, Pierre. *The Impossible Railway: The Building of the Canadian Pacific.* New York, 1972.

Blegen, Theodore C. *Minnesota: A History of the State.* Minneapolis, 1963.

Campbell, Marius R. and others. *Guidebook of the Western United States, Part A. The Northern Pacific Route.* Washington, 1916.

Clark, W.H. *Railroads and Rivers.* Boston, 1939.

Cochran, Thomas C. *Railroad Leaders, 1845–1890: The Business Mind In Action.* Cambridge, 1953.

Emerson, Edward Waldo and Forbes, Waldo Emerson, eds. *Journals of Ralph Waldo Emerson.* Boston, 1909–1914.

Fahey, John. *Inland Empire: D.C. Corbin and Spokane.* Seattle, 1965.

Fogel, Robert W. *Railroads and American Economic Growth: Essays in Econometric History.* Baltimore, 1964.

Folwell, William W. *A History of Minnesota.* Vol. 3. St. Paul, 1969.

Gibbon, John M. *Steel of Empire: Romantic History of the Canadian Pacific, the Northwest Passage of Today.* Toronto, 1935.

Ginger, Ray. *The Age of Excess.* New York, 1965.

Grodinsky, Julius. *Transcontinental Railway Strategy, 1869–1893: A Study of Businessmen.* Philadelphia, 1962.

Hedges, James B. *Henry Villard and the Railways of the Northwest.* New Haven, 1930.

Hidy, Ralph, Hill, Frank E., and Nevins, Allan. *Timber and Men: The Weyerhaeuser Story.* New York, 1963.

Hill, James J. *Highways of Progress.* New York, 1910.

Holbrook, Stewart H. *The Age of the Moguls.* New York, 1953.

———. *James J. Hill: A Great Life in Brief.* New York, 1955.

———. *The Story of American Railroads.* New York, 1947.

Howard, Joseph K. *Montana: High, Wide, and Handsome.* New Haven, 1943.

Innis, Harold A. *A History of the Canadian Pacific Railway.* Toronto, 1923.

Kennan, George. *E.H. Harriman: A Biography.* 2 vols. Boston, 1922.

Larson, Henrietta. *Jay Cooke, Private Banker.* Cambridge, 1936.

Lavender, David. *Land of Giants: The Drive to the Pacific Northwest, 1750–1950.* New York, 1956.

Lewis, Oscar. *The Big Four: The Story of Huntington, Stanford, Hopkins, and Crocker, And of the Building of the Central Pacific.* New York, 1938.

McDougall, J. Lorne. *Canadian Pacific: A Brief History.* Montreal, 1968.

Martin, Albro. *Enterprise Denied: Origins of the Decline of American Railroads, 1897–1917.* New York, 1971.

Mazlish, Bruce, ed. *The Railroad and the Space Program: An Exploration in Historical Analogy.* Cambridge, 1965.

Miner, H. Craig. *The St. Louis-San Francisco Transcontinental Railroad: The Thirty-Fifth Parallel Project, 1853–1890.* Lawrence, Kansas, 1972.

Moody, John. *The Railroad Builders.* New Haven, 1919.

Pyle, Joseph G. *The Life of James J. Hill.* 2 vols. New York, 1917.

Quiett, Glenn C. *They Built the West: An Epic of Rails and Cities.* New York, 1934.

Riegel, Robert E. *The Story of the Western Railroads: From 1852 Through the Reign of the Giants.* Lincoln, 1963.

Robinson, Elwyn. *History of North Dakota.* Lincoln, 1966.

Sobel, Robert. *Panic on Wall Street: A History of America's Financial Disasters.* New York, 1968.

Stover, John F. *The Life and Decline of the American Railroad.* New York, 1970.

Sullivan, Oscar M. *The Empire-Builder: A Biographical Novel of the Life of James J. Hill.* New York, 1928.

Taylor, George R. *The Transportation Revolution, 1815–1860.* New York, 1951.

Wilgus, William J. *The Railway Interrelations of the United States and Canada.* New York, 1937.

Chapter V. James Buchanan Duke: Opportunism is the Spur

Akehurst, B.C. *Tobacco.* New York, 1968.

American Tobacco Company. *"Sold American"—The First Fifty Years.* New York, 1954.

Barrett, John G. *The Civil War in North Carolina.* Chapel Hill, 1963.

Borden, Neil H. *The Economic Effects of Advertising.* Chicago, 1942.

Boyd, W.K. *The Story of Durham: City of the New South.* Durham, 1927.

Brooks, Jerome E. *The Mighty Leaf: Tobacco Through the Centuries.* Boston, 1952.

Cameron, J.D. *A Sketch of the Tobacco Interests of North Carolina.* Oxford, N.C., 1881.

Clark, Victor S. *History of Manufactures in the United States.* 2 vols. New York, 1929.

Cox, Reavis. *Competition in the American Tobacco Industry, 1911–1932.* New York, 1933.

Daniels, Josephus. *Editor in Politics.* Chapel Hill, 1941.

———. *Tar Hell Editor.* Chapel Hill, 1939.

Heiman, Robert K. *Tobacco and Americans.* New York, 1960.

Hower, Ralph M. *The History of An Advertising Agency: N.W. Ayer & Son at Work, 1869–1939.* Cambridge, 1939.

Jacobstein, Meyer. *The Tobacco Industry in the United States.* New York, 1907.

Jenkins, John W. *James B. Duke: Master Builder.* New York, 1927.

Lefler, Hugh T., ed. *North Carolina History Told by Contemporaries.* Chapel Hill, 1934.

Myers, Gustavus. *History of the Great American Fortunes.* 1936 ed. New York, 1936.

Nall, J.O. *The Tobacco Night Riders of Kentucky and Tennessee, 1905–1909.* Louisville, 1939.

Nicholls, William H. *Price Policies in the Cigarette Industry: A Study of "Concerted Action" and Its Social Control, 1911–1950.* Nashville, 1951.

Paul, Hiram V. *History of the Town of Durham, N.C.* Raleigh, 1884.

Porter, Glenn and Livesay, Harold C. *Merchants and Manufacturers: Studies in the Changing Structure of Nineteenth-Century Marketing.* Baltimore, 1971.

Report of the Commissioner of Corporations on the Tobacco Industry. 3 vols. Washington, 1909–1915.

Robert, Joseph C. *The Story of Tobacco in America.* New York, 1949.

Tennant, Richard B. *The American Cigarette Industry: A Study in Economic Analysis and Public Policy.* New York, 1971.

Thomas, James A. *A Pioneer Tobacco Merchant in the Orient.* Durham, 1928.

Tilley, Nannie May. *The Bright-Tobacco Industry, 1860–1929.* Chapel Hill, 1948.

Young, W.W. *The Story of the Cigarette.* New York, 1916.

United States Industrial Commission. *Report of the Industrial Commission on Trusts and Industrial Combinations.* Washington, 1901.

United States v. American Tobacco Co. 164 F. 700, 704 (1908); reversed and remanded, 221 U.S. 106 (1911); 191 F. 371 (1911)

United States v. American Tobacco Co. 163 F. 701 (1908)

Wagner, Susan. *Cigarette Country: Tobacco in American History and Politics.* New York, 1971.

Werner, Carl A. *Tobaccoland.* New York, 1922.

Wildman, Edwin, ed. *Famous Leaders of Industry.* New York, 1920.

Winkler, John K. *Tobacco Tycoon: The Story of James Buchanan Duke.* New York, 1942.

Chapter VI. Theodore N. Vail: The Subtle Serendipidist

Casson, Herbert N. *The History of the Telephone.* Chicago, 1910.

Coolidge, T. Jefferson. *T. Jefferson Coolidge, 1831–1920: An Autobiography.* Boston, 1923.

Coon, Horace. *American Tel & Tel: The Story of a Great Monopoly.* New York, 1939.

Corey, Lewis. *The House of Morgan.* New York, 1930.

Danielian, N.R. *A.T. & T.: The Story of Industrial Conquest.* New York, 1939.

Federal Communications Commission. *Proposed Report, Telephone Investigation (Pursuant to Public Resolution No. 8, 74th Congress).* Washington, D.C., 1938.

————. *Report on the Investigation of the Telephone Industry in the United States.* Washington, D.C., 1938.

————. *Staff Reports: Special Investigations Docket No. 1: No. 1360. A.T. & T. Co., Corporate and Financial History*. 3 vols.

Gabel, Richard. *Development of Separations Principles in the Telephone Industry*. East Lansing, 1967.

Glaeser, Martin G. *Public Utilities in American Capitalism*. New York, 1957.

Goulden, Joseph C. *Monopoly*. New York, 1968.

Harlow, Alvin. *Old Wires and New Waves*. New York, 1936.

Holcombe, A.N. *Public Ownership of Telephones on the Continent of Europe*. Cambridge, 1911.

Lavine, A. Lincoln. *Circuits of Victory*. New York, 1921.

MacKenzie, Catherine. *Alexander Graham Bell: The Man Who Contracted Space*. New York, 1928.

Mavor, James A. *Government Telephones*. New York, 1916.

Page, Arthur W. *The Bell Telephone System*. New York, 1941.

Paine, Albert B. *In One Man's Life: Being Chapters from the Personal & Business Career of Theodore N. Vail*. New York, 1921.

Pier, Arthur S. *Forbes: Telephone Pioneer*. New York, 1953.

Pound, Arthur. *The Telephone Idea*. New York, 1926.

Prescott, George P. *The Speaking Telephone*. Boston, 1879.

Rhodes, Frederick L. *Beginnings of Telephony*. New York, 1929.

Stehman, J. Warren. *The Financial History of the American Telephone and Telegraph Company*. New York, 1925.

Vail, Theodore N. *Views on Public Questions, 1907–1917*. New York, 1917.

Watson, Thomas A. *Exploring Life: The Autobiography of Thomas A. Watson*. Boston, 1926.

Chapter VII. Marcus Loew: An Artist In Spite Of Himself

Annals of the American Academy of Political and Social Science. *The Motion Picture In Its Economic and Social Aspects*. Philadelphia, 1926.

Balshofer, Fred J. and Miller, Arthur C. *One Reel a Week*. Berkeley, 1967.

Bardeche, Maurice and Brasillach, Robert. *The History of Motion Pictures*. New York, 1938.

Blesh, Rudi. *Keaton*. New York, 1968.

Brownlow, Keith. *The Parade's Gone By.* New York, 1968.

Crowther, Bosley. *Hollywood Rajah: The Life and Times of Louis B. Mayer.* New York, 1960.

_____. *The Lion's Share: The Story of an Entertainment Empire.* New York, 1957.

DeMille, Cecil. *The Autobiography of Cecil B. DeMille.* New York, 1959.

Drinkwater, John. *The Life and Adventures of Carl Laemmle.* New York, 1931.

French, Philip. *The Movie Moguls: An Informal History of the Hollywood Tycoons.* Chicago, 1969.

Lasky, Jesse L. *I Blow My Own Horn.* New York, 1957.

Goldwyn, Samuel. *Behind the Screen.* New York, 1923.

Green, Abel and Laurie, Joe Jr. *Show Biz: From Vaude to Video.* New York, 1951.

Hampton, Benjamin B. *A History of the Movies.* New York, 1931.

Huettig, Mae D. *Economic Control of the Motion Picture Industry.* Philadelphia, 1944.

Irwin, Will. *The House That Shadows Built: The Story of Adolph Zukor and His Circle.* New York, 1928.

Jacobs, Lewis. *The Rise of the American Film: A Critical History.* New York, 1939.

Jobes, Gertrude. *Motion Picture Empire.* Hampton, Conn., 1966.

Johnston, Alva. *The Great Goldwyn.* New York, 1937.

Josephson, Matthew. *Edison.* New York, 1959.

Kennedy, Joseph P., ed. *The Story of the Films.* Chicago, 1927.

Lewis, Howard T. *The Motion Picture Industry.* New York, 1933.

Mayer, Arthur. *Merely Colossal.* New York, 1953.

Powdermaker, Hortense. *Hollywood: The Dream Factory.* New York, 1950.

Ramsaye, Terry. *A Million and One Nights: A History of the Motion Picture.* New York, 1926.

Robinson, David. *Hollywood in the Twenties.* New York, 1968.

Rosenberg, Bernard and Silverstein, Harry. *The Real Tinsel.* New York, 1970.

Rosten, Leo C. *Hollywood: The Movie Colony, the Movie Makers.* New York, 1941.

Runes, Dagobert D., ed. *The Diary and Sundry Observations of Thomas Alva Edison.* New York, 1948.

Seabury, William M. *Motion Picture Problems.* New York, 1929.

————. *The Public and the Motion Picture Industry.* New York, 1926.
Seldes, Gilbert. *The Movies Come From America.* New York, 1931.
Sennett, Ted. *Warner Brothers Presents.* New Rochelle, 1971.
Sinclair, Upton. *Upton Sinclair Presents William Fox.* Los Angeles, 1933.
Thomas, Bob. *King Cohn: The Life and Times of Harry Cohn.* New York, 1967.
————. *Thalberg: Life and Legend.* New York, 1969.
Zierold, Norman. *The Hollywood Tycoons.* London, 1969.
Zukor, Adolph (with Dale Kramer). *The Public Is Never Wrong: The Autobiography of Adolph Zukor.* New York, 1953.

Chapter VIII. Donald Douglas: The Fortunes of War

Aeronautical Chamber of Commerce of America, Inc. *The Aircraft Year Book, 1926–1958.* New York, 1927–1958.
Boeing Company. *Pedigree of Champions.* Seattle, 1963.
Bollinger, Lynn L. and Lilley, Tom. *Financial Position of the Aircraft Industry.* Cambridge, Mass., 1943.
Brooks, Peter W. *The Modern Airliner.* London, 1961.
Bruno, Harry. *Wings Over America: The Inside Story of American Aviation.* New York, 1942.
Craven, Wesley F. and Cate, James L. *The Army Air Forces in World War II.* Vol. 6. *Men and Planes.* Chicago, 1955.
Cunningham, Frank. *Skymaster: The Story of Donald Douglas and Douglas Aircraft Co.* Philadelphia, 1943.
Cunningham, William G. *The Aircraft Industry: A Study in Industrial Location.* Los Angeles, 1951.
Davies, R.E.G. *A History of the World's Airlines.* London, 1964.
Davis, Kenneth S. *The Hero: Charles A. Lindbergh and the American Dream.* New York, 1955.
Day, John S. *Subcontracting in the Airframe Industry.* Cambridge, 1956.
Douglas Aircraft Company. *Fiftieth Anniversary of Naval Aviation.* El Segundo, Calif., 1962.
Fokker, Anthony H.G. and Gould, Bruce. *Flying Dutchman.* New York, 1931.
Francis, Devon. *Mr. Piper and His Cubs.* Ames, Iowa, 1973.
Frederick, John H. *Commercial Air Transportation.* Homewood, Ill., 1955.

Freudenthal, Elsbeth E. *The Aviation Business: From Kitty Hawk to Wall Street.* New York, 1940.

———. *Flight Into History: The Wright Brothers and the Air Age.* Norman, Oklahoma, 1949.

Gibbs-Smith, Charles H. *Aviation: An Historical Survey from its Origins to the End of World War II.* London, 1970.

Hatch, Alden. *Glenn Curtiss: Pioneer of Naval Aviation.* New York, 1942.

Heron, S.D. *History of the Aircraft Piston Engine.* Detroit, 1961.

Holland, Maurice. *Architects of Aviation.* New York, 1951.

Holley, Irving B., Jr. *United States Army in World War II, Special Studies, Buying Aircraft: Material Procurement for the Army Air Forces.* Washington, 1964.

———. *Ideas and Weapons: Exploitation of the Aerial Weapon by the United States During World War I.* New Haven, 1953.

Hubler, Richard G. *Big Eight: The Biography of an Airplane.* New York, 1960.

Ingells, Douglas J. *The Plane That Changed the World.* Fallbrook, Calif., 1966.

Josephson, Matthew. *Empire of the Air: Juan Trippe and the Struggle for World Airways.* New York, 1943.

Kaiser, William K. *The Development of the Aerospace Industry on Long Island, 1904–1964.* Hempstead, N.Y., 1968.

Kaufman, Richard F. *The War Profiteers.* New York, 1970.

Kelly, Charles J., Jr. *The Sky's the Limit: The History of the Airlines.* New York, 1963.

Keyes, Lucile S. *Federal Control of Entry into Air Transportation.* Cambridge, Mass., 1951.

Lawrance, Charles L. *Our National Aviation Program.* New York, 1932.

Lockheed Aircraft Corporation. *Of Men and Stars.* Burbank, 1958.

Loening, Grover. *Our Wings Grow Faster.* Garden City, N.Y., 1935.

Loosbrock, John F. and Skinner, Richard M., eds. *The Wild Blue: The Story of American Airpower.* New York, 1960.

McFarland, Marvin W., ed. *The Papers of Wilbur and Orville Wright, Including the Chanute-Wright Letters and Other Papers of Octave Chanute.* 2 vols. New York, 1953.

Mansfield, Harold. *Vision.* New York, 1956.

Maynard, Crosby. *Flight Plan for Tomorrow: The Douglas Story. A Condensed History.* Santa Monica, 1966.

Morris, Lloyd and Smith, Kendall. *Ceiling Unlimited: The Story of*

American Aviation From Kitty Hawk to Supersonics. New York, 1953.

Rae, John B. *Climb To Greatness: The American Aircraft Industry, 1920–1960.* Cambridge, Mass., 1968.

Rice, Berkeley. *The C-5A Scandal: An Inside Story of the Military-Industrial Complex.* Boston, 1971.

Roseberry, C.R. *Glenn Curtiss: Pioneer of Flight.* New York, 1972.

Ross, Walter S. *The Last Hero: Charles A. Lindbergh.* New York, 1964.

Shrader, Welman A. *Fifty Years of Flight: A Chronicle of the Aviation Industry in America, 1903–1953.* Cleveland, 1963.

Shamburger, Page and Christy, Joe. *Command The Horizon: A Pictorial History of Aviation.* New York, 1968.

Sikorsky, Igor. *The Story of the Winged-S.* London, 1939.

Simonson, G.R., ed. *The History of the American Aircraft Industry: An Anthology.* Cambridge, Mass., 1968.

Swanborough, F.G. *United States Military Aircraft Since 1909.* New York, 1963.

Wilson, Eugene E. *From Kitty Hawk to Sputnik to Polaris.* Palm Beach, Fla., 1967.

————. *Slipstream: The Autobiography of an Aircraftsman.* New York, 1965.

Weiss, David A. *The Saga of the Tin Goose: The Plane that Revolutionized American Civil Aviation.* New York, 1971.

Woods, George B. *The Aircraft Manufacturing Industry: Present and Future Prospects.* New York, 1946.

Chapter IX. Royal Little: The Spider and His Webs

Alberts, William and Segall, Joel. *The Corporate Merger.* Chicago, 1966.

Barber, Richard. *The American Corporation.* New York, 1970.

Barmash, Insadore. *Welcome to Our Conglomerate—You're Fired!* New York, 1971.

Brooks, John. *The Go-Go Years.* New York, 1973.

Butter, J. Keith, Lintner, John, and Cary, William. *Effects of Taxation on Corporate Mergers.* Boston, 1951.

Chandler, Alfred D., Jr. *Strategy and Structure: Chapters in the History of the Industrial Enterprise.* Cambridge, Mass., 1962.

Drayton, Clarence, Jr. *Mergers and Acquisitions: Planning and Action.* New York, 1963.

Federal Trade Commission. *Report of the Federal Trade Commission on the Merger Movement.* Washington, D.C., 1948.

———. *Report of the Federal Trade Commission on Corporate Mergers and Acquisitions.* Washington, D.C., 1955.

Fortune. The Conglomerate Commotion. New York, 1970.

Garoian, Leon, ed. *Economics of Conglomerate Growth.* Corvallis, Ore., 1969.

Gilbert, Charles, ed. *The Making of a Conglomerate.* Hempstead, N.Y., 1972.

Hacker, Andrew, ed. *The Corporate Take-Over.* New York, 1964.

Kelley, Aemon. *The Profitability of Growth Through Merger.* New York, 1967.

Kripke, Homer, ed. *Conglomerates and Congenerics.* New York, 1969.

Lynch, Harry. *Financial Performance of Conglomerates.* Boston, 1971.

Nelson, Ralph. *Merger Movements in American Industry, 1895–1956.* Princeton, 1959.

Sauerhaft, Stan. *The Merger Game.* New York, 1971.

Vance, Stanley. *Managers in the Conglomerate Era.* New York, 1971.

Weston, J. Fred and Peltzman, Sam, eds. *Public Policy Toward Mergers.* Pacific Palisades, Calif., 1969.

Journals and Other:

"The Royal Little Story." Cambridge, Mass., 1966.

Barron's
Business Week
Commercial and Financial Chronicle
Dun's Review
Economist
Financial Executive
Forbes
Fortune
Harvard Business Review
Journal of Accounting
Newsweek
Time

Index

Arkwright, Richard: 14, 17
Armat, Thomas: 255–56
Armour, Philip: 149
Arrowsmith, G. A.: 81
Ash, Roy: 348
Asia *see* China *and* Japan *and* Oriental trade
Atomic bomb: 250, 290, 328
AT&T *see* American Telephone and Telegraph
Automobiles and automobile industry: *xii*, 250, 251, 289–90, 292, 298, 347; airplane manufacture, 298–99, 303, 304, 313
AVCO: 312, 314, 318
Aviation and aviation industry: 250, 289–340, 341, 342, 347; antitrust actions, 318; and auto firms, 298–99, 303, 304, 313; commercial market, *xi, xii, xiii*, 296, 306, 310, 312, 315, 317–24, 328–29; compared to motion picture industry, 289, 290–92; Liberty engine, 299, 303, 304, 309, 310, 315; in Great Depression, 314–16; jet race, 332–38; management, 300; marketing, 292, 293, 294, 305–7; mergers, 339–40; military and government markets, 290, 292–94, 297–98, 299, 303, 304–7, 310, 311, 312, 313; New Deal, 318; pioneers, *xiii*, 290–91, 293, 294–300, 338–39; post-World War II, 378–79; production, 290, 291, 299; scientific-business-government alliance, 296–97, 299–300; and Wall Street, 312–13; World War I, 291, 293, 297–98; World War II, 325–26, 328. *See also* Douglas, Donald

Baehr, Herman: 265, 266
Baker, George F.: 228, 230
Baker, Ray Stannard: 188
Balaban, Barney: 263
Bangs, George: 203
Bankers and banking: 39, 143, 212. *See also* Investment banking
Bell, Alexander Graham: *xi, xiii*, 206–9, 213, 244, 245, 253; patents, 206–7, 208,

209, 210, 213, 214, 216, 218
Bell, Lawrence Dale: *xiii*, 290, 302, 304, 307, 308
Bell, Mabel Hubbard: 207
Bell Telephone Company: *xiii*, 206, 209–12; difficulties, 210–11; franchises, 208–9, 210, 213; merger with New England Telephone, 212; Western Union struggles, 210–11, 213. *See also* American Bell Telephone Company
Bethell, Union N.: 243, 244
Beveridge, Albert: 190
Beverly Cotton Manufactory: 18, 22, 23
Biograph Studios: 254–55, 261
Bishop, Cortlandt: 297
Blackwell, William T.: 159, 162, 165, 177
Bluhdorn, Charles: 176, 343, 349, 350, 352, 374, 377
Boeing Company: 292, 308, 312, 318, 319, 320, 321, 322, 324–25, 326, 329, 332–33, 334, 335–38, 341, 343, 379
Boeing, William: 300
Bonsack, James A.: 165; machines, 166, 168, 170, 172, 174, 183
Bossidy, John Collins: 1
Boston: 2, 5–6, 8, 9, 13, 21, 22, 32, 33, 36, 39, 206, 207, 209, 213, 219, 221, 225, 297; immigrants, 249; late eighteenth-century, 3, 5–6; retailing, 94, 104, 105; stock exchange, 39, 213
Boston aristocrats: 1, 3–5, 14, 42, 295–97; Boston Associates, 39; in international commerce, 5–9; Lowell and, 38–39; as manufacturers, 18, 23–24; in telephone industry, 210, 212–13, 215–16, 219, 220, 222, 223, 224, 226, 227–28, 230
Boston Manufacturing Company: *xiv*, 22–24, 26–31, 33–34, 36, 37, 38, 39, 41, 248, 342, 383
Brady, Anthony N.: 176, 178
Brady, George: 225
Brown, Moses: 14–17, 18, 24, 25, 32
Brown, A. C.: 58
Brown, Nathan: 80, 81, 88
Buchanan, James: 68, 111
Buell, Jesse: 54